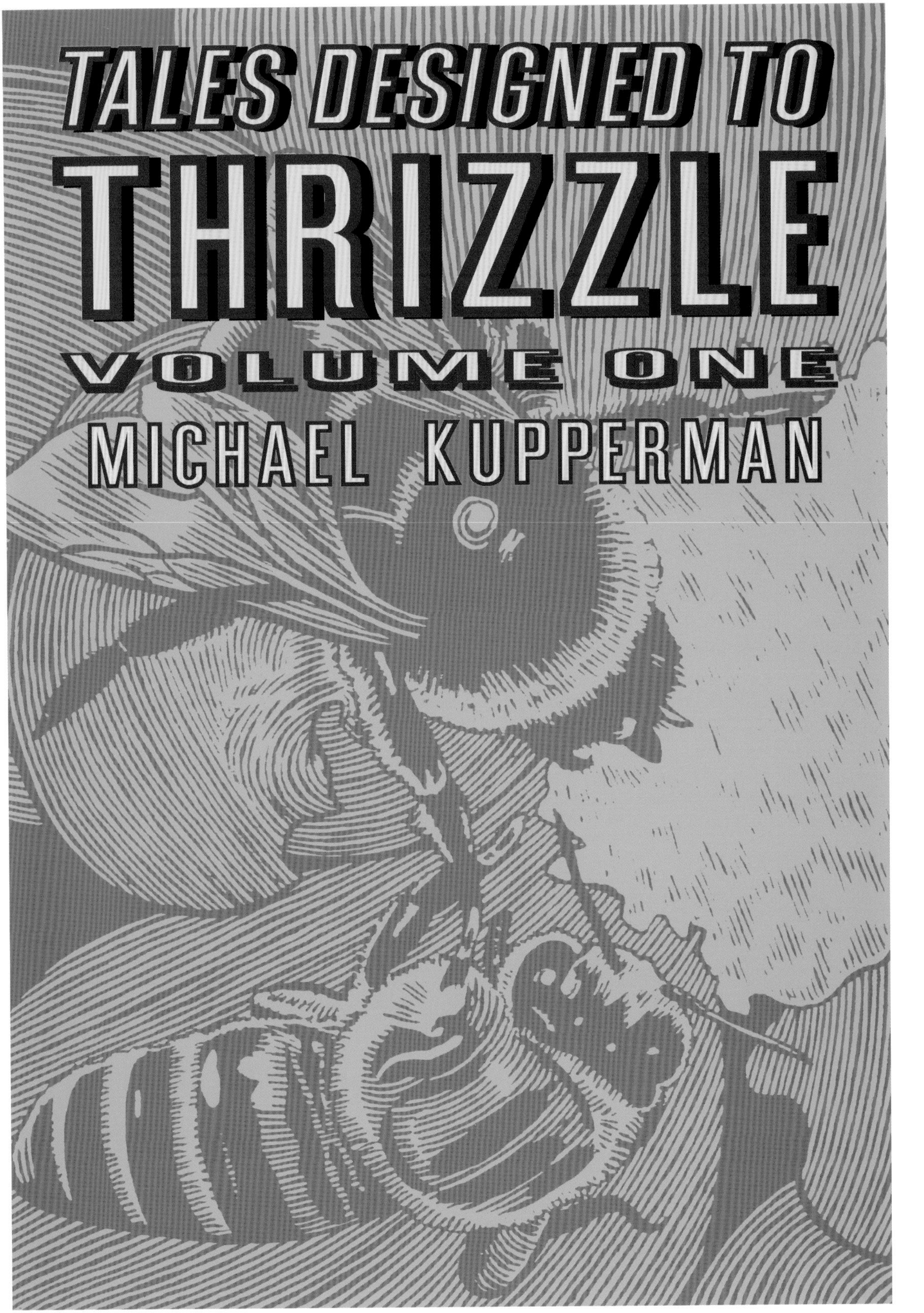
TALES DESIGNED TO
THRIZZLE
VOLUME ONE
MICHAEL KUPPERMAN

FANTAGRAPHICS BOOKS
7563 Lake City Way NE
Seattle WA 98115

Original comics edited by Eric Reynolds
Production assistance by John Kuramoto
Promotion by Eric Reynolds
Published by Gary Groth and Kim Thompson

Distributed in the U.S. by W.W. Norton and Company, Inc. (212-354-5500)
Distributed in Canada by Canadian Manda Group (416-516-0911)
Distributed in the United Kingdom by Turnaround Distribution (208-829-3009)

Visit the Fantagraphics website: www.fantagraphics.com

First printing: May, 2009

ISBN: 978-1-60699-164-0

Printed in China by PrintWORKS

FOREWORD
by Robert Smigel

I have diarrhea, so I'll be brief. Michael Kupperman is back! Yes, the author of *Snake 'N' Bacon's Cartoon Cabaret* is back. He was away. I'm not sure where. I think Greece, for a while. He said it was very nice.

Apparently they have beautiful islands in Greece, with clear water. The water is on the beaches. Am I on trial? This is making me very uncomfortable. I didn't campaign to write this foreword. I was just minding my own business, pleasuring myself in front of my sister-in-law, when my email alert signaled. Sure enough, it was a request from Michael Kupperman to write a foreword. I didn't even know he was back! Now I feel like I've been put in a position where I'm writing something that people are going to read. It's just messed up.

I just realized that I can figure out where else he was before he was back, besides, of course, Greece. If I can trace where the phone call he made asking me to write the foreword came from, I'll know exactly where he was while he was away. I'll let you know. I just remembered it was an email, not a phone call. To trace an email, simply look up the IP address in the header, next to "Received from." A common IP tracker will then trace the origin and location of the IP address. Voilà: where he was.

It just occurred to me that he was probably already back when he emailed asking me to write the foreword. Let's talk for a moment about Kupperman's skills. He is very good. Very, very, very, very good. That is to say, at what he does.

I sense this foreword has been a waste of your time. For that, and only for that, I apologize. What you've just read is the culmination of three years of work, from conception to finished product. It's possible that I overthought it. Or, in the words of Forwy the Foreword, "I come before the real book." But rather than examining it any further (which would be self-indulgent) I'm going to leave it to the historians to determine what went wrong with this foreword. The important thing is, that Michael Kupperman is back. And for that, he is richer.

I just reread the entire foreword. I wonder if the book is a letdown after it. Here's what I'm going to pitch: let's cut the first three sentences of the second paragraph. I think it would make it tighter, cleaner, etc. Plus there's a nice sound to "first three sentences of the second paragraph." It sounds confident, assured, etc. Or, as Forwy the Foreword would say, "I come before the real book." Let's also lose the sections about my sister-in-law, and any references to Kupperman. One last suggestion — and please don't be offended — more information about the internet. Otherwise, though, really, really good. I especially like the way it ended ("he is richer"). Okay, I really need to go.

"FORWY"

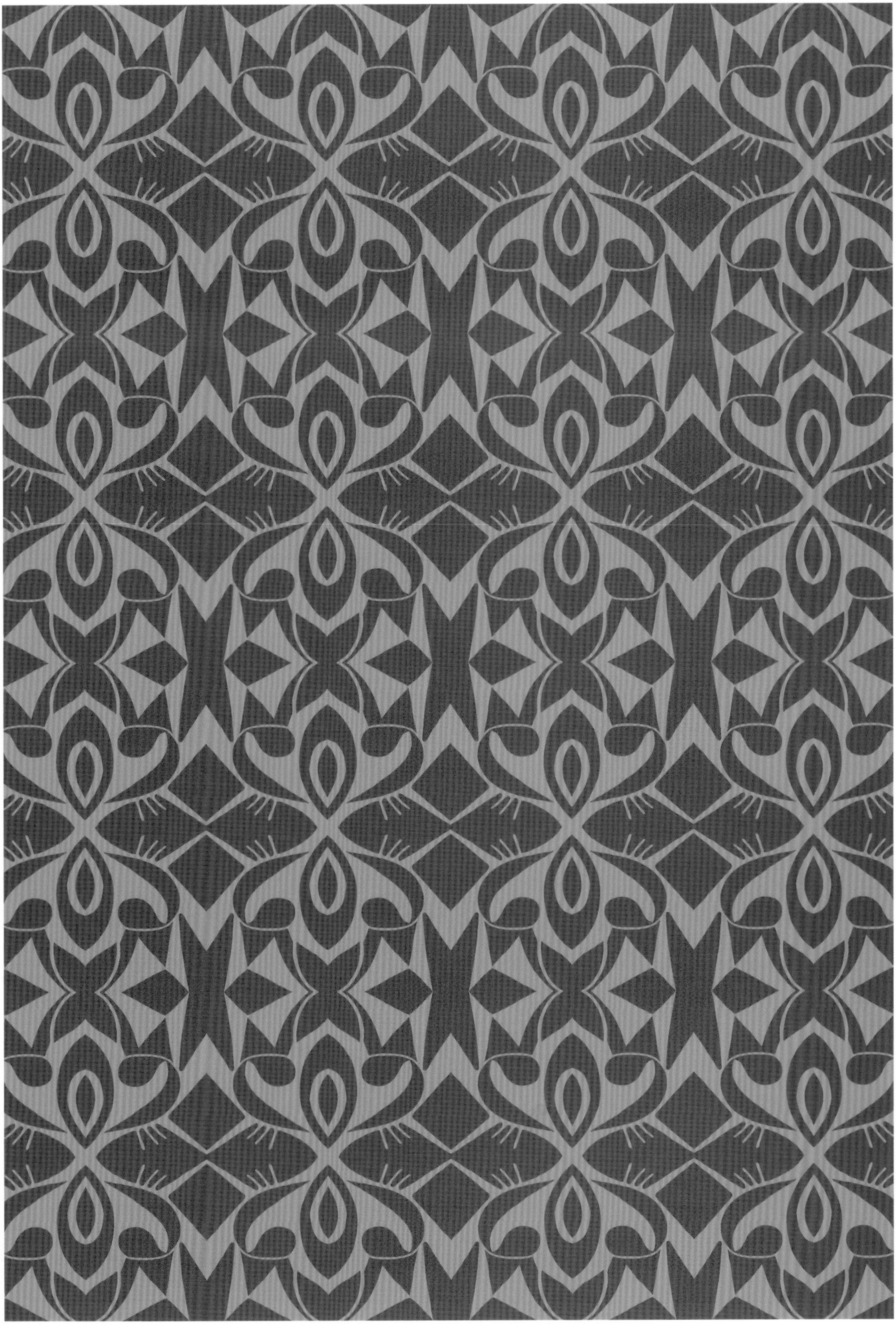

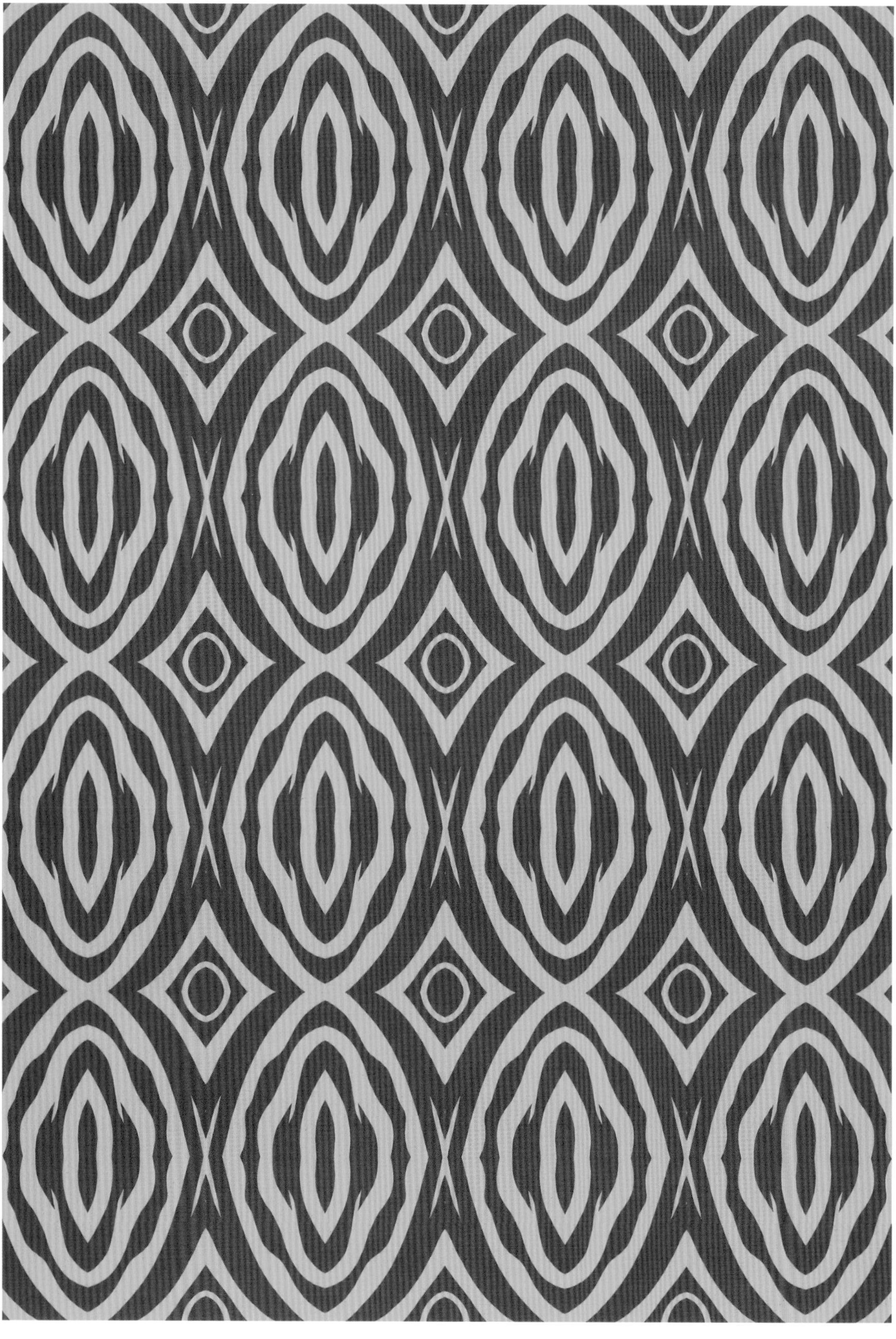

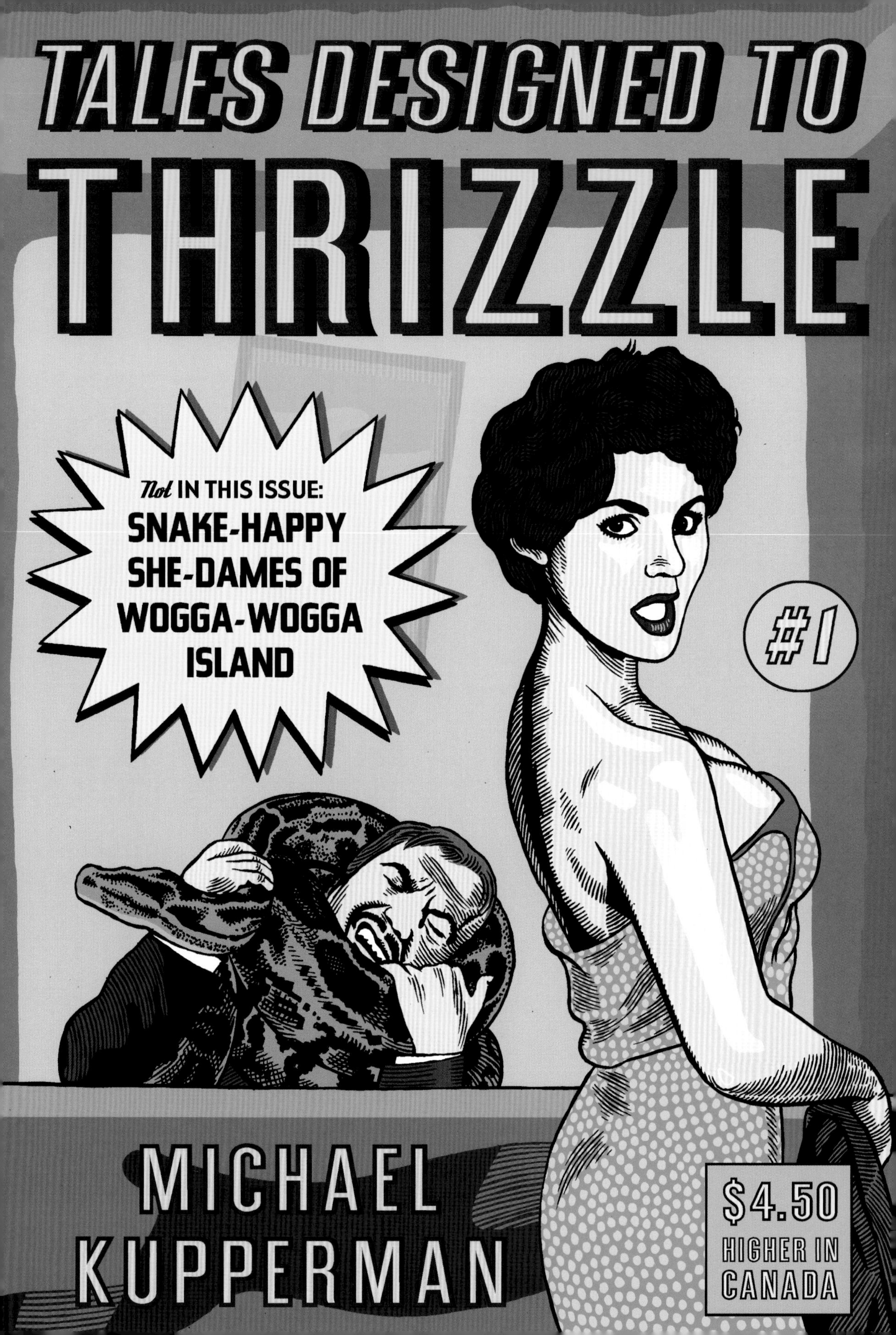
TALES DESIGNED TO
THRIZZLE
Not IN THIS ISSUE:
SNAKE-HAPPY
SHE-DAMES OF
WOGGA-WOGGA
ISLAND
#1
MICHAEL
KUPPERMAN
$4.50
HIGHER IN
CANADA

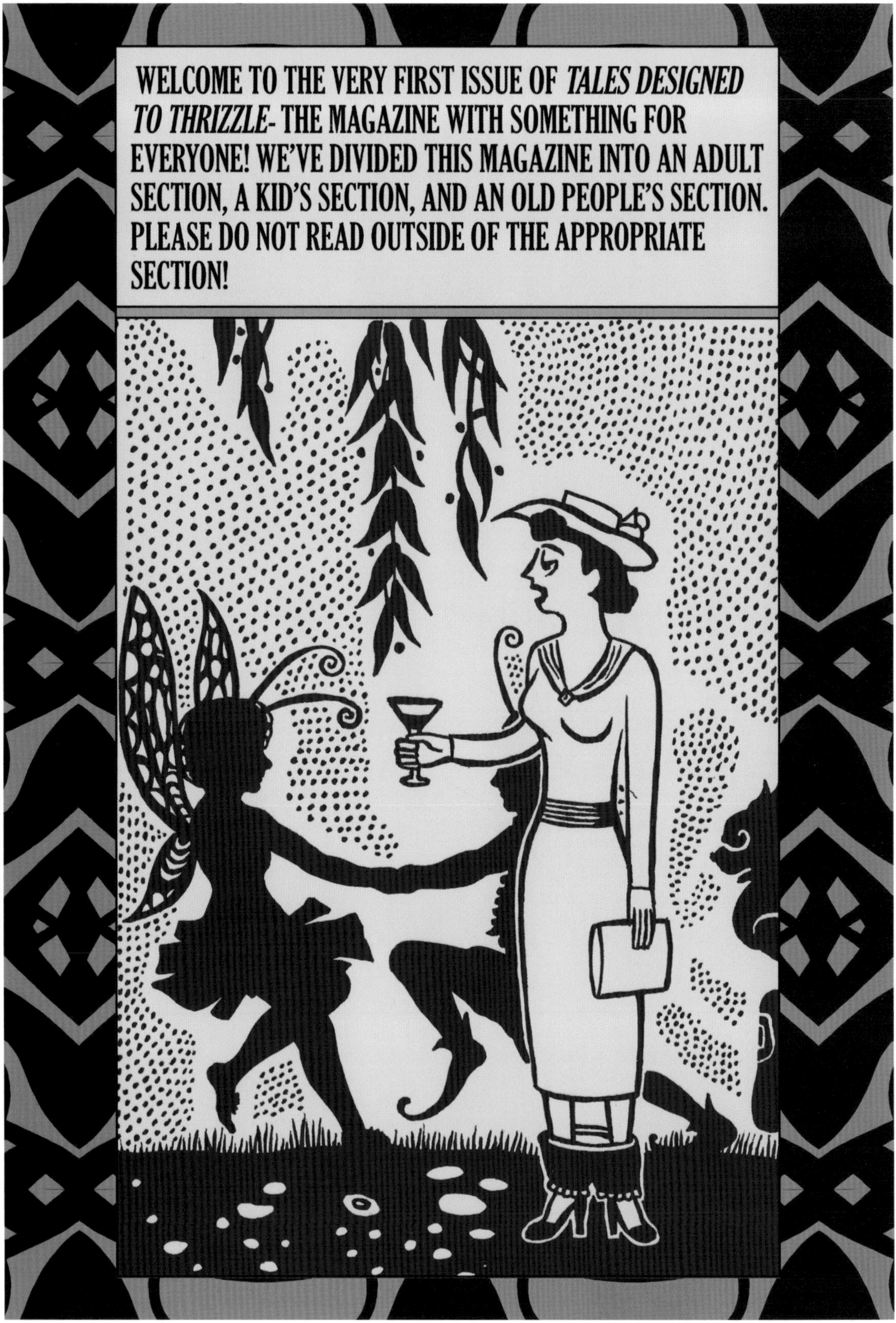
WELCOME TO THE VERY FIRST ISSUE OF *TALES DESIGNED TO THRIZZLE*- THE MAGAZINE WITH SOMETHING FOR EVERYONE! WE'VE DIVIDED THIS MAGAZINE INTO AN ADULT SECTION, A KID'S SECTION, AND AN OLD PEOPLE'S SECTION. PLEASE DO NOT READ OUTSIDE OF THE APPROPRIATE SECTION!

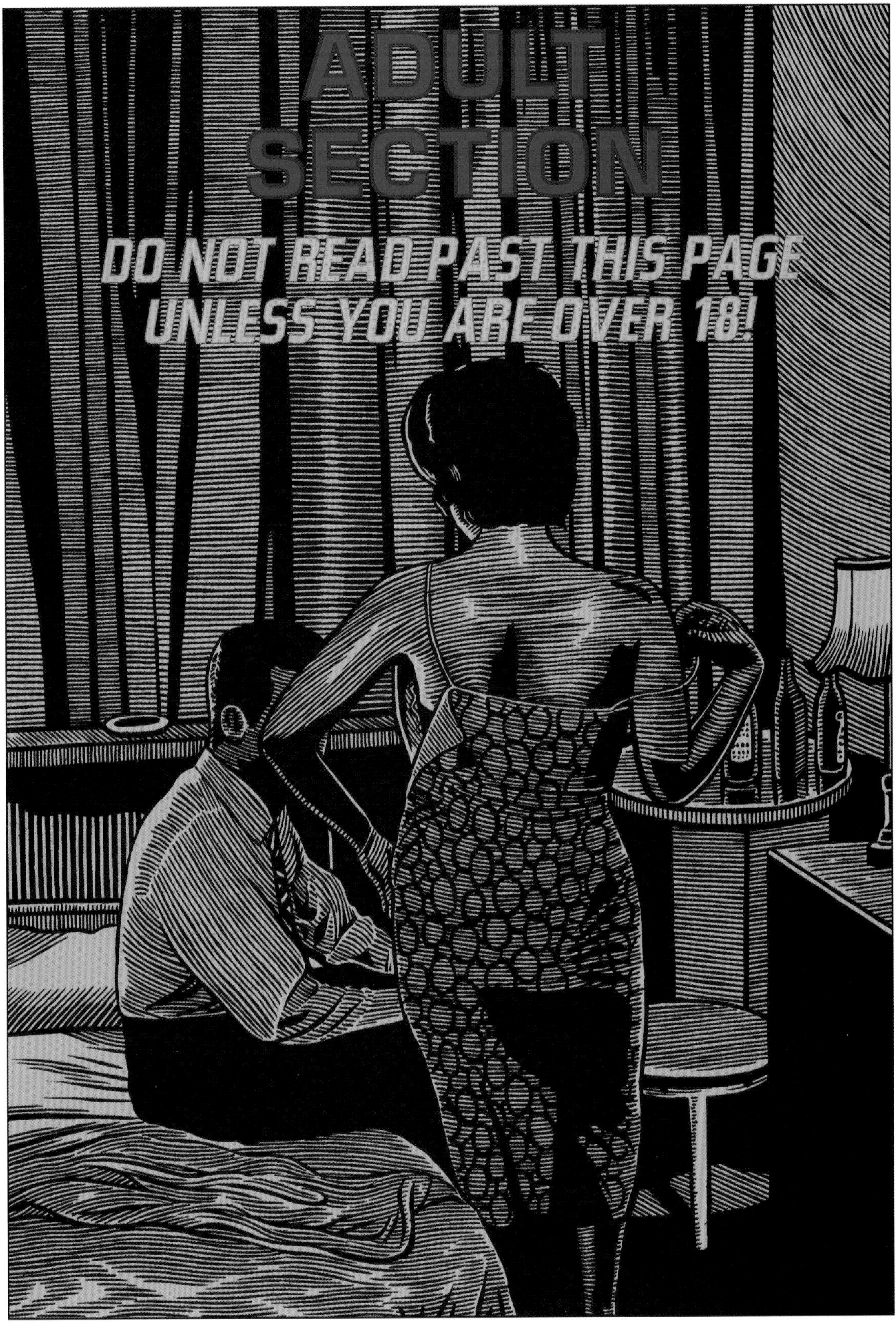
ADULT SECTION
DO NOT READ PAST THIS PAGE UNLESS YOU ARE OVER 18!

ADVERTISEMENT - ADVERTISEMENT - ADVERTISEMENT - ADVERTISEMENT - ADVERTISEMENT -

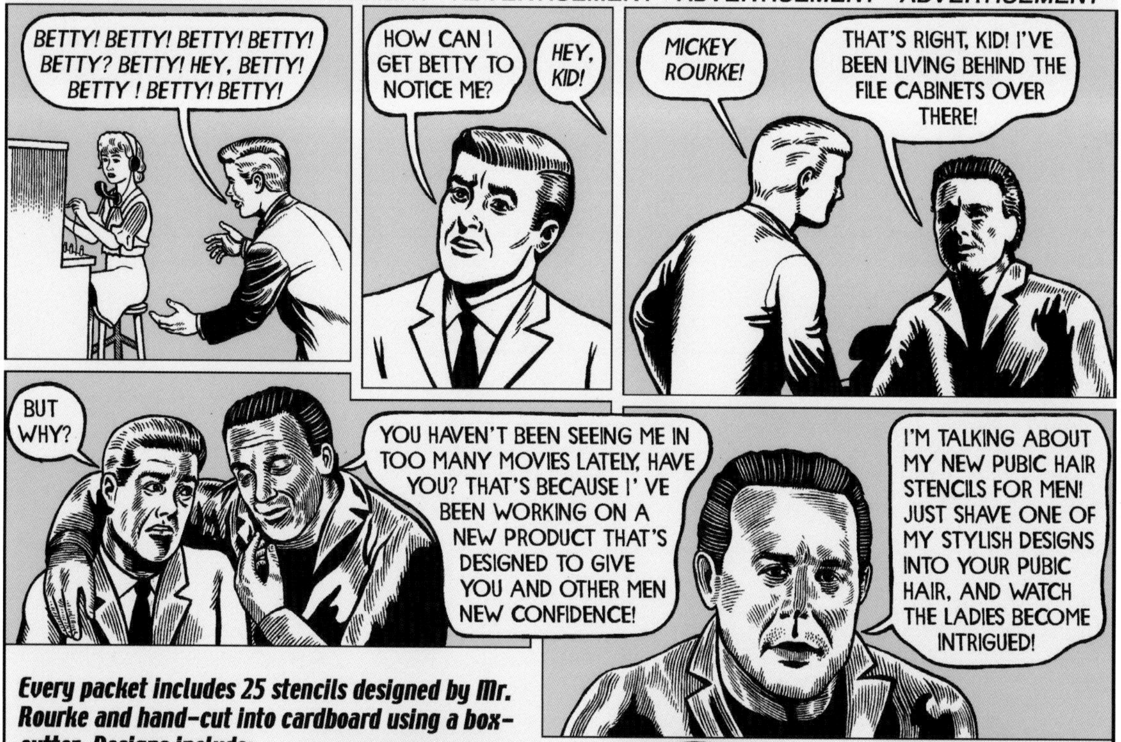
BETTY! BETTY! BETTY! BETTY! BETTY? BETTY! HEY, BETTY! BETTY ! BETTY! BETTY!
HOW CAN I GET BETTY TO NOTICE ME?
HEY, KID!
MICKEY ROURKE!
THAT'S RIGHT, KID! I'VE BEEN LIVING BEHIND THE FILE CABINETS OVER THERE!
BUT WHY?
YOU HAVEN'T BEEN SEEING ME IN TOO MANY MOVIES LATELY, HAVE YOU? THAT'S BECAUSE I' VE BEEN WORKING ON A NEW PRODUCT THAT'S DESIGNED TO GIVE YOU AND OTHER MEN NEW CONFIDENCE!
I'M TALKING ABOUT MY NEW PUBIC HAIR STENCILS FOR MEN! JUST SHAVE ONE OF MY STYLISH DESIGNS INTO YOUR PUBIC HAIR, AND WATCH THE LADIES BECOME INTRIGUED!

Every packet includes 25 stencils designed by Mr. Rourke and hand-cut into cardboard using a box-cutter. Designs include:

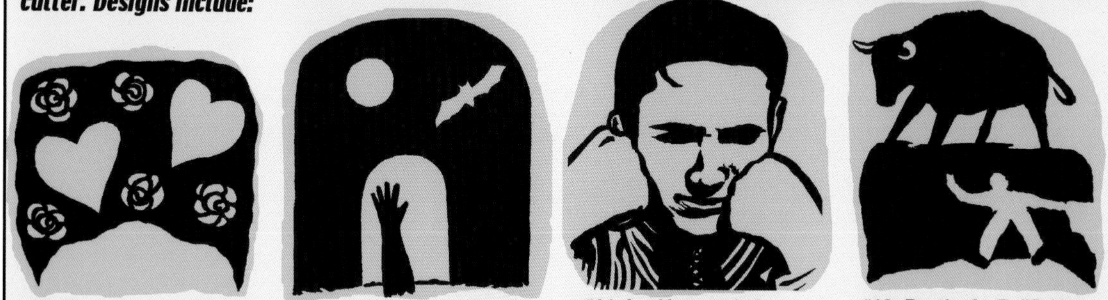

#6- Romantic Honeymoon

"This design will make your crotch into the equivalent of a bouquet of flowers."

#12- Zombie Nightmare

"You want your groin to be seriously scary? This one'll do the trick."

#14- Looking worried

"When the girl sees this, she'll ask why the guy is worried. And you say, "My penis owes money to gangsters." Classic!"

#18- Death of a Bullfighter

"This one I started as a novel, then I realized the story would work better within the medium of pubic hair."

Send $5.95 plus $1.62 postage & handling fee to: Mickey Rourke, Behind the filing cabinets at Wilshire & Bennett, 12 Rodeo Drive, Los Angeles, CA, 94105.

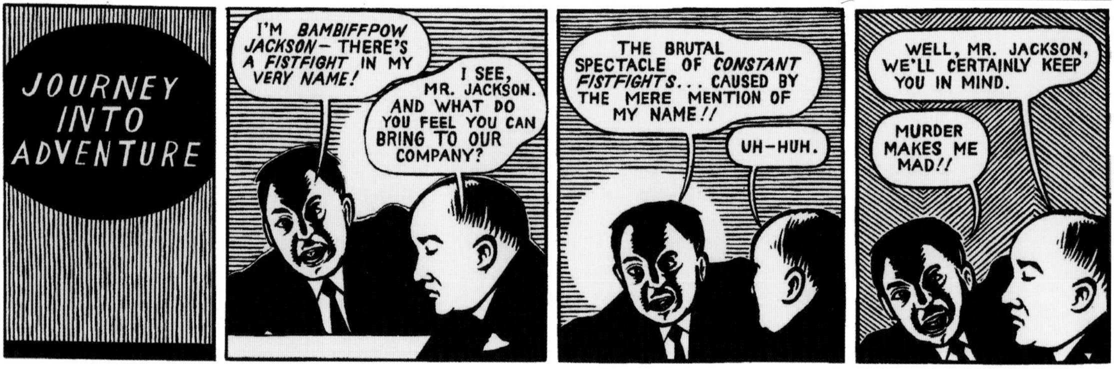
JOURNEY INTO ADVENTURE
I'M BAMBIFFPOW JACKSON— THERE'S A FISTFIGHT IN MY VERY NAME!
I SEE, MR. JACKSON. AND WHAT DO YOU FEEL YOU CAN BRING TO OUR COMPANY?
THE BRUTAL SPECTACLE OF CONSTANT FISTFIGHTS... CAUSED BY THE MERE MENTION OF MY NAME!!
UH-HUH.
WELL, MR. JACKSON, WE'LL CERTAINLY KEEP YOU IN MIND.
MURDER MAKES ME MAD!!

PICASSO
HIS ASTONISHING LIFE
Narrated by a Hamburger

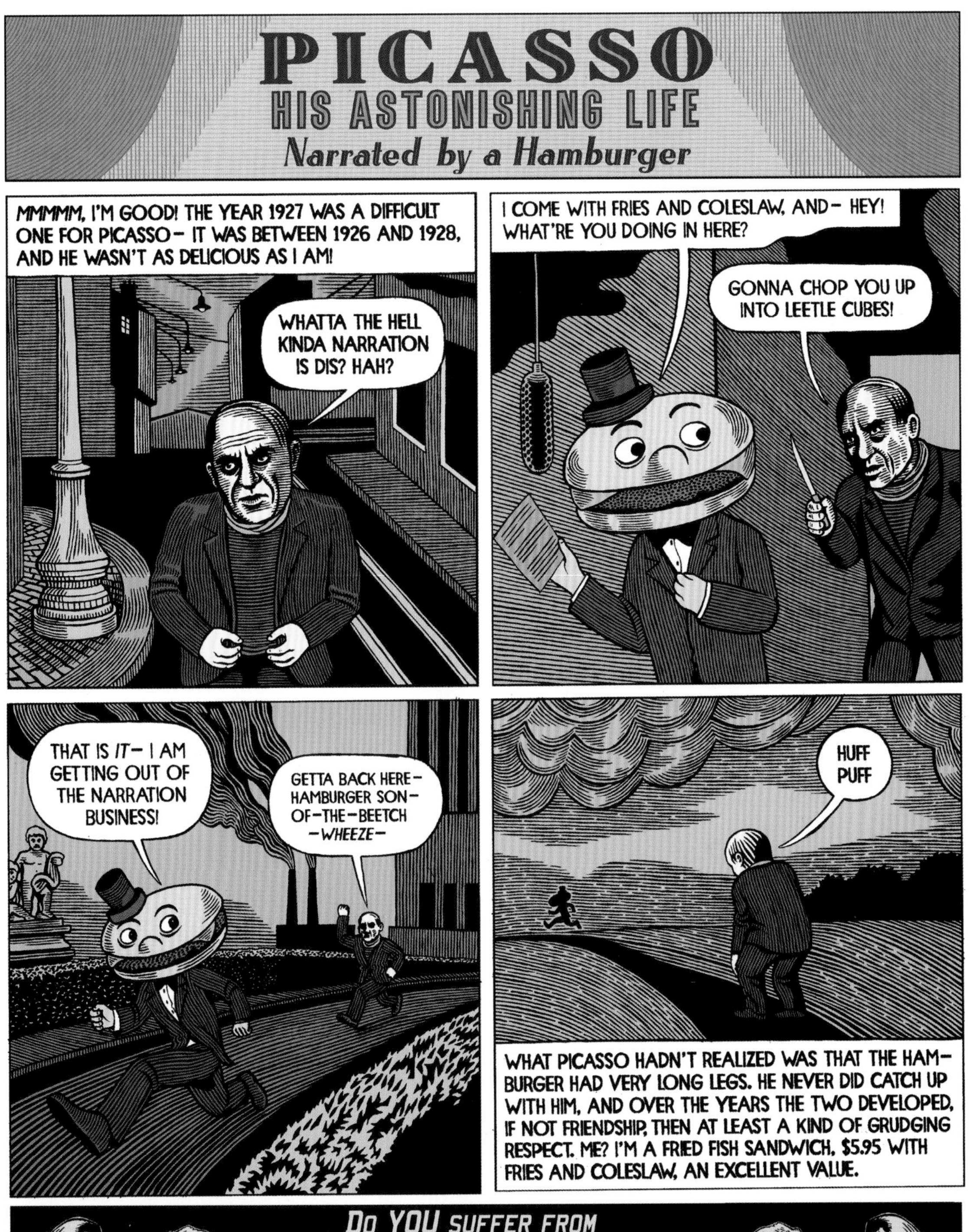
MMMMM, I'M GOOD! THE YEAR 1927 WAS A DIFFICULT ONE FOR PICASSO– IT WAS BETWEEN 1926 AND 1928, AND HE WASN'T AS DELICIOUS AS I AM!
WHATTA THE HELL KINDA NARRATION IS DIS? HAH?
I COME WITH FRIES AND COLESLAW, AND– HEY! WHAT'RE YOU DOING IN HERE?
GONNA CHOP YOU UP INTO LEETLE CUBES!
THAT IS *IT*– I AM GETTING OUT OF THE NARRATION BUSINESS!
GETTA BACK HERE– HAMBURGER SON–OF–THE–BEETCH –*WHEEZE*–
HUFF PUFF
WHAT PICASSO HADN'T REALIZED WAS THAT THE HAMBURGER HAD VERY LONG LEGS. HE NEVER DID CATCH UP WITH HIM, AND OVER THE YEARS THE TWO DEVELOPED, IF NOT FRIENDSHIP, THEN AT LEAST A KIND OF GRUDGING RESPECT. ME? I'M A FRIED FISH SANDWICH, $5.95 WITH FRIES AND COLESLAW, AN EXCELLENT VALUE.

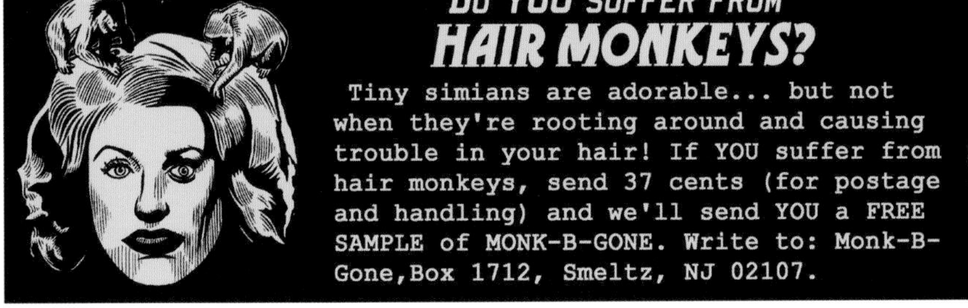

Do YOU suffer from HAIR MONKEYS?

Tiny simians are adorable... but not when they're rooting around and causing trouble in your hair! If YOU suffer from hair monkeys, send 37 cents (for postage and handling) and we'll send YOU a FREE SAMPLE of MONK-B-GONE. Write to: Monk-B-Gone,Box 1712, Smeltz, NJ 02107.

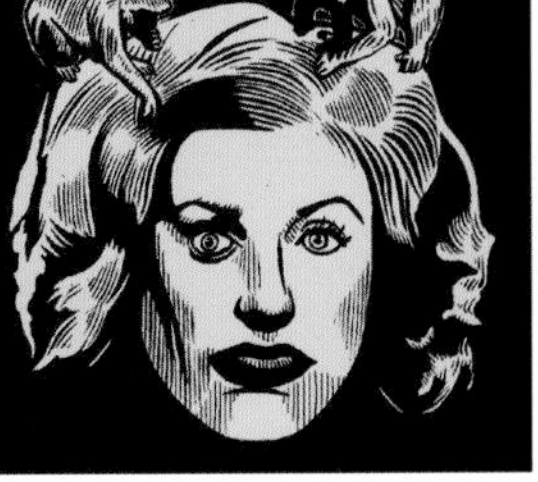

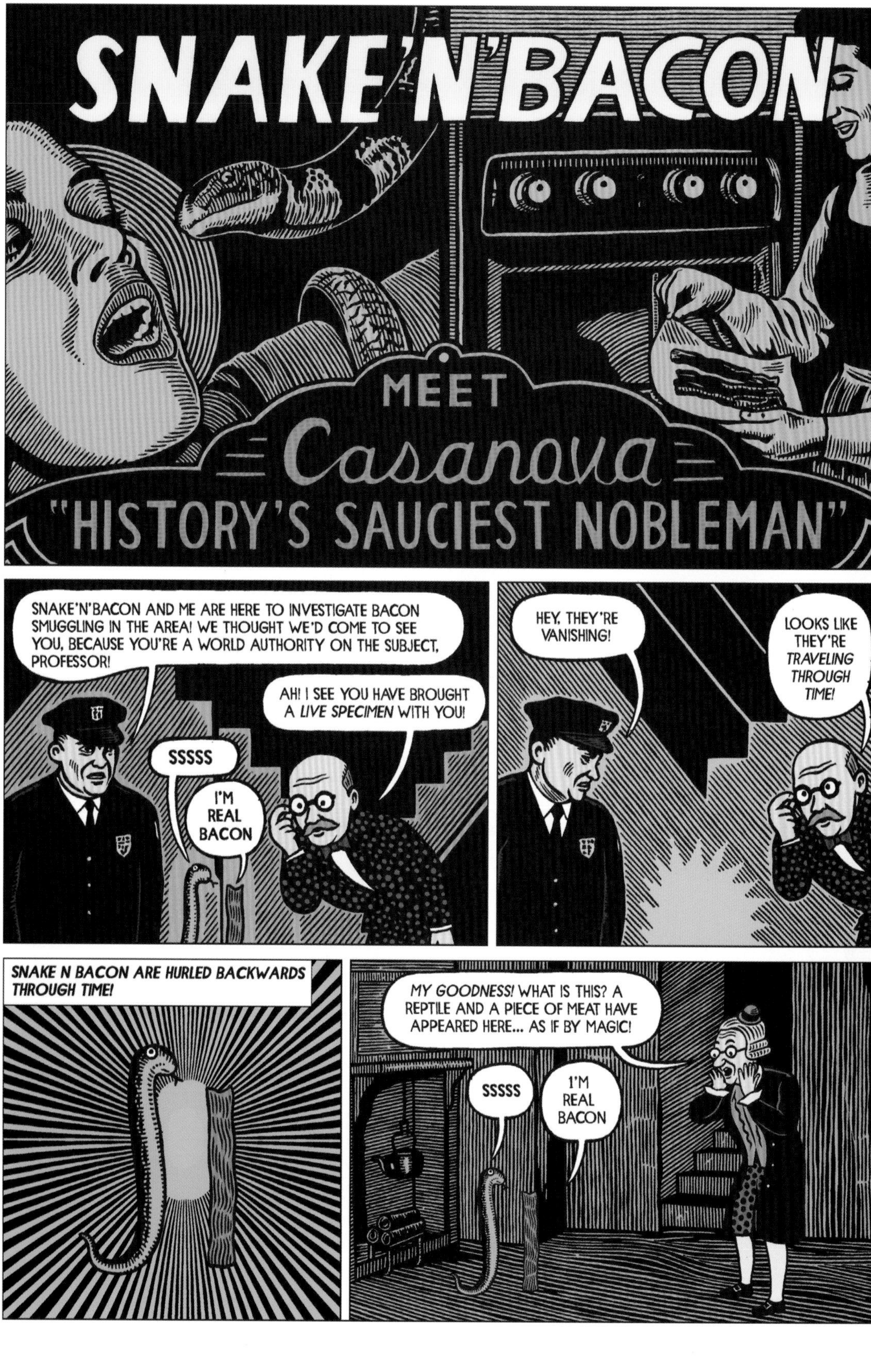
SNAKE'N'BACON
MEET
Casanova
"HISTORY'S SAUCIEST NOBLEMAN"
SNAKE'N'BACON AND ME ARE HERE TO INVESTIGATE BACON SMUGGLING IN THE AREA! WE THOUGHT WE'D COME TO SEE YOU, BECAUSE YOU'RE A WORLD AUTHORITY ON THE SUBJECT, PROFESSOR!
AH! I SEE YOU HAVE BROUGHT A *LIVE SPECIMEN* WITH YOU!
SSSSS
I'M REAL BACON
HEY, THEY'RE VANISHING!
LOOKS LIKE THEY'RE *TRAVELING THROUGH TIME!*
SNAKE N BACON ARE HURLED BACKWARDS THROUGH TIME!
MY GOODNESS! WHAT IS THIS? A REPTILE AND A PIECE OF MEAT HAVE APPEARED HERE... AS IF BY MAGIC!
SSSSS
I'M REAL BACON

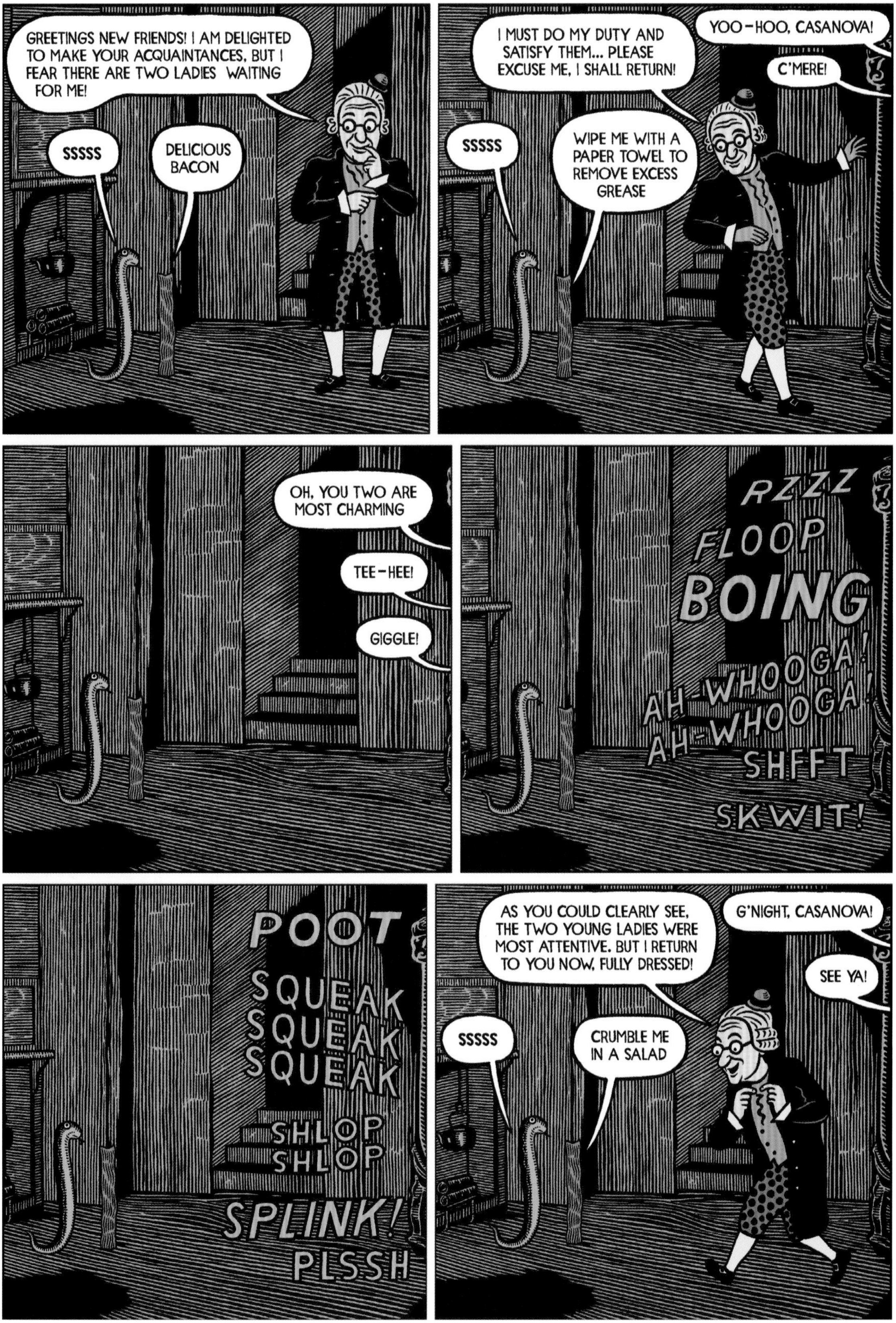

GREETINGS NEW FRIENDS! I AM DELIGHTED TO MAKE YOUR ACQUAINTANCES, BUT I FEAR THERE ARE TWO LADIES WAITING FOR ME!
SSSSS
DELICIOUS BACON
I MUST DO MY DUTY AND SATISFY THEM... PLEASE EXCUSE ME, I SHALL RETURN!
YOO-HOO, CASANOVA!
C'MERE!
SSSSS
WIPE ME WITH A PAPER TOWEL TO REMOVE EXCESS GREASE
OH, YOU TWO ARE MOST CHARMING
TEE-HEE!
GIGGLE!
RZZZ
FLOOP
BOING
AH-WHOOGA!
AH-WHOOGA!
SHFFT
SKWIT!
POOT
SQUEAK
SQUEAK
SQUEAK
SHLOP
SHLOP
SPLINK!
PLSSH
AS YOU COULD CLEARLY SEE, THE TWO YOUNG LADIES WERE MOST ATTENTIVE. BUT I RETURN TO YOU NOW, FULLY DRESSED!
G'NIGHT, CASANOVA!
SEE YA!
SSSSS
CRUMBLE ME IN A SALAD

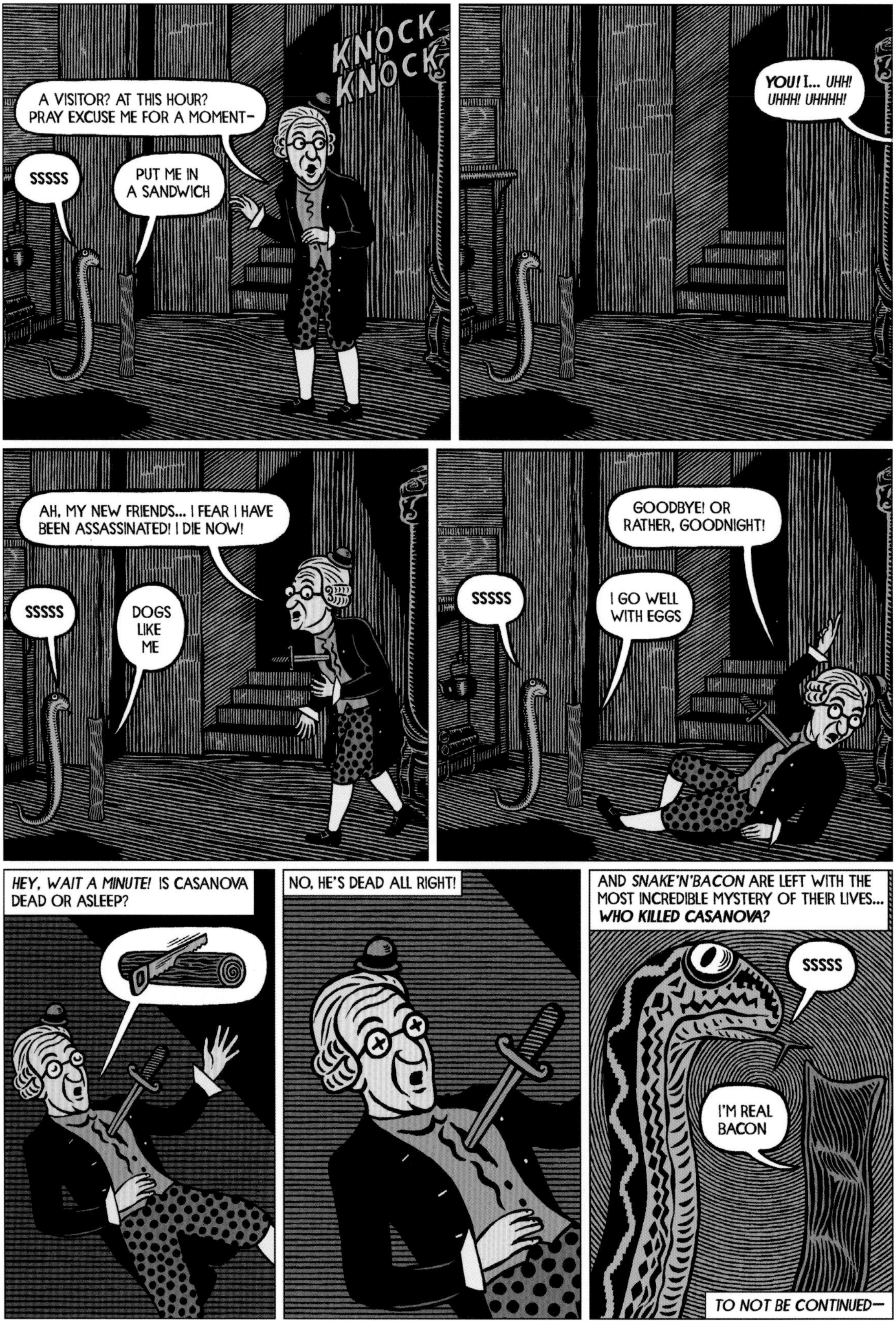
KNOCK KNOCK
A VISITOR? AT THIS HOUR? PRAY EXCUSE ME FOR A MOMENT–
SSSSS
PUT ME IN A SANDWICH
YOU! I... UHH! UHHH! UHHHH!
AH, MY NEW FRIENDS... I FEAR I HAVE BEEN ASSASSINATED! I DIE NOW!
SSSSS
DOGS LIKE ME
GOODBYE! OR RATHER, GOODNIGHT!
SSSSS
I GO WELL WITH EGGS
HEY, WAIT A MINUTE! IS CASANOVA DEAD OR ASLEEP?
NO, HE'S DEAD ALL RIGHT!
AND SNAKE'N'BACON ARE LEFT WITH THE MOST INCREDIBLE MYSTERY OF THEIR LIVES... WHO KILLED CASANOVA?
SSSSS
I'M REAL BACON
TO NOT BE CONTINUED—

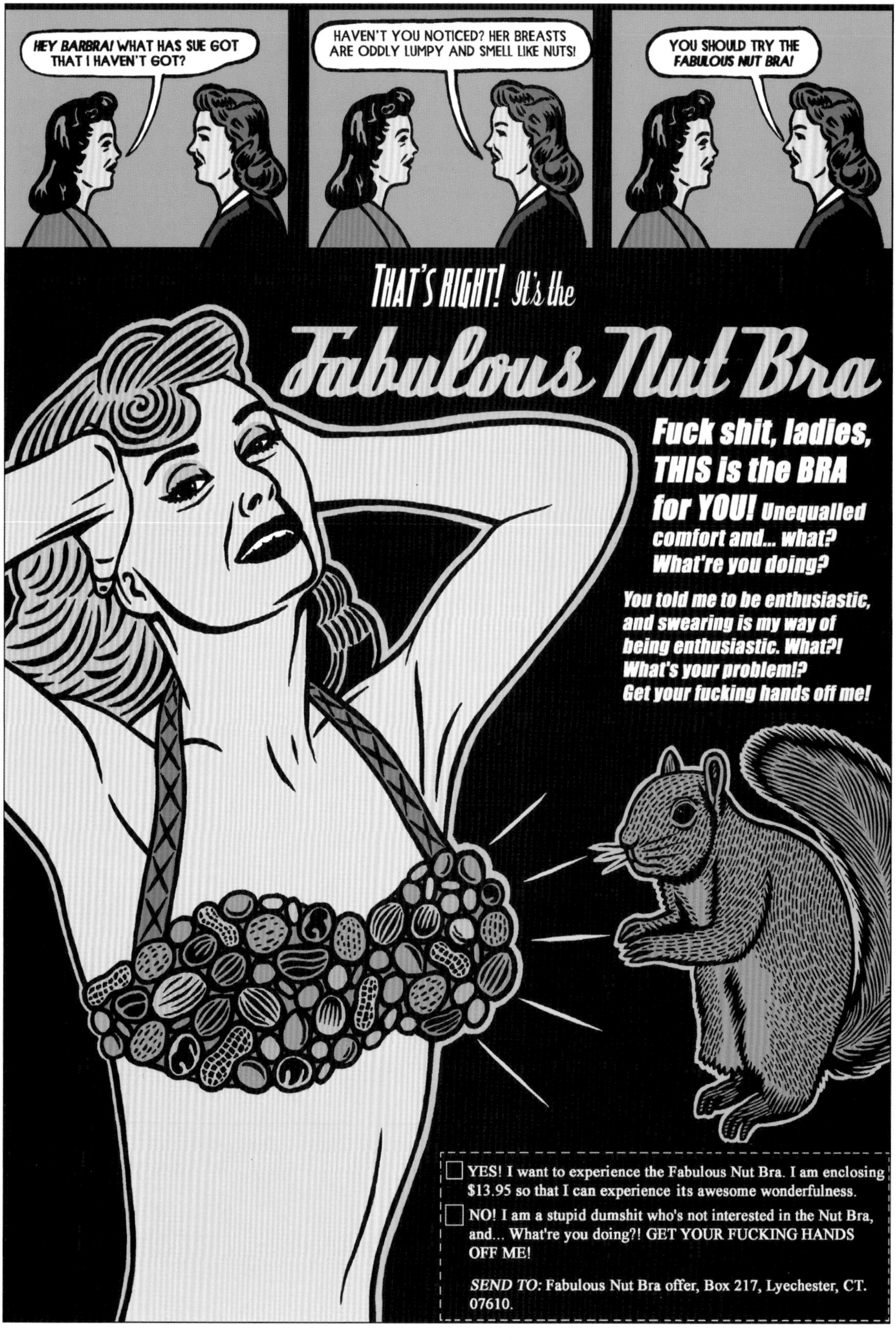
HEY BARBRA! WHAT HAS SUE GOT THAT I HAVEN'T GOT?
HAVEN'T YOU NOTICED? HER BREASTS ARE ODDLY LUMPY AND SMELL LIKE NUTS!
YOU SHOULD TRY THE FABULOUS NUT BRA!
THAT'S RIGHT! It's the
Fabulous Nut Bra
Fuck shit, ladies, THIS is the BRA for YOU! Unequalled comfort and... what? What're you doing?
You told me to be enthusiastic, and swearing is my way of being enthusiastic. What?! What's your problem!? Get your fucking hands off me!
YES! I want to experience the Fabulous Nut Bra. I am enclosing $13.95 so that I can experience its awesome wonderfulness.
NO! I am a stupid dumshit who's not interested in the Nut Bra, and... What're you doing?! GET YOUR FUCKING HANDS OFF ME!
SEND TO: Fabulous Nut Bra offer, Box 217, Lyechester, CT. 07610.

************************************ OUR SEXY PAST ***

SEX HOLES *and* SEX BLIMPS

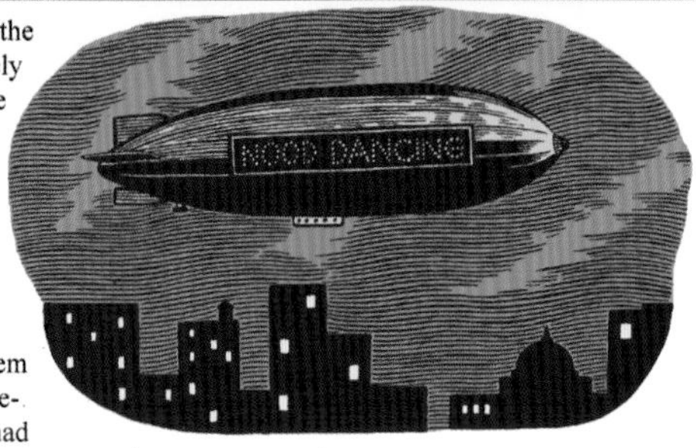
NOOD DANCING

SEX HOLES AND SEX BLIMPS! Who among us remembers them today? They were the "dirty little secret" of the first half of the twentieth century, and as a result are completely forgotten now. Yet millions of Americans were at one time or another familiar with one or both of these unique adult entertainment environments.

IT WAS THE 1920S WHEN IT STARTED. Prohibition was in effect, cocaine had recently been outlawed, and the leftovers of Victorian morality squashed any public displays of sexuality. But there was a loophole in the laws: anything was legal as long as it took place more than 15 feet above or below ground level. The first person to take advantage of this was a man named Rupert Bottenberg. In 1921 he bought a lot of five de-commissioned air force blimps, had them outfitted as crude adult taverns, and set them to work above the skyline of Newark. Soon most American cities had Sex Blimps in operation, and bluenoses were helpless. It wasn't long before other independent operators had taken inspiration and were digging tunnels into the earth, creating subterranean cellars where anything could take place.

THEY WERE CERTAINLY DANGEROUS. Sex Blimps were liable to explode or collapse; people usually boarded them on shaky unsafe ramps propped on windowsills or rooftops. Sex Holes were as often as not constructed by people with little or no engineering experience, and were likely to collapse or fill up with raw sewage at any moment. The newpapers rarely reported such disasters, because any news involving the Holes or Blimps was held to be distasteful. So it's not known exactly how many people died. The Hindenburg disaster in 1938 was major news; but Sex Blimp explosions, such as the one in Weehawken that claimed 28 lives in 1941, merited merely a sentence on the back page.

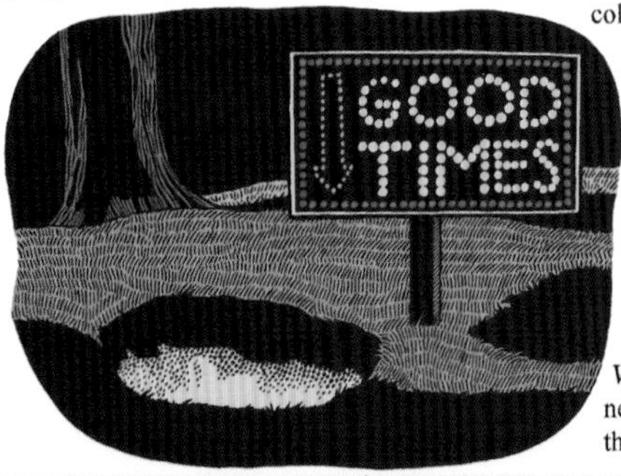
GOOD TIMES

HOW DID THEY WORK? Sex Blimps floated low over the rooftops, scouting for customers. Interested individuals would shout or wave handkerchiefs, and the blimp would extend a ramp. To find a Sex Hole, you merely had to go looking for the sign next to the hole. Many were on people's front lawns, but just as often they were situated in public parks. All customers were welcome, as long as they had money.

WHERE DID THEY GO? As laws at ground level became relaxed, there was no longer any need to risk death for a little pleasure. The last reported Sex Hole closed in Baltimore in 1954; the last Sex Blimp was the "Slippery Woo", which exited the skies of Chicago in 1956.

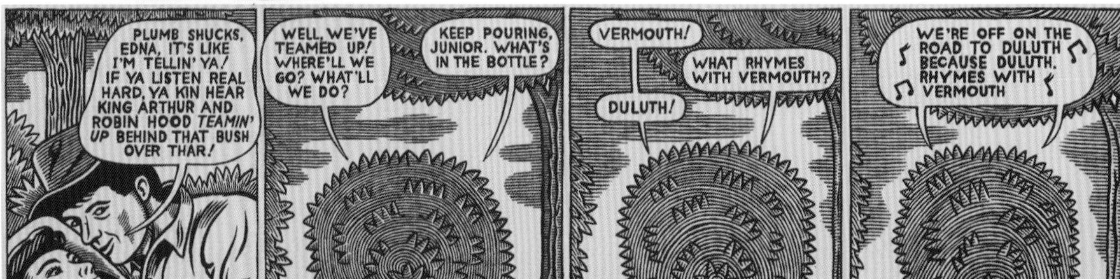
PLUMB SHUCKS, EDNA, IT'S LIKE I'M TELLIN' YA! IF YA LISTEN REAL HARD, YA KIN HEAR KING ARTHUR AND ROBIN HOOD TEAMIN' UP BEHIND THAT BUSH OVER THAR!
WELL, WE'VE TEAMED UP! WHERE'LL WE GO? WHAT'LL WE DO?
KEEP POURING, JUNIOR. WHAT'S IN THE BOTTLE?
VERMOUTH!
WHAT RHYMES WITH VERMOUTH?
DULUTH!
WE'RE OFF ON THE ROAD TO DULUTH BECAUSE DULUTH. RHYMES WITH VERMOUTH

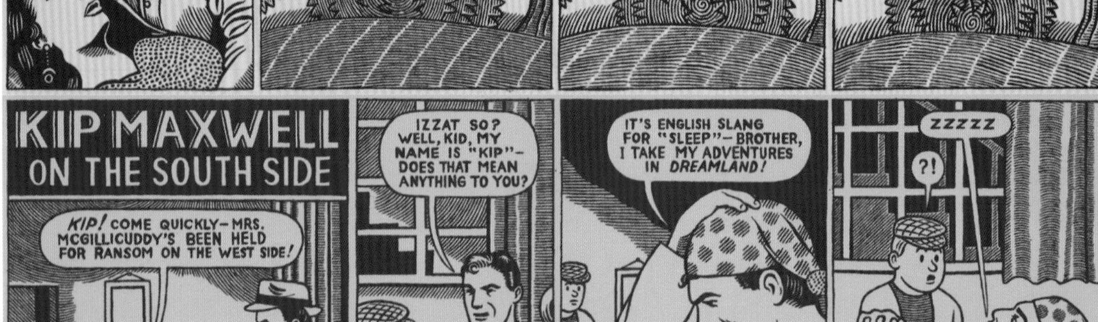
KIP MAXWELL
ON THE SOUTH SIDE
KIP! COME QUICKLY– MRS. MCGILLICUDDY'S BEEN HELD FOR RANSOM ON THE WEST SIDE!
IZZAT SO? WELL, KID, MY NAME IS "KIP"– DOES THAT MEAN ANYTHING TO YOU?
IT'S ENGLISH SLANG FOR "SLEEP"– BROTHER, I TAKE MY ADVENTURES IN DREAMLAND!
ZZZZZ
?!

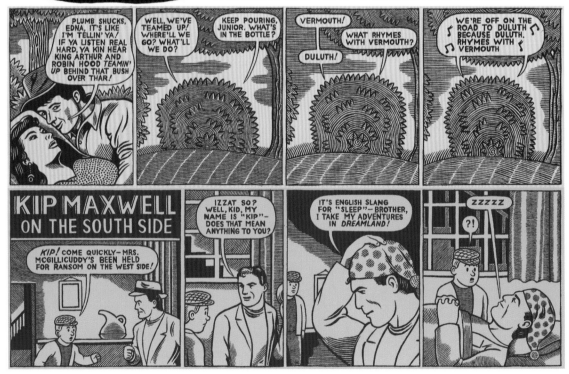

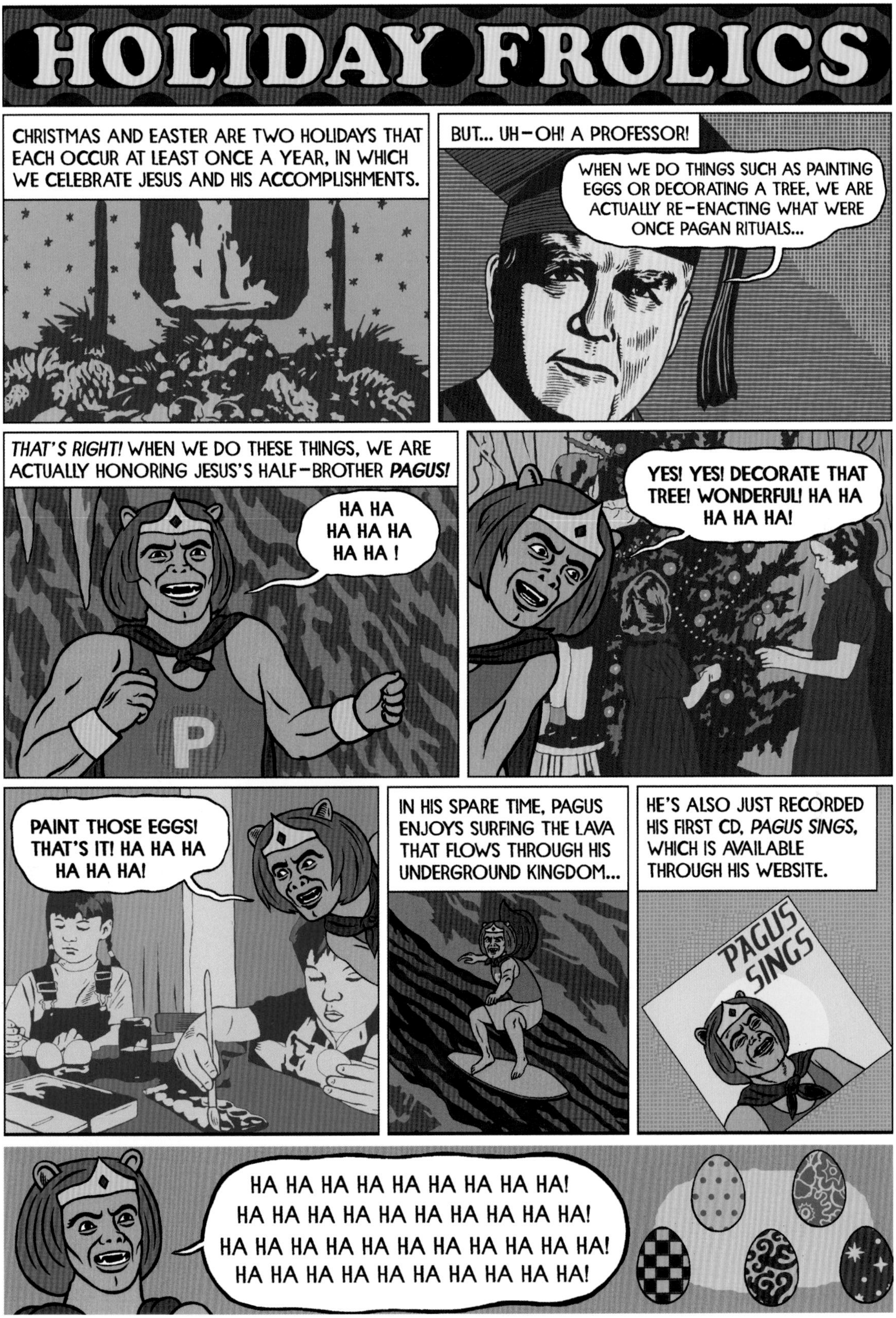
HOLIDAY FROLICS
CHRISTMAS AND EASTER ARE TWO HOLIDAYS THAT EACH OCCUR AT LEAST ONCE A YEAR, IN WHICH WE CELEBRATE JESUS AND HIS ACCOMPLISHMENTS.
BUT... UH-OH! A PROFESSOR!
WHEN WE DO THINGS SUCH AS PAINTING EGGS OR DECORATING A TREE, WE ARE ACTUALLY RE-ENACTING WHAT WERE ONCE PAGAN RITUALS...
THAT'S RIGHT! WHEN WE DO THESE THINGS, WE ARE ACTUALLY HONORING JESUS'S HALF-BROTHER *PAGUS!*
HA HA HA HA HA HA HA !
YES! YES! DECORATE THAT TREE! WONDERFUL! HA HA HA HA HA!
PAINT THOSE EGGS! THAT'S IT! HA HA HA HA HA HA!
IN HIS SPARE TIME, PAGUS ENJOYS SURFING THE LAVA THAT FLOWS THROUGH HIS UNDERGROUND KINGDOM...
HE'S ALSO JUST RECORDED HIS FIRST CD, *PAGUS SINGS*, WHICH IS AVAILABLE THROUGH HIS WEBSITE.
PAGUS SINGS
HA HA HA HA HA HA HA HA HA!
HA HA HA HA HA HA HA HA HA HA!
HA HA HA HA HA HA HA HA HA HA HA!
HA HA HA HA HA HA HA HA HA HA!

ADVERTISEMENT: "UNCLE SAM SPEAKS HIS MIND"

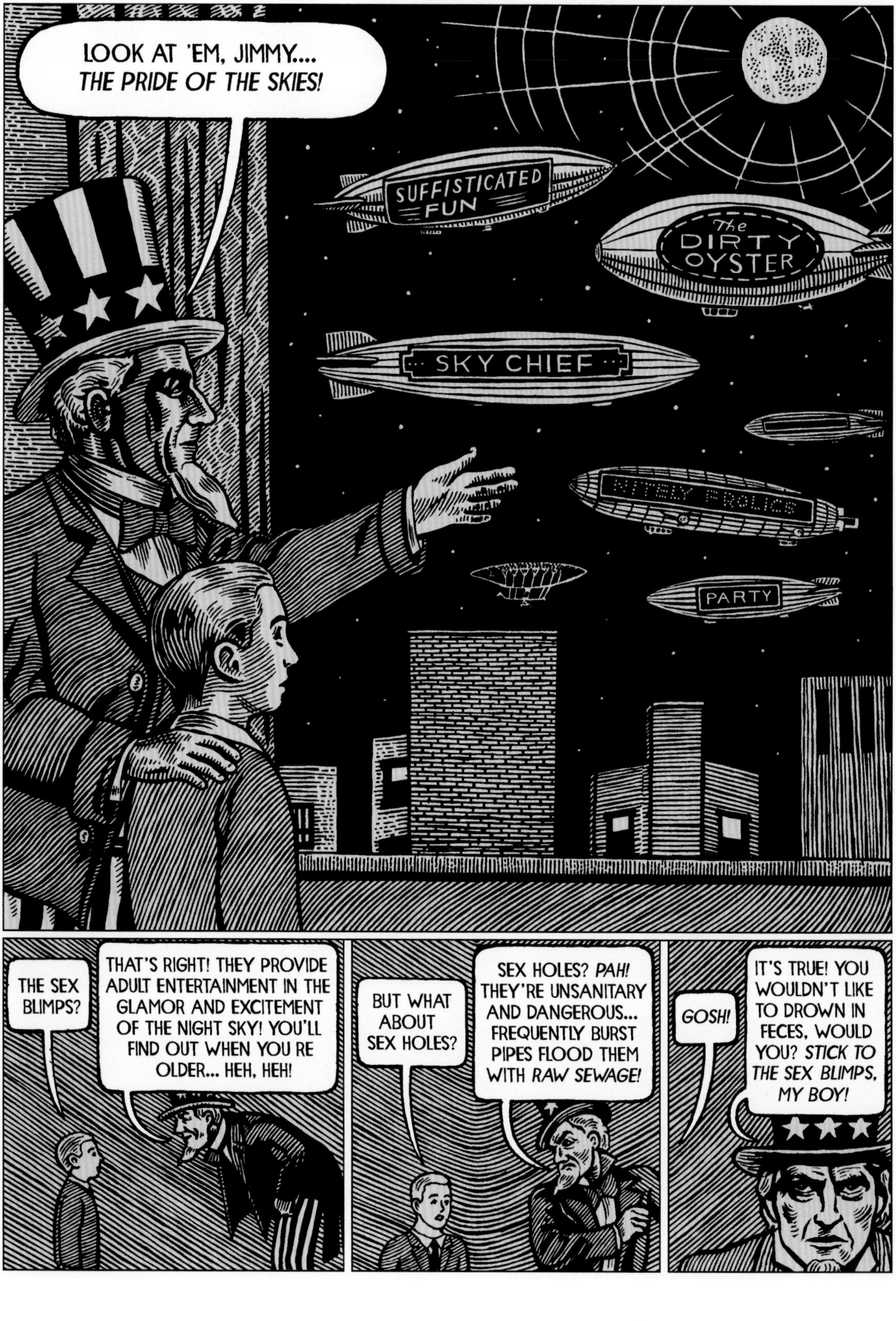
LOOK AT 'EM, JIMMY.... THE PRIDE OF THE SKIES!
SUFFISTICATED FUN
The DIRTY OYSTER
SKY CHIEF
NITELY FROLICS
PARTY
THE SEX BLIMPS?
THAT'S RIGHT! THEY PROVIDE ADULT ENTERTAINMENT IN THE GLAMOR AND EXCITEMENT OF THE NIGHT SKY! YOU'LL FIND OUT WHEN YOU RE OLDER... HEH, HEH!
BUT WHAT ABOUT SEX HOLES?
SEX HOLES? PAH! THEY'RE UNSANITARY AND DANGEROUS... FREQUENTLY BURST PIPES FLOOD THEM WITH RAW SEWAGE!
GOSH!
IT'S TRUE! YOU WOULDN'T LIKE TO DROWN IN FECES, WOULD YOU? STICK TO THE SEX BLIMPS, MY BOY!

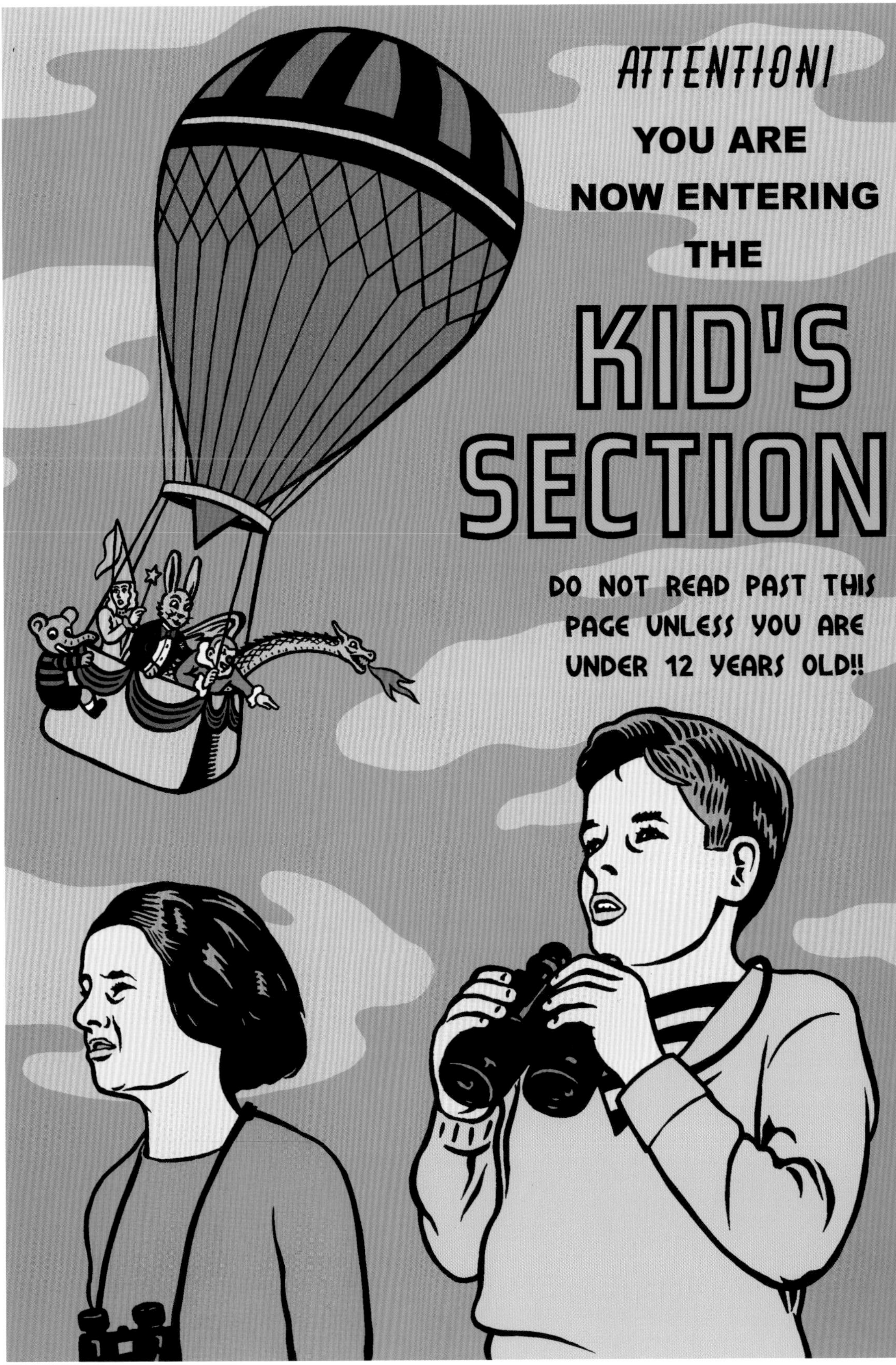
ATTENTION!
YOU ARE NOW ENTERING THE
KID'S SECTION
DO NOT READ PAST THIS PAGE UNLESS YOU ARE UNDER 12 YEARS OLD!!

UNCLE BILLY'S
DRUNKEN, BITTER GUIDE TO THE ANIMAL KINGDOM

A *ZEBRA* IS LIKE A HORSE THAT'S REAL STRIPEY. YOU KNOW WHO LIKES STRIPEY THINGS? WOMEN! MY EX-WIFE SURE DID. AND JEWELS. I BET IF SHE HAD A ZEBRA WITH JEWELS ALL OVER IT, THAT'D MAKE HER HAPPY, IF ANYTHING COULD.

THE *RACOON* EATS GARBAGE, BUT IT WASHES IT IN WATER FIRST. SOUNDS LIKE A BOSS I USED TO HAVE! HE'LL GET WHAT'S COMING TO HIM, YOU CAN BET ON THAT. SON OF A BITCH CAUGHT ME STEALING PAPERCLIPS.

THE *WARTHOG* IS KIND OF A WEIRD-LOOKING PIG, AND THE BOOK HERE SAYS IT DIGS HOLES IN THE GROUND WHICH ARE A NUISANCE TO TRA-VELERS. HAW HAW! I LIKE THAT! SOUNDS LIKE THE KIND OF ANIMAL I WOULDN'T MIND SHARING SOME BEERS WITH. YOU'RE ALRIGHT, WARTHOG!

THIS HERE'S THE *EUROPEAN POLECAT*, WHICH GIVES OFF A STINK WHEN IT'S ANNOYED. IT BETTER NOT TRY THAT WITH ME, I TELL YOU. I GOT A REAL SHORT FUSE WITH THINGS THAT TRY TO PUT A STINK ON ME. HEY, THIS BOTTLE'S EMPTY.

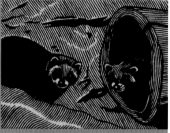

Mr. Flopears

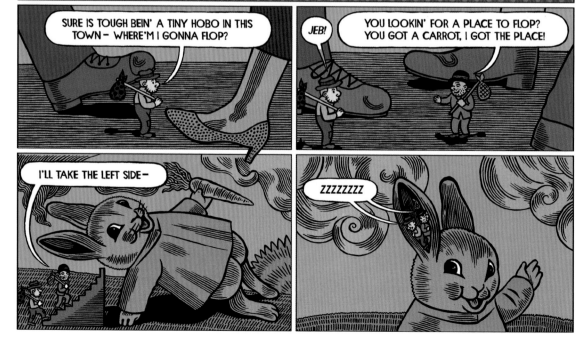

SURE IS TOUGH BEIN' A TINY HOBO IN THIS TOWN - WHERE'M I GONNA FLOP?

JEB!

YOU LOOKIN' FOR A PLACE TO FLOP? YOU GOT A CARROT, I GOT THE PLACE!

I'LL TAKE THE LEFT SIDE—

ZZZZZZZZ

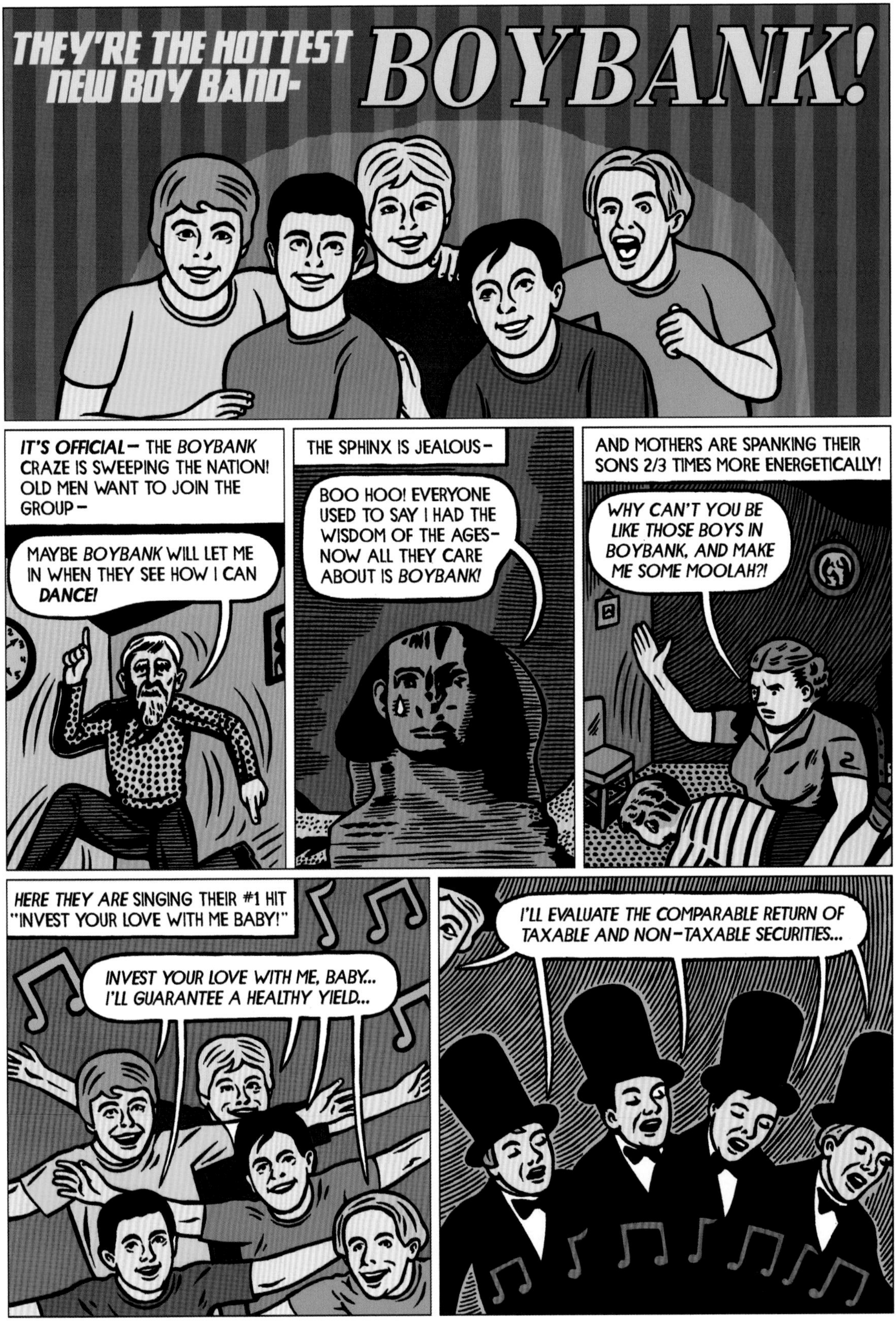

THEY'RE THE HOTTEST NEW BOY BAND-
BOYBANK!
IT'S OFFICIAL— THE BOYBANK CRAZE IS SWEEPING THE NATION! OLD MEN WANT TO JOIN THE GROUP—
MAYBE BOYBANK WILL LET ME IN WHEN THEY SEE HOW I CAN DANCE!
THE SPHINX IS JEALOUS—
BOO HOO! EVERYONE USED TO SAY I HAD THE WISDOM OF THE AGES— NOW ALL THEY CARE ABOUT IS BOYBANK!
AND MOTHERS ARE SPANKING THEIR SONS 2/3 TIMES MORE ENERGETICALLY!
WHY CAN'T YOU BE LIKE THOSE BOYS IN BOYBANK, AND MAKE ME SOME MOOLAH?!
HERE THEY ARE SINGING THEIR #1 HIT "INVEST YOUR LOVE WITH ME BABY!"
INVEST YOUR LOVE WITH ME, BABY... I'LL GUARANTEE A HEALTHY YIELD...
I'LL EVALUATE THE COMPARABLE RETURN OF TAXABLE AND NON-TAXABLE SECURITIES...

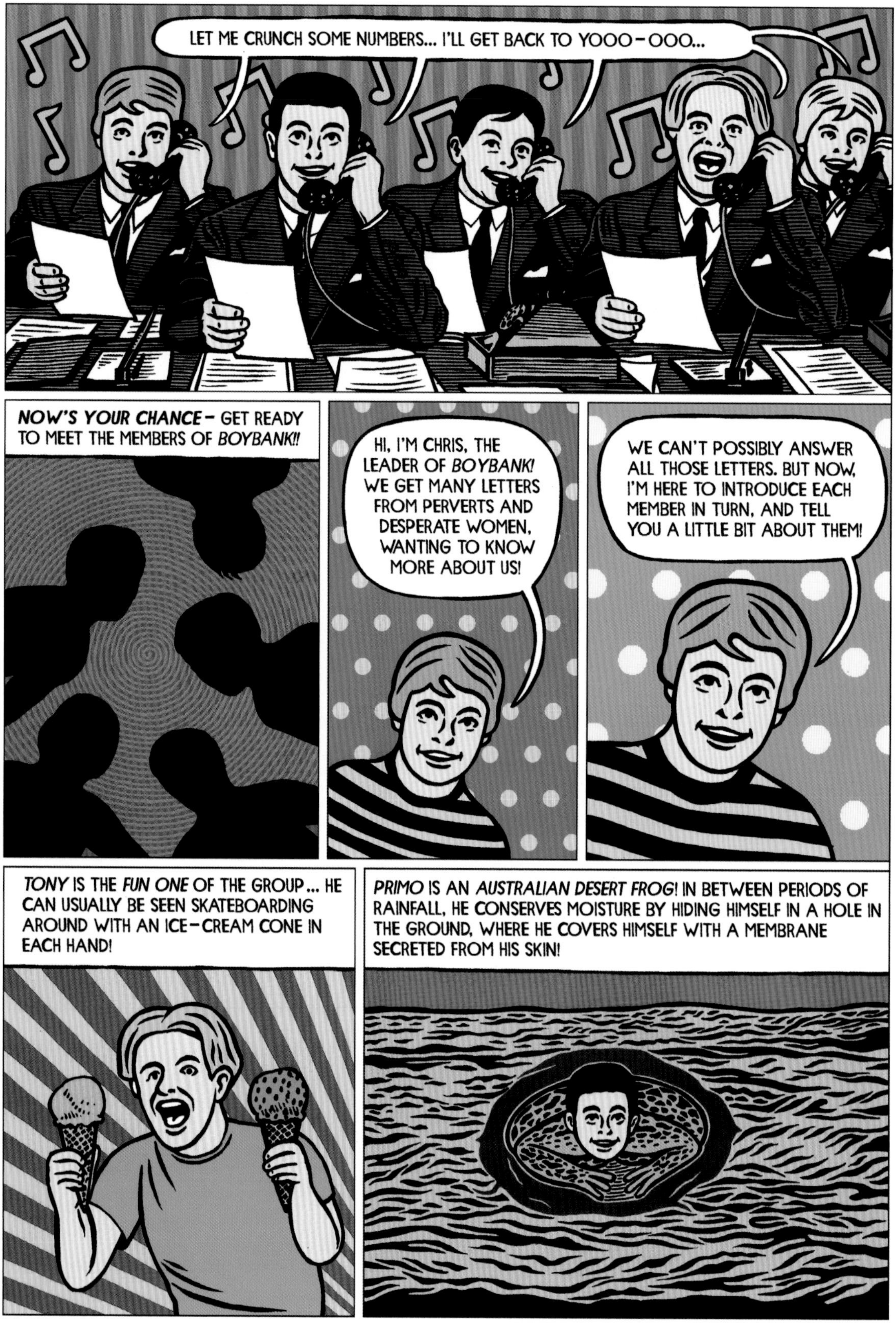
LET ME CRUNCH SOME NUMBERS... I'LL GET BACK TO YOOO-OOO...
NOW'S YOUR CHANCE - GET READY TO MEET THE MEMBERS OF BOYBANK!!
HI, I'M CHRIS, THE LEADER OF BOYBANK! WE GET MANY LETTERS FROM PERVERTS AND DESPERATE WOMEN, WANTING TO KNOW MORE ABOUT US!
WE CAN'T POSSIBLY ANSWER ALL THOSE LETTERS. BUT NOW, I'M HERE TO INTRODUCE EACH MEMBER IN TURN, AND TELL YOU A LITTLE BIT ABOUT THEM!
TONY IS THE FUN ONE OF THE GROUP... HE CAN USUALLY BE SEEN SKATEBOARDING AROUND WITH AN ICE-CREAM CONE IN EACH HAND!
PRIMO IS AN AUSTRALIAN DESERT FROG! IN BETWEEN PERIODS OF RAINFALL, HE CONSERVES MOISTURE BY HIDING HIMSELF IN A HOLE IN THE GROUND, WHERE HE COVERS HIMSELF WITH A MEMBRANE SECRETED FROM HIS SKIN!

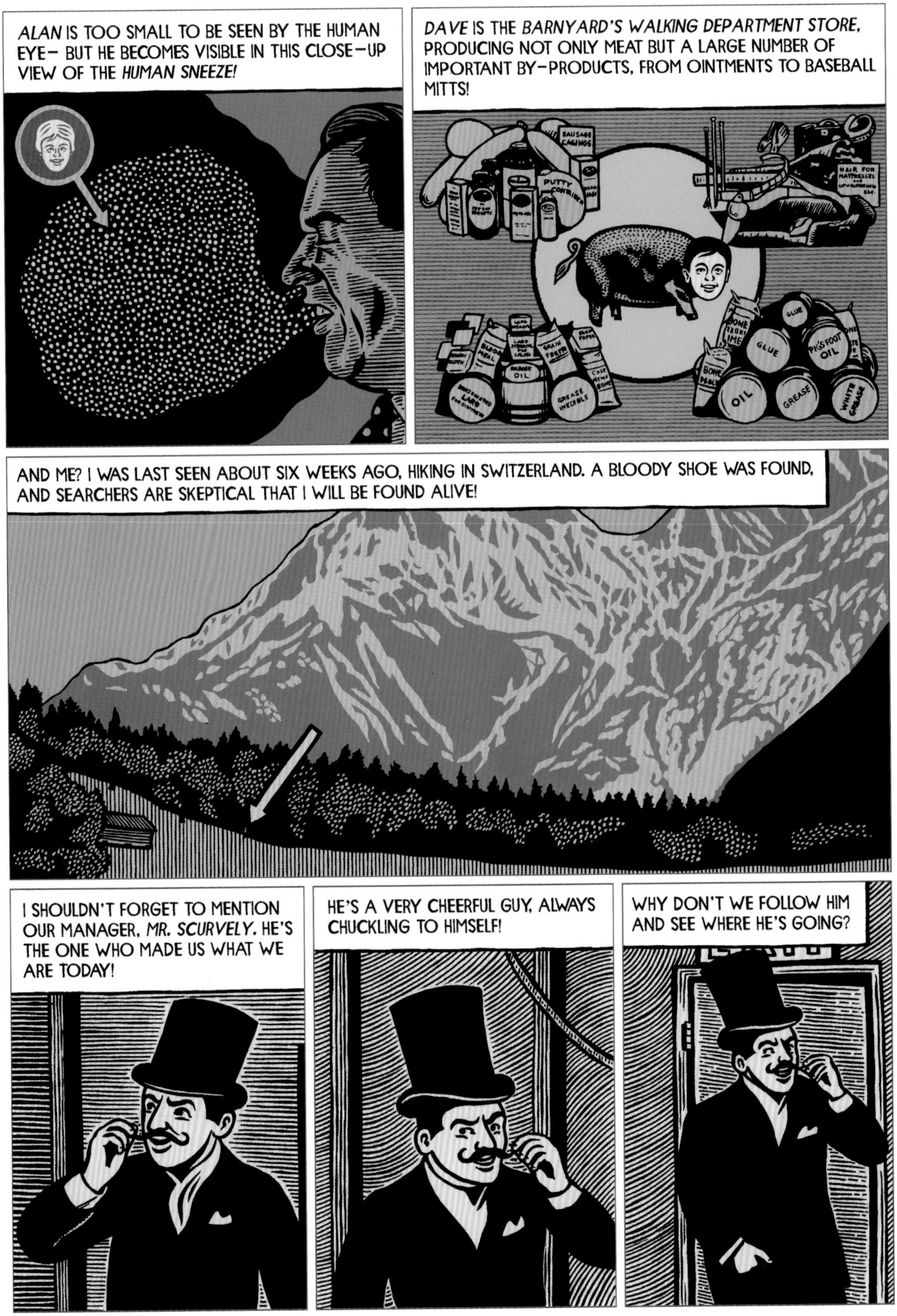

ALAN IS TOO SMALL TO BE SEEN BY THE HUMAN EYE— BUT HE BECOMES VISIBLE IN THIS CLOSE-UP VIEW OF THE HUMAN SNEEZE!
DAVE IS THE BARNYARD'S WALKING DEPARTMENT STORE, PRODUCING NOT ONLY MEAT BUT A LARGE NUMBER OF IMPORTANT BY-PRODUCTS, FROM OINTMENTS TO BASEBALL MITTS!
SAUSAGE CASINGS
GLUE
PIGS FOOT OIL
OIL
GREASE
WHITE GREASE
AND ME? I WAS LAST SEEN ABOUT SIX WEEKS AGO, HIKING IN SWITZERLAND. A BLOODY SHOE WAS FOUND, AND SEARCHERS ARE SKEPTICAL THAT I WILL BE FOUND ALIVE!
I SHOULDN'T FORGET TO MENTION OUR MANAGER, MR. SCURVELY. HE'S THE ONE WHO MADE US WHAT WE ARE TODAY!
HE'S A VERY CHEERFUL GUY, ALWAYS CHUCKLING TO HIMSELF!
WHY DON'T WE FOLLOW HIM AND SEE WHERE HE'S GOING?

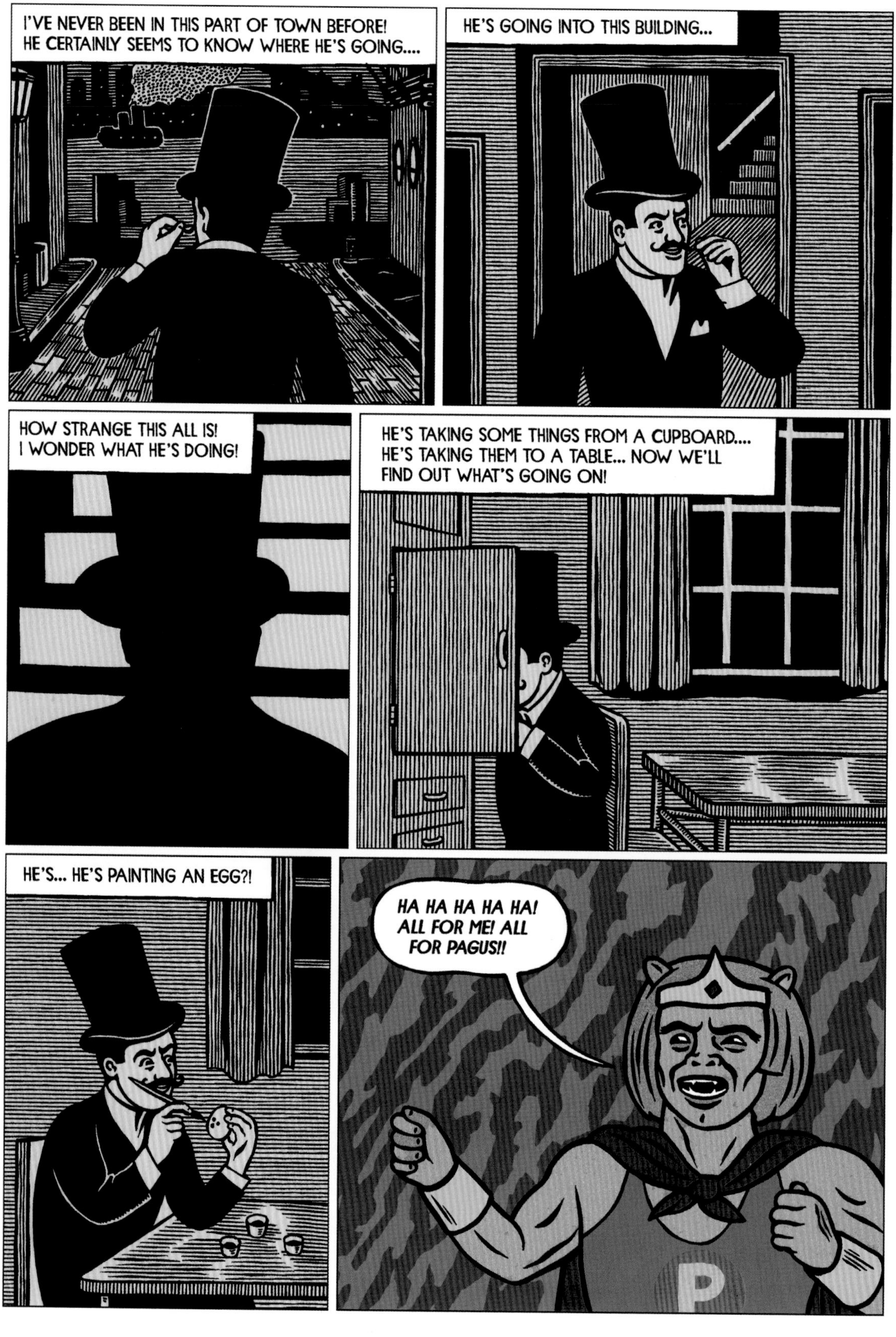
I'VE NEVER BEEN IN THIS PART OF TOWN BEFORE! HE CERTAINLY SEEMS TO KNOW WHERE HE'S GOING....
HE'S GOING INTO THIS BUILDING...
HOW STRANGE THIS ALL IS! I WONDER WHAT HE'S DOING!
HE'S TAKING SOME THINGS FROM A CUPBOARD.... HE'S TAKING THEM TO A TABLE... NOW WE'LL FIND OUT WHAT'S GOING ON!
HE'S... HE'S PAINTING AN EGG?!
HA HA HA HA HA! ALL FOR ME! ALL FOR PAGUS!!
P

CUT OUT'N'PLAY™

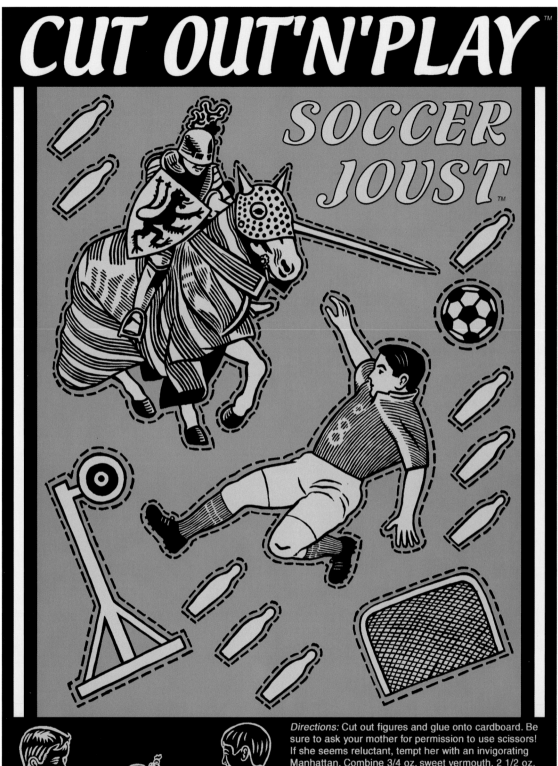

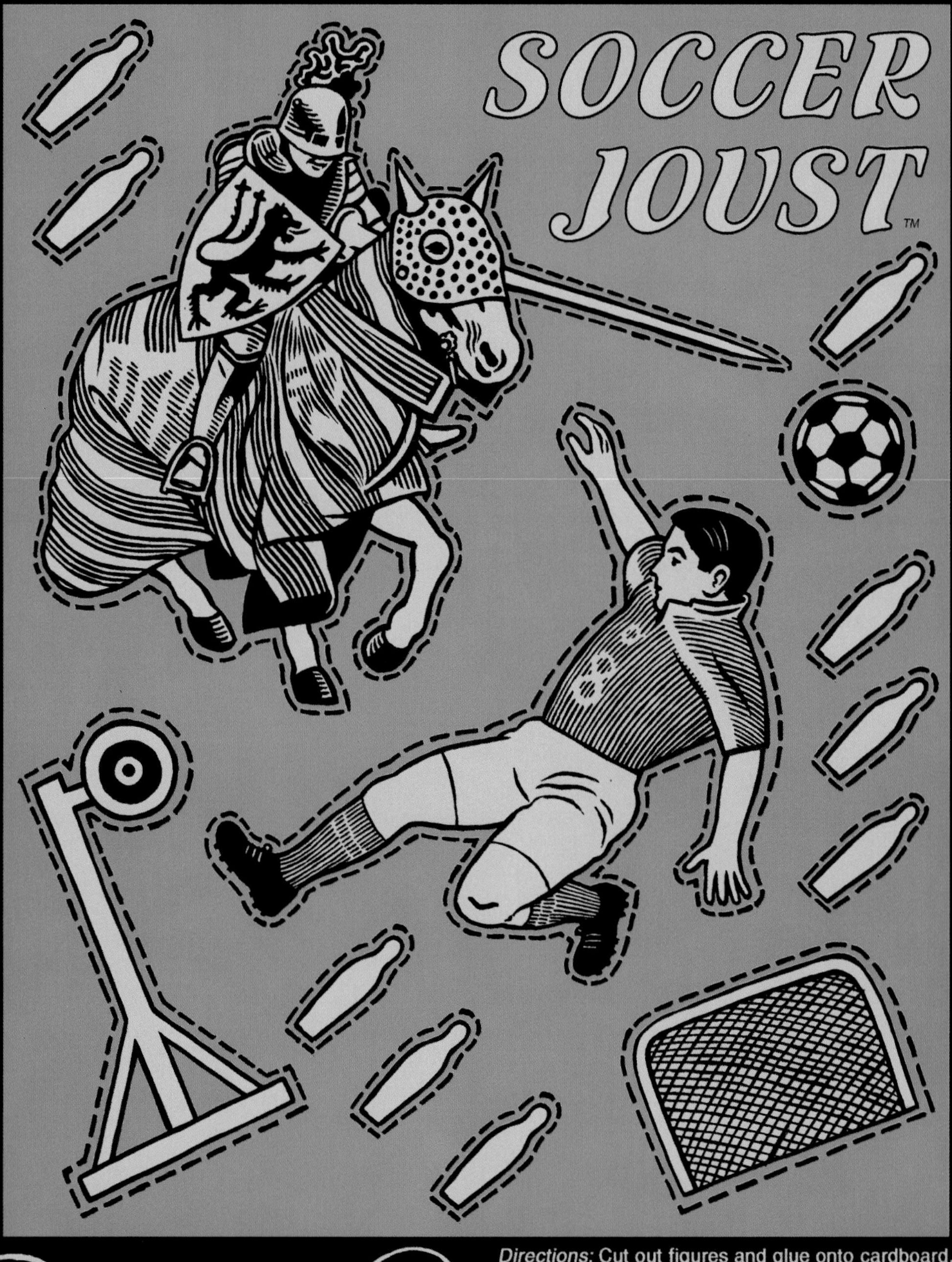
SOCCER JOUST™

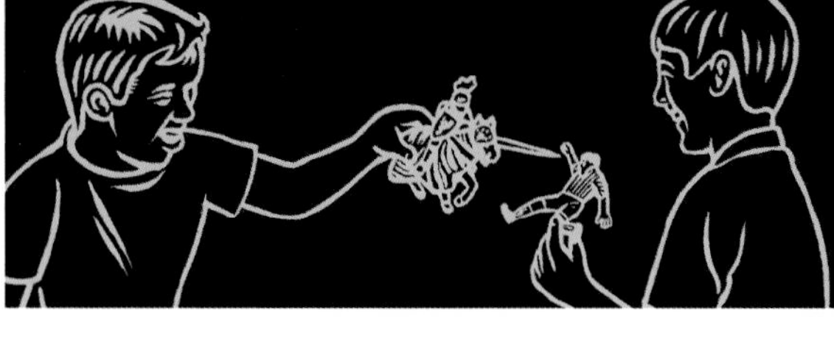

Directions: Cut out figures and glue onto cardboard. Be sure to ask your mother for permission to use scissors! If she seems reluctant, tempt her with an invigorating Manhattan. Combine 3/4 oz. sweet vermouth, 2 1/2 oz. Bourbon, and bitters with 2-3 ice cubes in a mixing glass. Stir gently. Place a cherry in a cocktail glass and strain the whiskey mixture over the cherry. Rub a piece of orange peel on the edge of the glass to add flavor, and serve. *Mmmm!*

HEY! KIDS! SHAKESPEARE!

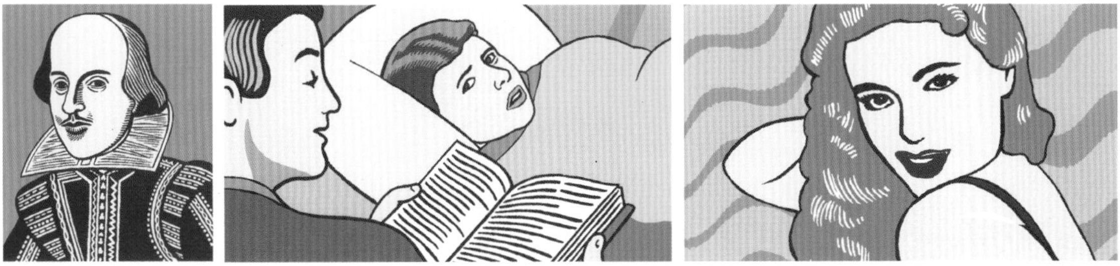

Experts have estimated that the average person thinks about Shakespeare about once every 3.6 minutes. Whether we're reading Titus Andronicus to our kids at bedtime or quoting from the Sonnets at some chick whom we wish to do, Shakespeare is eternally present in our lives.

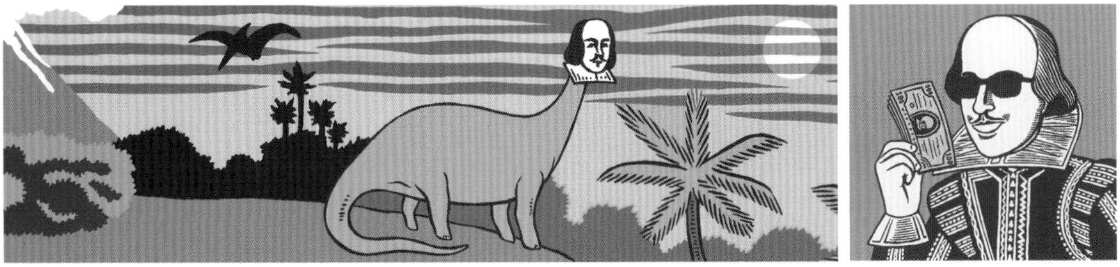

But who was Shakespeare? Many scholars now believe that he was actually a large, herbivorous lizard of the Pleistocene era; others disagree. "He was just an average guy," says writer Dom Bedooby. "He probably made a bet with his friends that he could get himself quoted a lot."

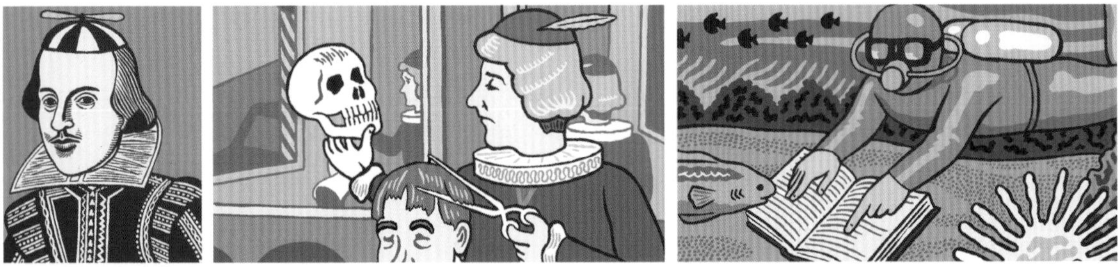

Us normal people love Shakespeare; a lot of eccentrics like him too. Take, for instance, the barber who goes to work dressed as Hamlet, or the schoolteacher who spends weekends and vacations underwater, trying to teach fish about iambic pentameter.

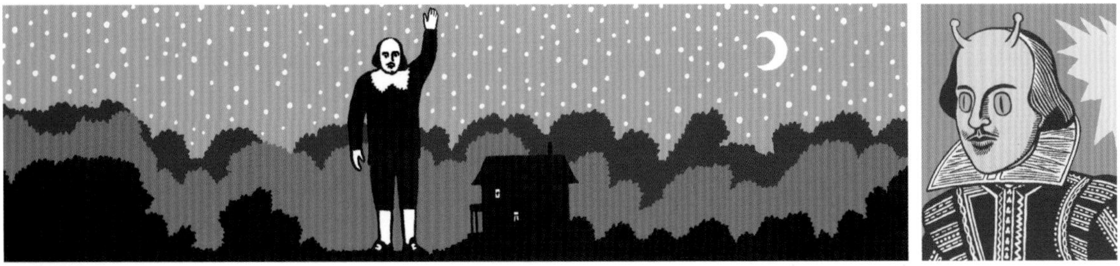

Then there's the farmer in Ohio who's built an 80-foot statue of the Bard using papier-mache and corn husks. Says he, "I want the aliens to come down and investigate, so I can be the first person to tell them all about Shakespeare."

EXTRA! WHERE IS SHAKESPEARE'S GOLD?

Imagine the scene. It is a quiet, moonlit night in 1607. Three men stand around a freshly dug hole. **At** the bottom of the hole is a wooden chest. Two of the men hold spades; the third is instantly recognizable as William Shakespeare, the David Mamet of his age. Now he speaks:

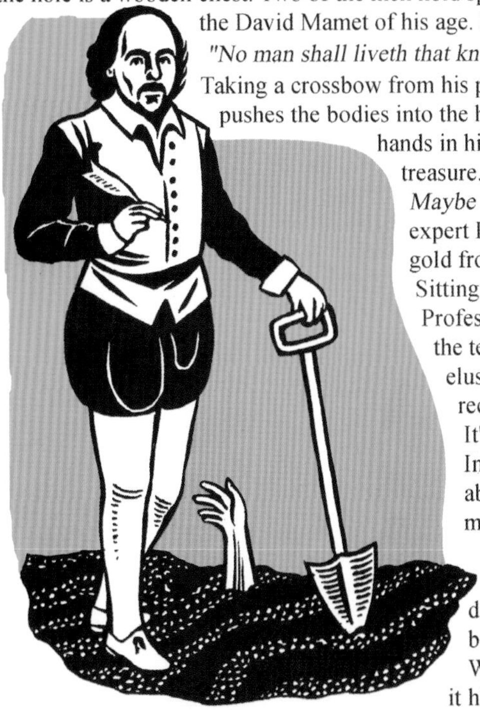

"No man shall liveth that knoweth of my gold."

Taking a crossbow from his pocket, he kills both men before they have time to protest.Then he pushes the bodies into the hole and fills it in. And, whistling nonchalantly, he strolls away, hands in his pockets. Now no-one but he knows the location of his buried treasure.

Maybe it didn't happen quite like this. But, points out Shakespeare expert Philip Silvers, "What's certain is that he probably made a lot of gold from writing those plays. And no-one knows where it is now."

Sitting in his office at the Center for Shakespeare Studies in Avon, Professor Silvers describd how generations of experts have combed the texts of his plays, searching for clues to the location of the Bard's elusive fortune. "I myself have recently been looking through this recently discovered long-lost play, *Romeo and Juliet: Full Throttle.* It's a sequel to another play of his, and I'm convinced it's genuine. In fact I had just marked this phrase, *'Great riches'.* And here, right above it: *'The first of Where most wondrous large.'* But that would mean... of course! A giant W!"

At this he jumped up and ran out of the office. Seconds later he was visible down in the parking lot, jumping into his car and driving away hurriedly. Within minutes, every scholar in the building was in pursuit, some of them on bicycles or in rowboats. We even saw one old coot push a child off his tricycle and jump on it himself, his bony knees sticking out as he pedalled away wildly.

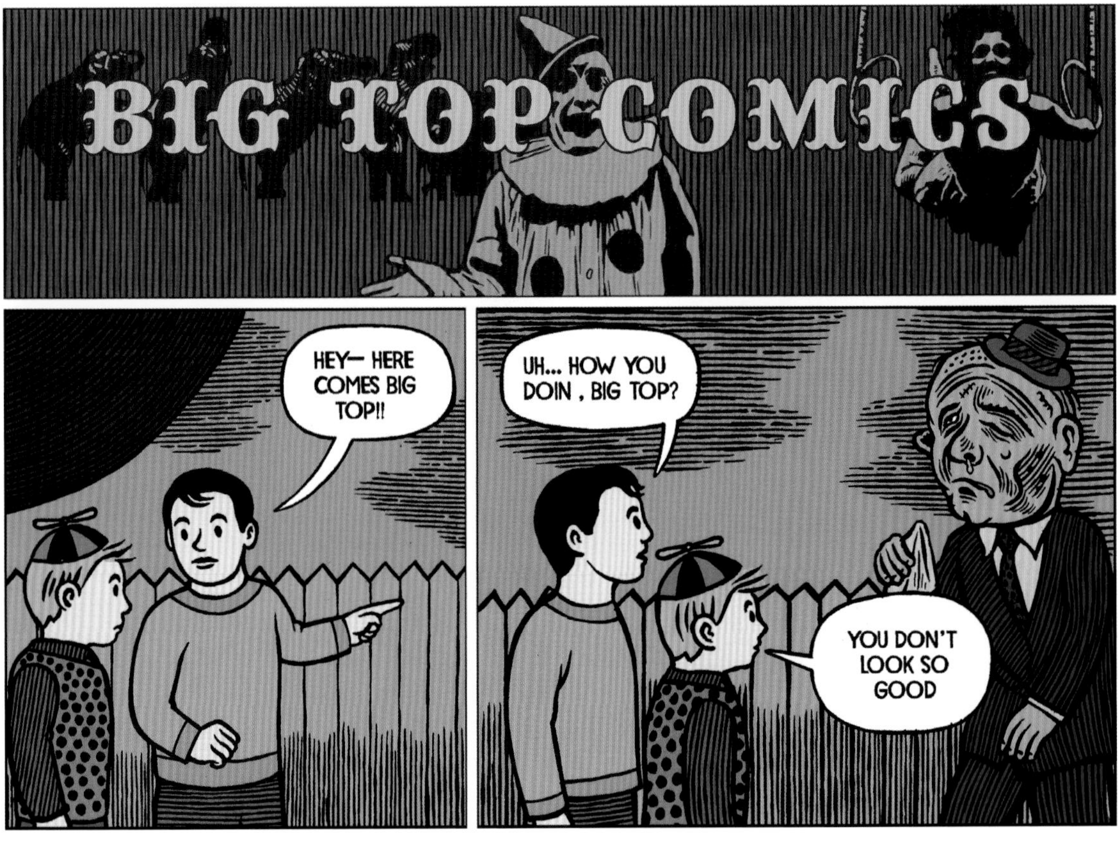
BIG TOP COMICS
HEY— HERE COMES BIG TOP!!
UH... HOW YOU DOIN , BIG TOP?
YOU DON'T LOOK SO GOOD

SHERLOCK HOLMES VERSUS JUNGLE BOY

PART 47

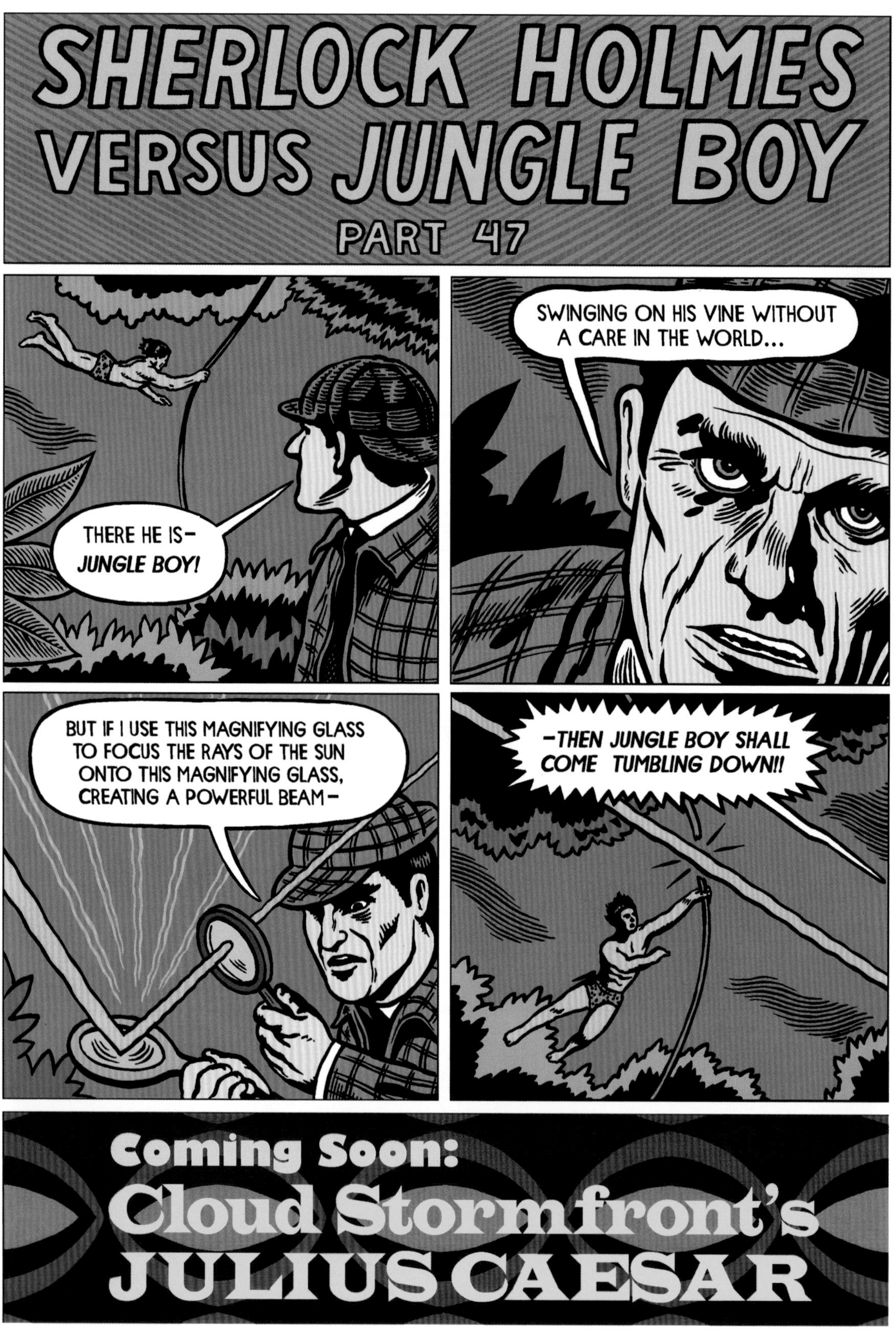
THERE HE IS–
JUNGLE BOY!
SWINGING ON HIS VINE WITHOUT A CARE IN THE WORLD...
BUT IF I USE THIS MAGNIFYING GLASS TO FOCUS THE RAYS OF THE SUN ONTO THIS MAGNIFYING GLASS, CREATING A POWERFUL BEAM–
–THEN JUNGLE BOY SHALL COME TUMBLING DOWN!!

Coming Soon:

Cloud Stormfront's JULIUS CAESAR

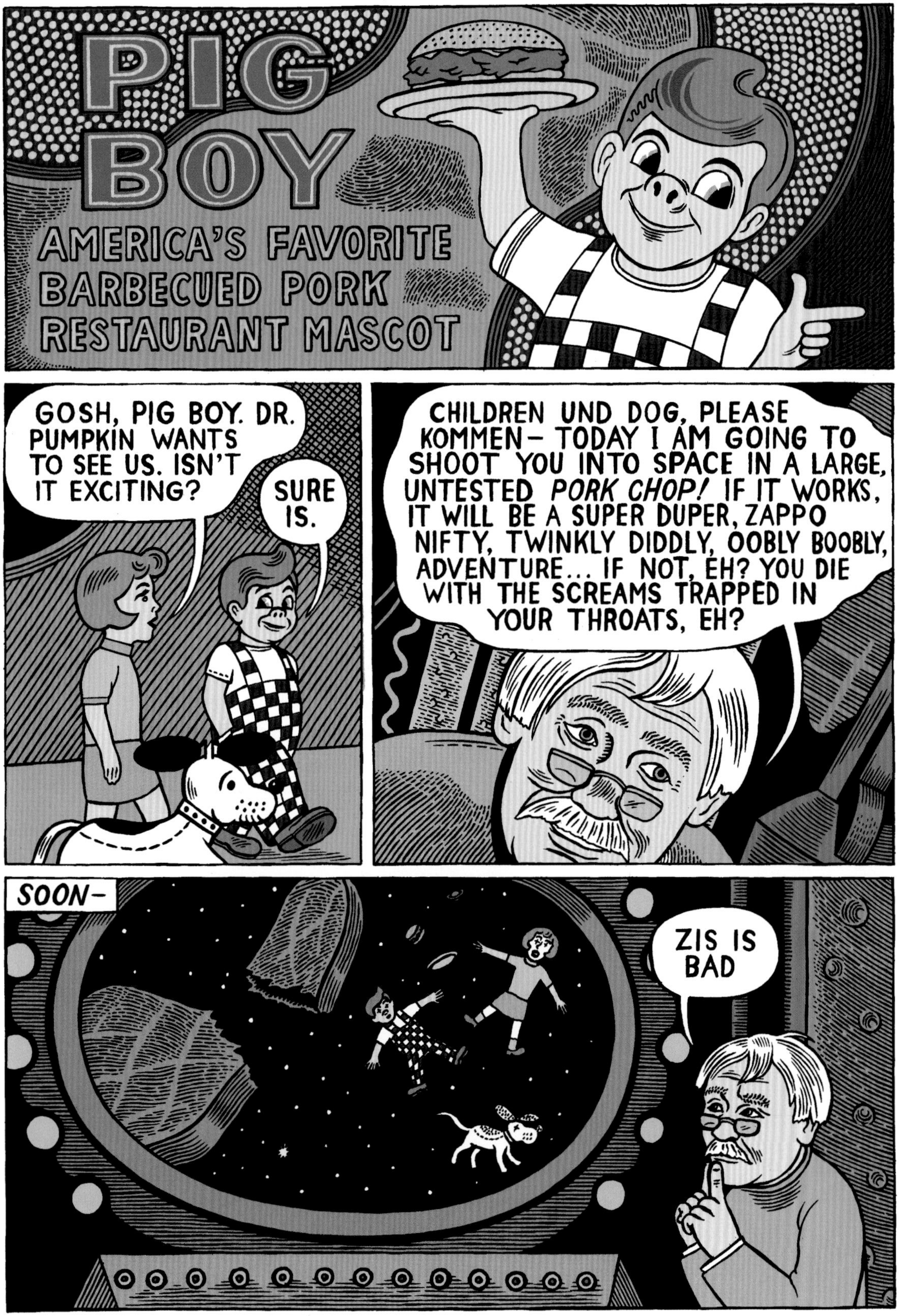
PIG BOY
AMERICA'S FAVORITE BARBECUED PORK RESTAURANT MASCOT
GOSH, PIG BOY. DR. PUMPKIN WANTS TO SEE US. ISN'T IT EXCITING?
SURE IS.
CHILDREN UND DOG, PLEASE KOMMEN– TODAY I AM GOING TO SHOOT YOU INTO SPACE IN A LARGE, UNTESTED *PORK CHOP!* IF IT WORKS, IT WILL BE A SUPER DUPER, ZAPPO NIFTY, TWINKLY DIDDLY, OOBLY BOOBLY, ADVENTURE... IF NOT, EH? YOU DIE WITH THE SCREAMS TRAPPED IN YOUR THROATS, EH?
SOON–
ZIS IS BAD

THE HARDLY BOYS *IN* "THE ADVENTURE OF THE HEADLESS CORPSE"

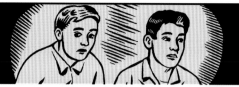

Bob and Jim Hardly had only been exploring for a few moments when they made their exciting discovery. The twin boys, their faces flushed with excitement, gazed upon their find, unearthed in a grove surrounded by a meadow: a naked, headless corpse.

"Wow! It's a lady!" breathed Jim.
"Gosh! Look at her!" marvelled Bob.

They never thought of calling the police. Their instant shared idea was to visit upon their Uncle Alex, whose domicile bordered the corpse-bearing meadow, and to solicit his advice and encouragement. They sprinted to their bicycles and raced each other to see who could get there fastest.

They burst in on Uncle Alex just as he was in the middle of one of his "experiments". He started, and shuddered abruptly, hastily covering the frog with a towel. "Boys!" he admonished loudly. "Knock, lads, how often have I told you to knock!"

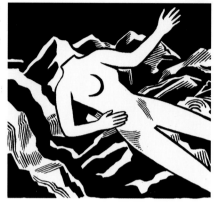

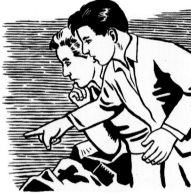

"But Uncle Alex" persisted Jim, "we saw a naked, headless corpse in a copse in the meadow!"
"Yes!" blurted Bob. "We need your sage advice on how to proceed investigationally."

Uncle Alex faced them now, a firm twinkle in his eye. "Boys, boys," he admonished them, "How many times have I told you to examine the evidence? If you had just looked a little closer at this "naked, headless corpse" of yours, you would have found it to be no more than a discarded mannequin, of the type used in department stores; and, upon inquiring here, could have been informed of the fact that such a mannequin had been discarded, with my permission, in the copse within my meadow. And it will probably have been removed by the next time you look. Not that I know anything of headless corpses," and at this last pronouncement his eyes darted wildly.

The twins exchanged wary glances, for both had noticed the darting eyes.

"No, no!" exclaimed Uncle Alex. "I read your wary glances; be not of such apprehensions, nay! My darting eyes meant merely that I - to confess my guilty secret- had watched last night, on television, a film the narrative of which involved headless corpses, and that your Aunt Ethel would surely rain invective upon my head were she but to suspect my viewing of such. My guilt lies in just this source, boys, and no other!" At this he raised his hands imploringly, and widened his eyes to show truthfulness.

The boys relaxed. "Sorry Uncle," said Bob. "Kind of got ahead of ourselves there."

"That's alright boys. Here, why don't you have some of these awful meal powder biscuits."

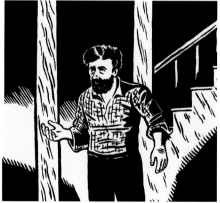

The boys put the biscuits in their mouth, and instantly responded with grimaces of disgust. "Ugh! These are awful!" Jim exclaimed, while Bob wasted no time in finding something he could spit into. "And look- it says right on the package, "Pathetically dreadful." What is the story behind these mediocre biscuits and their extraordinary packaging?"

"Well, boys," said Uncle Alex, and his face was somber. "You have to imagine the world these came out of. A world where a company that made perfectly awful biscuits hired a man to do the work of publicity for them, and to package and sell their product; this man tries his best, but they blame him for their failure, and mock him, and degrade him; and in this world the man becomes bitter and vengeful, and decides, since his masters are lazy and foolish, to mock their product, both in its packaging and in narrative print advertisements written in short story form."

"Then... are we in just such an advertisement?" breathed the twins together.

"I'm afraid so, boys," said Uncle Alfred, and his face was grim.

They each took another meal biscuit in silence, and then they forced them down, though the effort was painful. Then they all felt slightly ill, and went home to lie down.

LORD NORTH'S MEAL BISCUITS
"I cannot apologize enough for the quality of these revolting biscuits... I am heartily ashamed." - Lord North

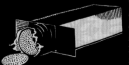

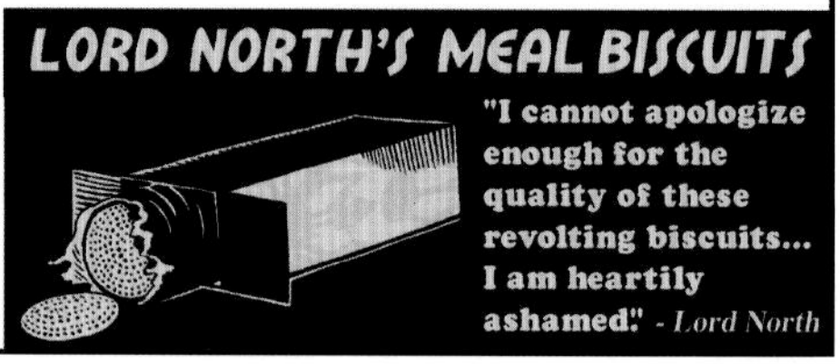

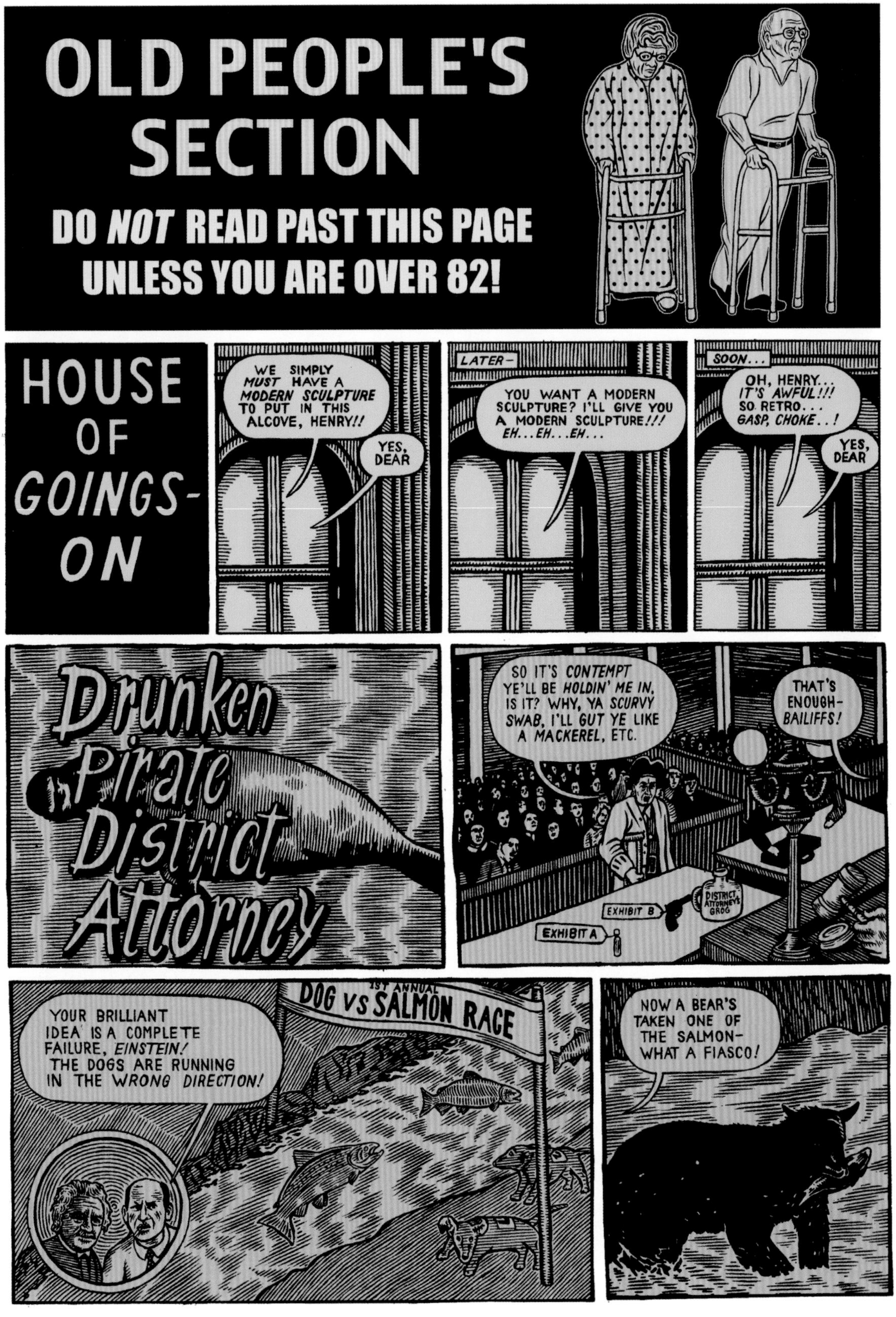
OLD PEOPLE'S SECTION
DO NOT READ PAST THIS PAGE UNLESS YOU ARE OVER 82!
HOUSE OF GOINGS-ON
WE SIMPLY MUST HAVE A MODERN SCULPTURE TO PUT IN THIS ALCOVE, HENRY!!
YES, DEAR
LATER–
YOU WANT A MODERN SCULPTURE? I'LL GIVE YOU A MODERN SCULPTURE!!! EH...EH...EH...
SOON...
OH, HENRY... IT'S AWFUL!!! SO RETRO... GASP, CHOKE..!
YES, DEAR
Drunken Pirate District Attorney
SO IT'S CONTEMPT YE'LL BE HOLDIN' ME IN, IS IT? WHY, YA SCURVY SWAB, I'LL GUT YE LIKE A MACKEREL, ETC.
THAT'S ENOUGH– BAILIFFS!
DISTRICT ATTORNEY'S GROG
EXHIBIT B
EXHIBIT A
1ST ANNUAL DOG VS SALMON RACE
YOUR BRILLIANT IDEA IS A COMPLETE FAILURE, EINSTEIN! THE DOGS ARE RUNNING IN THE WRONG DIRECTION!
NOW A BEAR'S TAKEN ONE OF THE SALMON– WHAT A FIASCO!

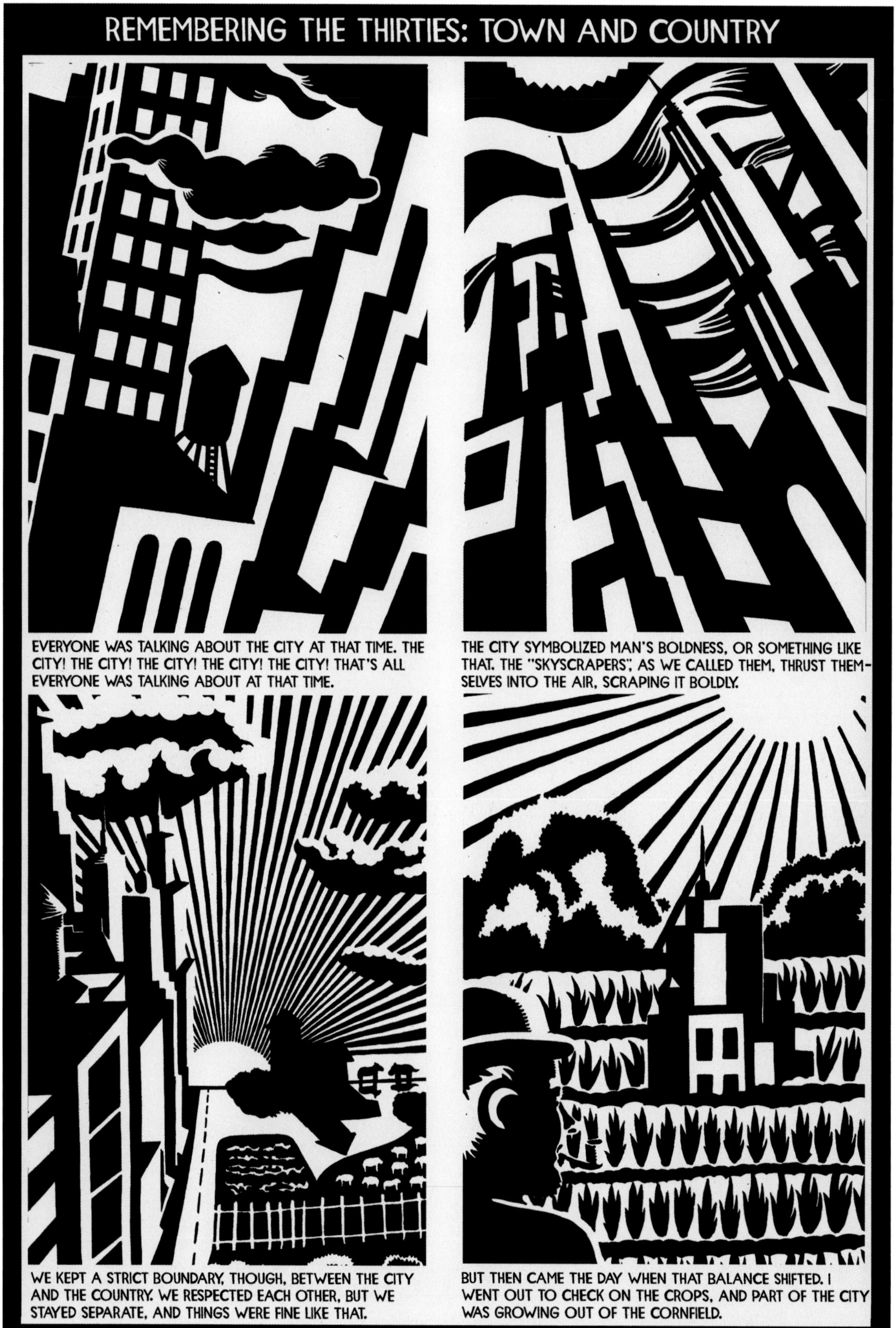
REMEMBERING THE THIRTIES: TOWN AND COUNTRY
EVERYONE WAS TALKING ABOUT THE CITY AT THAT TIME. THE CITY! THE CITY! THE CITY! THE CITY! THE CITY! THAT'S ALL EVERYONE WAS TALKING ABOUT AT THAT TIME.
THE CITY SYMBOLIZED MAN'S BOLDNESS, OR SOMETHING LIKE THAT. THE "SKYSCRAPERS", AS WE CALLED THEM, THRUST THEMSELVES INTO THE AIR, SCRAPING IT BOLDLY.
WE KEPT A STRICT BOUNDARY, THOUGH, BETWEEN THE CITY AND THE COUNTRY. WE RESPECTED EACH OTHER, BUT WE STAYED SEPARATE, AND THINGS WERE FINE LIKE THAT.
BUT THEN CAME THE DAY WHEN THAT BALANCE SHIFTED. I WENT OUT TO CHECK ON THE CROPS, AND PART OF THE CITY WAS GROWING OUT OF THE CORNFIELD.

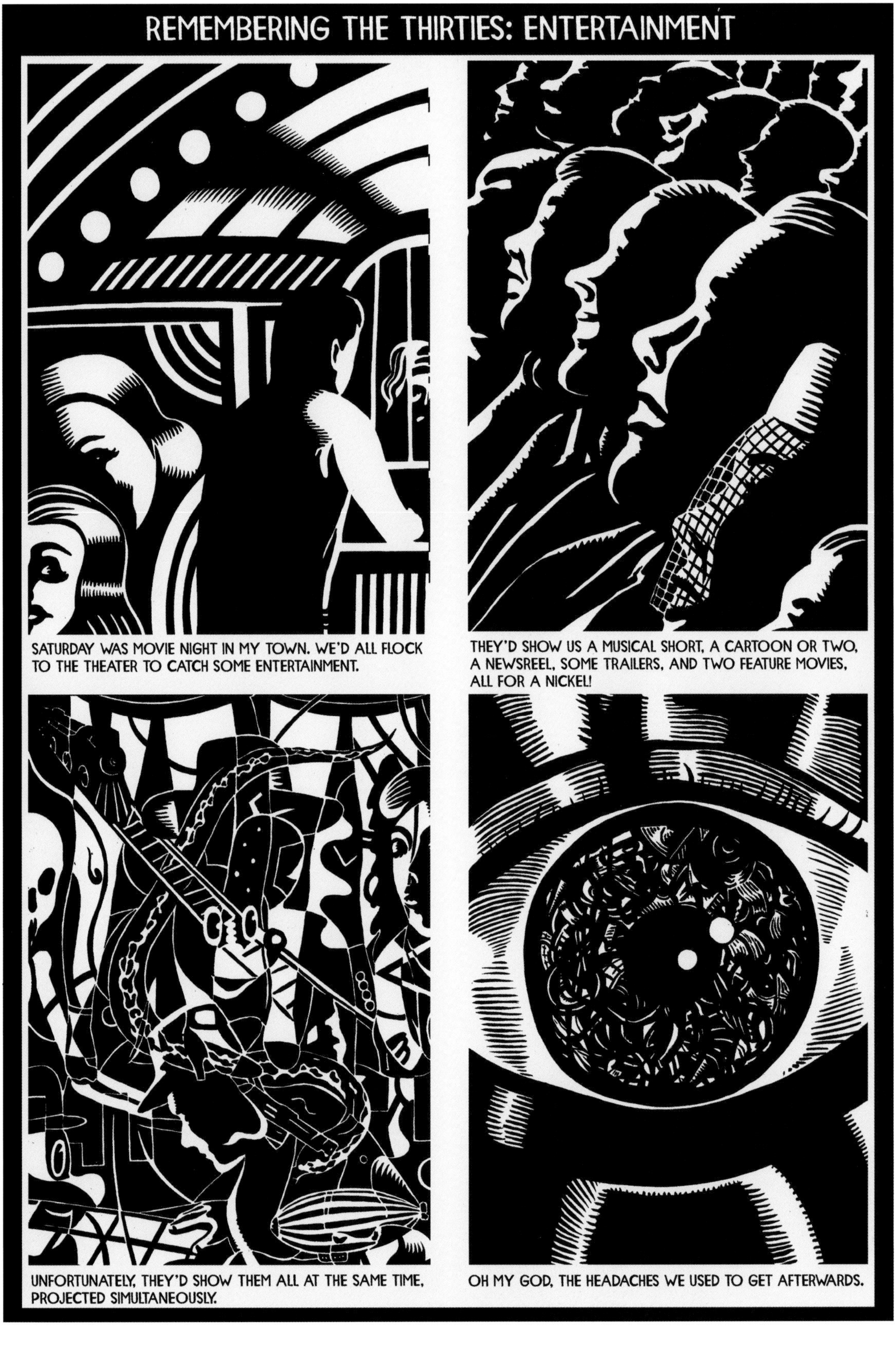
REMEMBERING THE THIRTIES: ENTERTAINMENT
SATURDAY WAS MOVIE NIGHT IN MY TOWN. WE'D ALL FLOCK TO THE THEATER TO CATCH SOME ENTERTAINMENT.
THEY'D SHOW US A MUSICAL SHORT, A CARTOON OR TWO, A NEWSREEL, SOME TRAILERS, AND TWO FEATURE MOVIES, ALL FOR A NICKEL!
UNFORTUNATELY, THEY'D SHOW THEM ALL AT THE SAME TIME, PROJECTED SIMULTANEOUSLY.
OH MY GOD, THE HEADACHES WE USED TO GET AFTERWARDS.

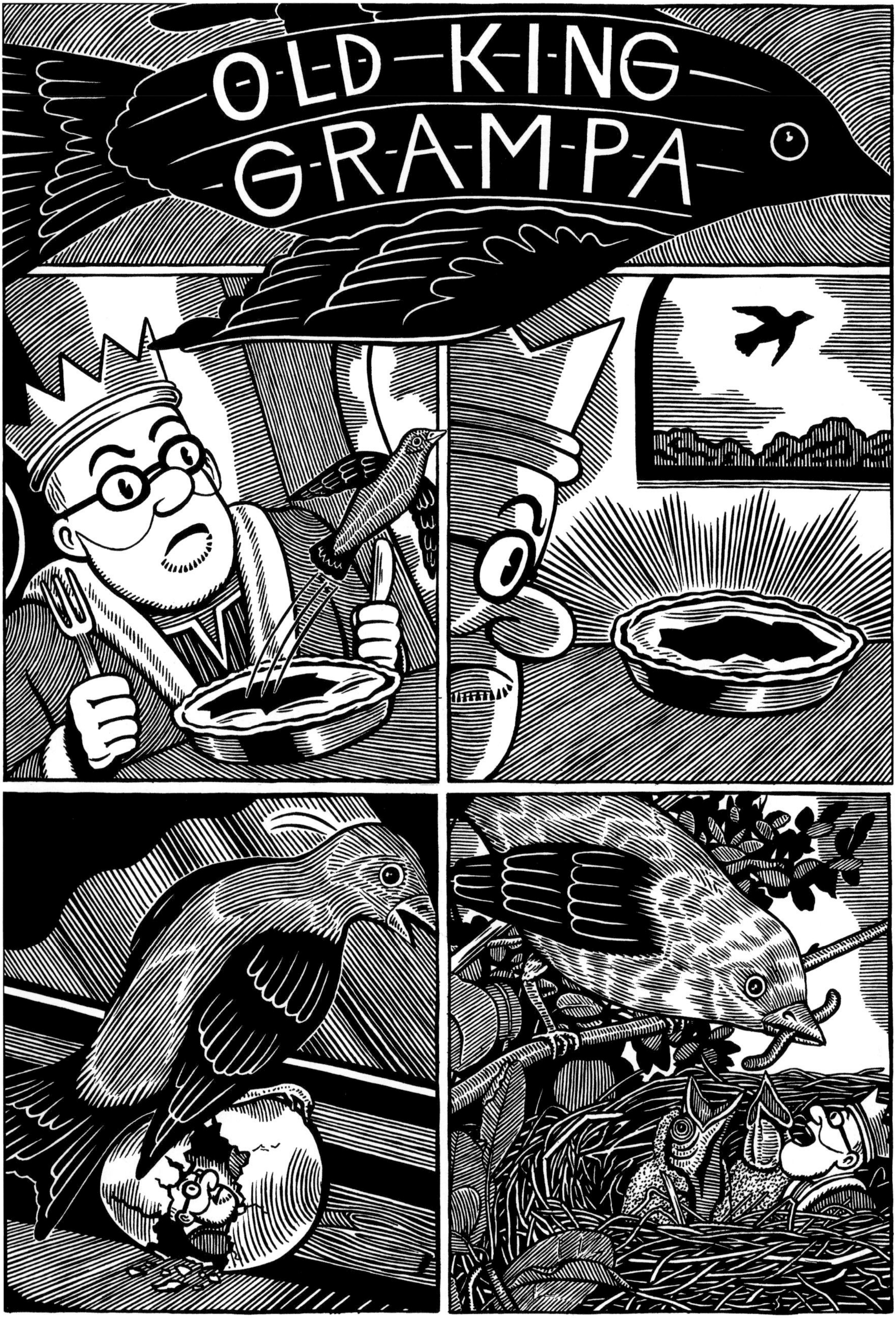
OLD KING GRAMPA

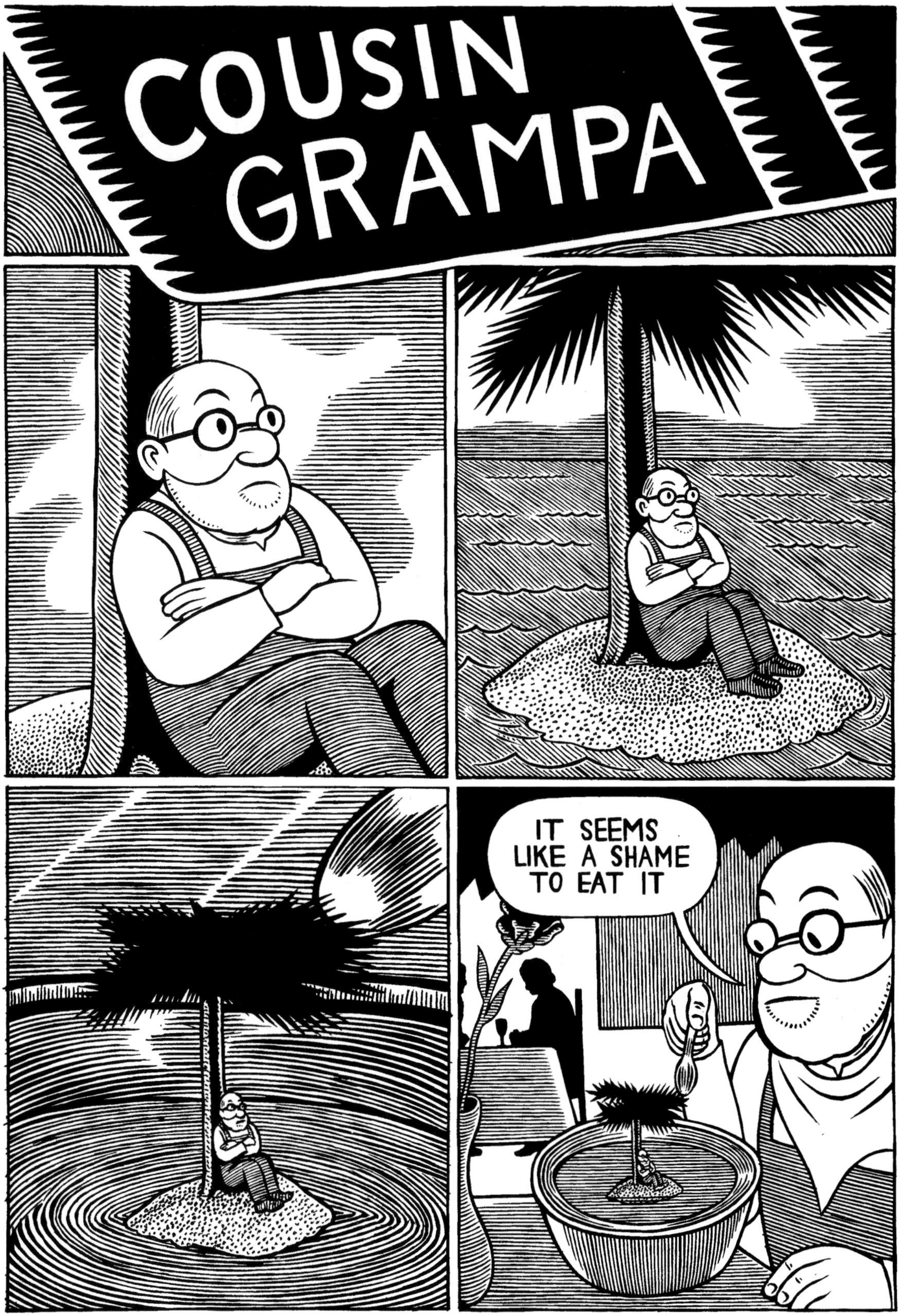
COUSIN GRAMPA
IT SEEMS LIKE A SHAME TO EAT IT

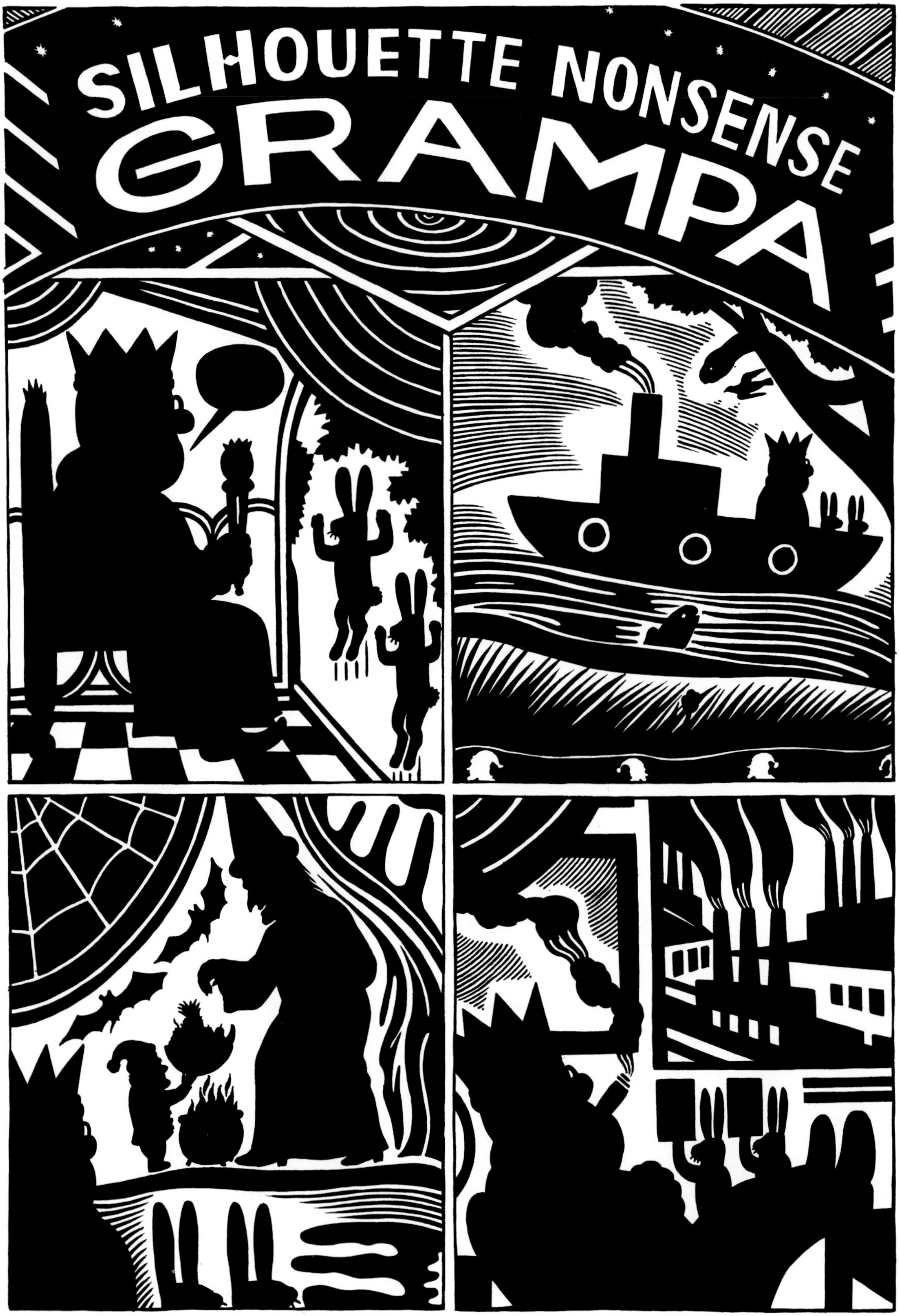
SILHOUETTE NONSENSE
GRAMPA

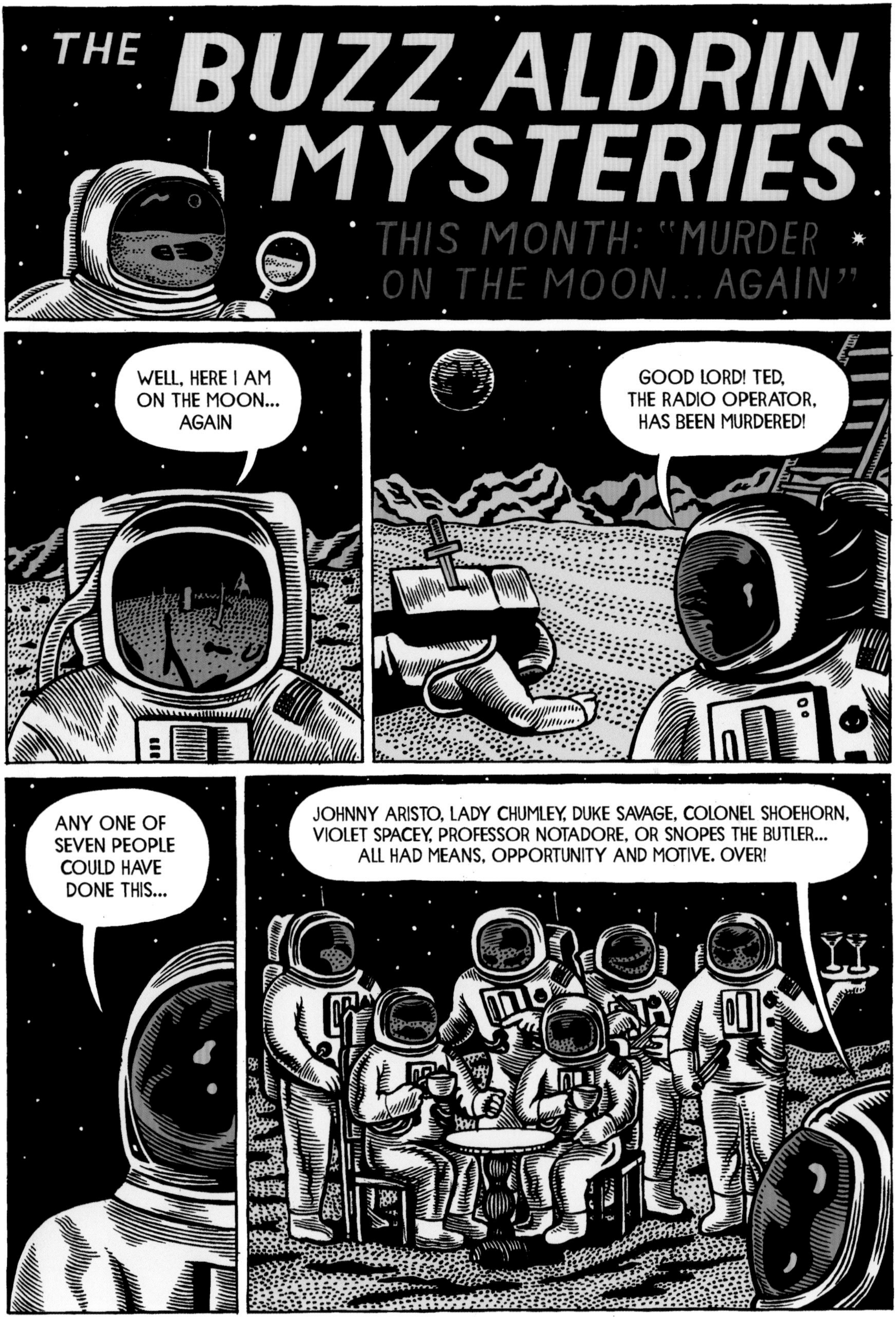

THE BUZZ ALDRIN MYSTERIES
THIS MONTH: "MURDER ON THE MOON... AGAIN"
WELL, HERE I AM ON THE MOON... AGAIN
GOOD LORD! TED, THE RADIO OPERATOR, HAS BEEN MURDERED!
ANY ONE OF SEVEN PEOPLE COULD HAVE DONE THIS...
JOHNNY ARISTO, LADY CHUMLEY, DUKE SAVAGE, COLONEL SHOEHORN, VIOLET SPACEY, PROFESSOR NOTADORE, OR SNOPES THE BUTLER... ALL HAD MEANS, OPPORTUNITY AND MOTIVE. OVER!

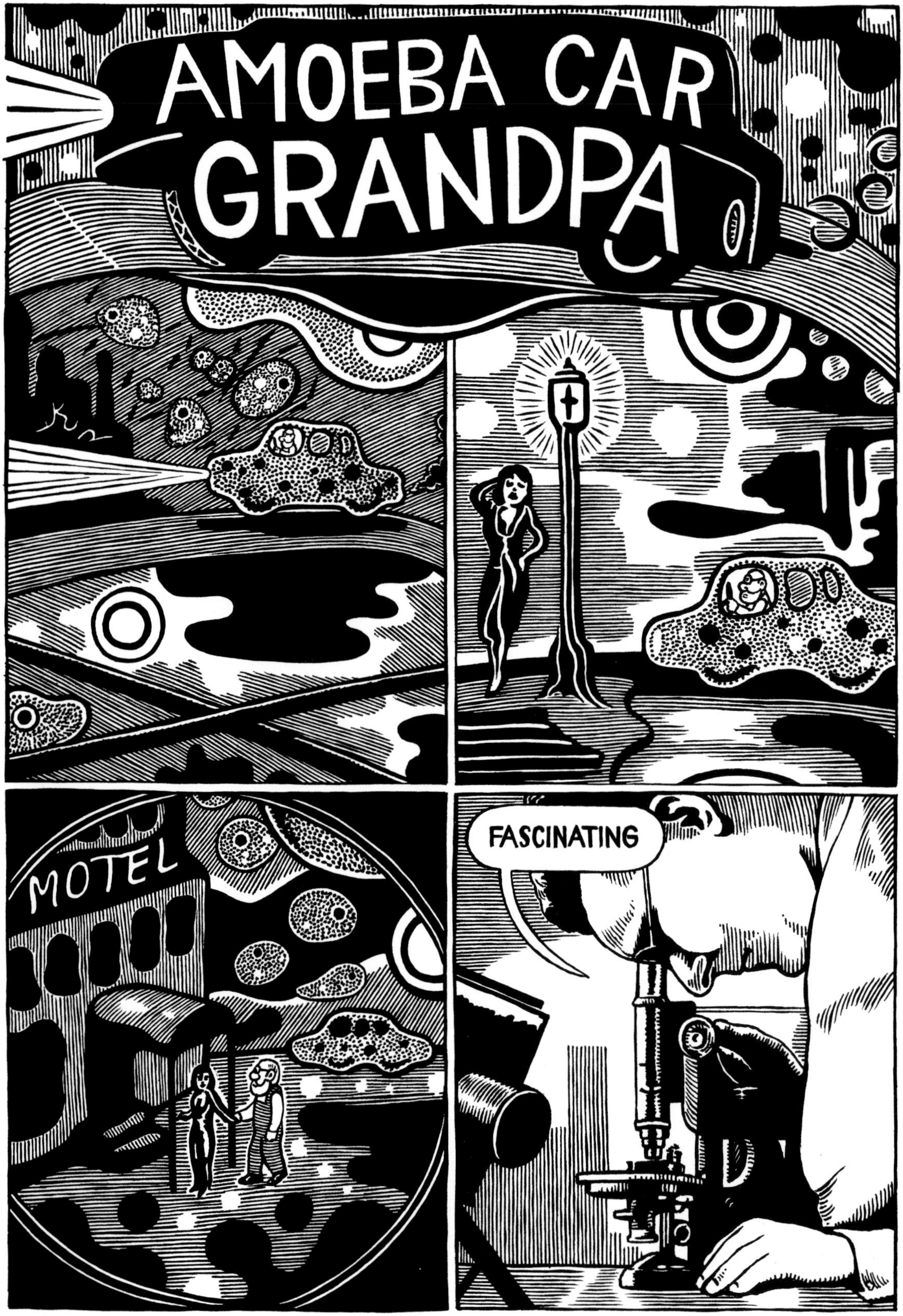
AMOEBA CAR GRANDPA
MOTEL
FASCINATING

ARE COMICS SERIOUS LITERATURE?

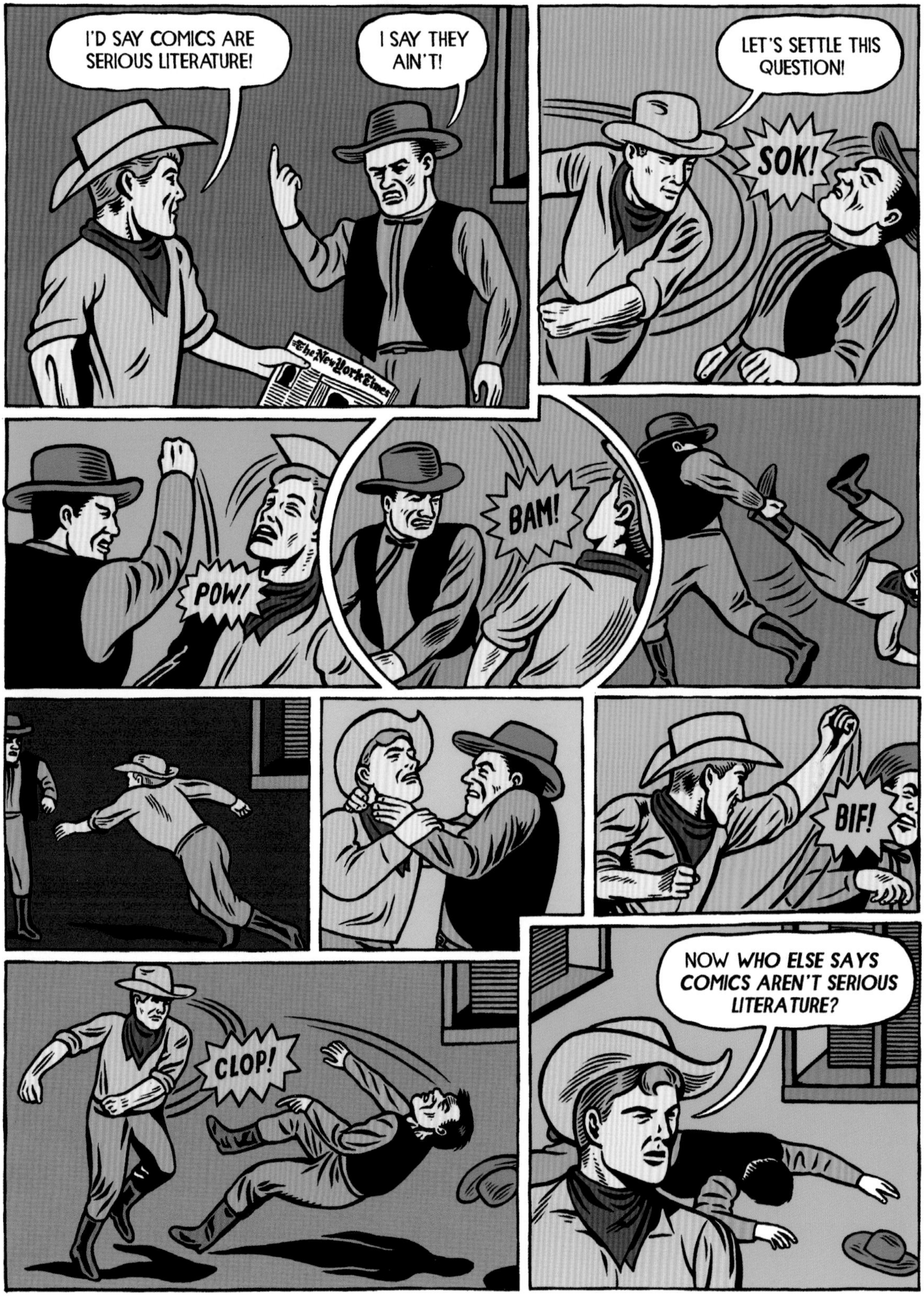
I'D SAY COMICS ARE SERIOUS LITERATURE!
I SAY THEY AIN'T!
The New York Times
LET'S SETTLE THIS QUESTION!
SOK!
POW!
BAM!
BIF!
CLOP!
NOW WHO ELSE SAYS COMICS AREN'T SERIOUS LITERATURE?

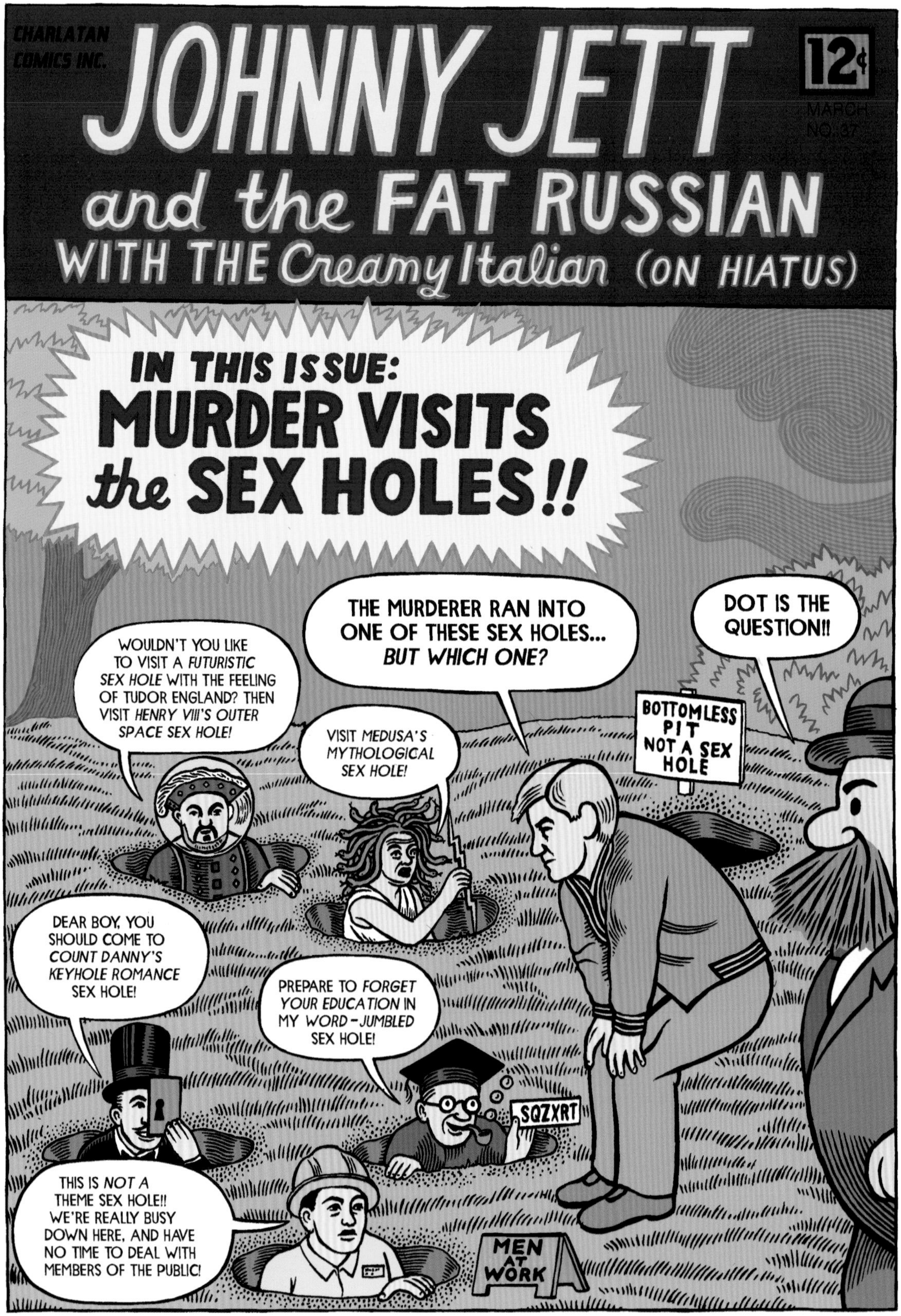
CHARLATAN COMICS INC.
JOHNNY JETT
12¢
MARCH NO. 37
and the FAT RUSSIAN
WITH THE Creamy Italian (ON HIATUS)
IN THIS ISSUE: MURDER VISITS the SEX HOLES!!
WOULDN'T YOU LIKE TO VISIT A FUTURISTIC SEX HOLE WITH THE FEELING OF TUDOR ENGLAND? THEN VISIT HENRY VIII'S OUTER SPACE SEX HOLE!
THE MURDERER RAN INTO ONE OF THESE SEX HOLES... BUT WHICH ONE?
DOT IS THE QUESTION!!
BOTTOMLESS PIT NOT A SEX HOLE
VISIT MEDUSA'S MYTHOLOGICAL SEX HOLE!
DEAR BOY, YOU SHOULD COME TO COUNT DANNY'S KEYHOLE ROMANCE SEX HOLE!
PREPARE TO FORGET YOUR EDUCATION IN MY WORD-JUMBLED SEX HOLE!
SQZXRT
THIS IS NOT A THEME SEX HOLE!! WE'RE REALLY BUSY DOWN HERE, AND HAVE NO TIME TO DEAL WITH MEMBERS OF THE PUBLIC!
MEN AT WORK

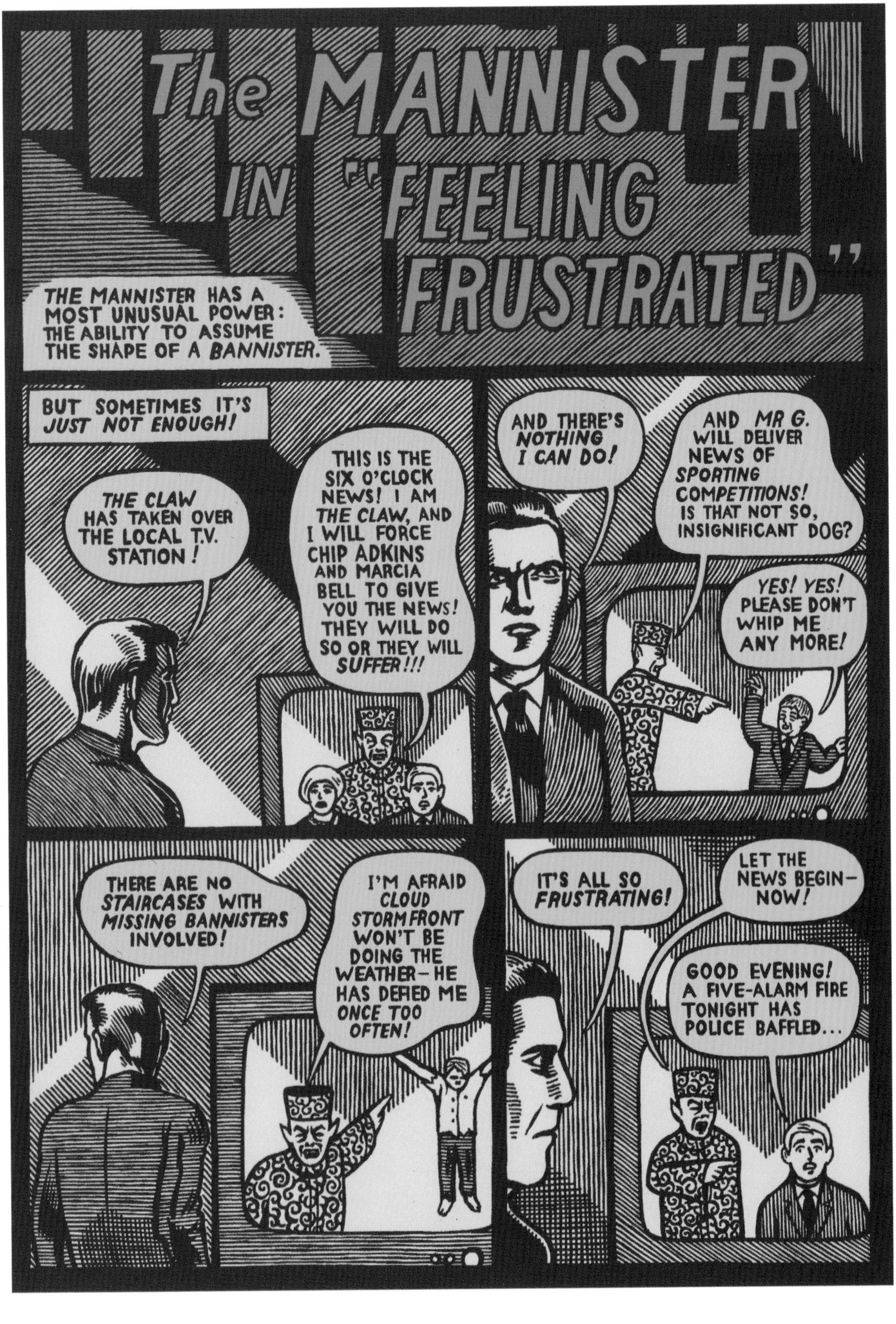
The MANNISTER IN "FEELING FRUSTRATED"
THE MANNISTER HAS A MOST UNUSUAL POWER: THE ABILITY TO ASSUME THE SHAPE OF A BANNISTER.
BUT SOMETIMES IT'S JUST NOT ENOUGH!
THE CLAW HAS TAKEN OVER THE LOCAL T.V. STATION!
THIS IS THE SIX O'CLOCK NEWS! I AM THE CLAW, AND I WILL FORCE CHIP ADKINS AND MARCIA BELL TO GIVE YOU THE NEWS! THEY WILL DO SO OR THEY WILL SUFFER!!!
AND THERE'S NOTHING I CAN DO!
AND MR G. WILL DELIVER NEWS OF SPORTING COMPETITIONS! IS THAT NOT SO, INSIGNIFICANT DOG?
YES! YES! PLEASE DON'T WHIP ME ANY MORE!
THERE ARE NO STAIRCASES WITH MISSING BANNISTERS INVOLVED!
I'M AFRAID CLOUD STORMFRONT WON'T BE DOING THE WEATHER— HE HAS DEFIED ME ONCE TOO OFTEN!
IT'S ALL SO FRUSTRATING!
LET THE NEWS BEGIN— NOW!
GOOD EVENING! A FIVE-ALARM FIRE TONIGHT HAS POLICE BAFFLED...

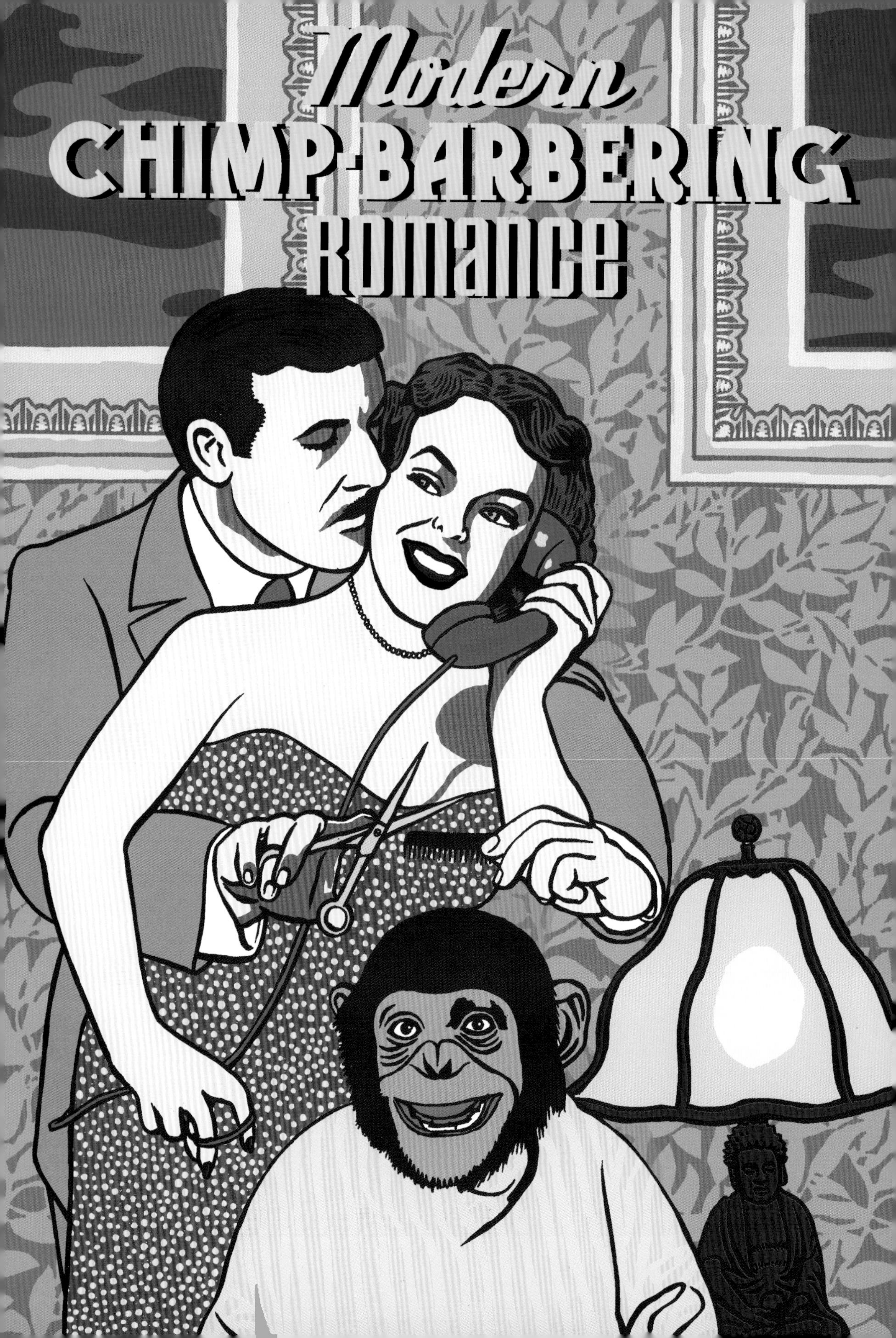

Modern
CHIMP-BARBERING
ROMANCE

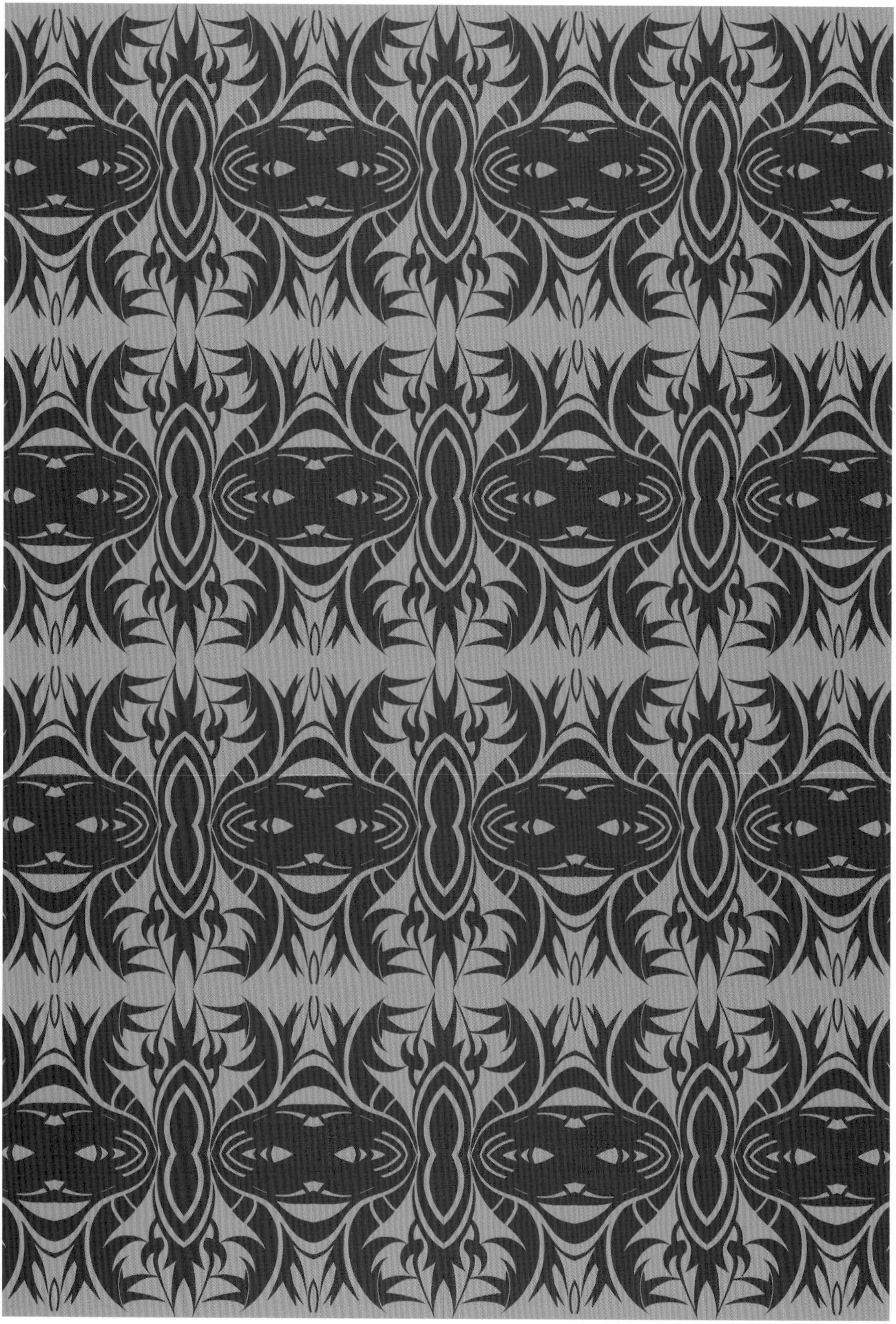

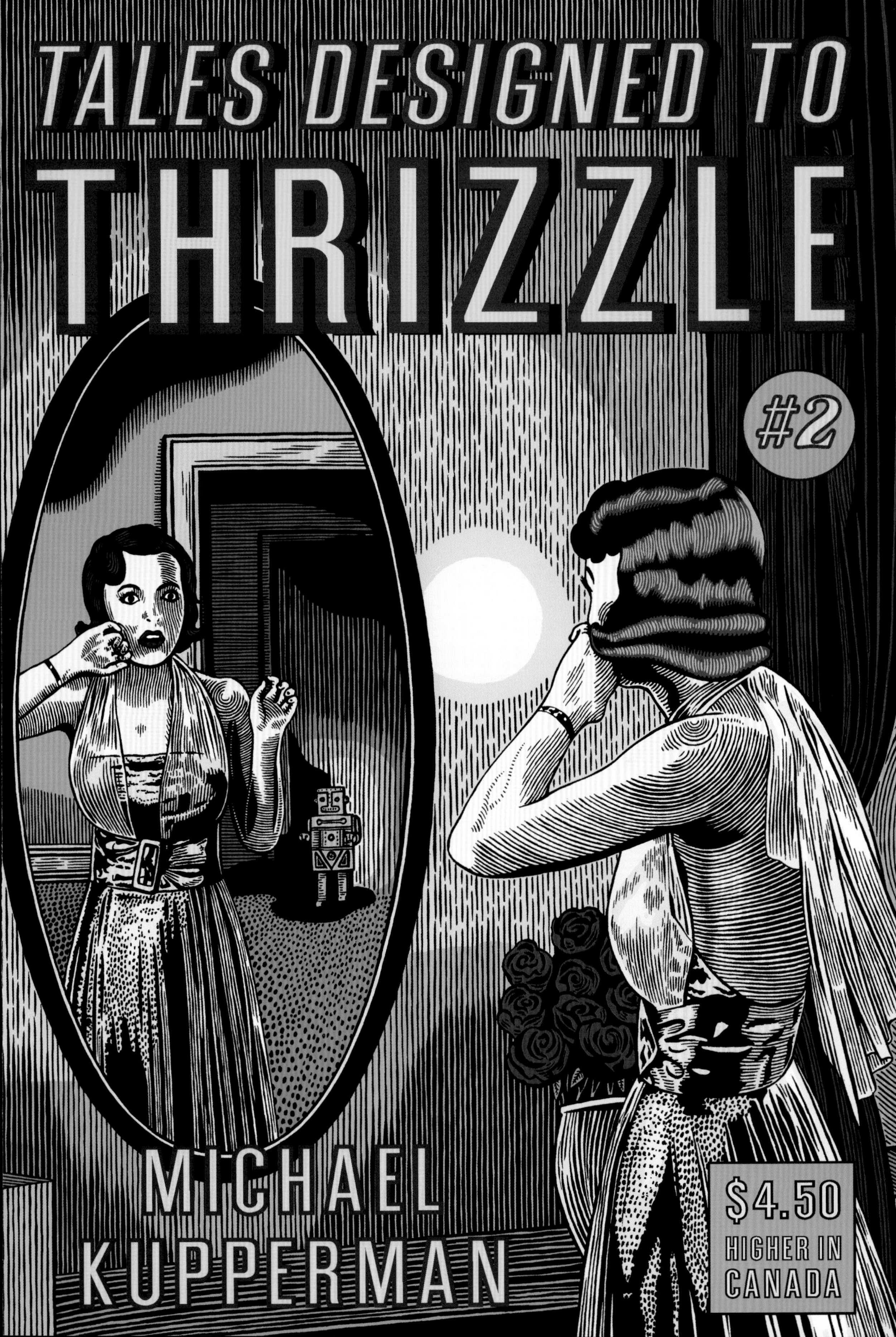
TALES DESIGNED TO
THRIZZLE
#2
MICHAEL
KUPPERMAN
$4.50
HIGHER IN
CANADA

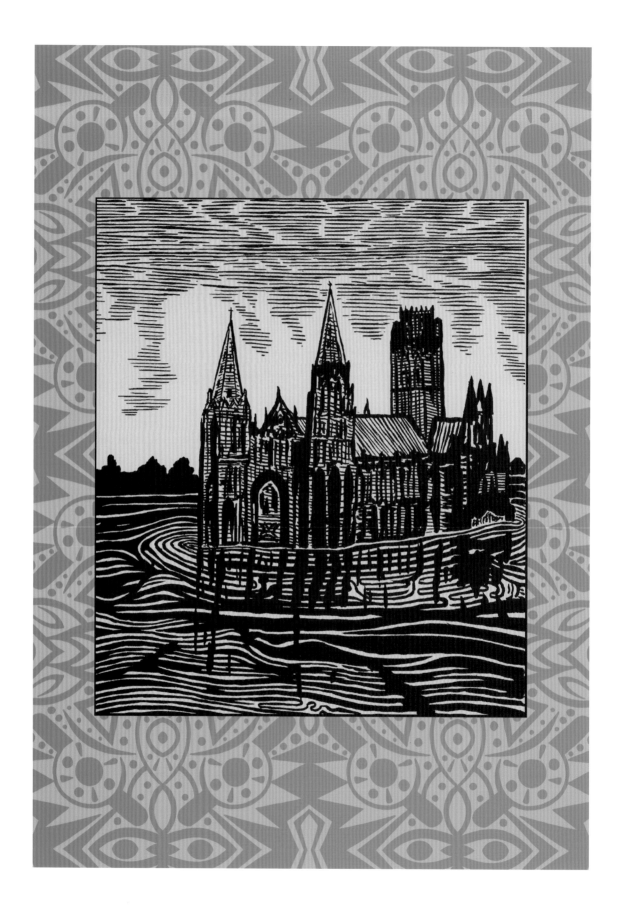

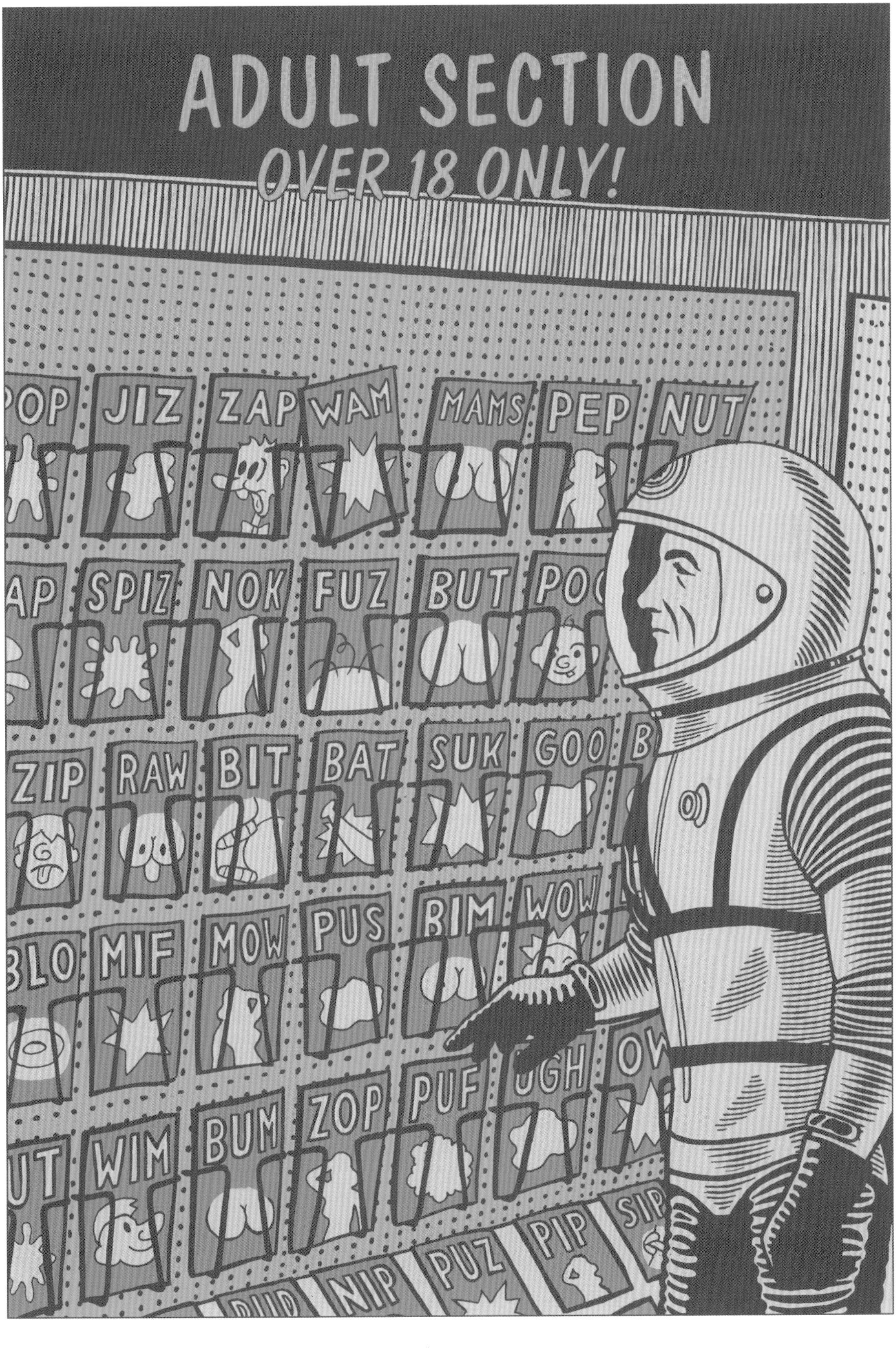
ADULT SECTION
OVER 18 ONLY!
JIZ
ZAP
WAM
MAMS
PEP
NUT
SPIZ
NOK
FUZ
BUT
ZIP
RAW
BIT
BAT
SUK
GOO
BLO
MIF
MOW
PUS
BIM
WOW
WIM
BUM
ZOP
PUF
UGH
SIP
PIP
PUZ
NIP

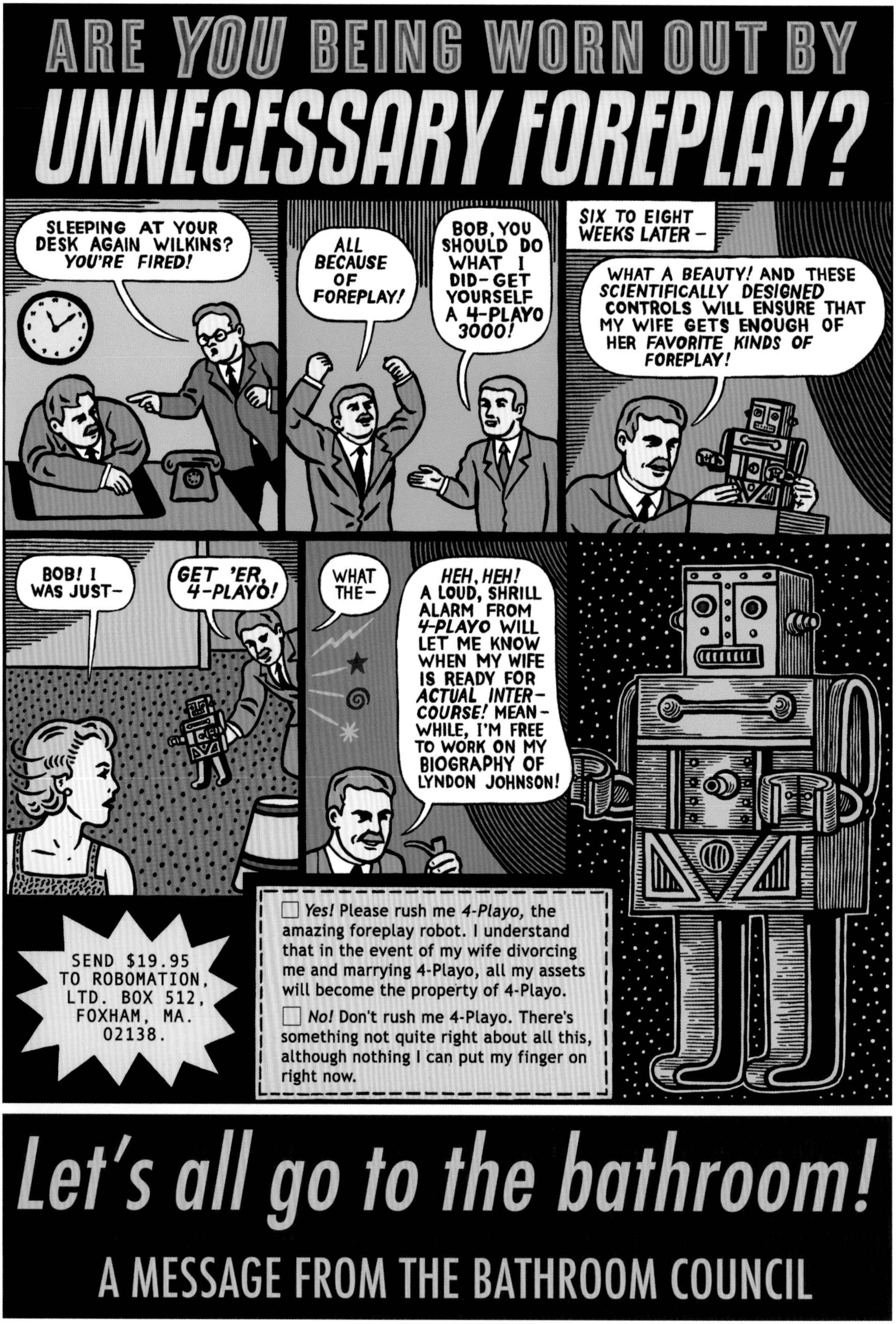
ARE YOU BEING WORN OUT BY
UNNECESSARY FOREPLAY?
SLEEPING AT YOUR DESK AGAIN WILKINS? YOU'RE FIRED!
ALL BECAUSE OF FOREPLAY!
BOB, YOU SHOULD DO WHAT I DID–GET YOURSELF A 4-PLAYO 3000!
SIX TO EIGHT WEEKS LATER–
WHAT A BEAUTY! AND THESE SCIENTIFICALLY DESIGNED CONTROLS WILL ENSURE THAT MY WIFE GETS ENOUGH OF HER FAVORITE KINDS OF FOREPLAY!
BOB! I WAS JUST–
GET 'ER, 4-PLAYO!
WHAT THE–
HEH, HEH! A LOUD, SHRILL ALARM FROM 4-PLAYO WILL LET ME KNOW WHEN MY WIFE IS READY FOR ACTUAL INTER-COURSE! MEAN-WHILE, I'M FREE TO WORK ON MY BIOGRAPHY OF LYNDON JOHNSON!
SEND $19.95 TO ROBOMATION, LTD. BOX 512, FOXHAM, MA. 02138.
☐ Yes! Please rush me 4-Playo, the amazing foreplay robot. I understand that in the event of my wife divorcing me and marrying 4-Playo, all my assets will become the property of 4-Playo.
☐ No! Don't rush me 4-Playo. There's something not quite right about all this, although nothing I can put my finger on right now.
Let's all go to the bathroom!
A MESSAGE FROM THE BATHROOM COUNCIL

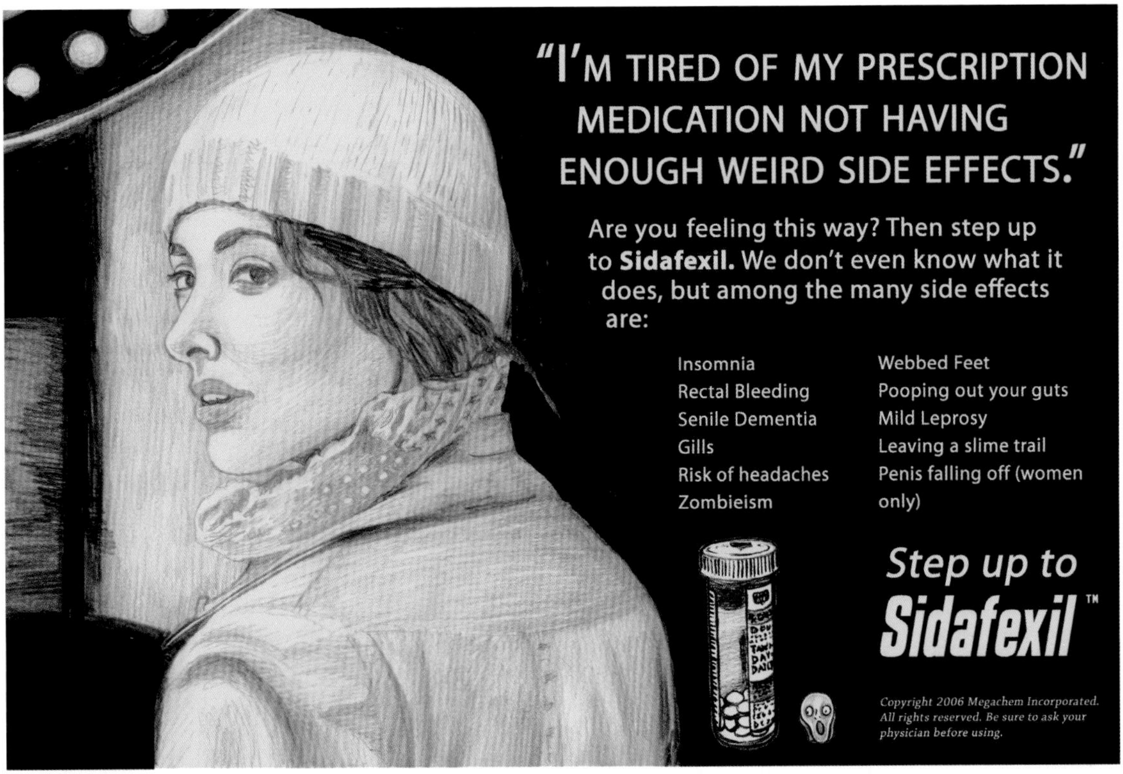
"I'M TIRED OF MY PRESCRIPTION MEDICATION NOT HAVING ENOUGH WEIRD SIDE EFFECTS."
Are you feeling this way? Then step up to **Sidafexil.** We don't even know what it does, but among the many side effects are:
Insomnia
Rectal Bleeding
Senile Dementia
Gills
Risk of headaches
Zombieism
Webbed Feet
Pooping out your guts
Mild Leprosy
Leaving a slime trail
Penis falling off (women only)
Step up to
Sidafexil™
Copyright 2006 Megachem Incorporated. All rights reserved. Be sure to ask your physician before using.

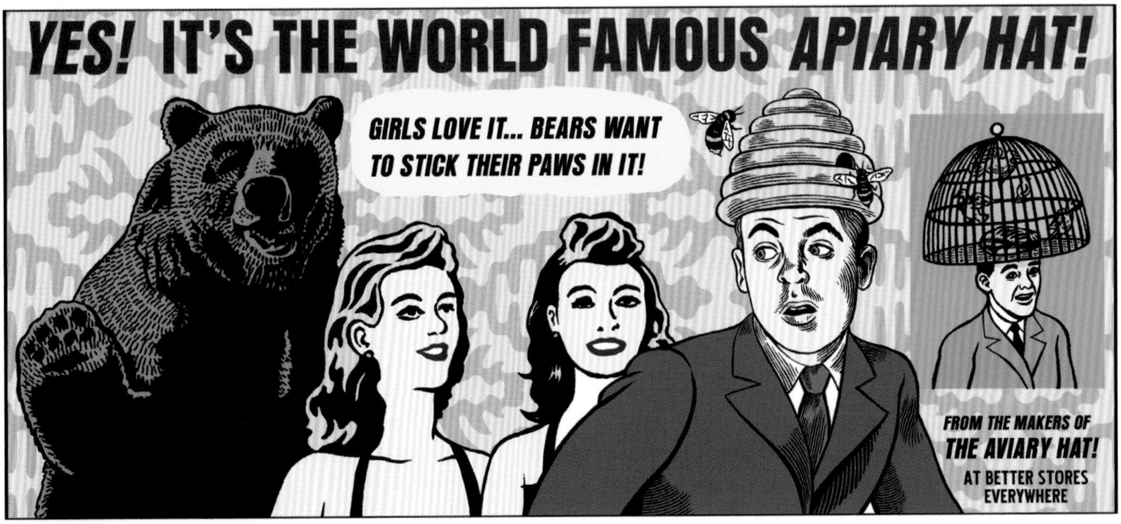
YES! IT'S THE WORLD FAMOUS APIARY HAT!
GIRLS LOVE IT... BEARS WANT TO STICK THEIR PAWS IN IT!
FROM THE MAKERS OF
THE AVIARY HAT!
AT BETTER STORES EVERYWHERE

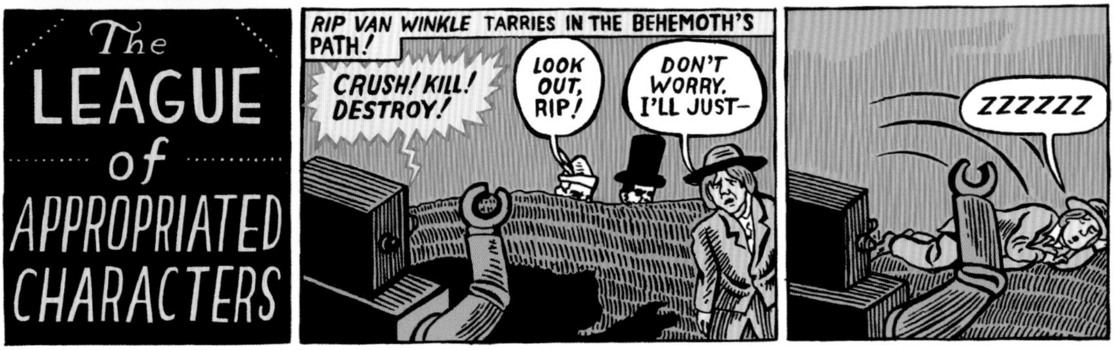
The LEAGUE of APPROPRIATED CHARACTERS
RIP VAN WINKLE TARRIES IN THE BEHEMOTH'S PATH!
CRUSH! KILL! DESTROY!
LOOK OUT, RIP!
DON'T WORRY. I'LL JUST—
ZZZZZZ

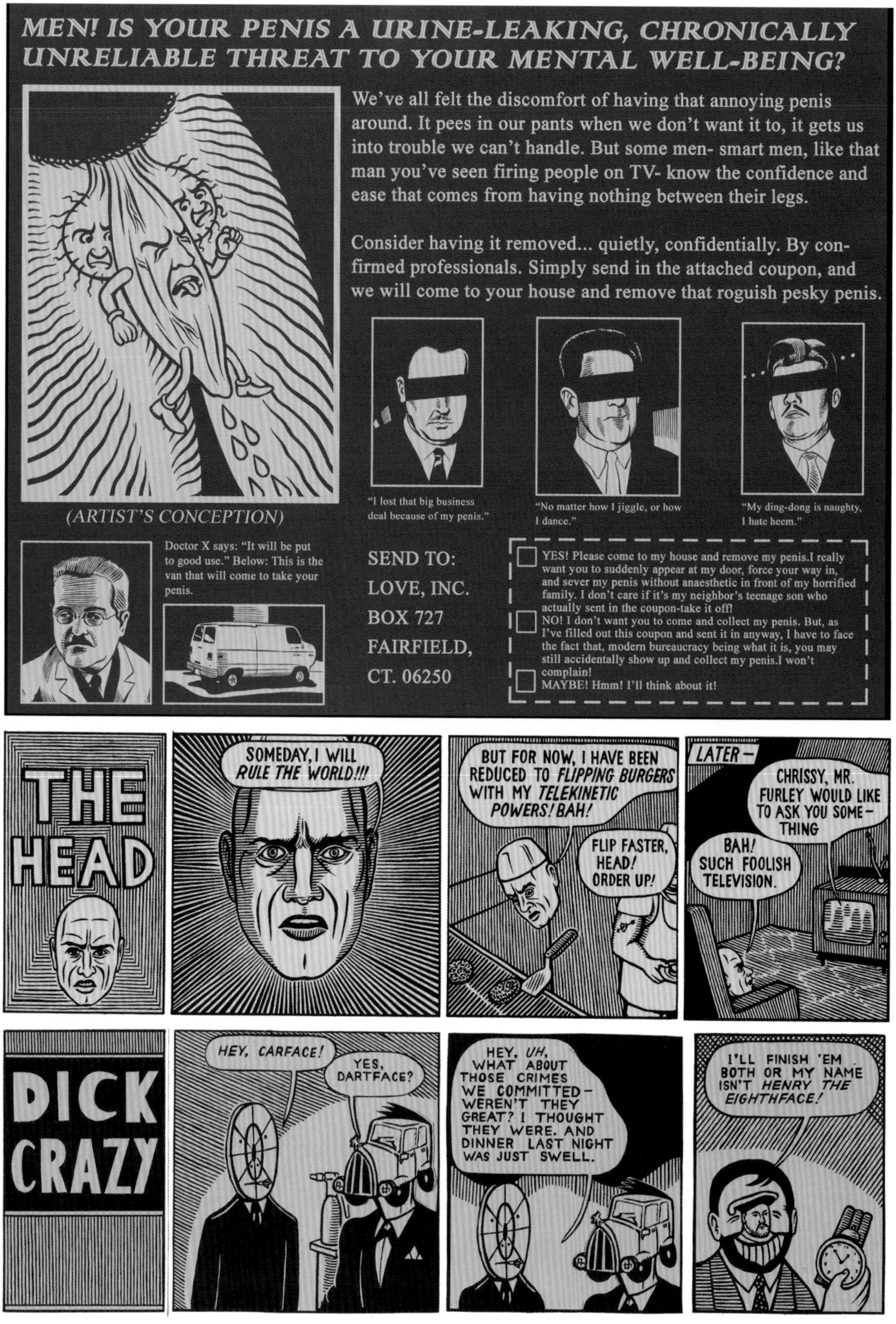
MEN! IS YOUR PENIS A URINE-LEAKING, CHRONICALLY UNRELIABLE THREAT TO YOUR MENTAL WELL-BEING?
We've all felt the discomfort of having that annoying penis around. It pees in our pants when we don't want it to, it gets us into trouble we can't handle. But some men- smart men, like that man you've seen firing people on TV- know the confidence and ease that comes from having nothing between their legs.
Consider having it removed... quietly, confidentially. By confirmed professionals. Simply send in the attached coupon, and we will come to your house and remove that roguish pesky penis.
(ARTIST'S CONCEPTION)
"I lost that big business deal because of my penis."
"No matter how I jiggle, or how I dance."
"My ding-dong is naughty, I hate heem."
Doctor X says: "It will be put to good use." Below: This is the van that will come to take your penis.
SEND TO: LOVE, INC. BOX 727 FAIRFIELD, CT. 06250
YES! Please come to my house and remove my penis.I really want you to suddenly appear at my door, force your way in, and sever my penis without anaesthetic in front of my horrified family. I don't care if it's my neighbor's teenage son who actually sent in the coupon-take it off!
NO! I don't want you to come and collect my penis. But, as I've filled out this coupon and sent it in anyway, I have to face the fact that, modern bureaucracy being what it is, you may still accidentally show up and collect my penis.I won't complain!
MAYBE! Hmm! I'll think about it!
THE HEAD
SOMEDAY, I WILL RULE THE WORLD!!!
BUT FOR NOW, I HAVE BEEN REDUCED TO FLIPPING BURGERS WITH MY TELEKINETIC POWERS! BAH!
FLIP FASTER, HEAD! ORDER UP!
LATER—
CHRISSY, MR. FURLEY WOULD LIKE TO ASK YOU SOME-THING
BAH! SUCH FOOLISH TELEVISION.
DICK CRAZY
HEY, CARFACE!
YES, DARTFACE?
HEY, UH, WHAT ABOUT THOSE CRIMES WE COMMITTED— WEREN'T THEY GREAT? I THOUGHT THEY WERE. AND DINNER LAST NIGHT WAS JUST SWELL.
I'LL FINISH 'EM BOTH OR MY NAME ISN'T HENRY THE EIGHTHFACE!

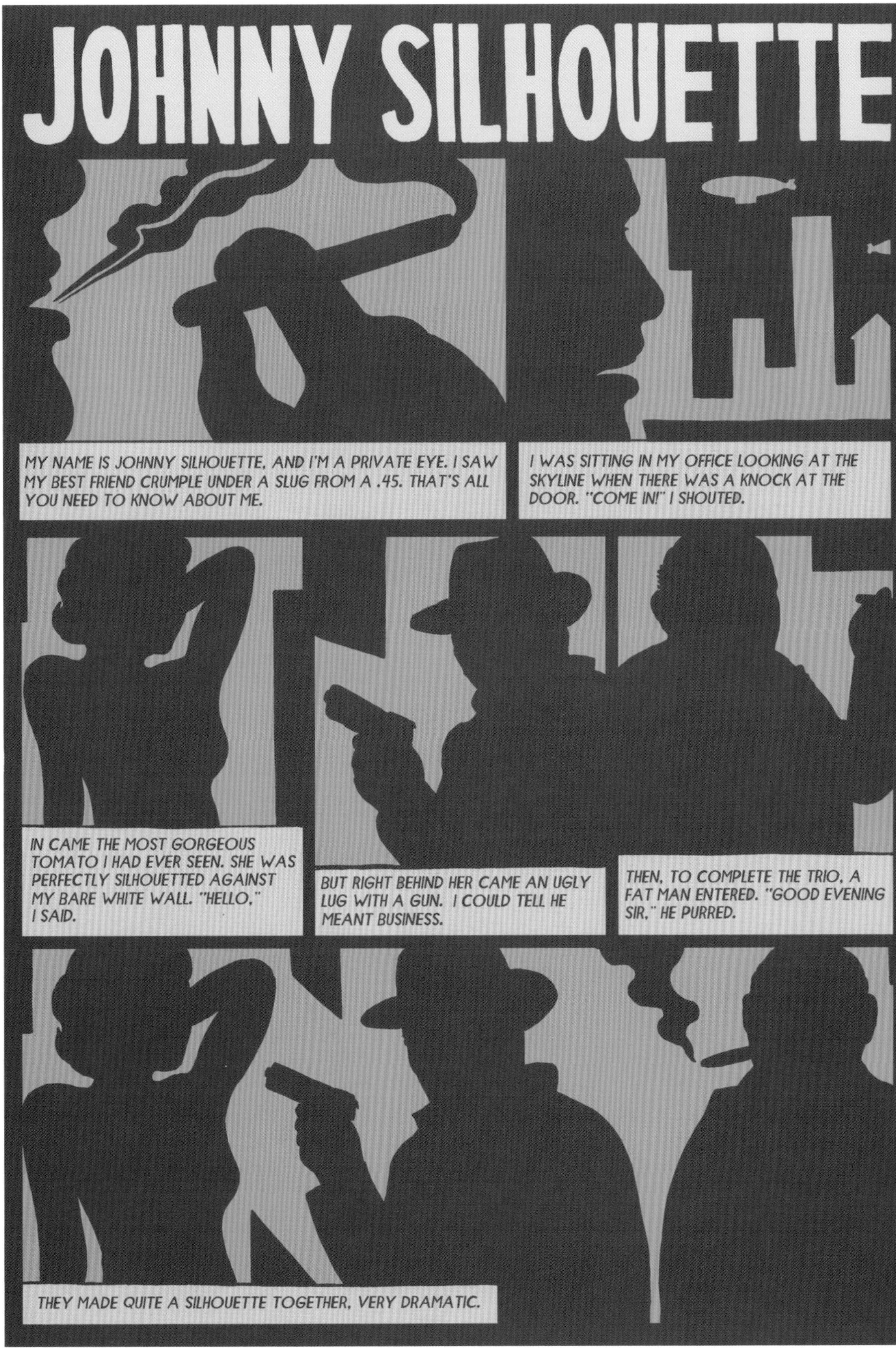
JOHNNY SILHOUETTE
MY NAME IS JOHNNY SILHOUETTE, AND I'M A PRIVATE EYE. I SAW MY BEST FRIEND CRUMPLE UNDER A SLUG FROM A .45. THAT'S ALL YOU NEED TO KNOW ABOUT ME.
I WAS SITTING IN MY OFFICE LOOKING AT THE SKYLINE WHEN THERE WAS A KNOCK AT THE DOOR. "COME IN!" I SHOUTED.
IN CAME THE MOST GORGEOUS TOMATO I HAD EVER SEEN. SHE WAS PERFECTLY SILHOUETTED AGAINST MY BARE WHITE WALL. "HELLO," I SAID.
BUT RIGHT BEHIND HER CAME AN UGLY LUG WITH A GUN. I COULD TELL HE MEANT BUSINESS.
THEN, TO COMPLETE THE TRIO, A FAT MAN ENTERED. "GOOD EVENING SIR," HE PURRED.
THEY MADE QUITE A SILHOUETTE TOGETHER. VERY DRAMATIC.

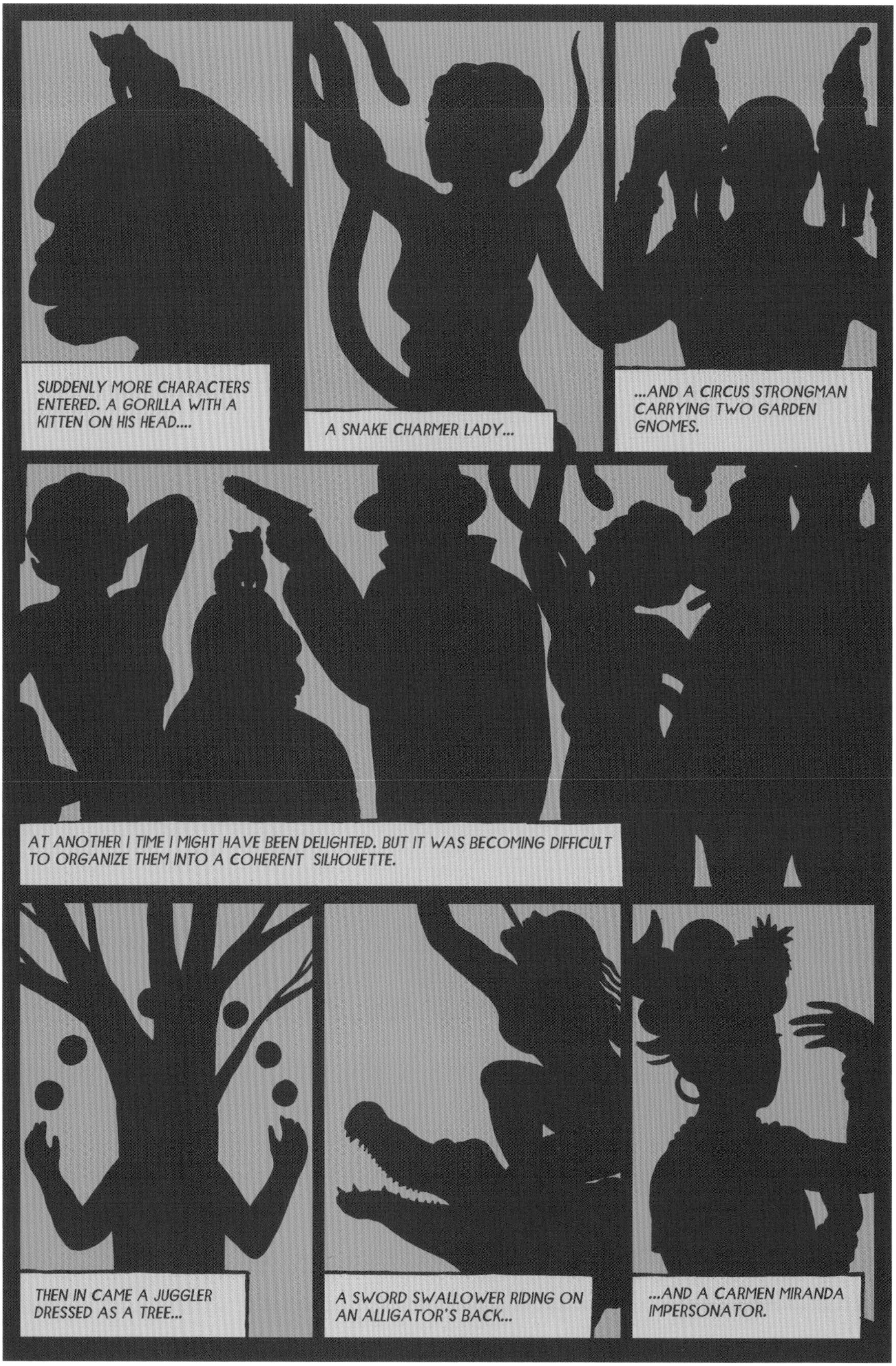
SUDDENLY MORE CHARACTERS ENTERED. A GORILLA WITH A KITTEN ON HIS HEAD....
A SNAKE CHARMER LADY...
...AND A CIRCUS STRONGMAN CARRYING TWO GARDEN GNOMES.
AT ANOTHER I TIME I MIGHT HAVE BEEN DELIGHTED. BUT IT WAS BECOMING DIFFICULT TO ORGANIZE THEM INTO A COHERENT SILHOUETTE.
THEN IN CAME A JUGGLER DRESSED AS A TREE...
A SWORD SWALLOWER RIDING ON AN ALLIGATOR'S BACK...
...AND A CARMEN MIRANDA IMPERSONATOR.

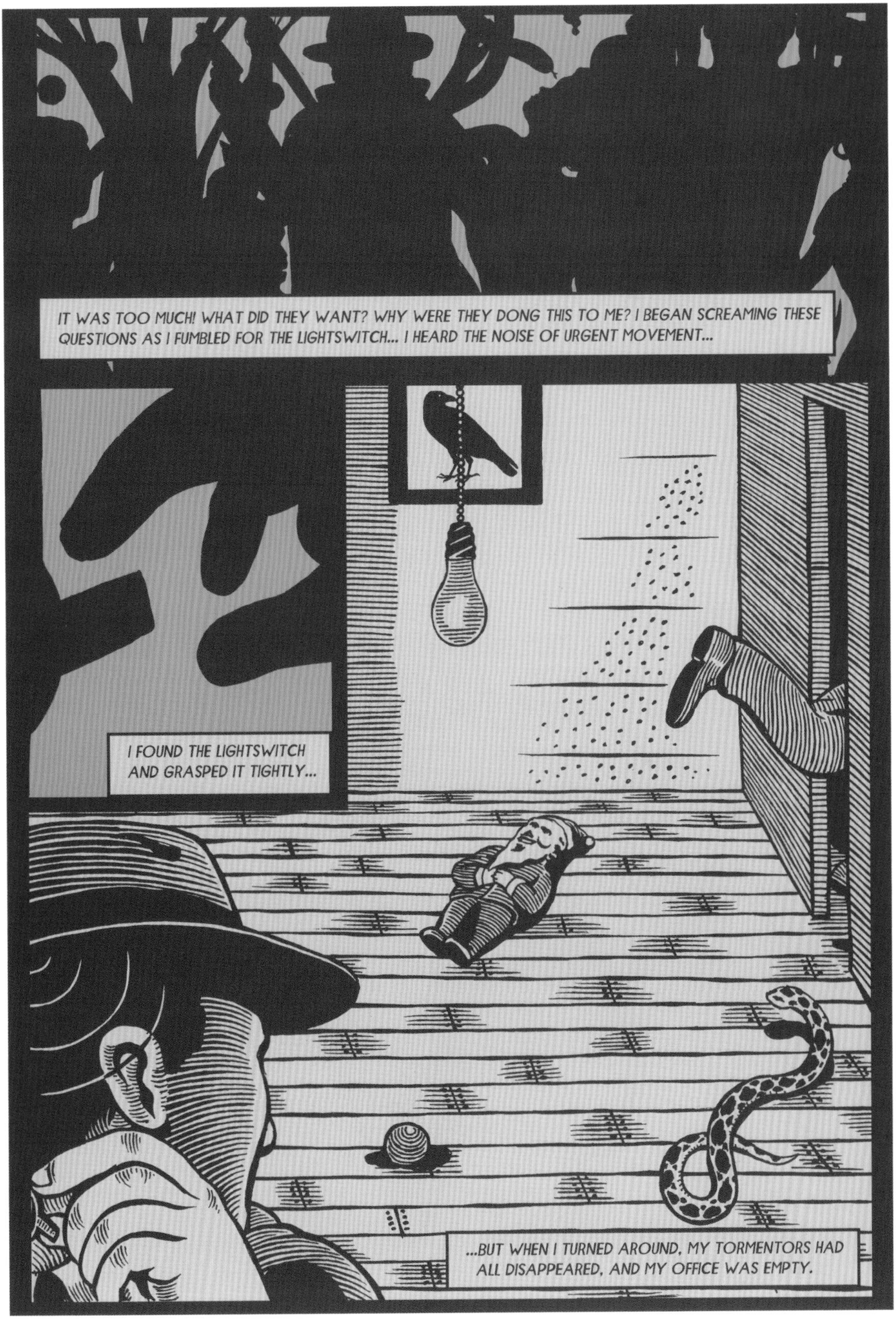
IT WAS TOO MUCH! WHAT DID THEY WANT? WHY WERE THEY DONG THIS TO ME? I BEGAN SCREAMING THESE QUESTIONS AS I FUMBLED FOR THE LIGHTSWITCH... I HEARD THE NOISE OF URGENT MOVEMENT...
I FOUND THE LIGHTSWITCH AND GRASPED IT TIGHTLY...
...BUT WHEN I TURNED AROUND, MY TORMENTORS HAD ALL DISAPPEARED, AND MY OFFICE WAS EMPTY.

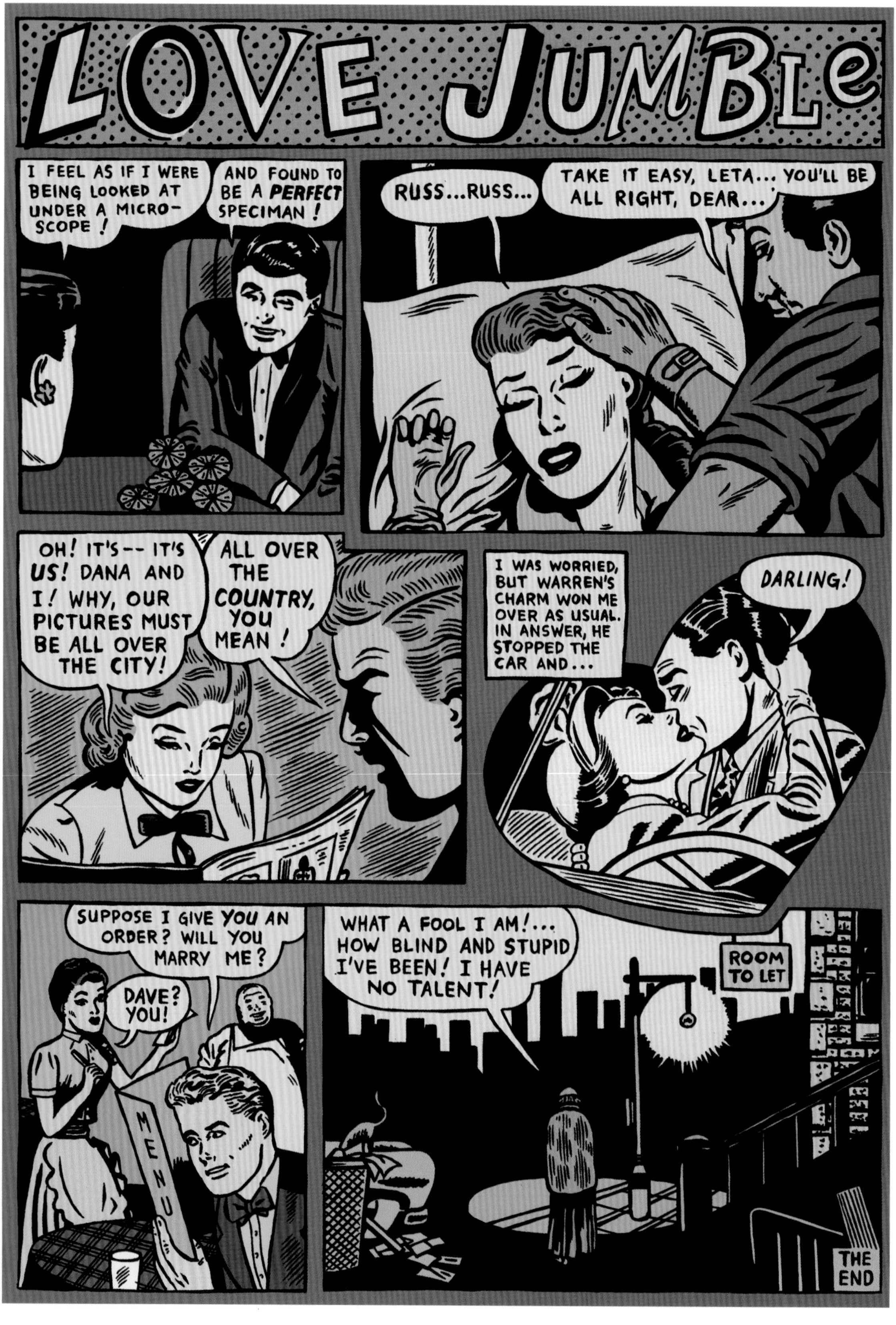
LOVE JUMBLE
I FEEL AS IF I WERE BEING LOOKED AT UNDER A MICRO-SCOPE!
AND FOUND TO BE A PERFECT SPECIMAN!
RUSS...RUSS...
TAKE IT EASY, LETA... YOU'LL BE ALL RIGHT, DEAR...
OH! IT'S-- IT'S US! DANA AND I! WHY, OUR PICTURES MUST BE ALL OVER THE CITY!
ALL OVER THE COUNTRY, YOU MEAN!
I WAS WORRIED, BUT WARREN'S CHARM WON ME OVER AS USUAL. IN ANSWER, HE STOPPED THE CAR AND...
DARLING!
SUPPOSE I GIVE YOU AN ORDER? WILL YOU MARRY ME?
DAVE? YOU!
MENU
WHAT A FOOL I AM!... HOW BLIND AND STUPID I'VE BEEN! I HAVE NO TALENT!
ROOM TO LET
THE END

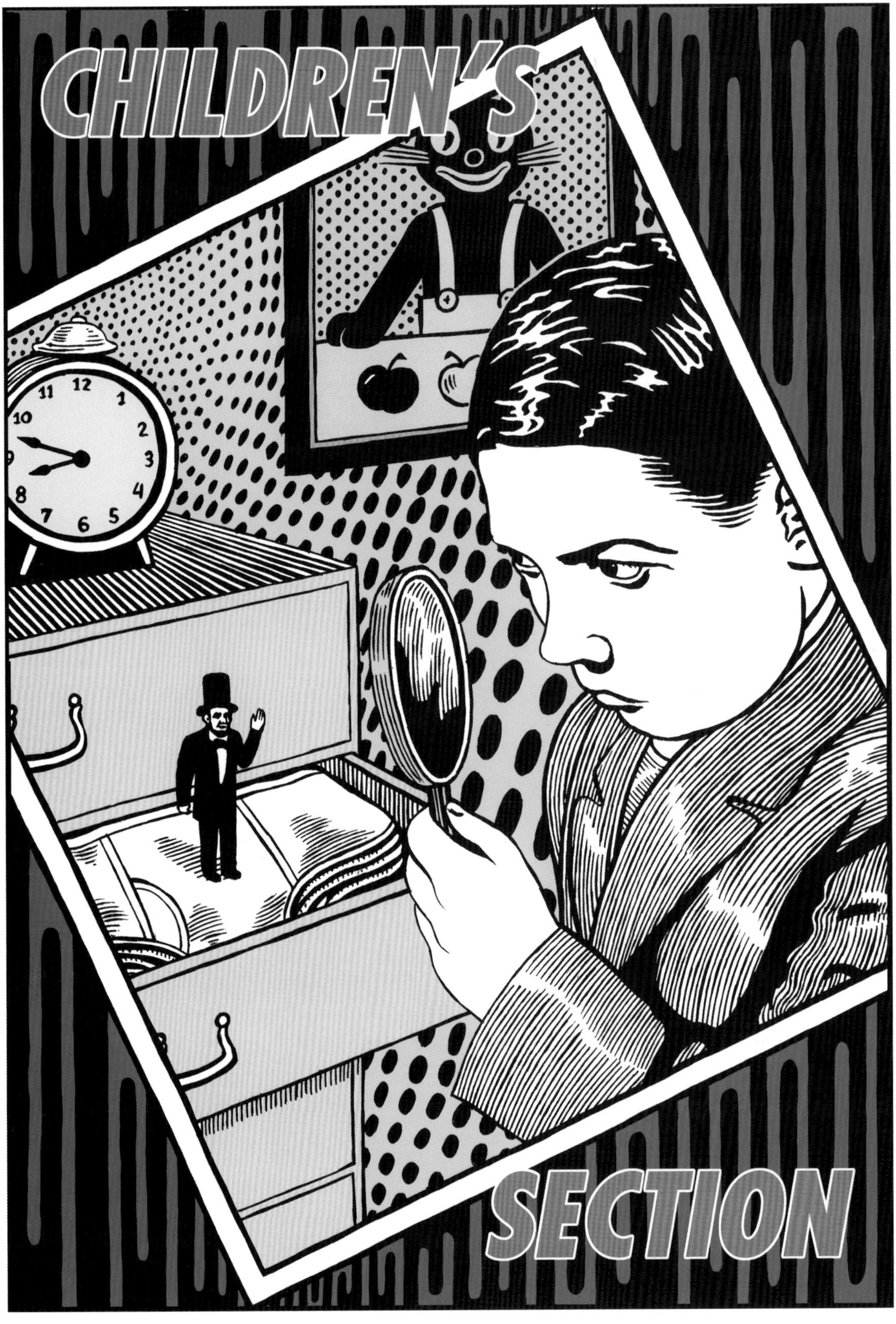
CHILDREN'S
SECTION

PARENTS! YOUR KIDS WILL LOVE
NEW BABY POOP'N'TELL!™

SHE PROUDLY ANNOUNCES EVERY NUMBER TWO!

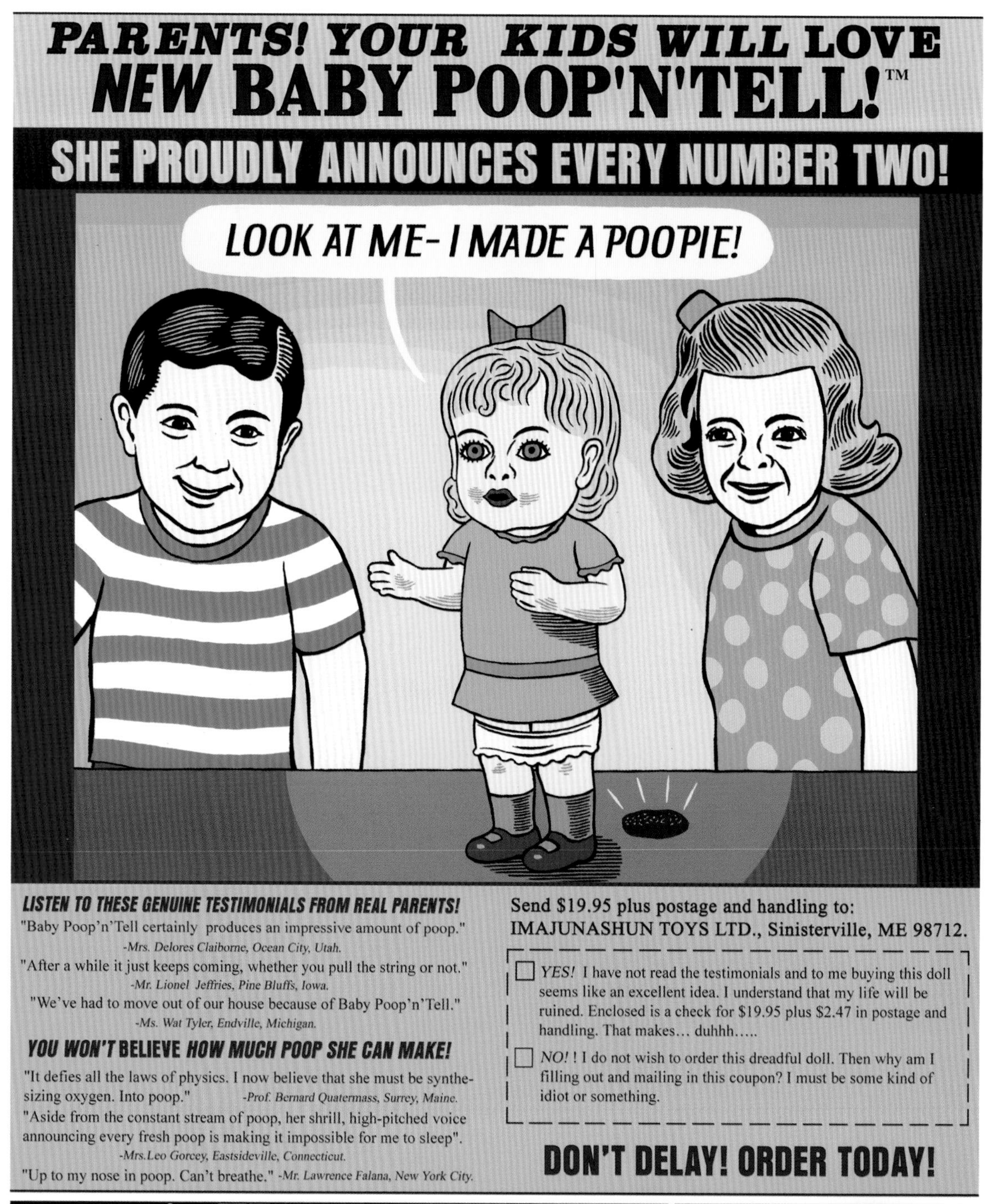
LOOK AT ME- I MADE A POOPIE!

LISTEN TO THESE GENUINE TESTIMONIALS FROM REAL PARENTS!

"Baby Poop'n'Tell certainly produces an impressive amount of poop."
-Mrs. Delores Claiborne, Ocean City, Utah.

"After a while it just keeps coming, whether you pull the string or not."
-Mr. Lionel Jeffries, Pine Bluffs, Iowa.

"We've had to move out of our house because of Baby Poop'n'Tell."
-Ms. Wat Tyler, Endville, Michigan.

YOU WON'T BELIEVE HOW MUCH POOP SHE CAN MAKE!

"It defies all the laws of physics. I now believe that she must be synthesizing oxygen. Into poop." *-Prof. Bernard Quatermass, Surrey, Maine.*

"Aside from the constant stream of poop, her shrill, high-pitched voice announcing every fresh poop is making it impossible for me to sleep".
-Mrs.Leo Gorcey, Eastsideville, Connecticut.

"Up to my nose in poop. Can't breathe." *-Mr. Lawrence Falana, New York City.*

Send $19.95 plus postage and handling to:
IMAJUNASHUN TOYS LTD., Sinisterville, ME 98712.

☐ *YES!* I have not read the testimonials and to me buying this doll seems like an excellent idea. I understand that my life will be ruined. Enclosed is a check for $19.95 plus $2.47 in postage and handling. That makes... duhhh.....

☐ *NO!* ! I do not wish to order this dreadful doll. Then why am I filling out and mailing in this coupon? I must be some kind of idiot or something.

DON'T DELAY! ORDER TODAY!

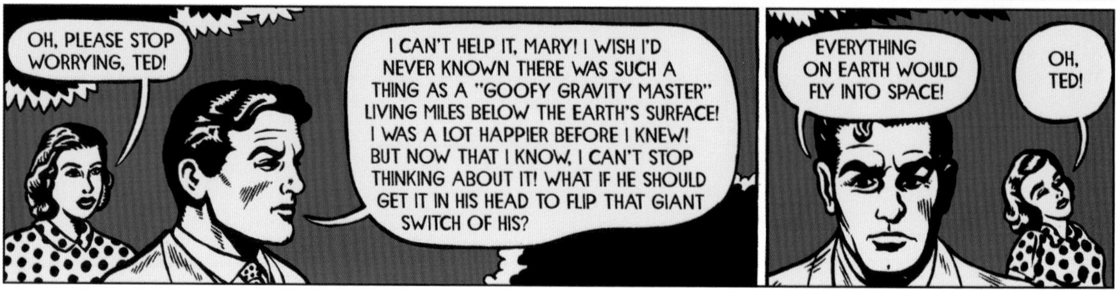
OH, PLEASE STOP WORRYING, TED!
I CAN'T HELP IT, MARY! I WISH I'D NEVER KNOWN THERE WAS SUCH A THING AS A "GOOFY GRAVITY MASTER" LIVING MILES BELOW THE EARTH'S SURFACE! I WAS A LOT HAPPIER BEFORE I KNEW! BUT NOW THAT I KNOW, I CAN'T STOP THINKING ABOUT IT! WHAT IF HE SHOULD GET IT IN HIS HEAD TO FLIP THAT GIANT SWITCH OF HIS?
EVERYTHING ON EARTH WOULD FLY INTO SPACE!
OH, TED!

The Adventures of The SILVER KNIGHT FEATURING MERLIN

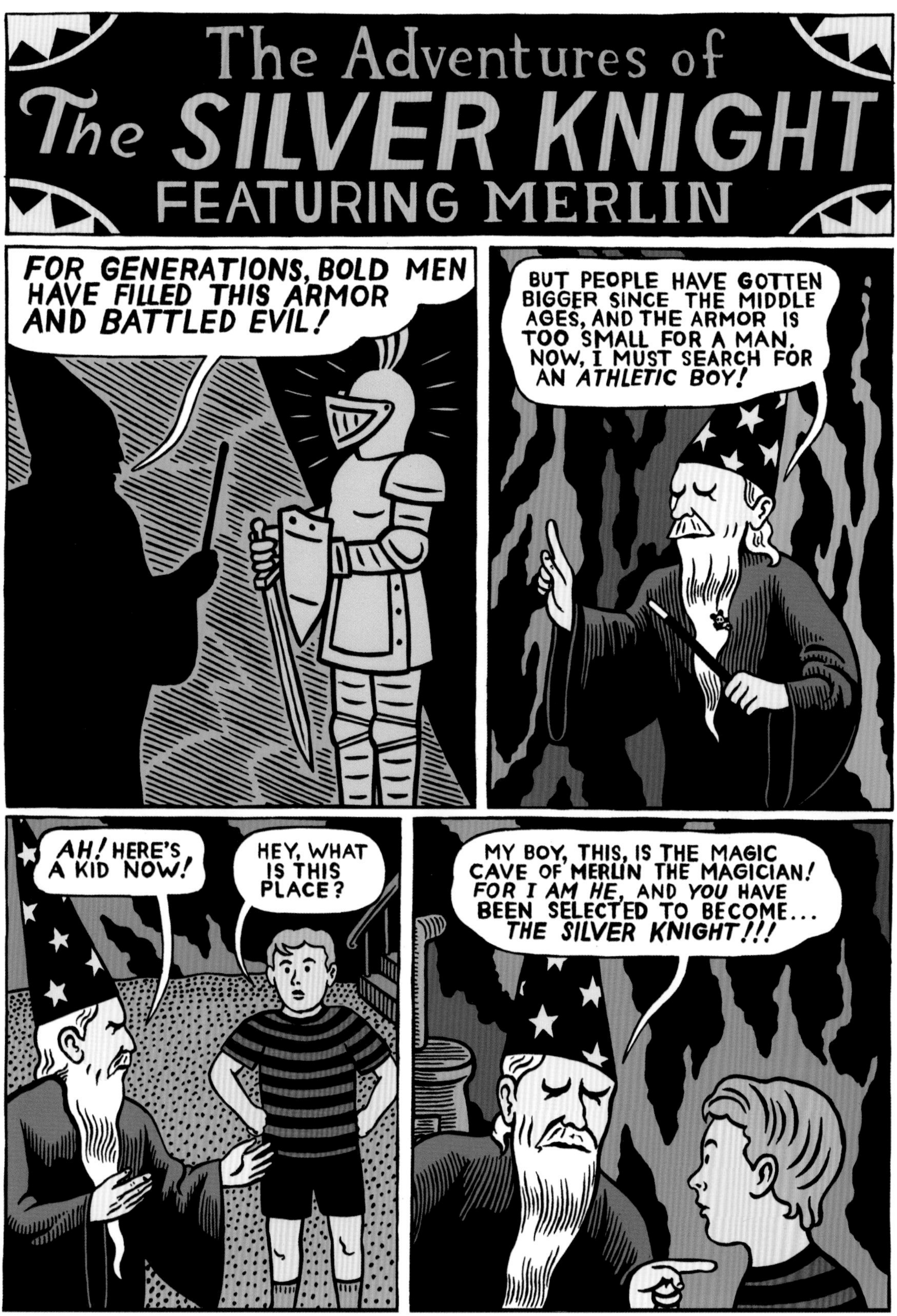

FOR GENERATIONS, BOLD MEN HAVE FILLED THIS ARMOR AND BATTLED EVIL!
BUT PEOPLE HAVE GOTTEN BIGGER SINCE THE MIDDLE AGES, AND THE ARMOR IS TOO SMALL FOR A MAN. NOW, I MUST SEARCH FOR AN ATHLETIC BOY!
AH! HERE'S A KID NOW!
HEY, WHAT IS THIS PLACE?
MY BOY, THIS, IS THE MAGIC CAVE OF MERLIN THE MAGICIAN! FOR I AM HE, AND YOU HAVE BEEN SELECTED TO BECOME... THE SILVER KNIGHT!!!

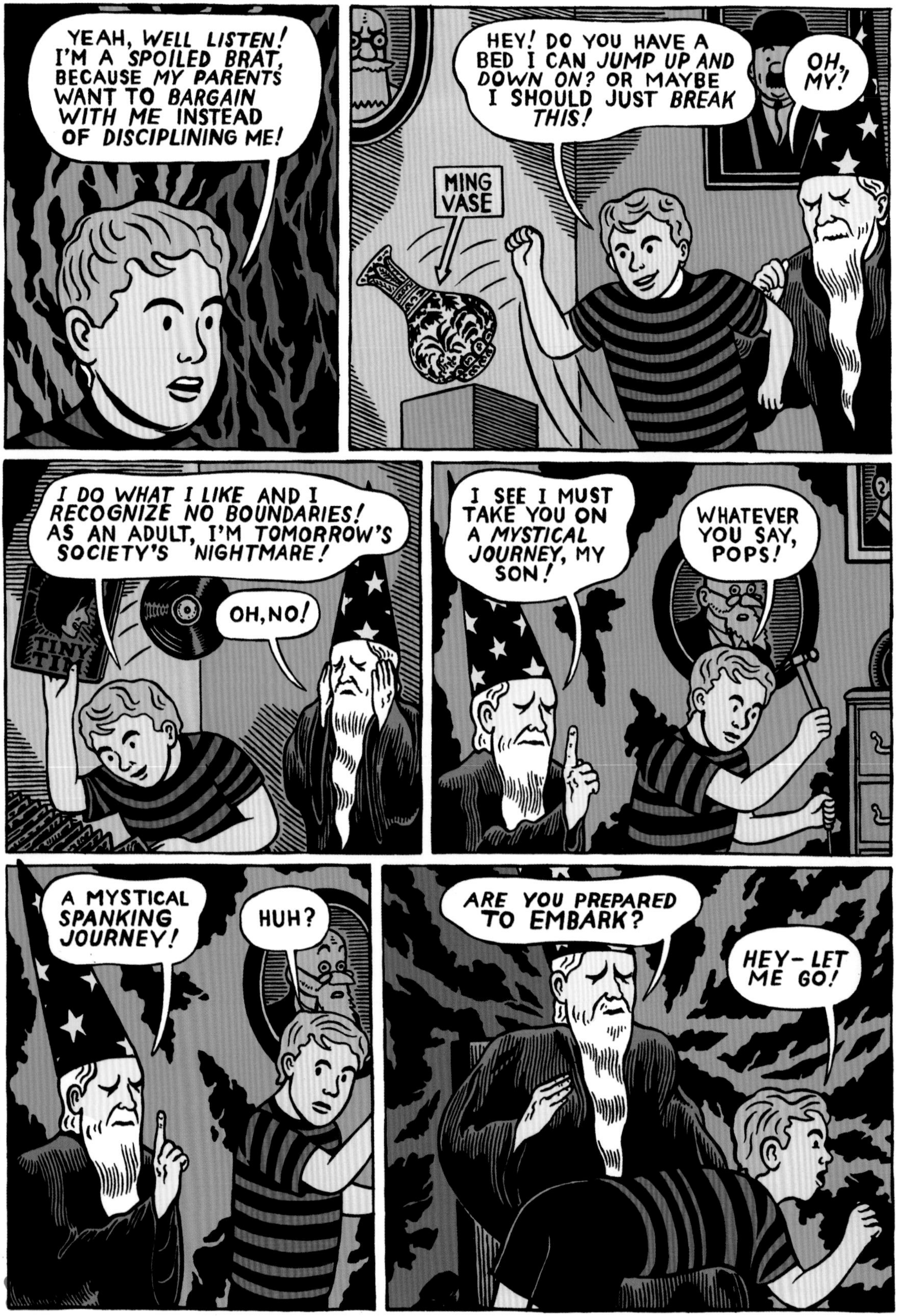
YEAH, WELL LISTEN! I'M A SPOILED BRAT, BECAUSE MY PARENTS WANT TO BARGAIN WITH ME INSTEAD OF DISCIPLINING ME!
HEY! DO YOU HAVE A BED I CAN JUMP UP AND DOWN ON? OR MAYBE I SHOULD JUST BREAK THIS!
OH, MY!
MING VASE
I DO WHAT I LIKE AND I RECOGNIZE NO BOUNDARIES! AS AN ADULT, I'M TOMORROW'S SOCIETY'S NIGHTMARE!
TINY TIM
OH, NO!
I SEE I MUST TAKE YOU ON A MYSTICAL JOURNEY, MY SON!
WHATEVER YOU SAY, POPS!
A MYSTICAL SPANKING JOURNEY!
HUH?
ARE YOU PREPARED TO EMBARK?
HEY-LET ME GO!

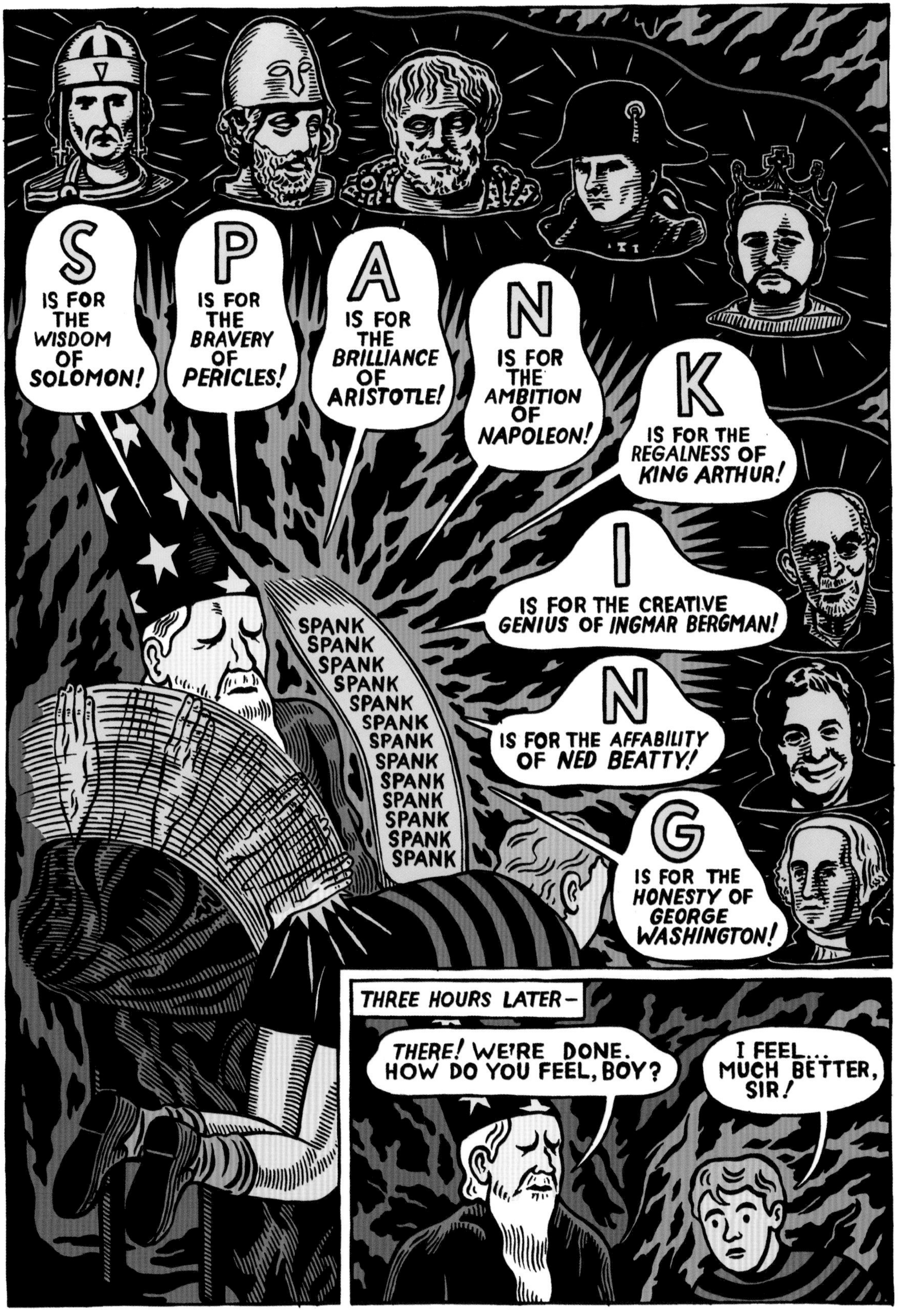
S IS FOR THE WISDOM OF SOLOMON!
P IS FOR THE BRAVERY OF PERICLES!
A IS FOR THE BRILLIANCE OF ARISTOTLE!
N IS FOR THE AMBITION OF NAPOLEON!
K IS FOR THE REGALNESS OF KING ARTHUR!
I IS FOR THE CREATIVE GENIUS OF INGMAR BERGMAN!
N IS FOR THE AFFABILITY OF NED BEATTY!
G IS FOR THE HONESTY OF GEORGE WASHINGTON!
SPANK SPANK SPANK SPANK SPANK SPANK SPANK SPANK SPANK SPANK SPANK SPANK SPANK
THREE HOURS LATER—
THERE! WE'RE DONE. HOW DO YOU FEEL, BOY?
I FEEL... MUCH BETTER, SIR!

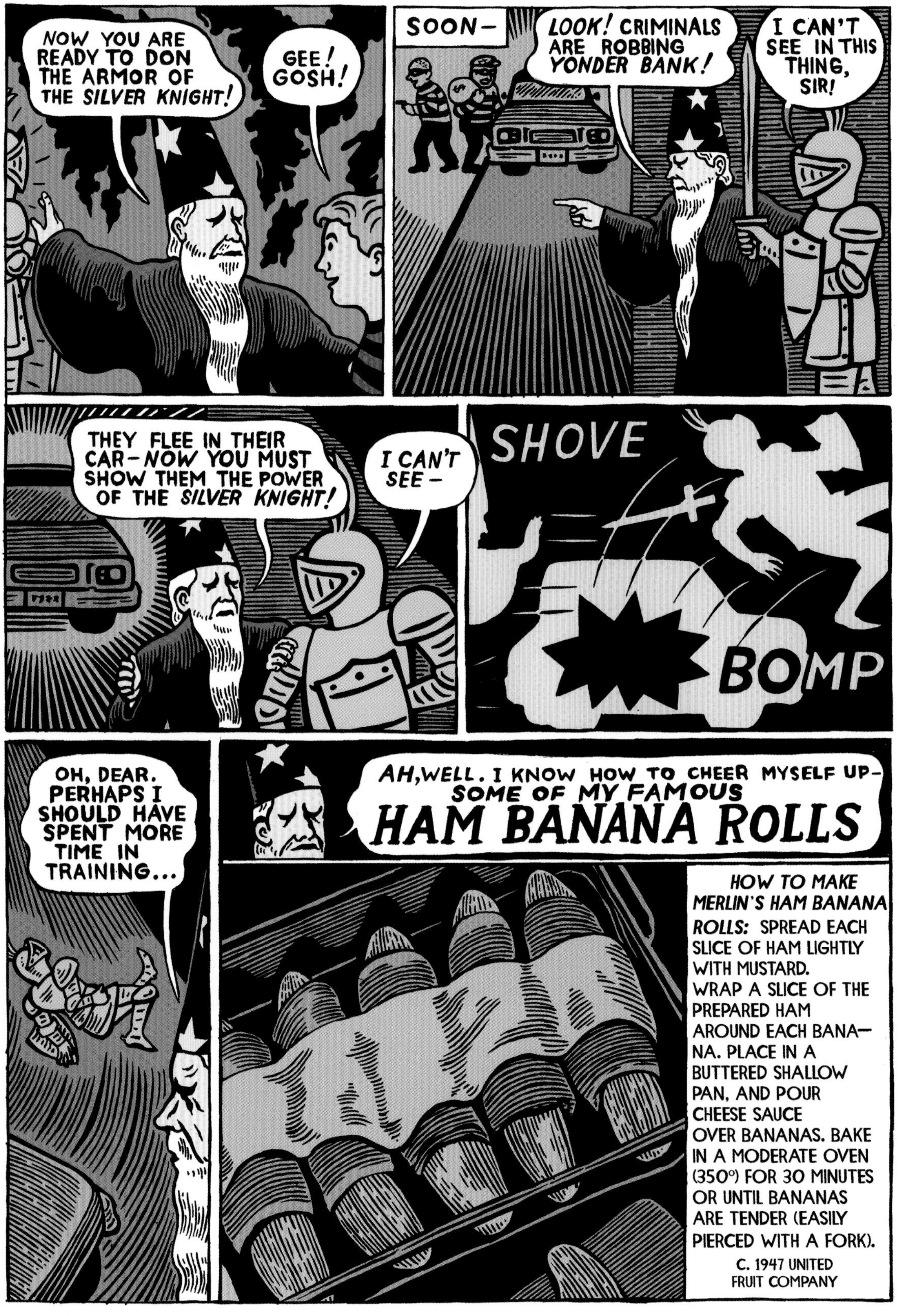
NOW YOU ARE READY TO DON THE ARMOR OF THE SILVER KNIGHT!
GEE! GOSH!
SOON–
LOOK! CRIMINALS ARE ROBBING YONDER BANK!
I CAN'T SEE IN THIS THING, SIR!
THEY FLEE IN THEIR CAR–NOW YOU MUST SHOW THEM THE POWER OF THE SILVER KNIGHT!
I CAN'T SEE–
SHOVE
BOMP
OH, DEAR. PERHAPS I SHOULD HAVE SPENT MORE TIME IN TRAINING...
AH, WELL. I KNOW HOW TO CHEER MYSELF UP– SOME OF MY FAMOUS
HAM BANANA ROLLS
HOW TO MAKE MERLIN'S HAM BANANA ROLLS: SPREAD EACH SLICE OF HAM LIGHTLY WITH MUSTARD. WRAP A SLICE OF THE PREPARED HAM AROUND EACH BANANA. PLACE IN A BUTTERED SHALLOW PAN, AND POUR CHEESE SAUCE OVER BANANAS. BAKE IN A MODERATE OVEN (350°) FOR 30 MINUTES OR UNTIL BANANAS ARE TENDER (EASILY PIERCED WITH A FORK).
C. 1947 UNITED FRUIT COMPANY

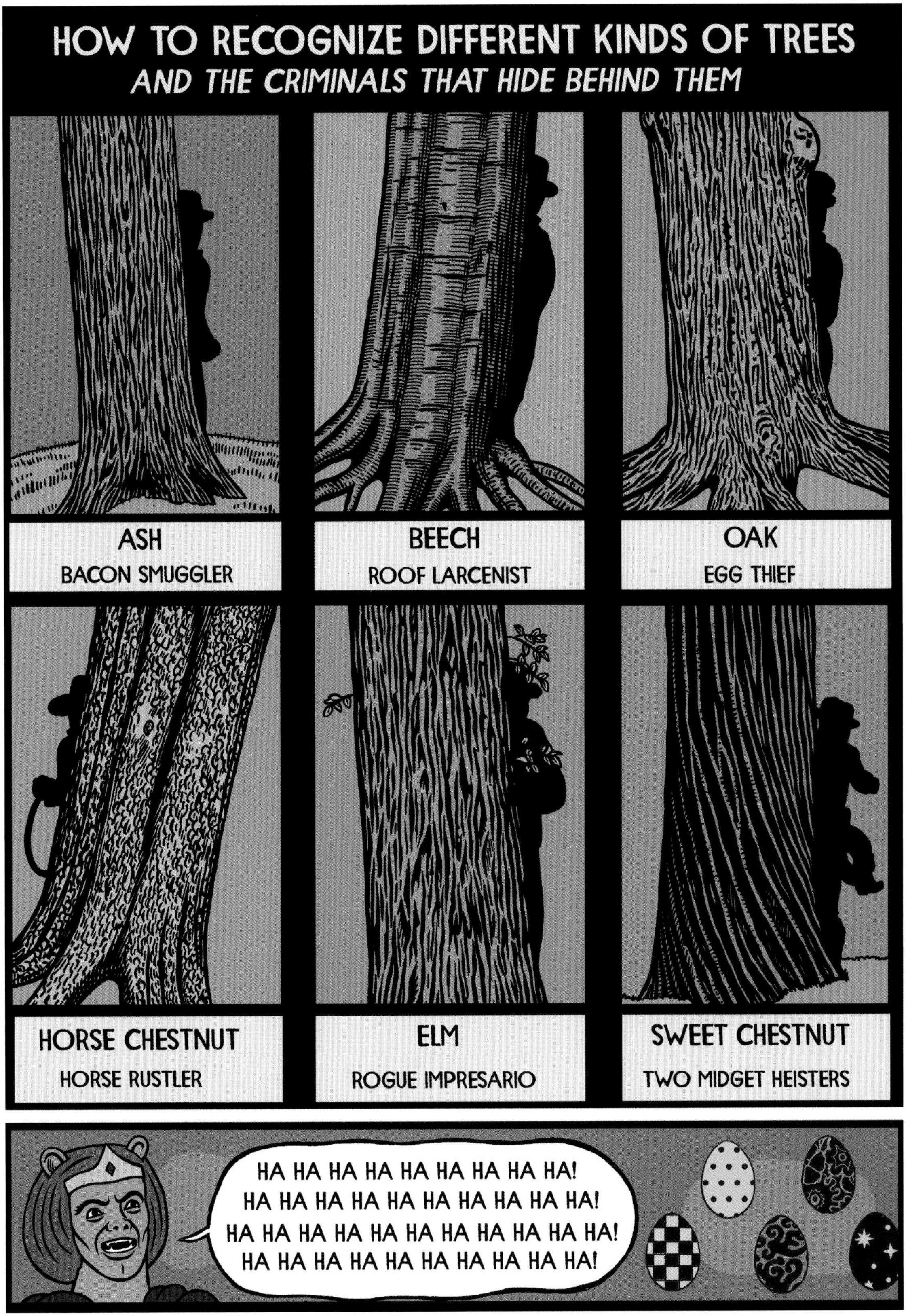
HOW TO RECOGNIZE DIFFERENT KINDS OF TREES
AND THE CRIMINALS THAT HIDE BEHIND THEM
ASH
BACON SMUGGLER
BEECH
ROOF LARCENIST
OAK
EGG THIEF
HORSE CHESTNUT
HORSE RUSTLER
ELM
ROGUE IMPRESARIO
SWEET CHESTNUT
TWO MIDGET HEISTERS
HA HA HA HA HA HA HA HA HA! HA HA HA HA HA HA HA HA HA HA! HA HA HA HA HA HA HA HA HA HA HA! HA HA HA HA HA HA HA HA HA HA!

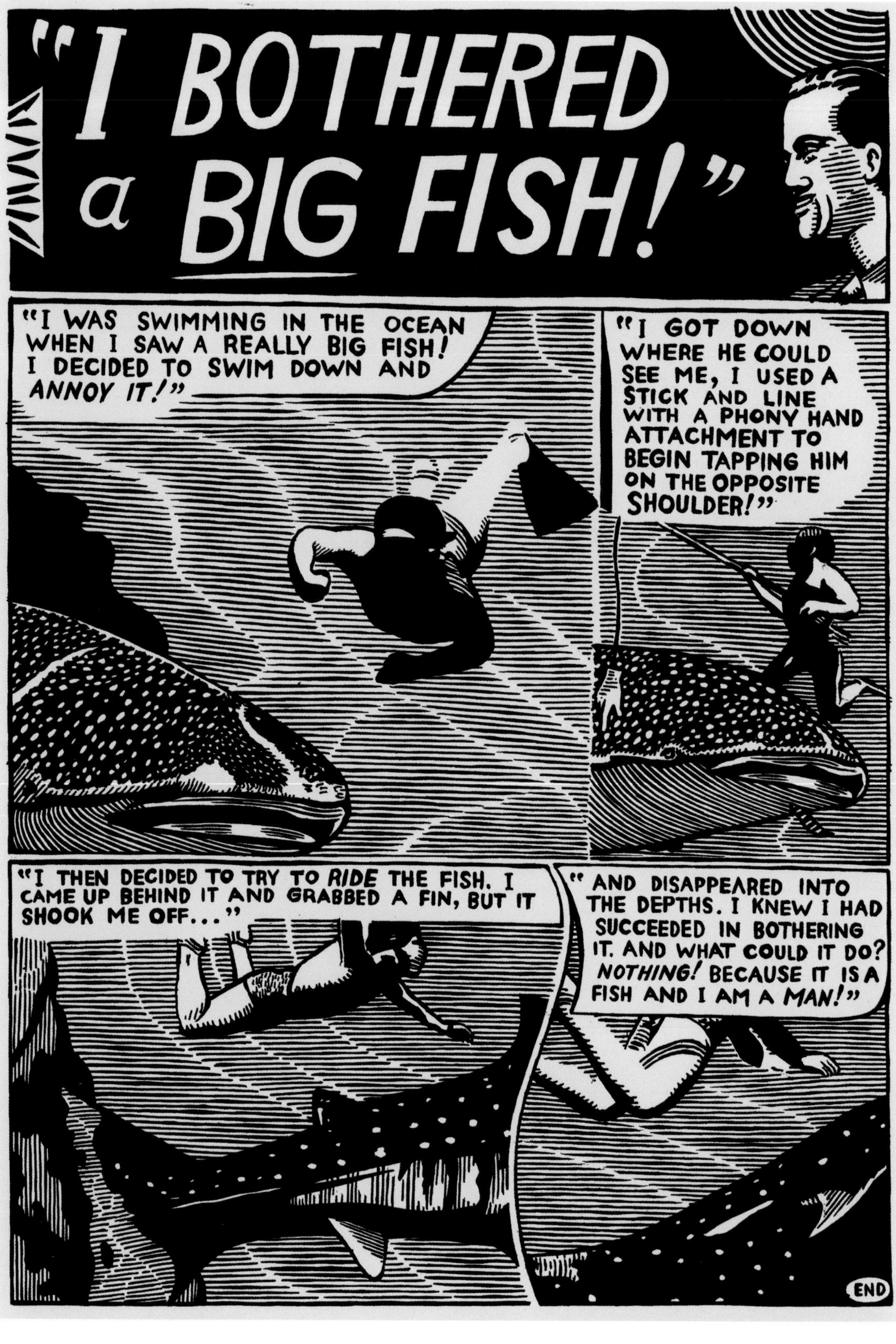
"I BOTHERED a BIG FISH!"
"I WAS SWIMMING IN THE OCEAN WHEN I SAW A REALLY BIG FISH! I DECIDED TO SWIM DOWN AND ANNOY IT!"
"I GOT DOWN WHERE HE COULD SEE ME, I USED A STICK AND LINE WITH A PHONY HAND ATTACHMENT TO BEGIN TAPPING HIM ON THE OPPOSITE SHOULDER!"
"I THEN DECIDED TO TRY TO RIDE THE FISH. I CAME UP BEHIND IT AND GRABBED A FIN, BUT IT SHOOK ME OFF..."
" AND DISAPPEARED INTO THE DEPTHS. I KNEW I HAD SUCCEEDED IN BOTHERING IT. AND WHAT COULD IT DO? NOTHING! BECAUSE IT IS A FISH AND I AM A MAN!"
END

* . INVENT YOUR OWN ADVENTURE! .

THE SPACE MOTHS *IN* "Who's

Minding the Earth?"

A FANTASTIC STORY WHERE YOU MAKE THE DECISIONS! CONTAINS UP TO 19 HOURS OF POTENTIAL READING!

WITH ILLUSTRATIONS TAKEN FROM OTHER STORIES TO SAVE MONEY!

YOU are the central figure in this incredible tale. And **YOU** make the decisions that lead this incredible narrative to its many surprising conclusions. For **YOU** are Yournamehere, a member of the elite space corps known as The Space Moths. You are the last and best defense of Earth in the crazy days of the late 23rd century. You are lazy and stupid, and nobody likes you. Our story opens at 8:13 on a **Wednesday** morning.

PARAGRAPH 1
Your peaceful sleep is being disturbed by a splash of lukewarm soup being dribbled off your face. At least you hope it's soup. Through it all you recognize the energetic voice of your bunkmate, Zebra Nixon. "Wake up, fool!" he's yelling, and begins kicking you with his third leg. "We got that big briefing to go to! On that new big-ass secret space mission! You better get dressed in a hurry if you wish to go! Or are you gonna spend all day in bed?"

Turn to paragraph 2 if you want to stay in bed all day.
Turn to paragraph 3 if you want to go to the big briefing.

PARAGRAPH 2
You scrunch your face into your pillow and turn towards the wall. Zebra finally gives up, shaking his head in disgust, and you return to the dream you were having, a dream in which you were smart and respected. It is 2:30 before you get up, and you spend the rest of the day eating macaroni and cheese and watching TV in your underwear.
MISSION OVER

PARAGRAPH 3
You get up and get dressed, and trot along to the big space briefing. All your fellow Space Moths are already there, and you take your seat, feeling nervous. Space Major Bradford enters the room. Brushing some space dust from his silver-winged gauntlets, he swishes his cape theatrically as he ascends to the podium. As soon as he's behind the microphone, he begins shouting. "Listen up!" he shouts, and then he continues shouting, something about a big dangerous space mission. It makes your head hurt. Why does he always have to shout so loudly? Your mind drifts, and you start to imagine what life would be like if you were a lion tamer, or a 19th-century Cockney grave robber...

Turn to paragraph 4 if you want to be a 19th-century Cockney grave robber.
Turn to paragraph 5 if you want to continue being a Space Moth.

PARAGRAPH 4
You skulk through the narrow, fog-laden backstreets of Victorian London, a freshly-stolen corpse slung over your shoulder. "Blimey, this'll bring me a couple o'bob. 'E don't smell much," you observe to yourself. But this reverie is disturbed by the shrill sound of

"But he didn't die in water. He drowned in a bathtub full of... *Shamrock Shakes!*

a Bobby's whistle. "Bloomin' eck!" you think miserably to yourself as you are sentenced to be hanged.
MISSION OVER

PARAGRAPH 5
Apparently the mission Space Major Bradford has been shouting about is a really, really scary one. You can tell because even the bravest of the Space Moths are looking a bit green. Then he's shouting about "volunteers" and looking straight at you. "Are you willing to risk your life for this planet?" he shouts. "Or are you going to cry and pee in your pants?"

Turn to paragraph 6 if you want to cry and pee in your pants.

Turn to paragraph 7 if you want to go on the big scary Space mission.

PARAGRAPH 6

You begin to cry, and urine flows from your trousers. Your fellow Space Moths look at you with expressions of pity and disgust. Space Major Bradford stares at you, open-mouthed for a moment, and opens his mouth. "You-" he begins, and then, lost for words, his face becomes grim. "Get this man out of here. He's dishonorably discharged." As you are dragged out of the room, you have the satisfaction at least of knowing that you won't have to go on the dangerous space mission. You begin to defecate as well.

MISSION OVER

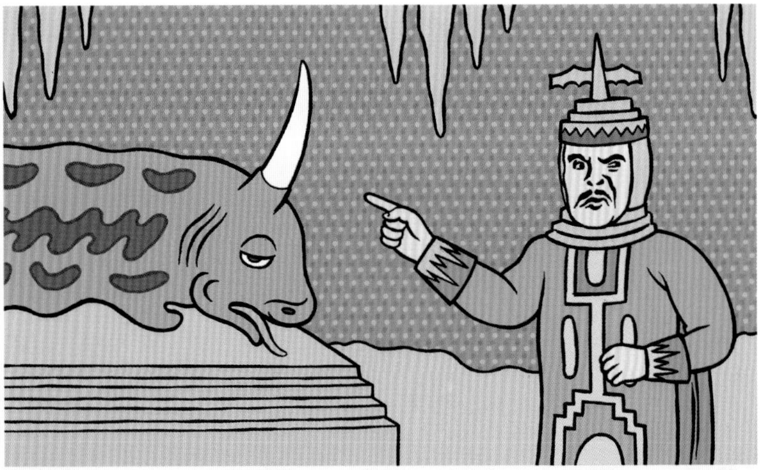

"Bah! The super-worm is still super-listless. Fetch me my witless, grovelling scientists!

PARAGRAPH 7

You say "Yes, sir, I volunteer," in a bold confident voice. The Space Major is pleased. "Good luck, son" he shouts gently, and then he jet-packs out of the room. You try to catch one of your fellow Space Moths as they run out of the room, but they are too fast, and you are quickly left alone. "Now what is this mission I'm supposed to be going on?" you wonder aloud. "Wish I'd learned to listen. Maybe I should go to the Spaceship room, where they keep the spaceships, and they can probably tell me there." You do so, and are informed that you are to leave in one hour to confront the Flesh-shredding Chocolate Chip Muffin people. "That doesn't sound so bad, except for the shredding part," you say, and then you wander out to buy some peanuts. Space Major Bradford's quarters are near the space newsstand, and as you pocket your change you notice Bradford's wife, standing in the door. She is dressed in a sexy negligee, and is beckoning to you provocatively.

TURN TO PARAGRAPH 8 IF YOU WANT TO HAVE SEX WITH MRS. BRADFORD
TURN TO PARAGRAPH 9 IF YOU DON'T WANT TO HAVE SEX WITH MRS. BRADFORD

PARAGRAPH 8

You saunter over to the Bradfords' door, and without a word she beckons you inside. "Goblet of peach brandy?" she asks, and you accept gratefully. As you guzzle the brandy, she begins to rub up against you. "Gosh, Mrs. Bradford," you say, and soon you are rolling around on the floor together. You are pulling your pants down when you hear the door being smashed open, and there is Space Major Bradford, his eyes blazing with hate."I'm gonna get 21st-century on your ass!" he screams, and he begins to pound and batter you with his massive fists, adding savage kicks as you fall to the floor, trying to curl up into a fetal position. As the savage beating continues, you can take comfort in one thing: soon you will lose consciousness.

MISSION OVER

PARAGRAPH 9

You give Mrs. Bradford a polite nod, and then you walk away. Nearby you notice a bush, and behind it is Major Bradford, crouching with a pair of binoculars. "Gosh! It's a good thing I didn't have sex with his wife," you say to yourself. Then you realize that he can hear you, and before you can explain, he is shouting at you. "How dare you! You want to have SEX with my WIFE? What kind of a place do you think this is? I've got a good mind to tear you to pieces! You little maggot! I've flushed better life forms than you down the toilet!" etc. Finally he pauses, short of breath. "Well? Is that enough, or should I yell at you some more?"

Turn to paragraph 10 if you want Space Major Bradford to yell at you some more.
Turn to paragraph 11 if you feel that you've had enough.

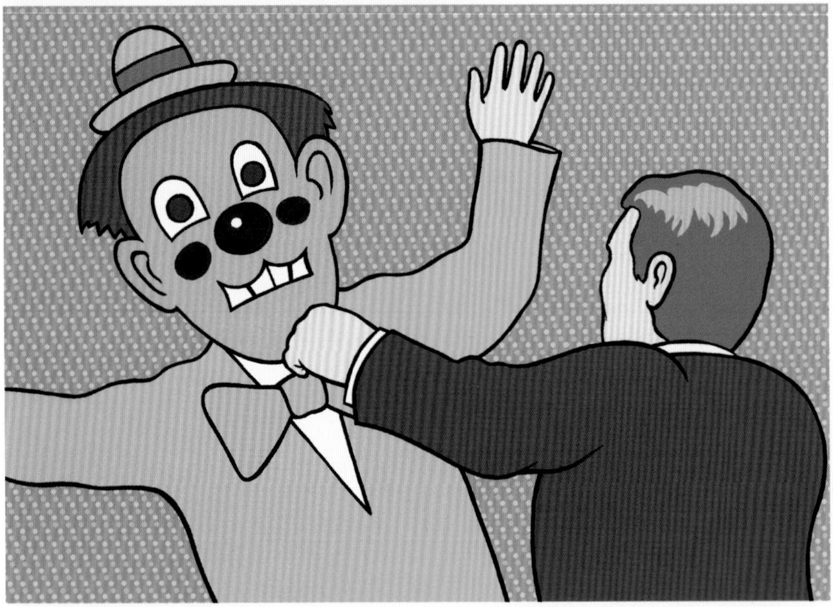

I punched and punched at that enormous papier-mache head. Sooner or later I knew I'd break through and reach face!

PARAGRAPH 10

You indicate to Bradford that you're ready for more abuse, and he launches into a fresh tirade. "Sex with my wife! The very idea! A disgusting worm like you! I don't like you, Yournamehere! I've NEVER liked you! You're the kind of pilot that gives the Space Moths a bad name! You're stupid, and lazy, and you eat with your mouth open! And YOU want to have sex with my wife! If you even come NEAR my wife, I'll cripple you! It won't be pretty, I tell you! You revolting bag of shit!" Etc., etc. He pauses, out of breath again. "Well! NOW have you had enough, or do you need for me to yell at you even more?"

Turn back to the beginning of paragraph 10 if you want to be yelled at some more.
Turn to paragraph 11 if you feel that you've had enough.

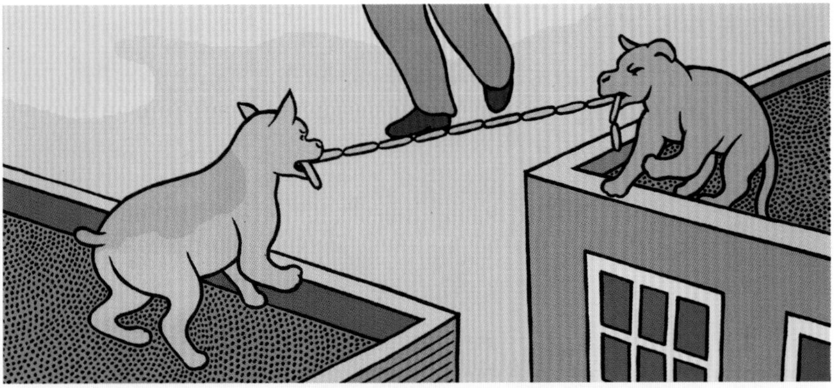

I moved slowly along my improvised tightrope, knowing that if either dog let go of the string of sausages, I would fall five stories to my death.

PARAGRAPH 11

"I guess I've had enough," you mumble, and he waves you away, anxious to resume his position behind the bush. You saunter back to the spaceship room, eating your peanuts. A hologram tries to sell you some life insurance, and you kick it away, disgusted by everything. "What a life!" you think. "I wish I was the narrator of *Moby Dick.*"

T urn to paragraph 12 if you want to become the narrator of Moby Dick.
Turn to paragraph 13 if you want to go on with the mission thing.

PARAGRAPH 12

"Call me Ishmail," you think to yourself. "Some years ago- never mind how long precisely- having little or no money in my purse, and nothing particular to interest me on shore, I thought I would sail about a little and see the watery part of the world..." *(get a copy of Moby Dick and continue reading from it, pretending that the words are your thoughts).*

PARAGRAPH 13

It's time for your big space mission! As the mechanics strap you into your ejector seat, you notice that none of your fellow Space moths have come to salute you as you fly off into space. Oh, well- they'll change their tunes when you come back, shrouded in glory! The hatch of your space flyer closes slowly with a defiant hiss, and the hatch to space begins to open. You realize that you have no idea how to fly your spaceship, having cheated in class, since then flying with a co-pilot to whom you unfailingly delegated all responsibilities. "Hey," you shout, but the ground crew sitting in the plastic box can't hear you. You look at the controls, and try hard to remember what they do.You've seen it done before; and slowly, haltingly, memories come to the surface. "This button makes it go," you murmur, and just then Space Major Bradford's voice grates from your console, disturbing your thoughts. "What are you waiting for?!" he screams. "Get that thing into space!" Steeling yourself, you press the button. You are jerked backwards as the vessel lifts straight off the ground- too fast! You just have time for a glimpse of the horrified faces in the control room, and then your ship smashes violently into the roof, instantly exploding, and killing you and five members of the ground crew.

MISSION OVER

THE END

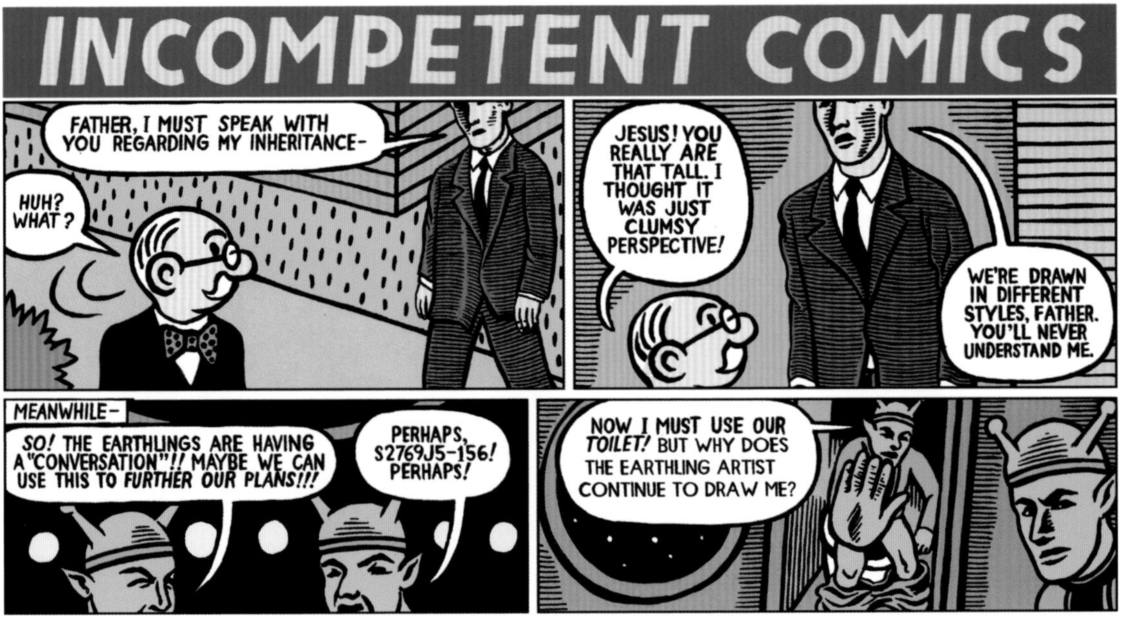
INCOMPETENT COMICS
FATHER, I MUST SPEAK WITH YOU REGARDING MY INHERITANCE-
HUH? WHAT?
JESUS! YOU REALLY ARE THAT TALL. I THOUGHT IT WAS JUST CLUMSY PERSPECTIVE!
WE'RE DRAWN IN DIFFERENT STYLES, FATHER. YOU'LL NEVER UNDERSTAND ME.
MEANWHILE-
SO! THE EARTHLINGS ARE HAVING A "CONVERSATION"!! MAYBE WE CAN USE THIS TO FURTHER OUR PLANS!!!
PERHAPS, S2769J5-156! PERHAPS!
NOW I MUST USE OUR TOILET! BUT WHY DOES THE EARTHLING ARTIST CONTINUE TO DRAW ME?

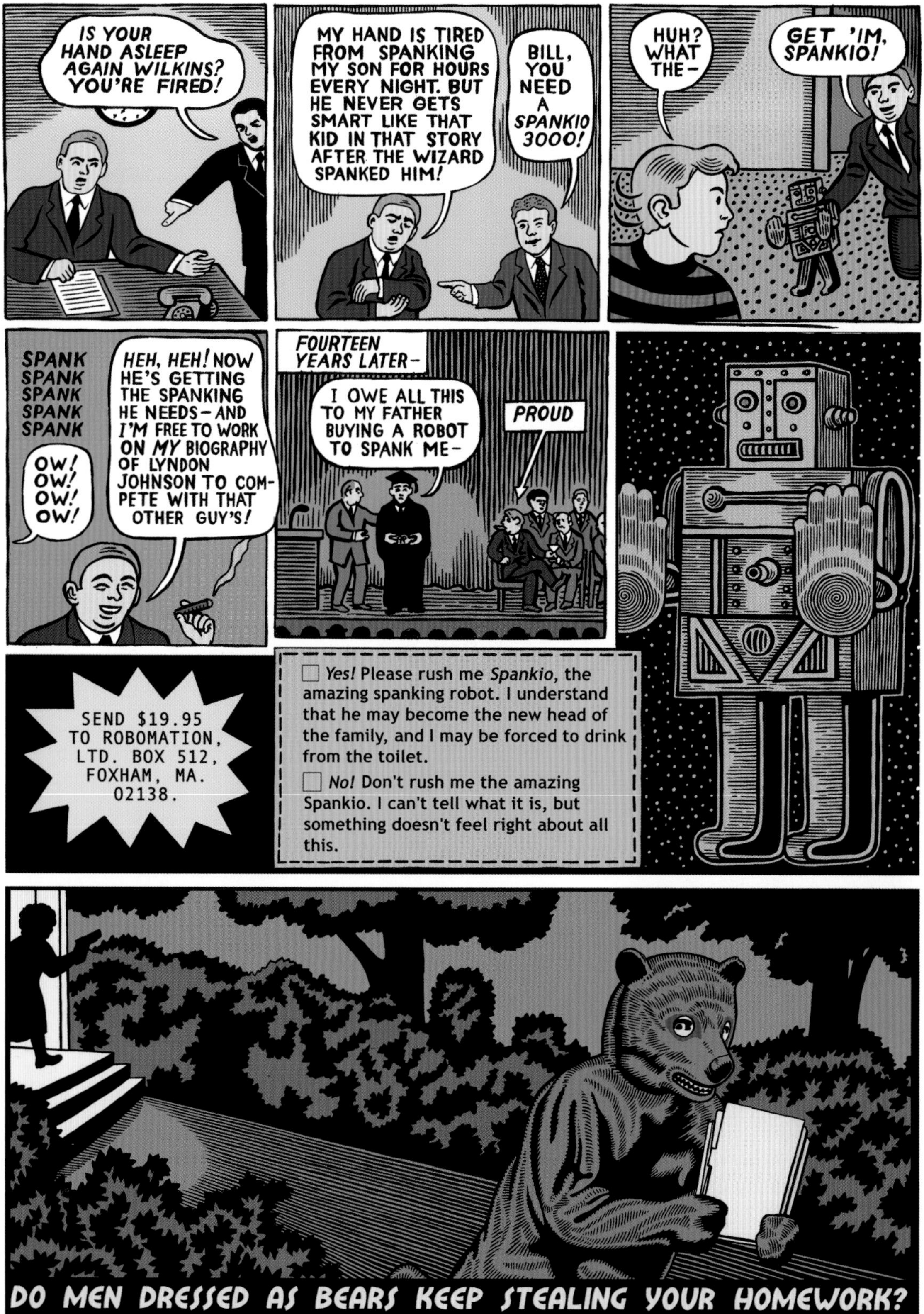
IS YOUR HAND ASLEEP AGAIN WILKINS? YOU'RE FIRED!
MY HAND IS TIRED FROM SPANKING MY SON FOR HOURS EVERY NIGHT. BUT HE NEVER GETS SMART LIKE THAT KID IN THAT STORY AFTER THE WIZARD SPANKED HIM!
BILL, YOU NEED A SPANKIO 3000!
HUH? WHAT THE–
GET 'IM, SPANKIO!
SPANK SPANK SPANK SPANK SPANK
HEH, HEH! NOW HE'S GETTING THE SPANKING HE NEEDS–AND I'M FREE TO WORK ON MY BIOGRAPHY OF LYNDON JOHNSON TO COMPETE WITH THAT OTHER GUY'S!
OW! OW! OW! OW!
FOURTEEN YEARS LATER–
I OWE ALL THIS TO MY FATHER BUYING A ROBOT TO SPANK ME–
PROUD
SEND $19.95 TO ROBOMATION, LTD. BOX 512, FOXHAM, MA. 02138.
☐ Yes! Please rush me Spankio, the amazing spanking robot. I understand that he may become the new head of the family, and I may be forced to drink from the toilet.
☐ No! Don't rush me the amazing Spankio. I can't tell what it is, but something doesn't feel right about all this.
DO MEN DRESSED AS BEARS KEEP STEALING YOUR HOMEWORK?
We can help. Write to Bearsaway, 577 Wormwowod Hill Embankment, Massapequany, Rhode Island 05739.

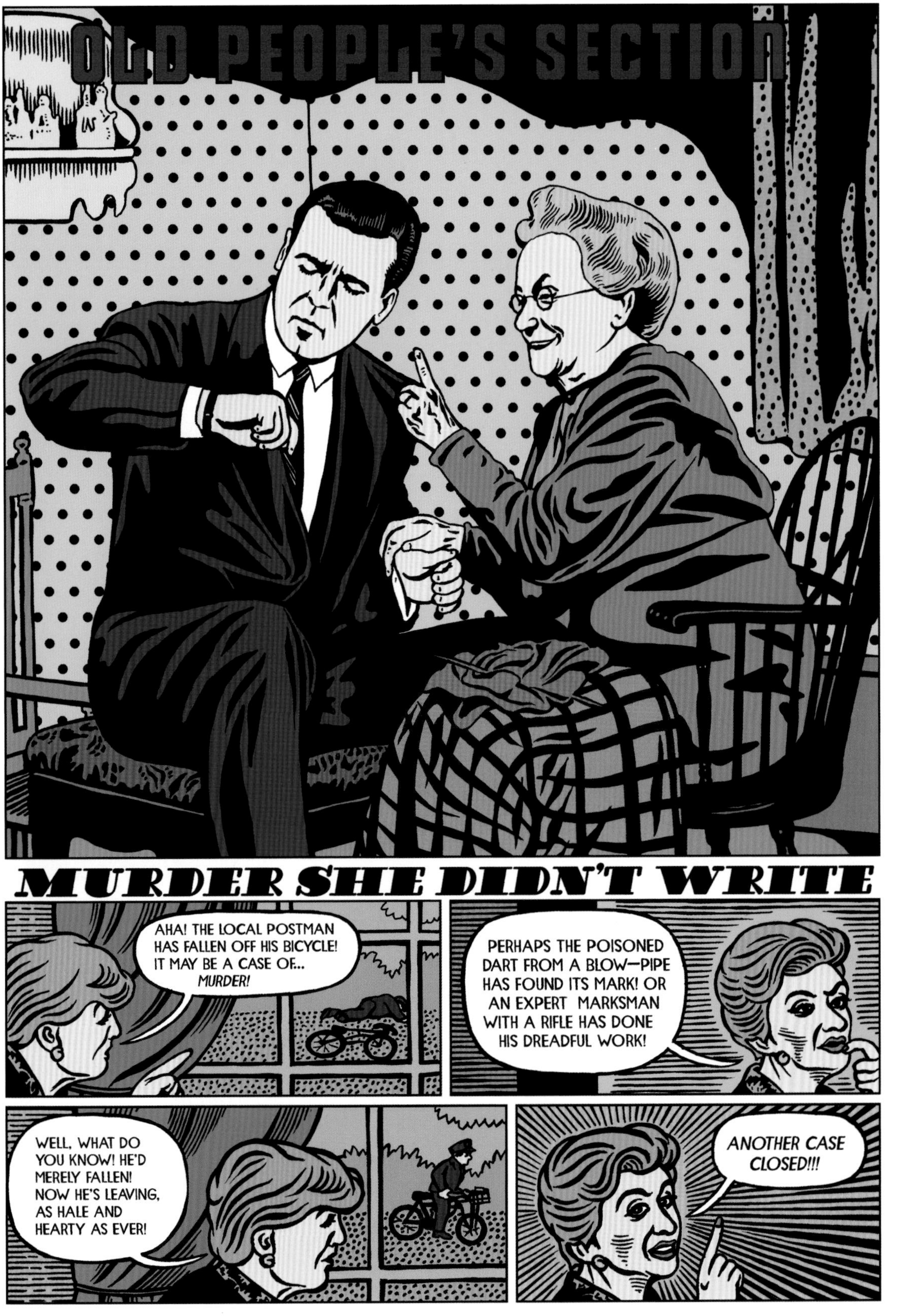
OLD PEOPLE'S SECTION
MURDER SHE DIDN'T WRITE
AHA! THE LOCAL POSTMAN HAS FALLEN OFF HIS BICYCLE! IT MAY BE A CASE OF... MURDER!
PERHAPS THE POISONED DART FROM A BLOW—PIPE HAS FOUND ITS MARK! OR AN EXPERT MARKSMAN WITH A RIFLE HAS DONE HIS DREADFUL WORK!
WELL, WHAT DO YOU KNOW! HE'D MERELY FALLEN! NOW HE'S LEAVING, AS HALE AND HEARTY AS EVER!
ANOTHER CASE CLOSED!!!

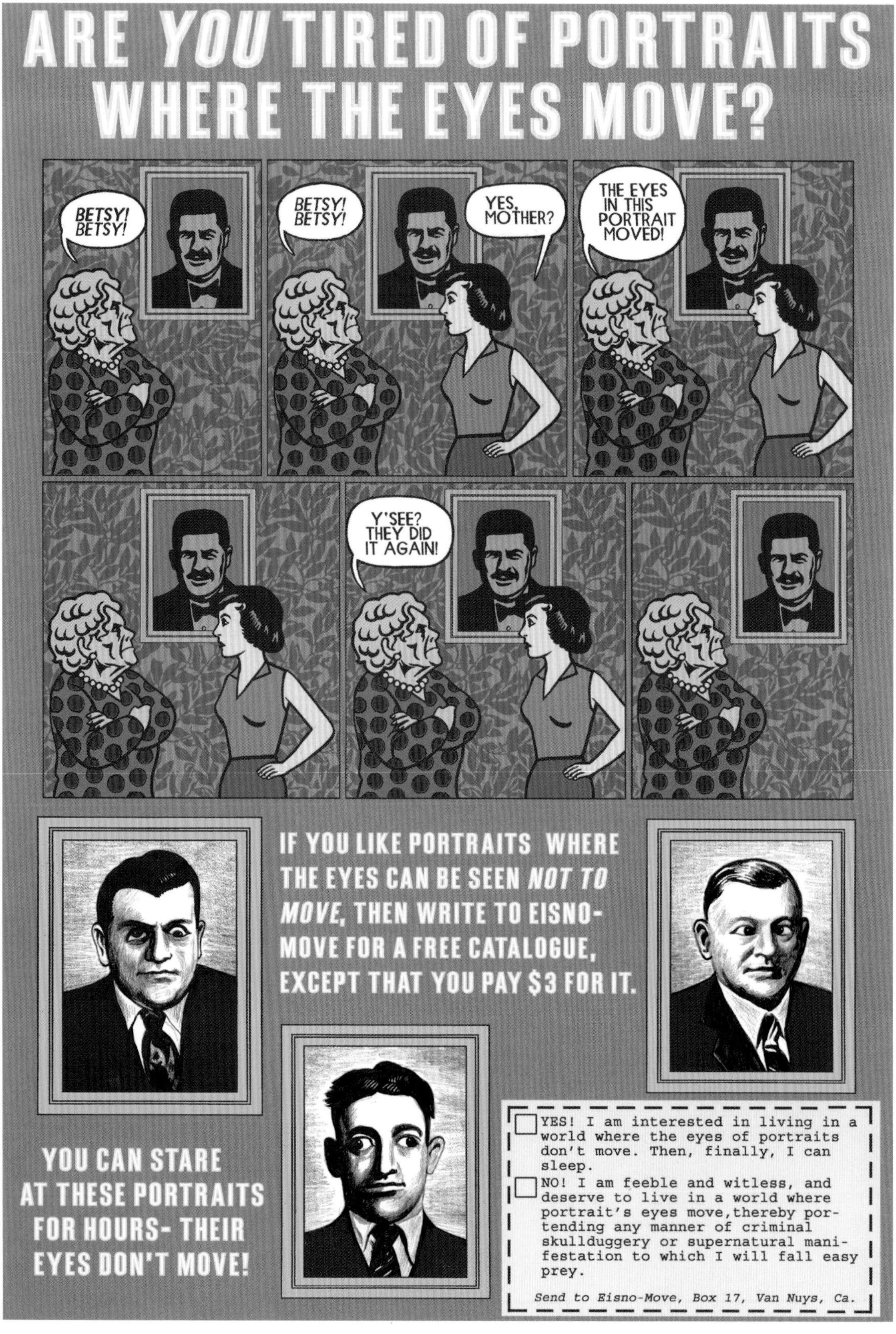
ARE YOU TIRED OF PORTRAITS WHERE THE EYES MOVE?
BETSY! BETSY!
BETSY! BETSY!
YES, MOTHER?
THE EYES IN THIS PORTRAIT MOVED!
Y'SEE? THEY DID IT AGAIN!
IF YOU LIKE PORTRAITS WHERE THE EYES CAN BE SEEN NOT TO MOVE, THEN WRITE TO EISNO-MOVE FOR A FREE CATALOGUE, EXCEPT THAT YOU PAY $3 FOR IT.
YOU CAN STARE AT THESE PORTRAITS FOR HOURS- THEIR EYES DON'T MOVE!
YES! I am interested in living in a world where the eyes of portraits don't move. Then, finally, I can sleep.
NO! I am feeble and witless, and deserve to live in a world where portrait's eyes move,thereby portending any manner of criminal skullduggery or supernatural manifestation to which I will fall easy prey.
Send to Eisno-Move, Box 17, Van Nuys, Ca.

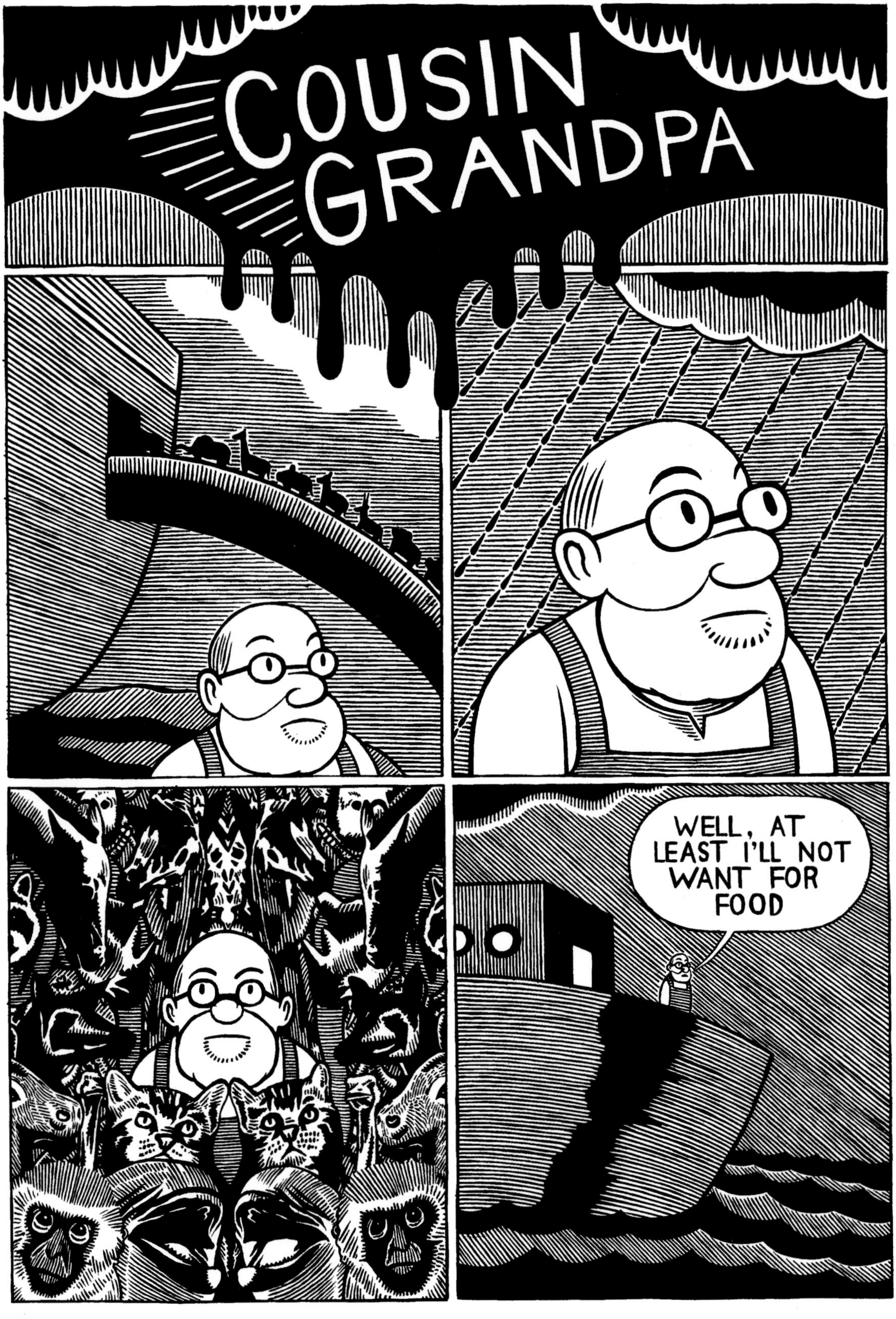
COUSIN GRANDPA
WELL, AT LEAST I'LL NOT WANT FOR FOOD

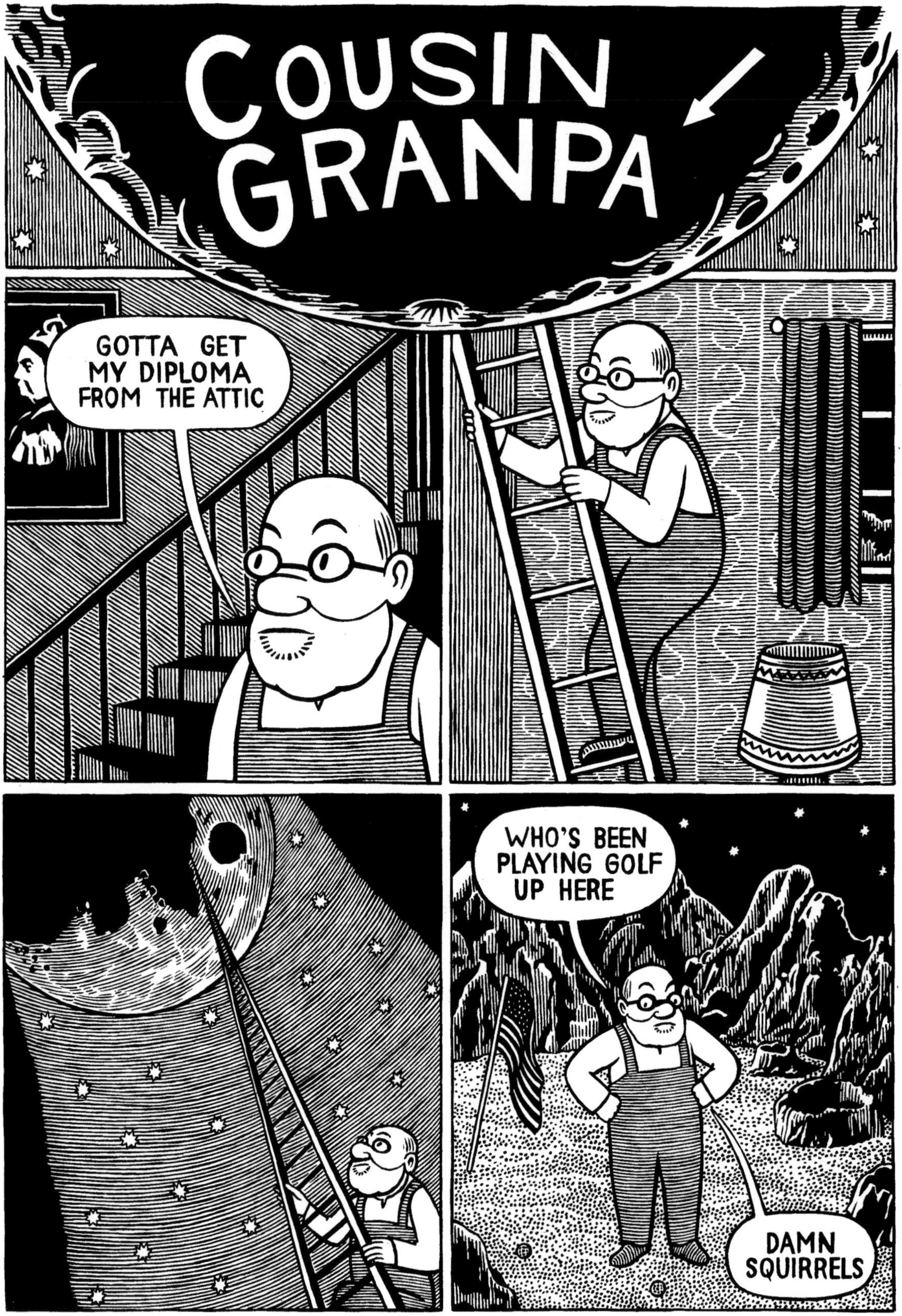
COUSIN GRANPA
GOTTA GET MY DIPLOMA FROM THE ATTIC
WHO'S BEEN PLAYING GOLF UP HERE
DAMN SQUIRRELS

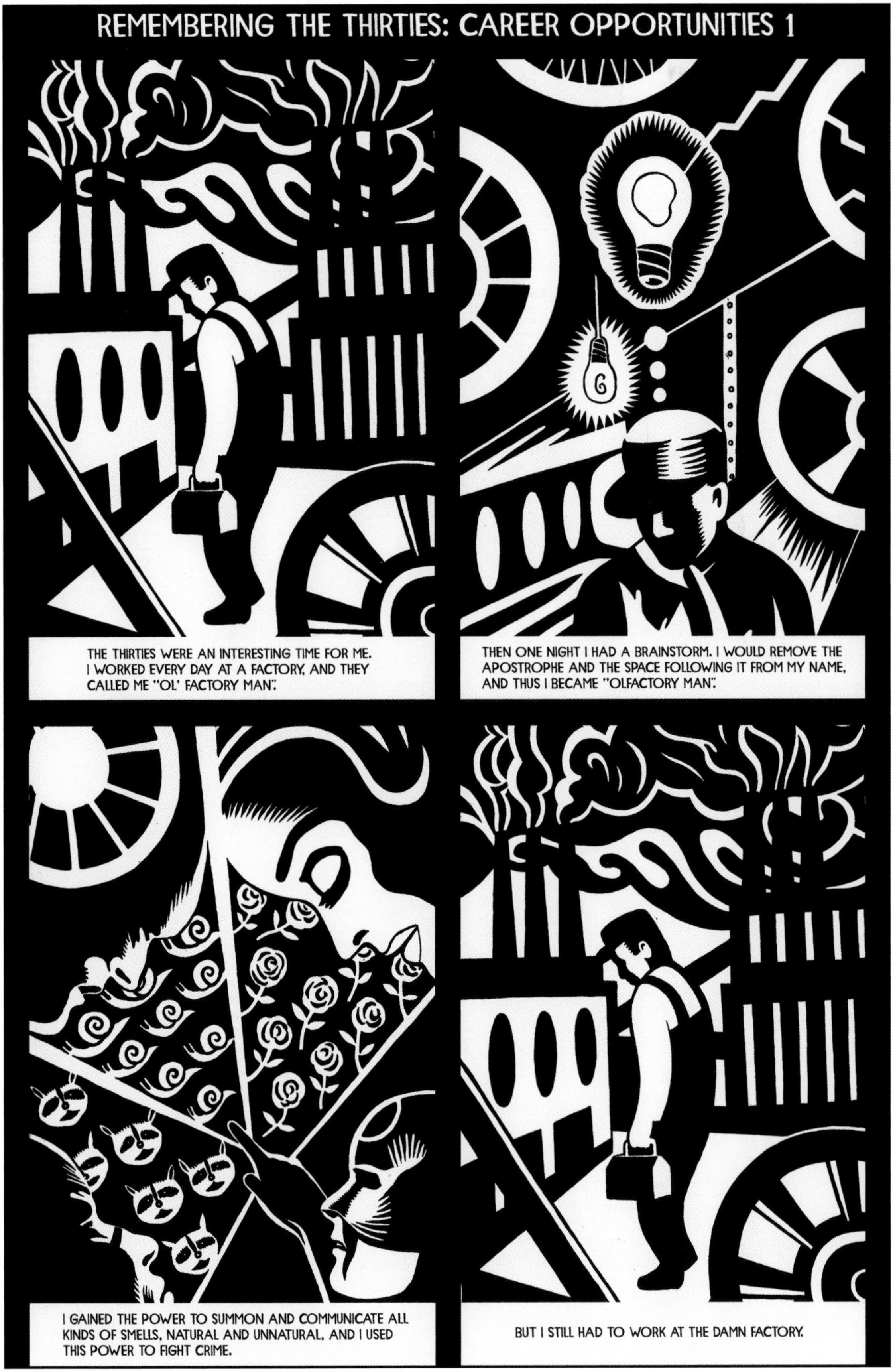
REMEMBERING THE THIRTIES: CAREER OPPORTUNITIES 1
THE THIRTIES WERE AN INTERESTING TIME FOR ME. I WORKED EVERY DAY AT A FACTORY, AND THEY CALLED ME "OL' FACTORY MAN".
THEN ONE NIGHT I HAD A BRAINSTORM. I WOULD REMOVE THE APOSTROPHE AND THE SPACE FOLLOWING IT FROM MY NAME, AND THUS I BECAME "OLFACTORY MAN".
I GAINED THE POWER TO SUMMON AND COMMUNICATE ALL KINDS OF SMELLS, NATURAL AND UNNATURAL, AND I USED THIS POWER TO FIGHT CRIME.
BUT I STILL HAD TO WORK AT THE DAMN FACTORY.

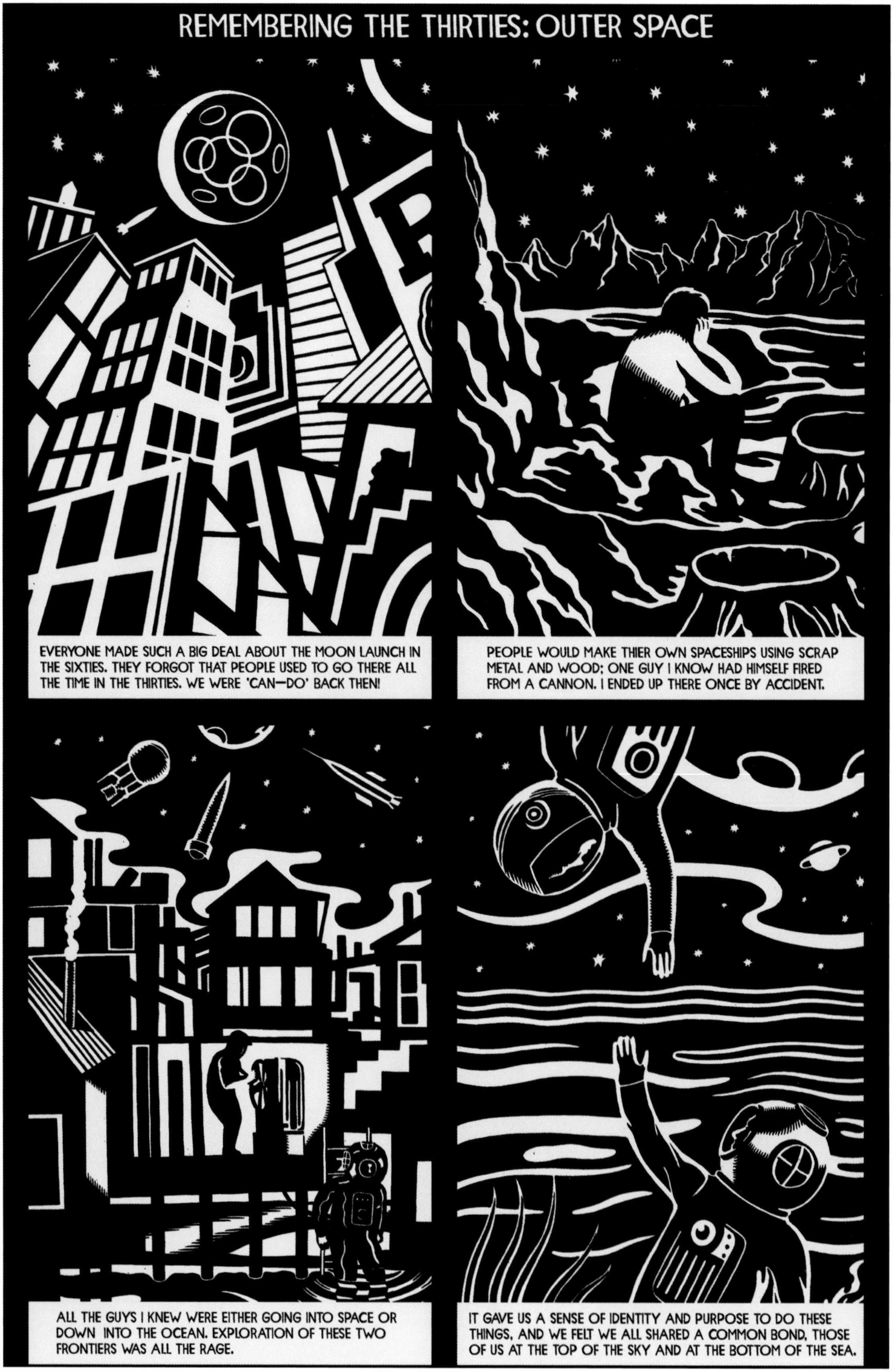
REMEMBERING THE THIRTIES: OUTER SPACE
EVERYONE MADE SUCH A BIG DEAL ABOUT THE MOON LAUNCH IN THE SIXTIES. THEY FORGOT THAT PEOPLE USED TO GO THERE ALL THE TIME IN THE THIRTIES. WE WERE 'CAN—DO' BACK THEN!
PEOPLE WOULD MAKE THIER OWN SPACESHIPS USING SCRAP METAL AND WOOD; ONE GUY I KNOW HAD HIMSELF FIRED FROM A CANNON. I ENDED UP THERE ONCE BY ACCIDENT.
ALL THE GUYS I KNEW WERE EITHER GOING INTO SPACE OR DOWN INTO THE OCEAN. EXPLORATION OF THESE TWO FRONTIERS WAS ALL THE RAGE.
IT GAVE US A SENSE OF IDENTITY AND PURPOSE TO DO THESE THINGS, AND WE FELT WE ALL SHARED A COMMON BOND, THOSE OF US AT THE TOP OF THE SKY AND AT THE BOTTOM OF THE SEA.

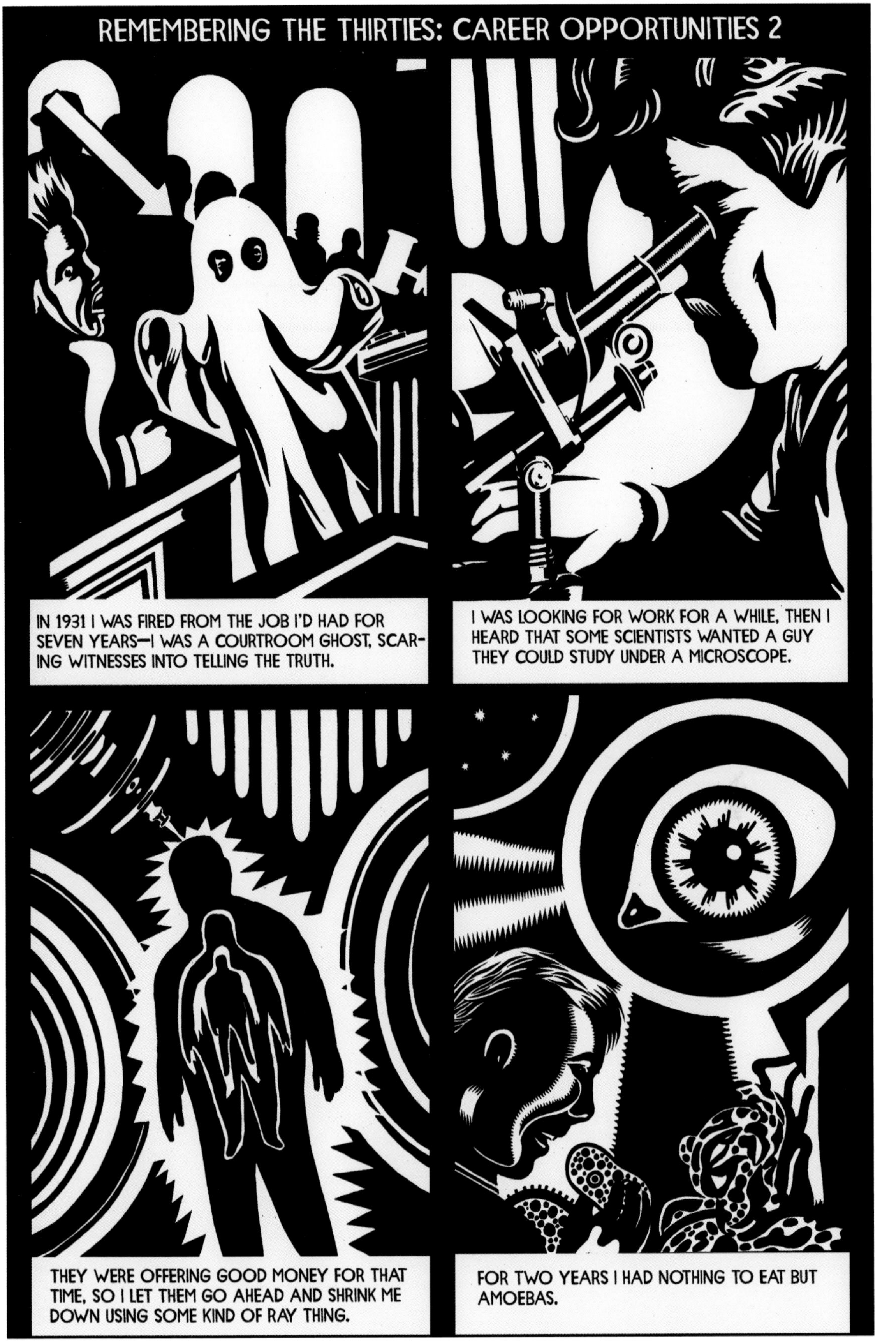
REMEMBERING THE THIRTIES: CAREER OPPORTUNITIES 2
IN 1931 I WAS FIRED FROM THE JOB I'D HAD FOR SEVEN YEARS—I WAS A COURTROOM GHOST, SCARING WITNESSES INTO TELLING THE TRUTH.
I WAS LOOKING FOR WORK FOR A WHILE, THEN I HEARD THAT SOME SCIENTISTS WANTED A GUY THEY COULD STUDY UNDER A MICROSCOPE.
THEY WERE OFFERING GOOD MONEY FOR THAT TIME, SO I LET THEM GO AHEAD AND SHRINK ME DOWN USING SOME KIND OF RAY THING.
FOR TWO YEARS I HAD NOTHING TO EAT BUT AMOEBAS.

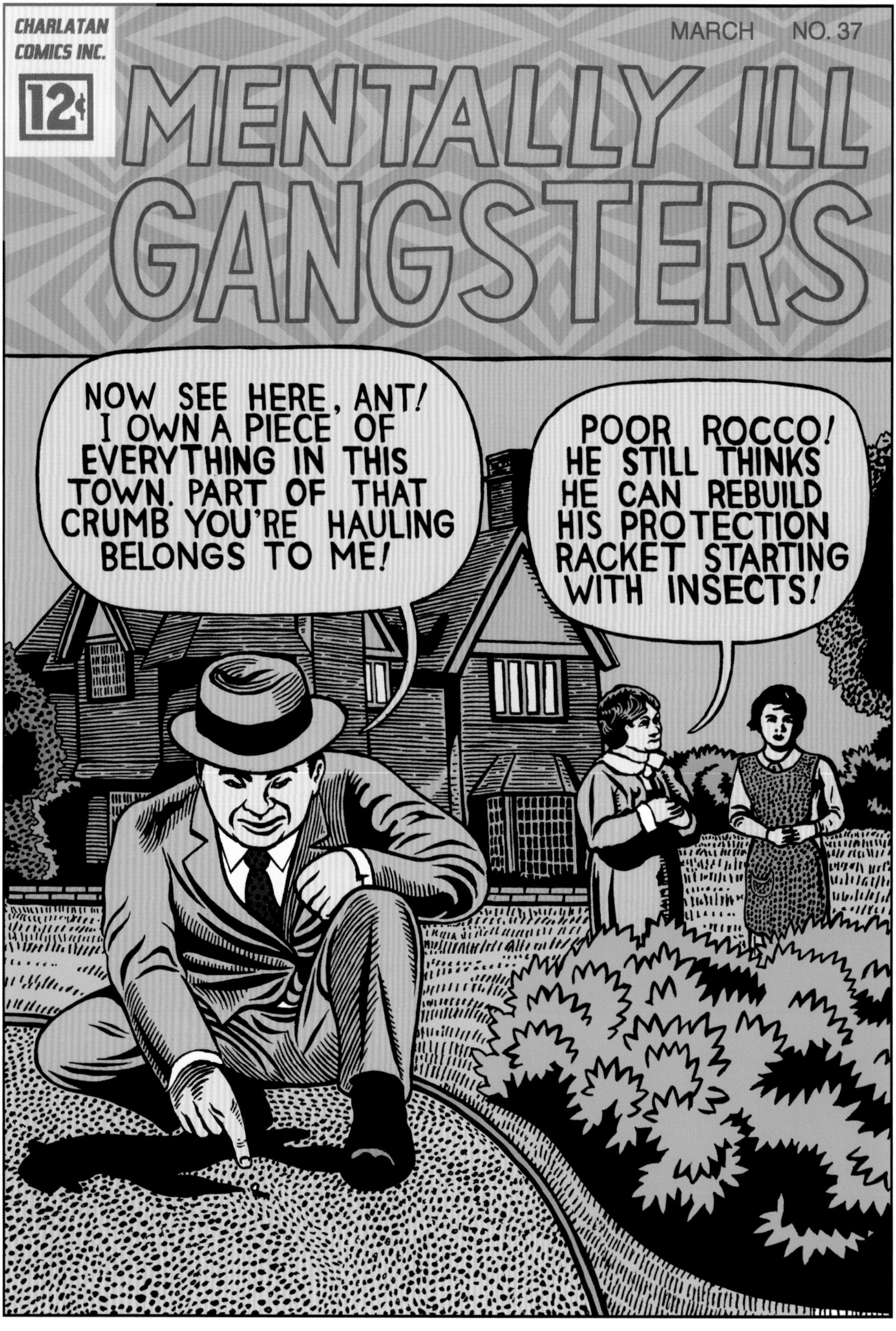
CHARLATAN COMICS INC.
12¢
MARCH NO. 37
MENTALLY ILL GANGSTERS
NOW SEE HERE, ANT! I OWN A PIECE OF EVERYTHING IN THIS TOWN. PART OF THAT CRUMB YOU'RE HAULING BELONGS TO ME!
POOR ROCCO! HE STILL THINKS HE CAN REBUILD HIS PROTECTION RACKET STARTING WITH INSECTS!

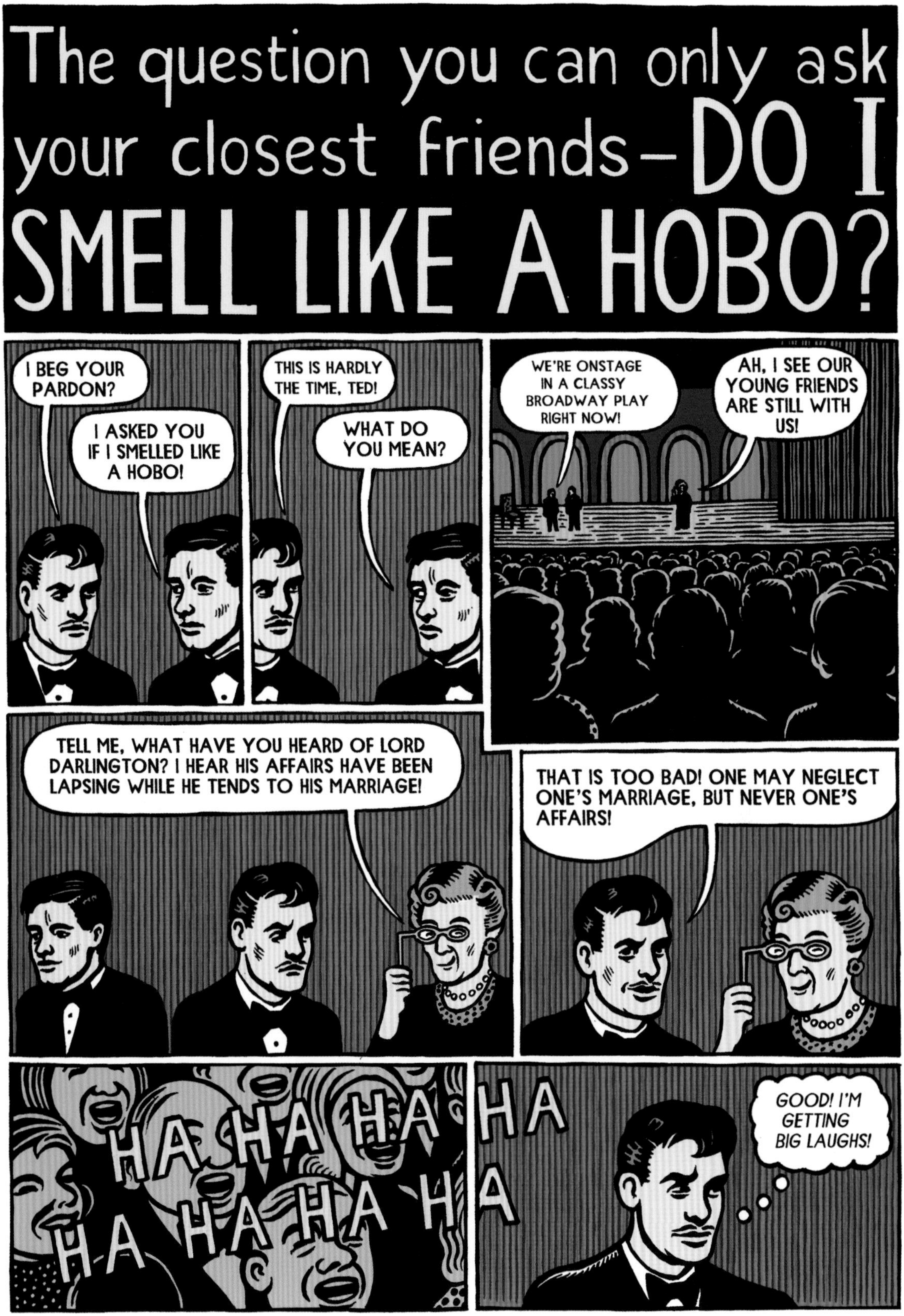
The question you can only ask your closest friends–DO I SMELL LIKE A HOBO?
I BEG YOUR PARDON?
I ASKED YOU IF I SMELLED LIKE A HOBO!
THIS IS HARDLY THE TIME, TED!
WHAT DO YOU MEAN?
WE'RE ONSTAGE IN A CLASSY BROADWAY PLAY RIGHT NOW!
AH, I SEE OUR YOUNG FRIENDS ARE STILL WITH US!
TELL ME, WHAT HAVE YOU HEARD OF LORD DARLINGTON? I HEAR HIS AFFAIRS HAVE BEEN LAPSING WHILE HE TENDS TO HIS MARRIAGE!
THAT IS TOO BAD! ONE MAY NEGLECT ONE'S MARRIAGE, BUT NEVER ONE'S AFFAIRS!
HA HA HA HA HA
HA HA HA HA HA
GOOD! I'M GETTING BIG LAUGHS!

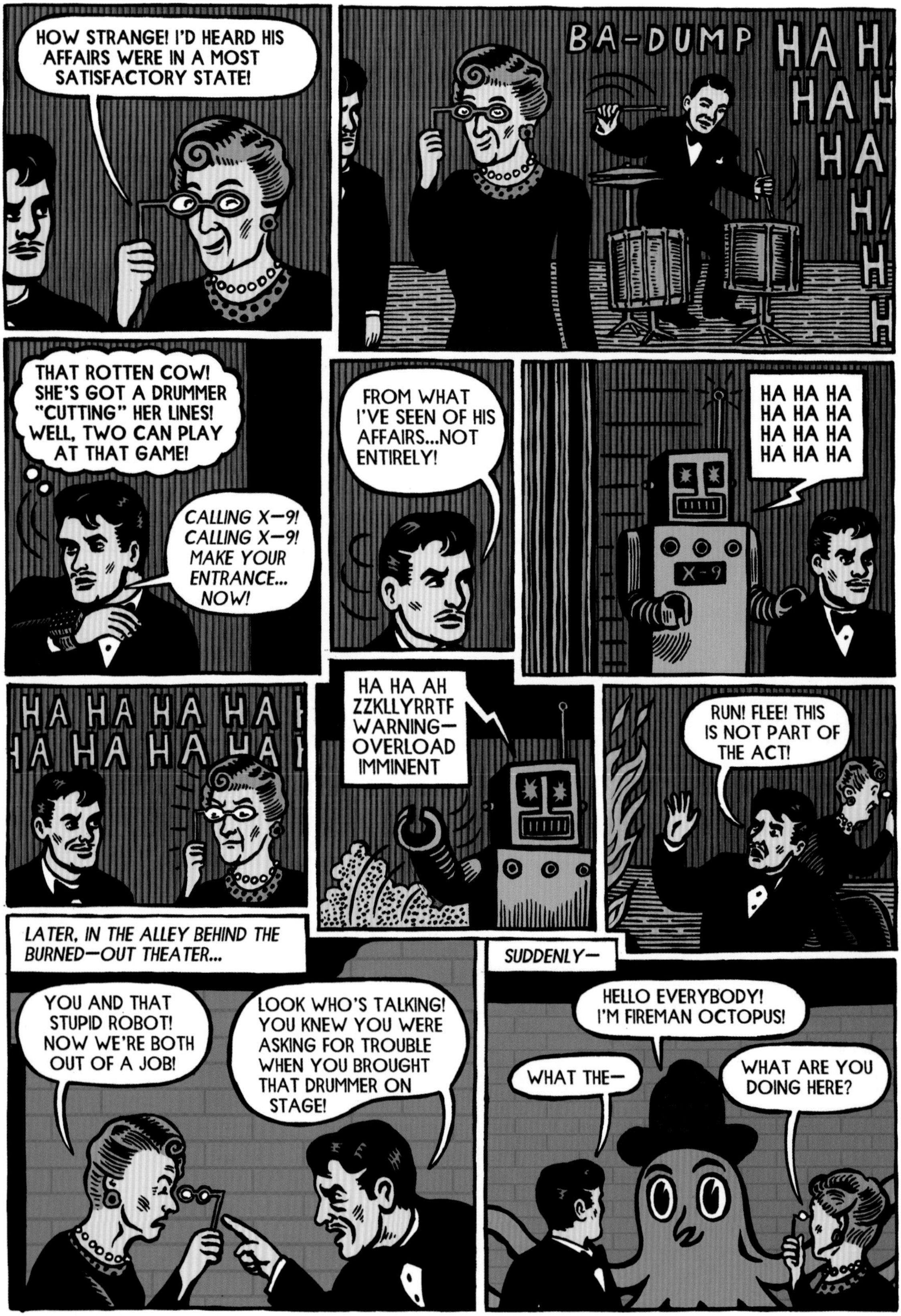

HOW STRANGE! I'D HEARD HIS AFFAIRS WERE IN A MOST SATISFACTORY STATE!
BA-DUMP HA HA HA HA HA HA H H
THAT ROTTEN COW! SHE'S GOT A DRUMMER "CUTTING" HER LINES! WELL, TWO CAN PLAY AT THAT GAME!
CALLING X-9! CALLING X-9! MAKE YOUR ENTRANCE... NOW!
FROM WHAT I'VE SEEN OF HIS AFFAIRS...NOT ENTIRELY!
HA HA HA HA HA HA HA HA HA HA HA HA
X-9
HA HA HA HA HA HA HA HA HA HA
HA HA AH ZZKLLYRRTF WARNING— OVERLOAD IMMINENT
RUN! FLEE! THIS IS NOT PART OF THE ACT!
LATER, IN THE ALLEY BEHIND THE BURNED-OUT THEATER...
YOU AND THAT STUPID ROBOT! NOW WE'RE BOTH OUT OF A JOB!
LOOK WHO'S TALKING! YOU KNEW YOU WERE ASKING FOR TROUBLE WHEN YOU BROUGHT THAT DRUMMER ON STAGE!
SUDDENLY—
HELLO EVERYBODY! I'M FIREMAN OCTOPUS!
WHAT THE—
WHAT ARE YOU DOING HERE?

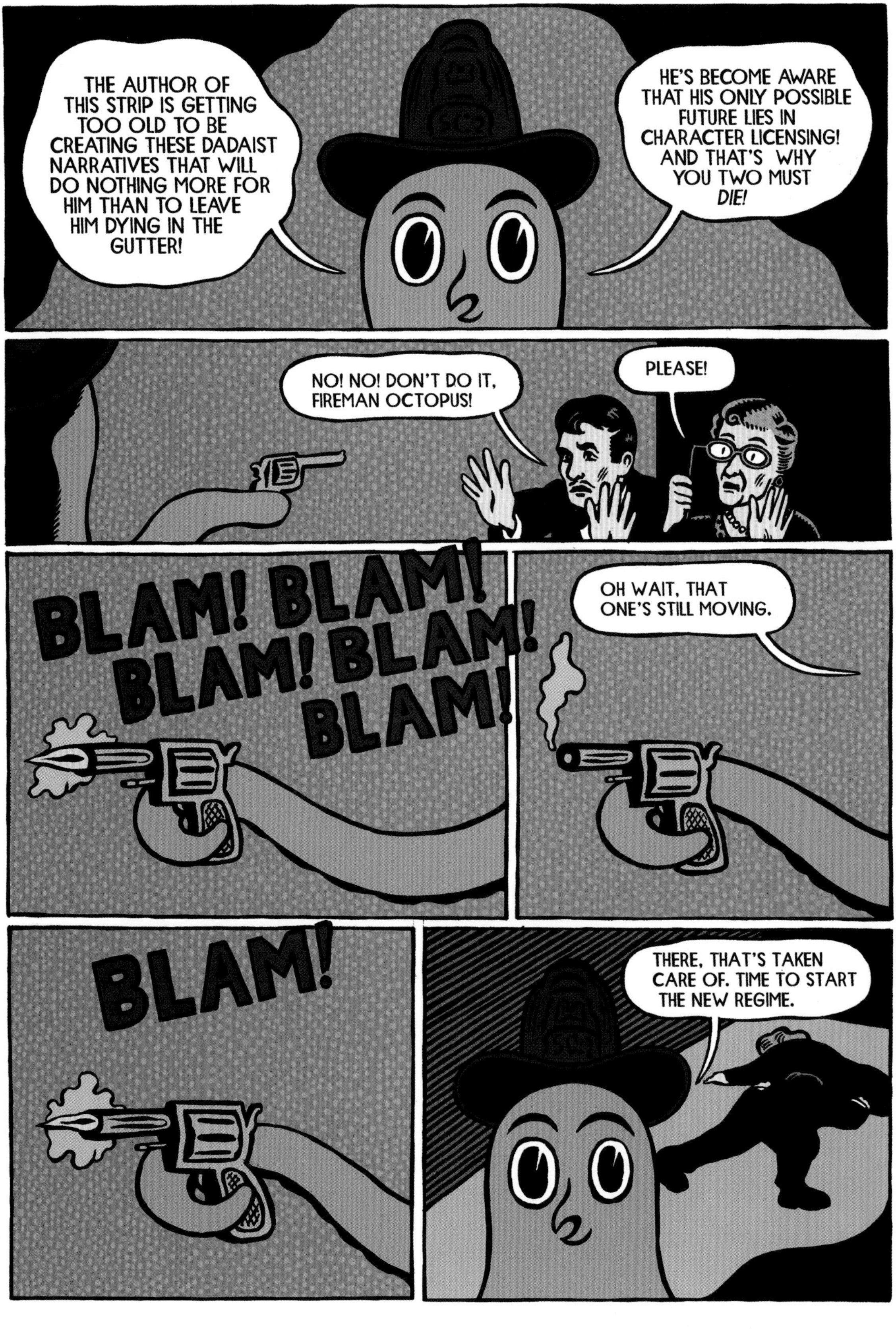
THE AUTHOR OF THIS STRIP IS GETTING TOO OLD TO BE CREATING THESE DADAIST NARRATIVES THAT WILL DO NOTHING MORE FOR HIM THAN TO LEAVE HIM DYING IN THE GUTTER!
HE'S BECOME AWARE THAT HIS ONLY POSSIBLE FUTURE LIES IN CHARACTER LICENSING! AND THAT'S WHY YOU TWO MUST *DIE!*
NO! NO! DON'T DO IT, FIREMAN OCTOPUS!
PLEASE!
BLAM! BLAM! BLAM! BLAM! BLAM!
OH WAIT, THAT ONE'S STILL MOVING.
BLAM!
THERE, THAT'S TAKEN CARE OF. TIME TO START THE NEW REGIME.

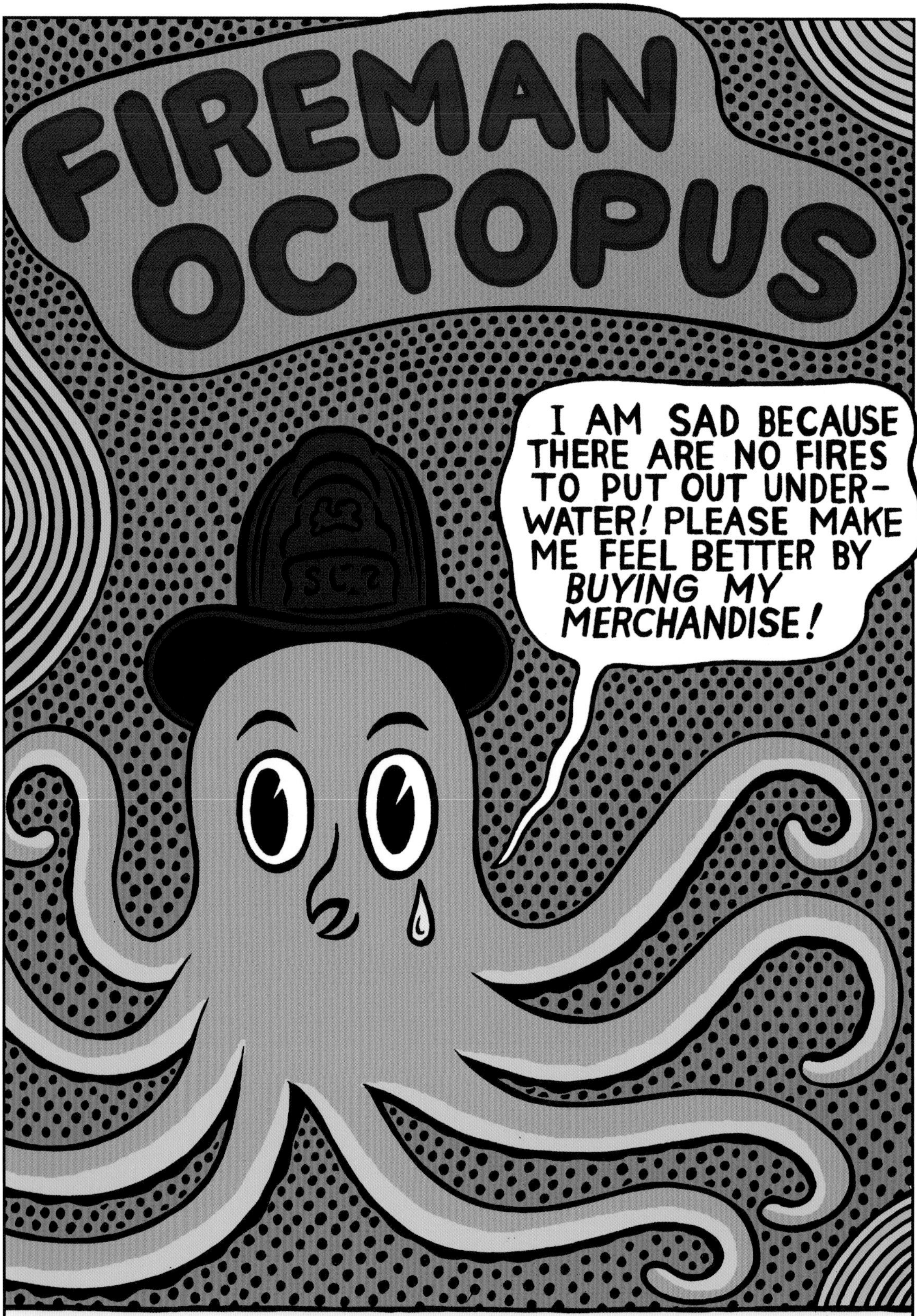
FIREMAN OCTOPUS
I AM SAD BECAUSE THERE ARE NO FIRES TO PUT OUT UNDER-WATER! PLEASE MAKE ME FEEL BETTER BY *BUYING MY MERCHANDISE!*
AVAILABLE AT BETTER BOUTIQUES EVERYWHERE?

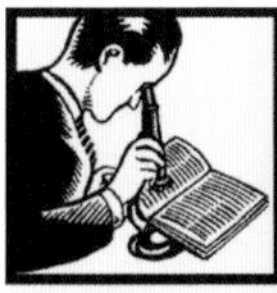

Improve yourself with
The DR. LEARNING SERIES OF BOOKLETS
"All knowledge is under the Sun."

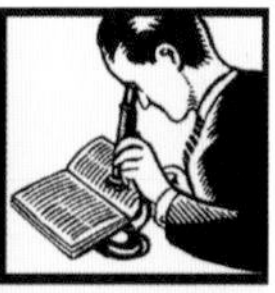

238. HOW TO DISCOVER NEW CONTINENTS, PLANETS ETC.Get in on the lucrative "explorer" racket. Listen in on conversations at bars and racetracks to discover tips on where you can discover hot new stuff and places.
116. PARDONING CRIMINALS. You don't have to be the governor to get involved. Pardon criminals in the privacy of your own home.
471. HOW TO RECOMMEND THINGS TO PEOPLE. People like a fella who's helpful in that way. Recommended.
224. WATCH REPAIR. Here are hints on how to and when to watch repair going on, on boats, clocks, buildings etc.
567. HOW TO GET HORRIBLY DRUNK. Enter a brave new world of magnificent adventure today.
097. HOW TO BE SLIPPERY. Coat yourself with grease, peanut butter, oil etc.
098. HOW NOT TO BE SLIPPERY.Coat yourself in flour, glue, oats etc.
453. LEARN HOW TO RESEMBLE WANTED POSTERS. Involve yourself in amusing situations with the police.
556. PRETENDING TO BE AN AIRPLANE. How to run bent over with your arms stuck out while going "Bshhpllptb-rrmphhrrr..." with your lips.
728. HOW TO BECOME AN ASTRONAUT. Many strategies, including standing in public places and saying loudly "Gee! I sure would like to go into space!"
324. HOW TO KNOCK THINGS OVER. "A man who can knock over many a thing is the wisest of all."- ***Benjamin Franklin.***
128. ENTICING RODENTS TO YOUR HOUSE. Some are easy, like rats or mice. But have you tried for the South American capybara, or the Indian mouse deer? Assemble a "fantasy world" of exotic rodentry in your own home.
554. MAKE BIG MONEY INVENTING NEW FINGER-PRINTS. Make big money.
731. REPAIRING ANOTHER PERSON'S CAR. We've all wanted to jump over and start repairing someone else's car. Here's how to do it when you're sure they won't notice.
298. FALLING DOWN HOLES FOR FUN AND PROFIT. The smaller the hole, the bigger the payoff.
145. RUBBING PEOPLE THE RIGHT WAY. How to rub against people in that secret, magical way.
626. IMITATING WILDLIFE. Imagine your friend's faces when you realistically portray a wounded gull.
394. UNDERWATER ESPIONAGE. Can you hold your breath for a long time? Become part of this exciting new field.
171. INSERTING RADISHES. You'll learn how and when.
248. SHRINKING HUMAN HEADS. Is your collection of human heads taking up too much space in your shabby furnished room?
402. NEW STYLES IN FACIAL EXPRESSIONS.With some bold combinations you might not have thought of.
208. HOW TO COMPETE IN SPACE TRAVEL. The Russians, Chinese, even the French are getting into the act. Why shouldn't you?
599. GESTICULATING WILDLY. While jabbering inanely.
273. LEARN HOW TO SEND PATENT APPLICATIONS BACK THROUGH TIME. They laughed when you sat down on things. Imagine their faces when it turns out you invented the lightbulb, or even chairs.
904. ARE YOU BEING BOTHERED BY TAUNTING HILL-BILLIES? Here are some effective remedies.
253. RECOGNIZING TURTLES. You might see the same turtle 90 years later- imagine the missed opportunity!
422. LEARNED ORATIONS. Mesmerize friends and strangers alike with your astute ramblings.
101. HOW TO HYPNOTIZE ANTS. Once you can control the ants you've got it made.
760. WHAT GOES ON INSIDE YOUR EAR? Wouldn't you like to know? The truth will amaze you.
129. IS YOUR CAR ON DRUGS? We all know if we're on drugs. But what about our cars? 37 ways to help you know once and for all.
323. OUTWITTING MACHINERY. With diagrams and a blank diary.
413. HOW TO APPEAR STUPID. Learn phrases such as "Duhh..." and "what the-".
047. SMELTING FUNNY. Working with liquid metal in a humorous fashion.
617. FOLLOWING SNAILS. It takes real patience to track a snail to it's lair.
298. IMAGINING PEOPLE IN THEIR UNDERPANTS. This will make you the "big man" in every situation.
819. URINATING IN PUBLIC. And doing it with style, confidence.
290. HOW TO TAME SNAKES. Make yourself a reptile pal.
306. TELLING BABOONS. They won't listen. But you'll know how to tell them.
563. MAKE MONEY WRITING. Ransom letters, stick-up notes, etc.
718. DOGS AND INVENTIONS. When and when not to mix the two.
436. BREAKING INTO SOCIETY. How to noisily smash your way through a french door, backing it up with fists and attitude.
025. INVEST YOUR MONEY IN NUTS. Let a squirrel be your broker. Fun!
340. NEW NAMES FOR CHILDREN. Flatula, Stinkums, Slo-mo, Gargantua, Stirfry, Potential, Figment.
513. LEARNING TO SURRENDER. Hand your sword to people; now you've become a "dependant nation".
800. DON'T RUN WITH SCISSORS! ILustrated with case histories and photographs.
211. SALIVATING GROTESQUELY. Train yourself like Pavlov's dog.
687. AMUSING NOISES FOR EVERY OCCASION. Lighten the mood with a well-timed sound.
261. SPITTING FOR PRIZES. You'll be amazed at what you can get.
720. SANITARY MAINTENANCE. How to use the latest spy technology to keep a lonely watch upon your toilet.
498. BECOME A STRESSTICIAN. Teach people to have more stress, worries etc.

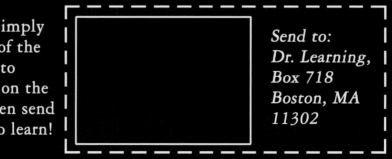

It's Easy to order! Simply write the numbers of the booklets wou want to order in the square on the coupon at right- then send it in, and prepare to learn!

Send to:
Dr. Learning,
Box 718
Boston, MA
11302

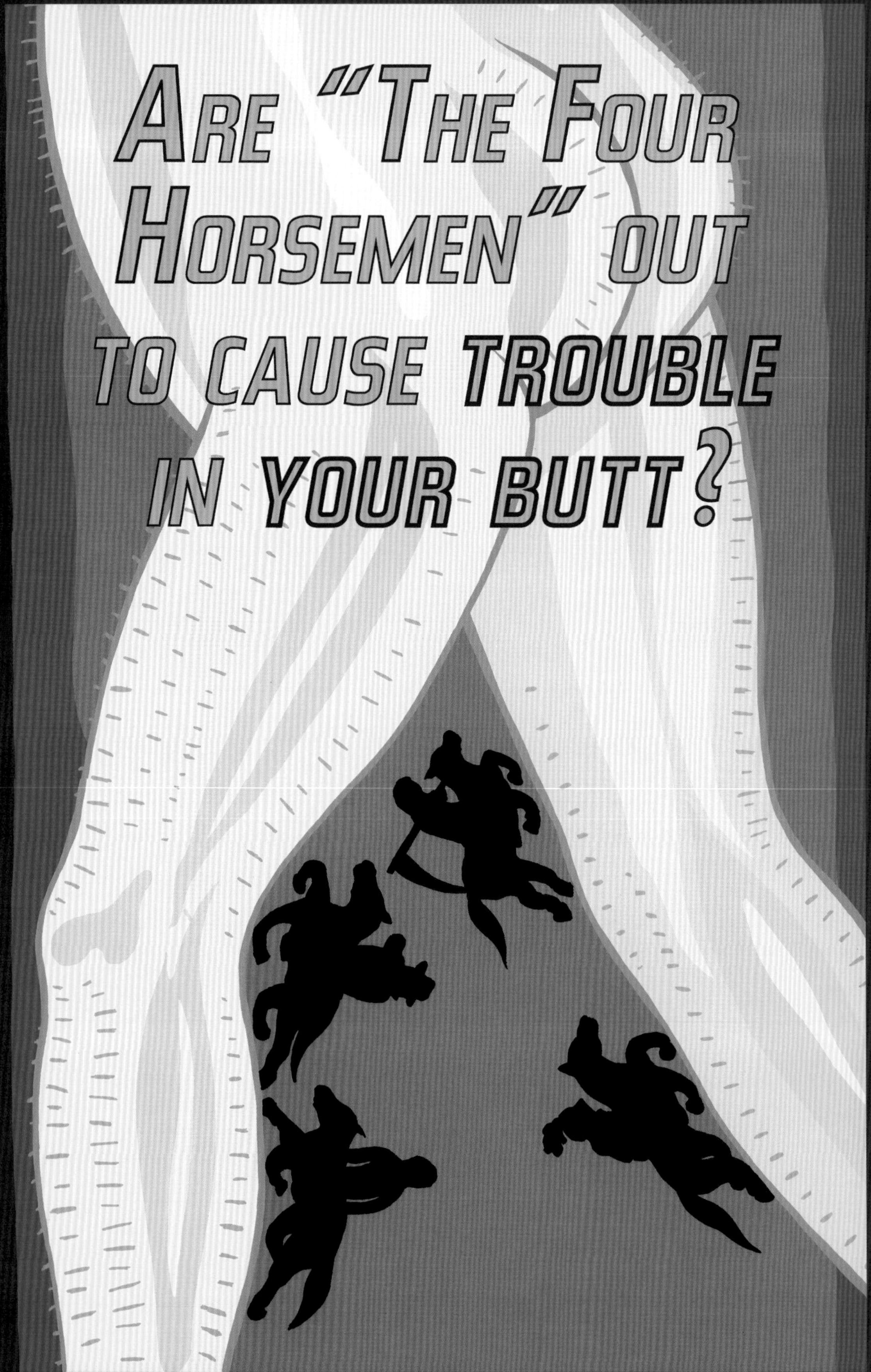
ARE "THE FOUR HORSEMEN" OUT
TO CAUSE TROUBLE
IN YOUR BUTT?

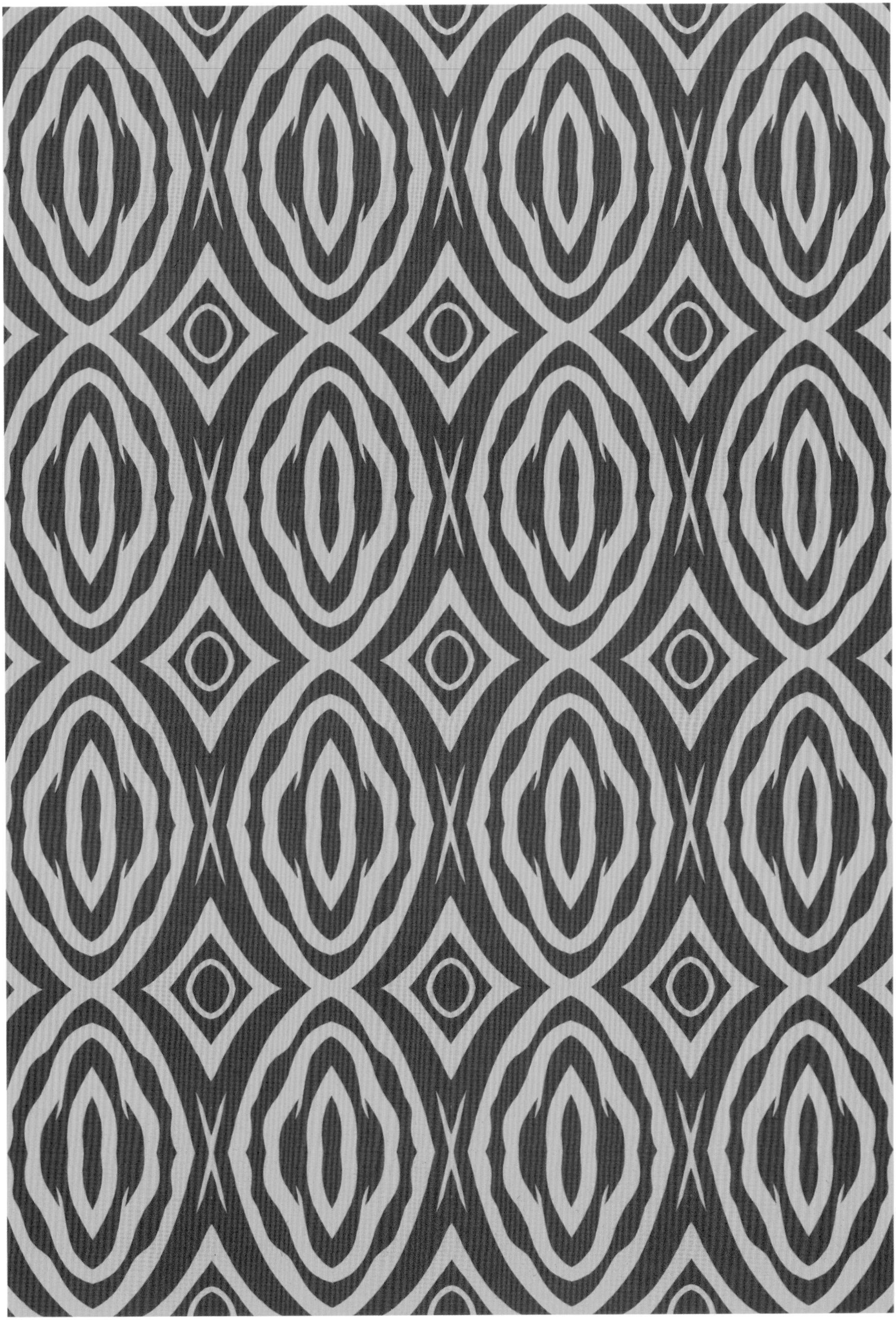

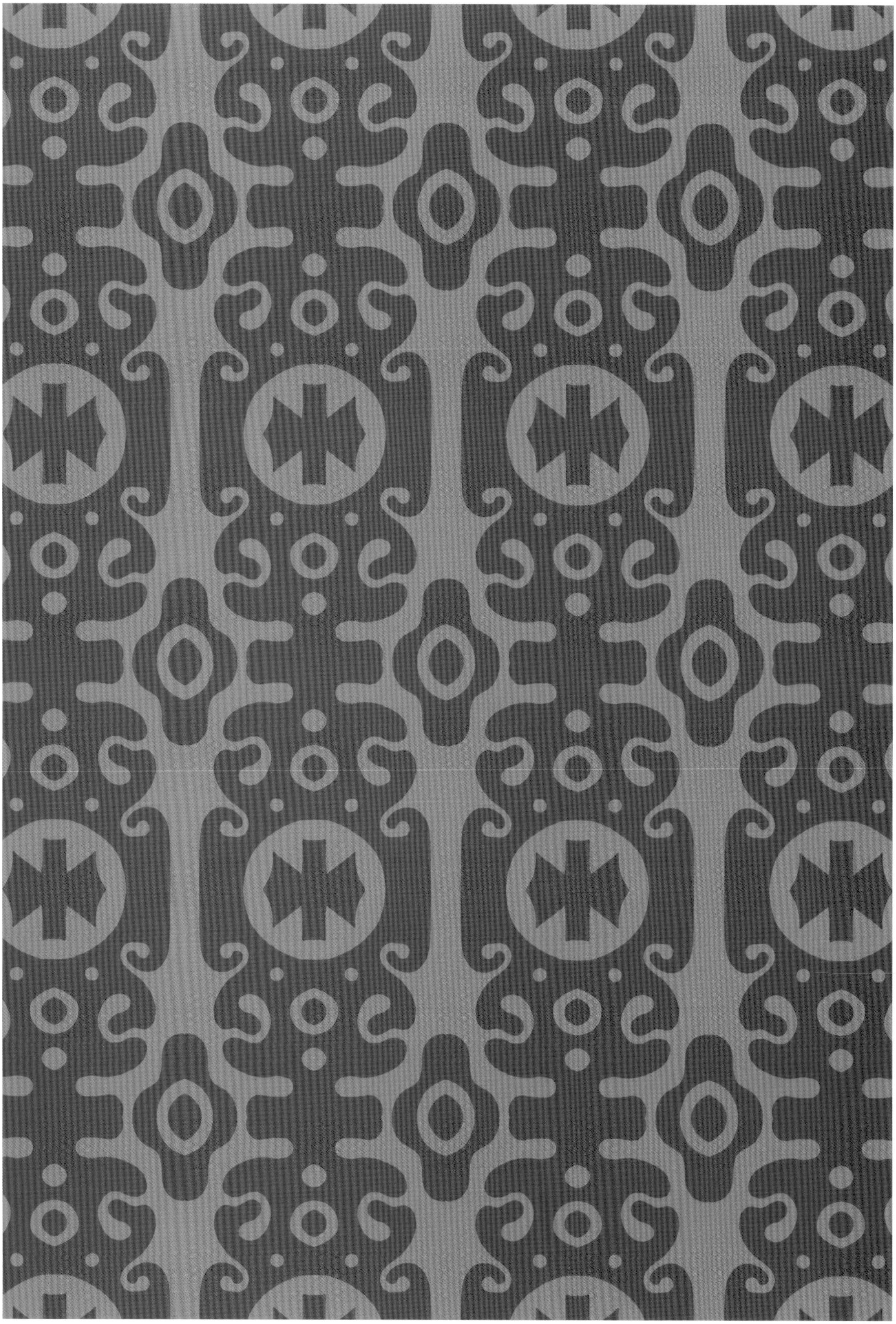

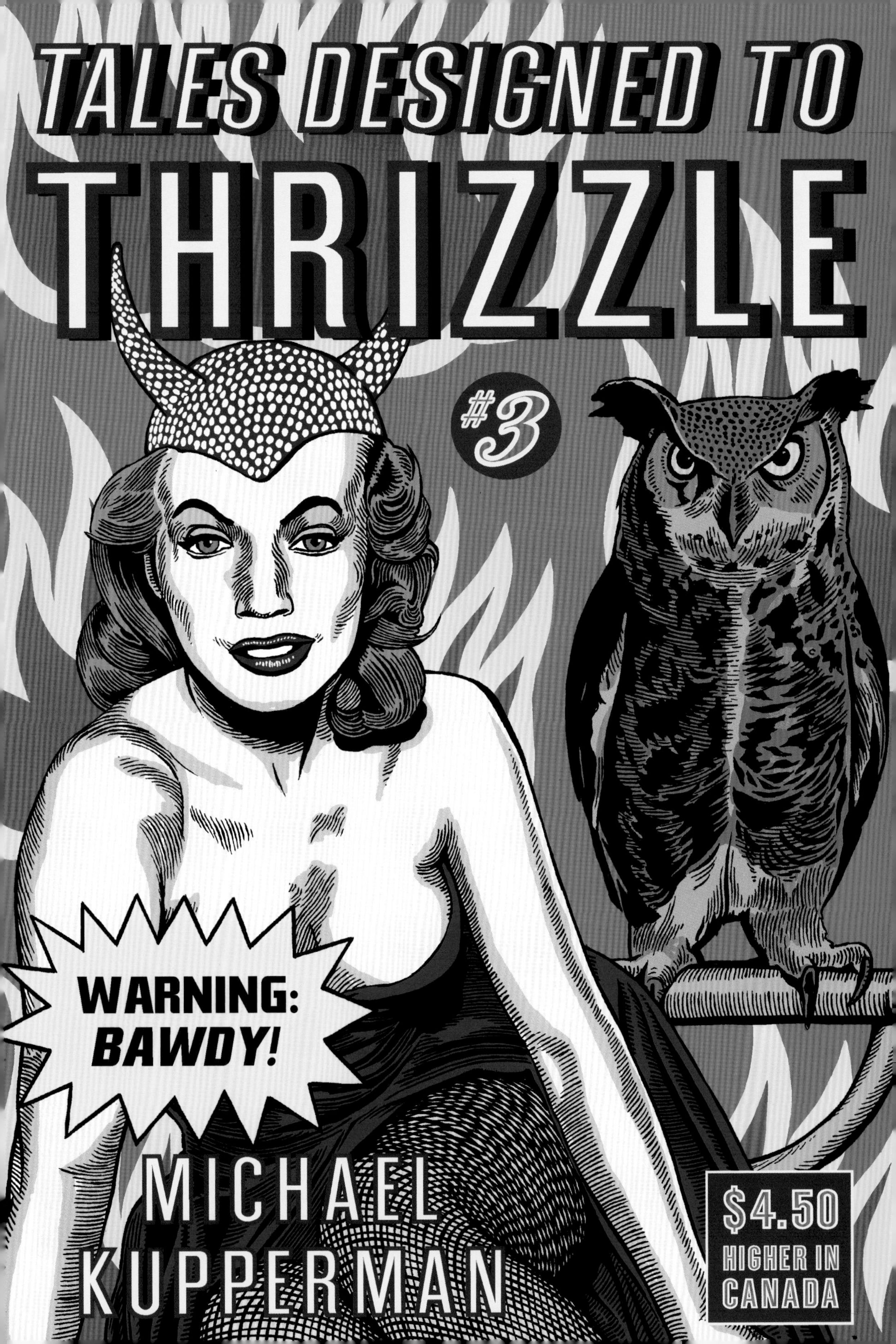
TALES DESIGNED TO
THRIZZLE
#3
WARNING:
BAWDY!
MICHAEL
KUPPERMAN
$4.50
HIGHER IN
CANADA

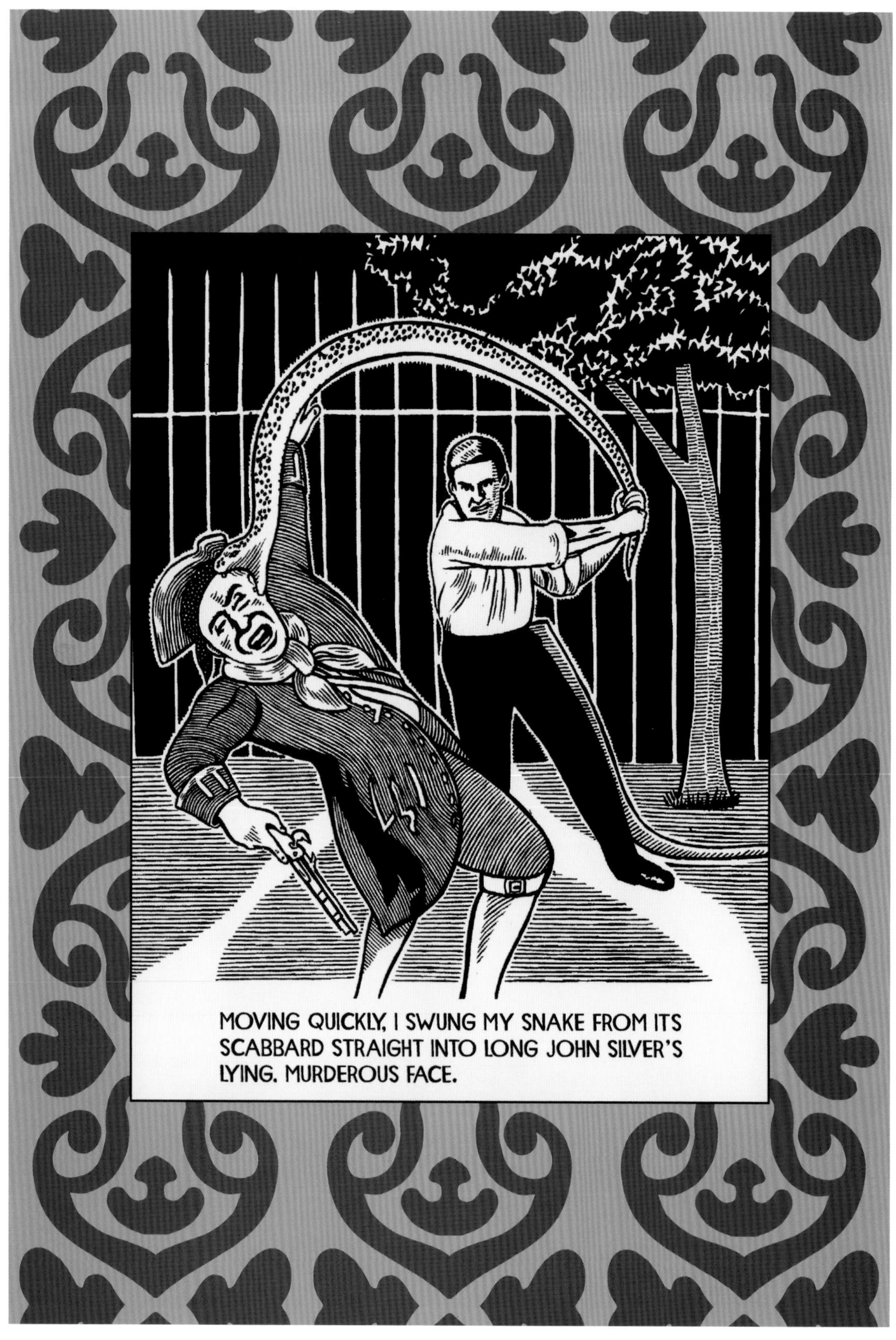
MOVING QUICKLY, I SWUNG MY SNAKE FROM ITS SCABBARD STRAIGHT INTO LONG JOHN SILVER'S LYING, MURDEROUS FACE.

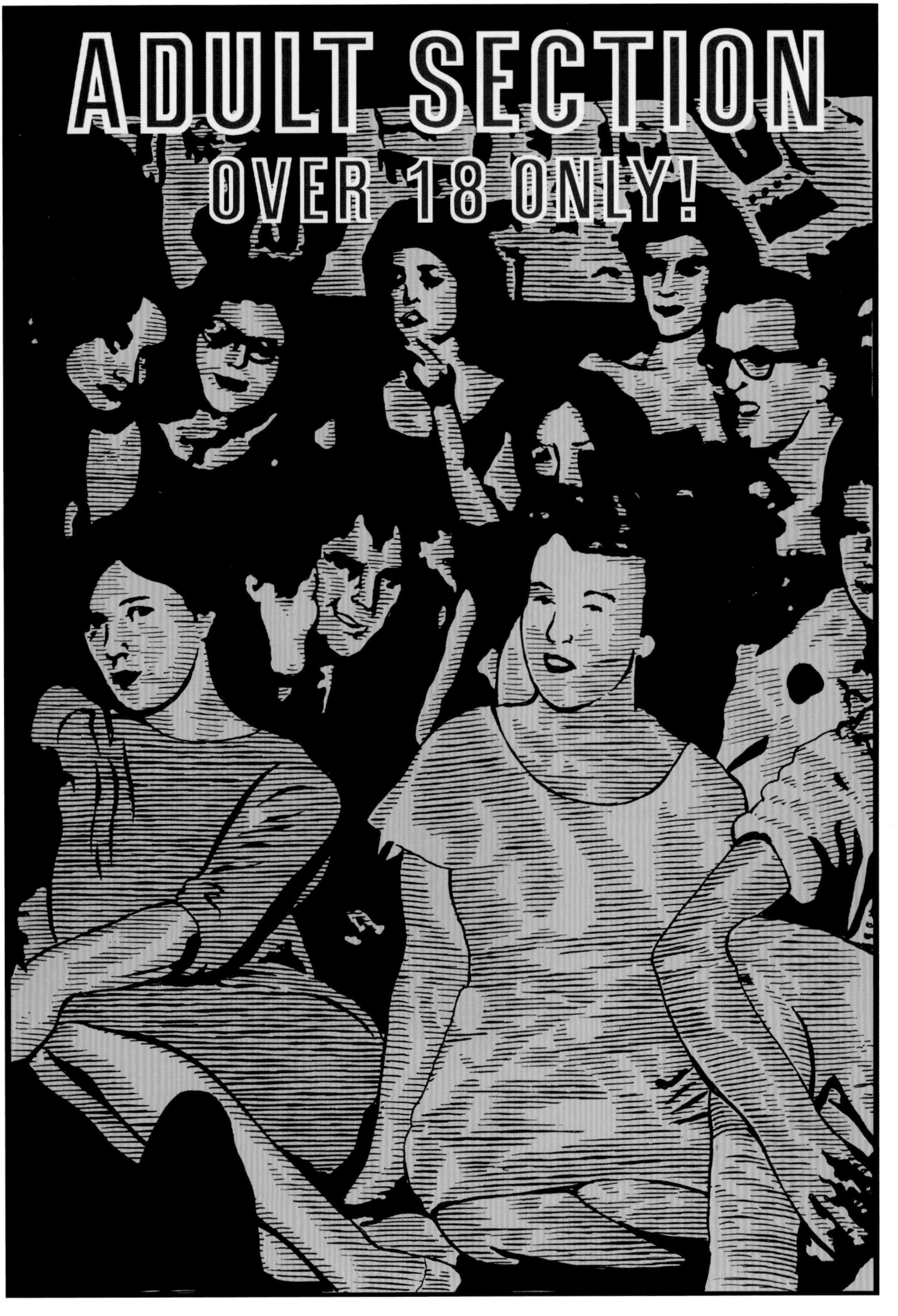
ADULT SECTION
OVER 18 ONLY!

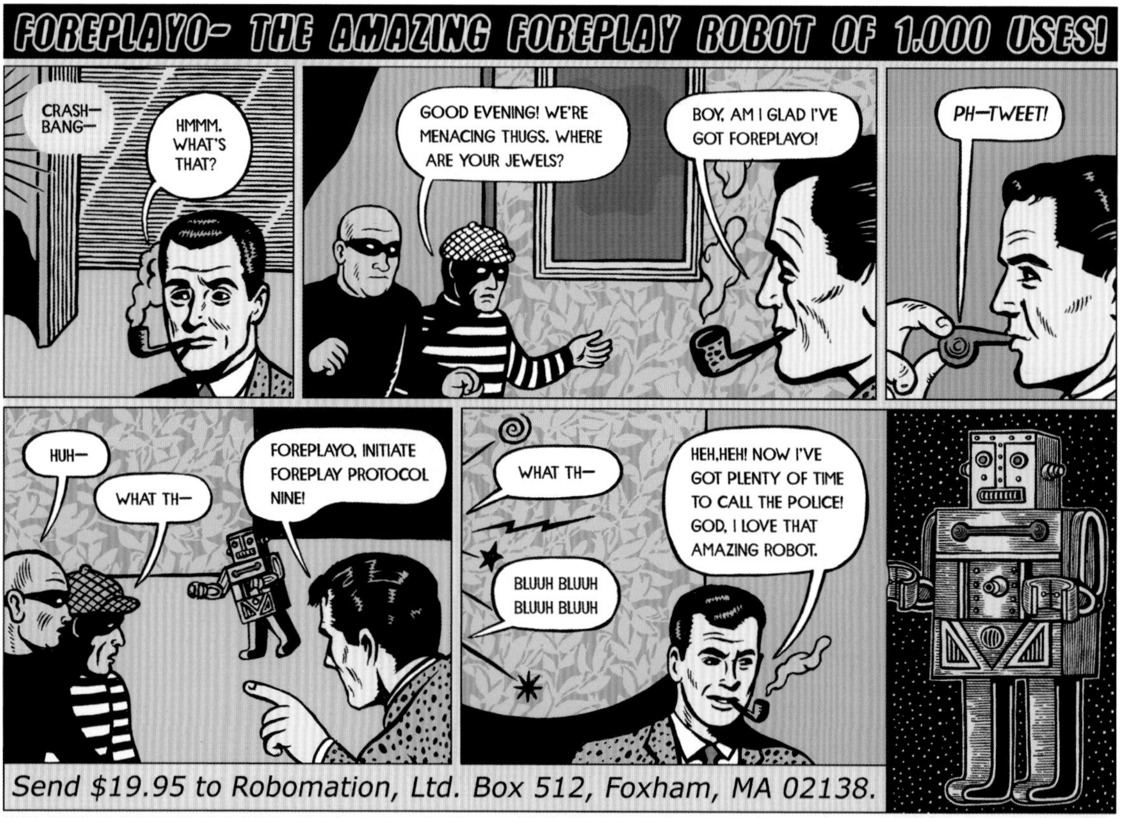

FOREPLAYO- THE AMAZING FOREPLAY ROBOT OF 1,000 USES!
CRASH— BANG—
HMMM. WHAT'S THAT?
GOOD EVENING! WE'RE MENACING THUGS. WHERE ARE YOUR JEWELS?
BOY, AM I GLAD I'VE GOT FOREPLAYO!
PH—TWEET!
HUH—
WHAT TH—
FOREPLAYO, INITIATE FOREPLAY PROTOCOL NINE!
WHAT TH—
BLUUH BLUUH BLUUH BLUUH
HEH,HEH! NOW I'VE GOT PLENTY OF TIME TO CALL THE POLICE! GOD, I LOVE THAT AMAZING ROBOT.
Send $19.95 to Robomation, Ltd. Box 512, Foxham, MA 02138.

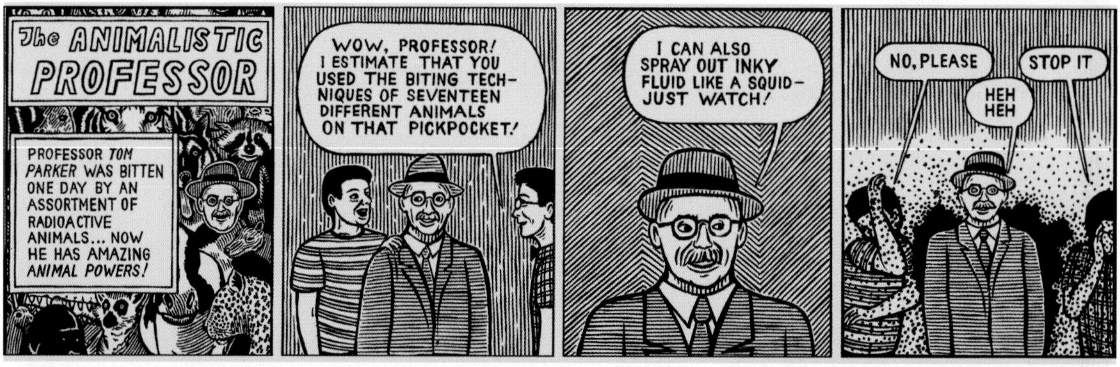

The ANIMALISTIC PROFESSOR
PROFESSOR TOM PARKER WAS BITTEN ONE DAY BY AN ASSORTMENT OF RADIOACTIVE ANIMALS... NOW HE HAS AMAZING ANIMAL POWERS!
WOW, PROFESSOR! I ESTIMATE THAT YOU USED THE BITING TECHNIQUES OF SEVENTEEN DIFFERENT ANIMALS ON THAT PICKPOCKET!
I CAN ALSO SPRAY OUT INKY FLUID LIKE A SQUID- JUST WATCH!
NO, PLEASE
HEH HEH
STOP IT

USING THE RIGHT WORDS PAYS OFF

When Shakespeare wrote the immortal classic "Hamlet", he had his hero say "To be or not to be."
He did not have him say "I am farting my way to a beatoff bonanza."

When Humphrey Bogart played Rick in Casablanca, he said "Play it again, Sam."
He did not say "Dribble me, flupnakes."

When Winston Churchill made his famous speech on the radio, he said "We shall fight on the beaches."
He didn't say "Mauling wankus jablonski."

Using the right words pays off. All these people did that, you can too. Send $4.95 for my free booklet: Wordsmart, Box 271, Cayanduga, NY.

THE HUMAN SNEEZE.

We all need to be reminded from time to time of what the human sneeze looks like. Here's a recent, high-definition picture.

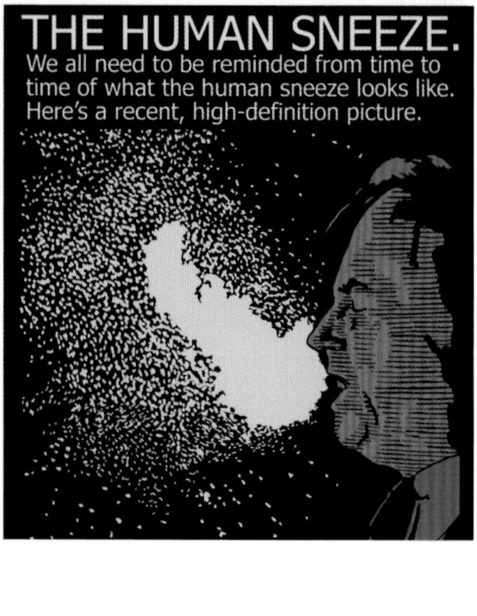

WHEN YOU VISIT THE CARNIVAL BE SURE TO GO TO THE

HOUSE of WHEELS

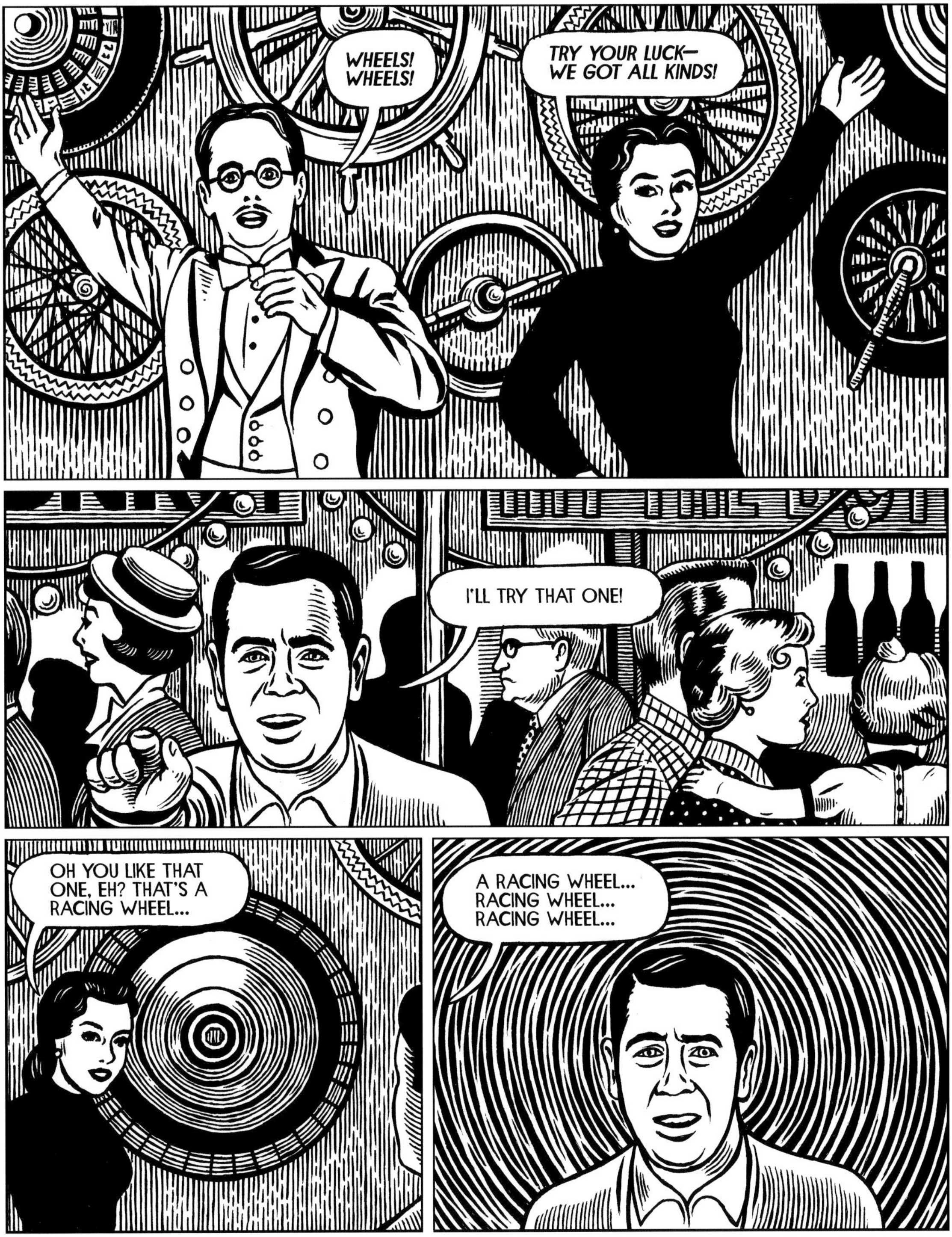

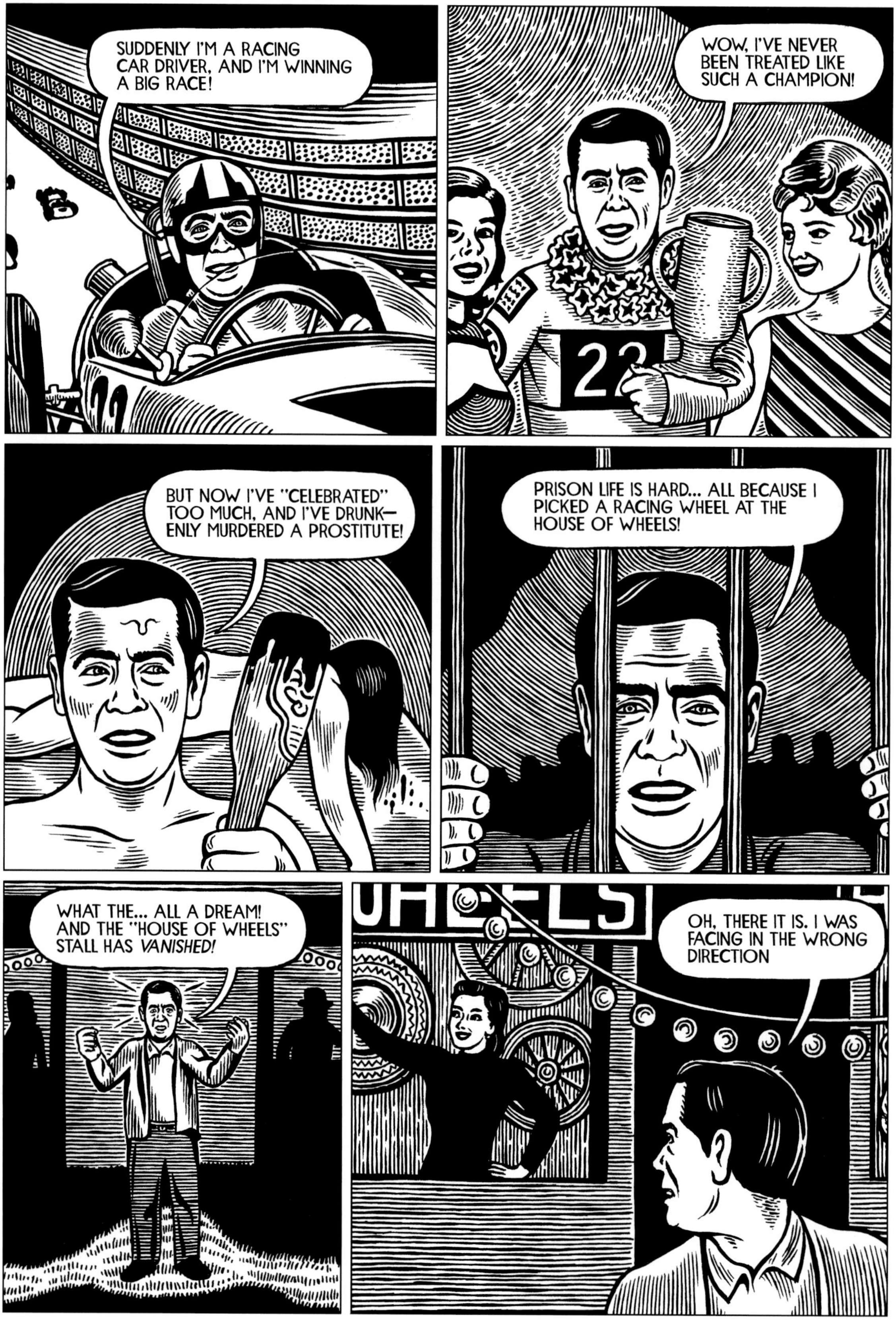
SUDDENLY I'M A RACING CAR DRIVER, AND I'M WINNING A BIG RACE!
WOW, I'VE NEVER BEEN TREATED LIKE SUCH A CHAMPION!
22
BUT NOW I'VE "CELEBRATED" TOO MUCH, AND I'VE DRUNK-ENLY MURDERED A PROSTITUTE!
PRISON LIFE IS HARD... ALL BECAUSE I PICKED A RACING WHEEL AT THE HOUSE OF WHEELS!
WHAT THE... ALL A DREAM! AND THE "HOUSE OF WHEELS" STALL HAS *VANISHED!*
WHEELS
OH, THERE IT IS. I WAS FACING IN THE WRONG DIRECTION

PORNO COLORING BOOKS

A brief tour through my collection.

I've been collecting pornographic coloring books since 1978- coincidentally the last year that one was published. Since then I've accumulated over 100 crumbling volumes. They were cheaply produced, and reflect society at that time (1967-1978). They are a constant source of inspiration for me.

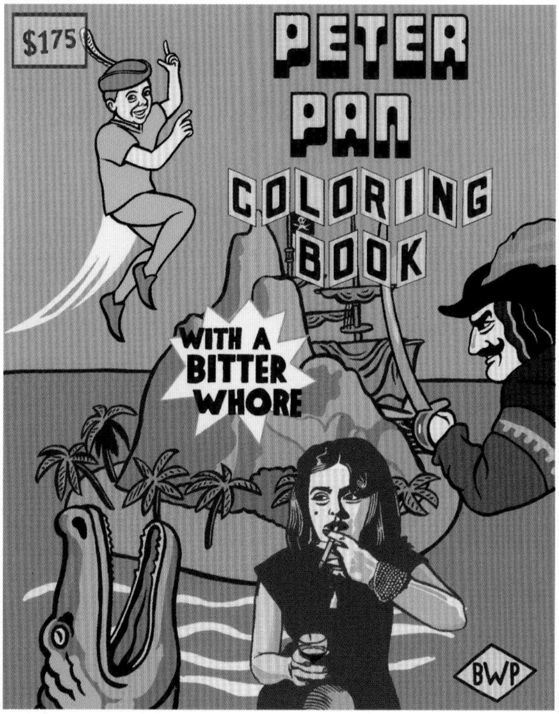

$175
PETER PAN
COLORING BOOK
WITH A BITTER WHORE
BWP

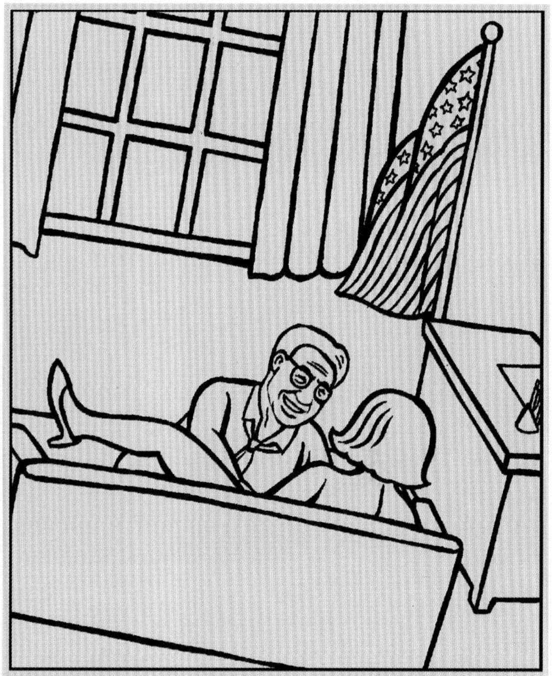

"Ohhh! Uhhh! went the Senator.

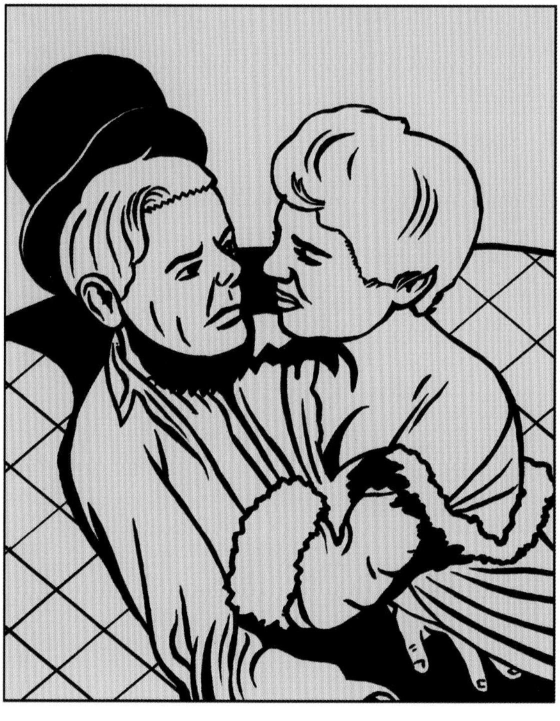

Upper left: BWP Publishing of St. Louis never officially became a publisher of porno coloring books; they did, however, begin inserting "A Bitter Whore" in every children's coloring book. Top right: Political satire: *Washington Follies*, 1975. Bottom left: *Young Horny Abe Lincoln: The Coloring Book of the Movie*, 1972. Lower right: A familiar television character makes an appearance.

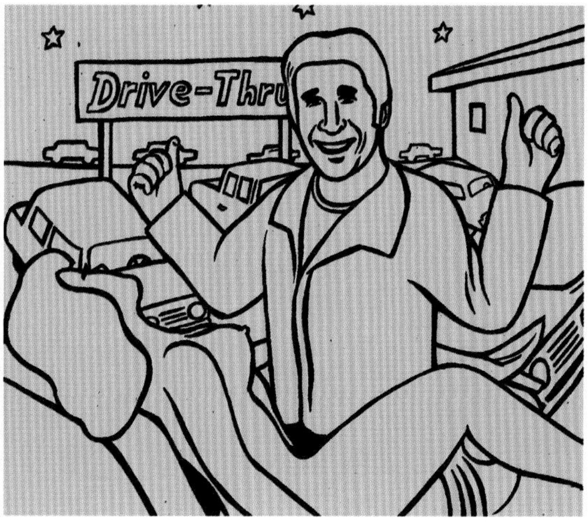

Drive-Thru

"Pornographic coloring books are so in right now, man... I just went to the drugstore and they were all out of pink crayons." -Sonny Hangman, 1972 (to rapturous applause).

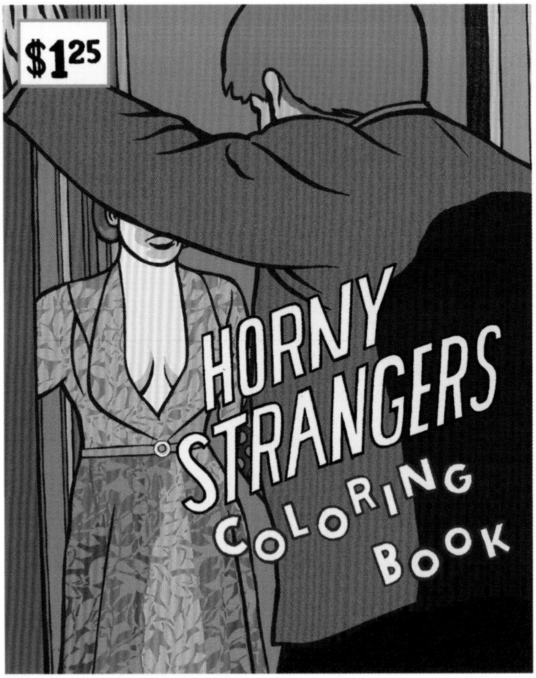
$1.25
HORNY STRANGERS
COLORING BOOK

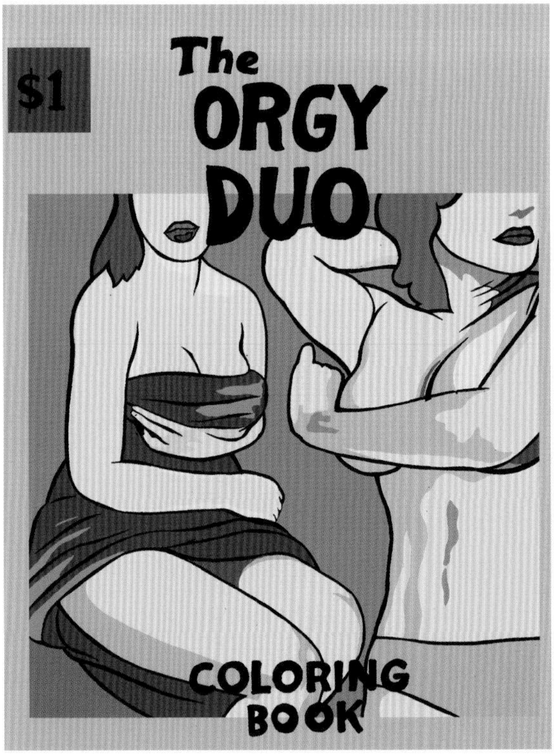
$1
The ORGY DUO
COLORING BOOK

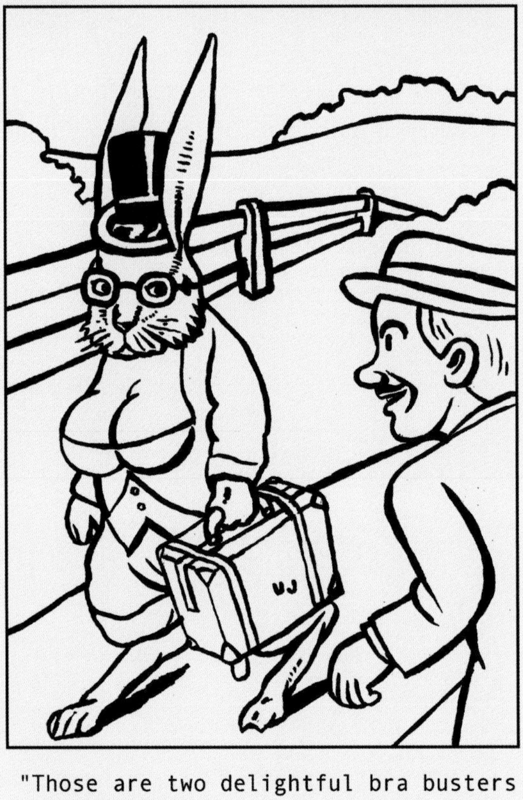
UJ

"Those are two delightful bra busters you've got there, Uncle Jiggly" said the naughty man.

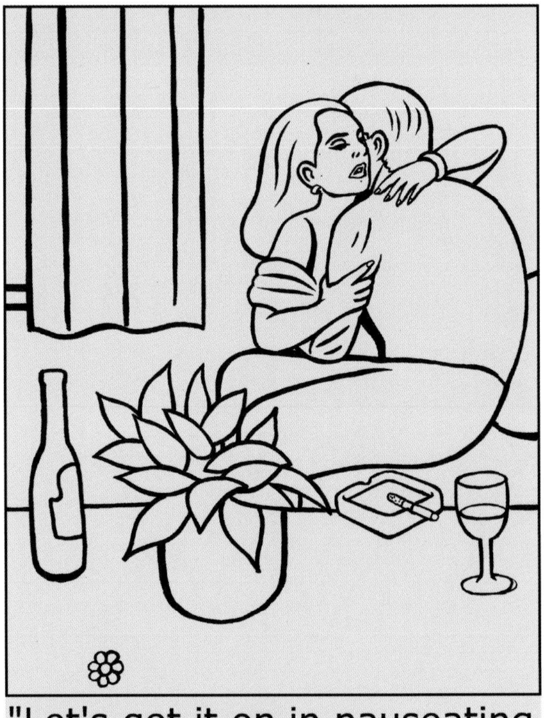

"Let's get it on in nauseating detail" says Sondra.

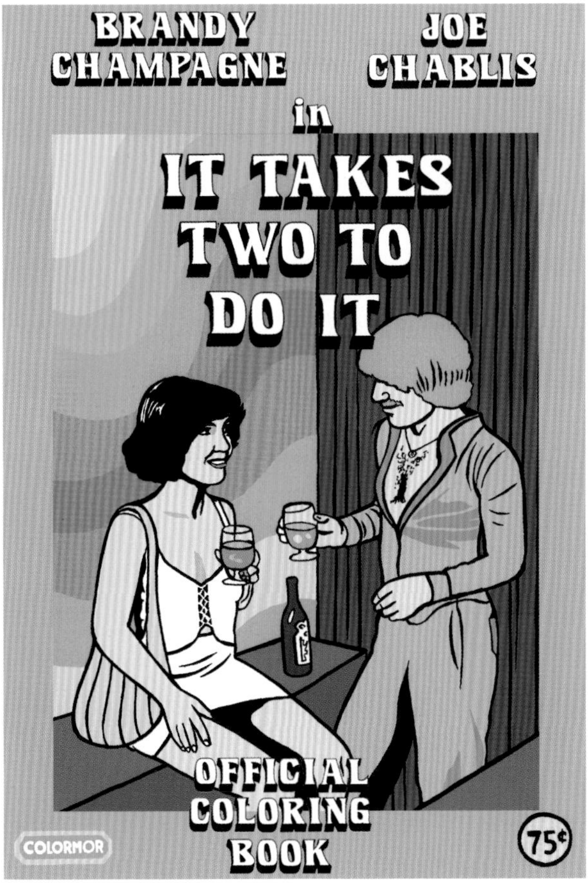
BRANDY CHAMPAGNE
JOE CHABLIS
in
IT TAKES TWO TO DO IT
OFFICIAL COLORING BOOK
COLORMOR
75¢

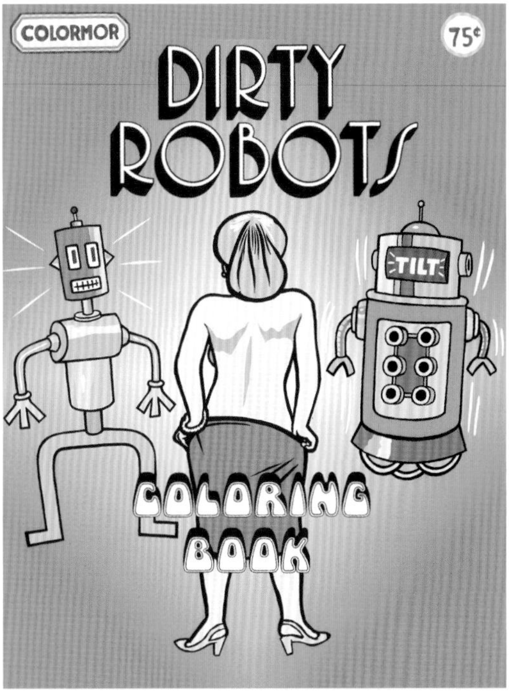
COLORMOR
75¢
DIRTY ROBOTS
TILT
COLORING BOOK

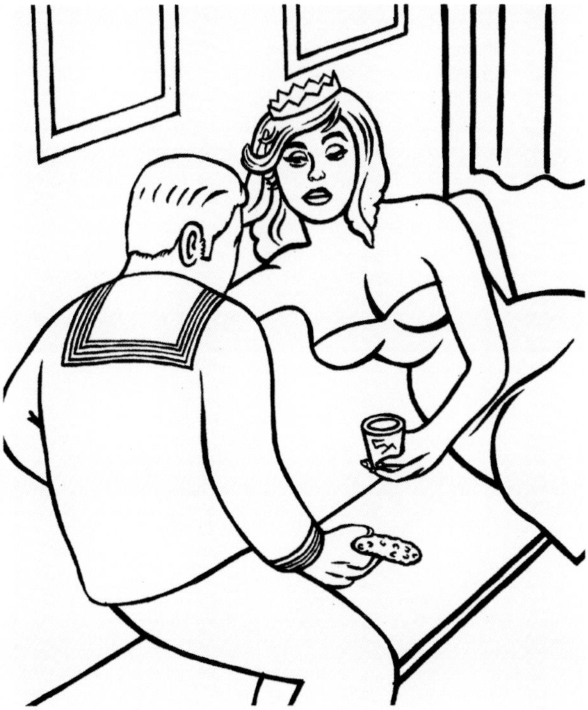

" I'm interested in your theories about Kierkegaard."

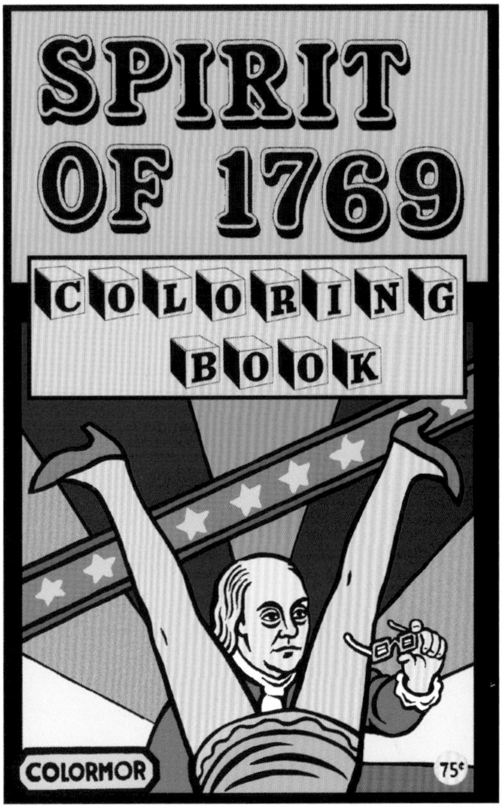
SPIRIT OF 1769
COLORING BOOK
COLORMOR
75¢

Colormor was the biggest publisher of porno coloring books. Their subjects ranged from the Bicentennial to science fiction, and also many movie adaptations; *It Takes Two to Do It* featured Brandy Champagne, "Porno's answer to Sally Struthers".

Every one of us has watched a pornographic film and thought, "They're in bed, and otherwise naked, so why are they wearing their shoes?" The truth is that, not that long ago, they had to be ready to run from the police... because, believe it or not, the making and distribution of pornography was *illegal.*

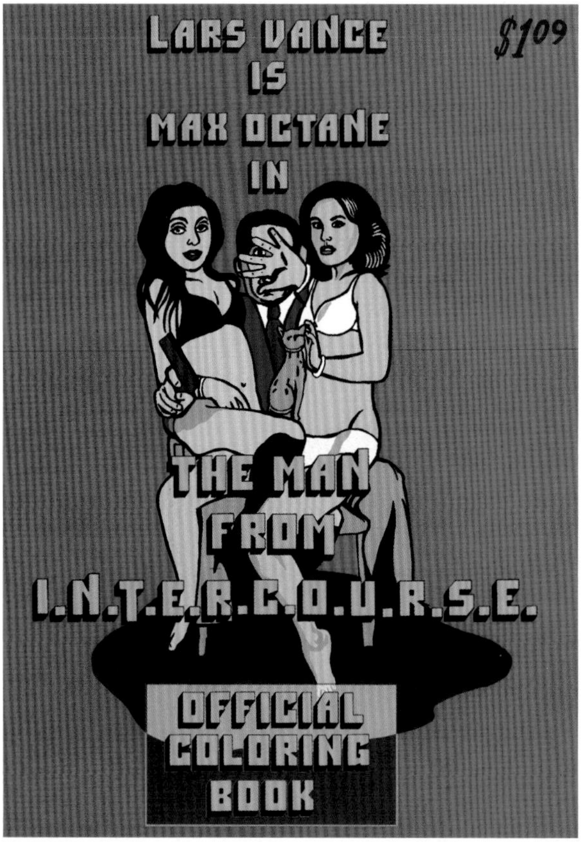
LARS VANCE
IS
MAX OCTANE
IN
$109
THE MAN
FROM
I.N.T.E.R.C.O.U.R.S.E.
OFFICIAL
COLORING
BOOK

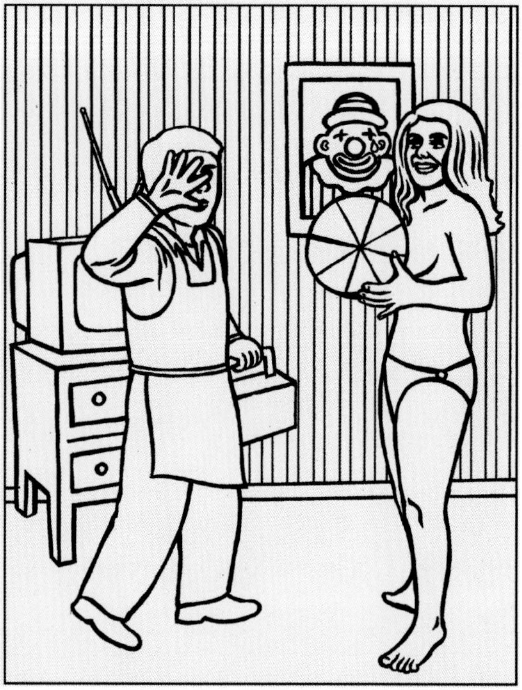

Actors in porn had to disguise their identities, so as not to lose their day jobs as rodeo clowns or Supreme Court Justices. Mostly they wore plastic glasses and false mustaches; the effect was disconcerting, especially on the women. The actor known as Lars Shvantz had a better idea: he simply held his hand in front of his face, and it worked in over 500 films. "Professor" Ralf "Waldo" "Emerson" of Chicago claims to have carefully viewed over 14,000 hours of the actor's output and never to have seen his face. After his retirement, rumors flew that he was a member of the Carter Cabinet (the governmental body, not the rock group). His unusual technique of disguise also made him the #1 male attraction in movie-based adult erotic coloring books, as artists got paid less for drawing hands than they did for drawing faces.

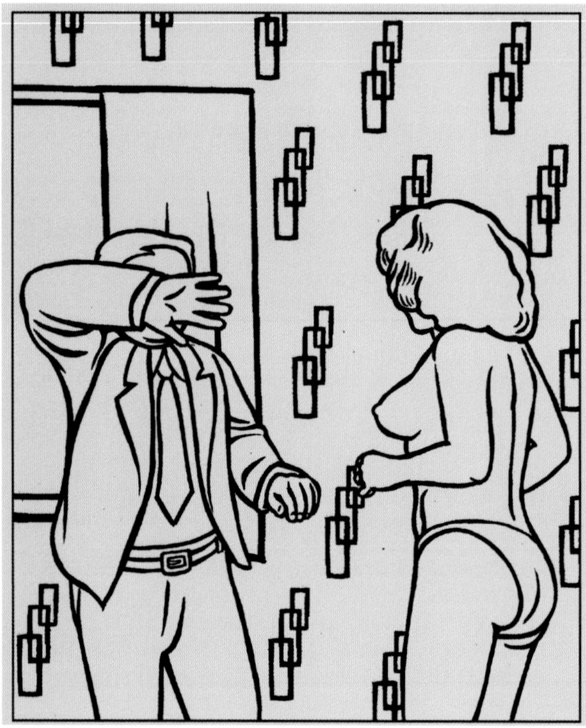

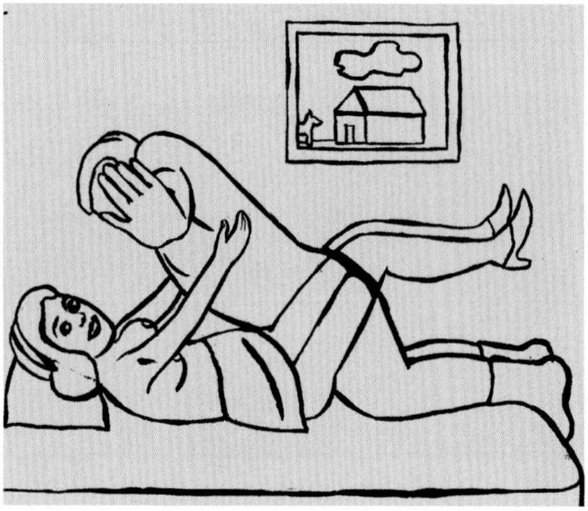

"How'd you do it?"

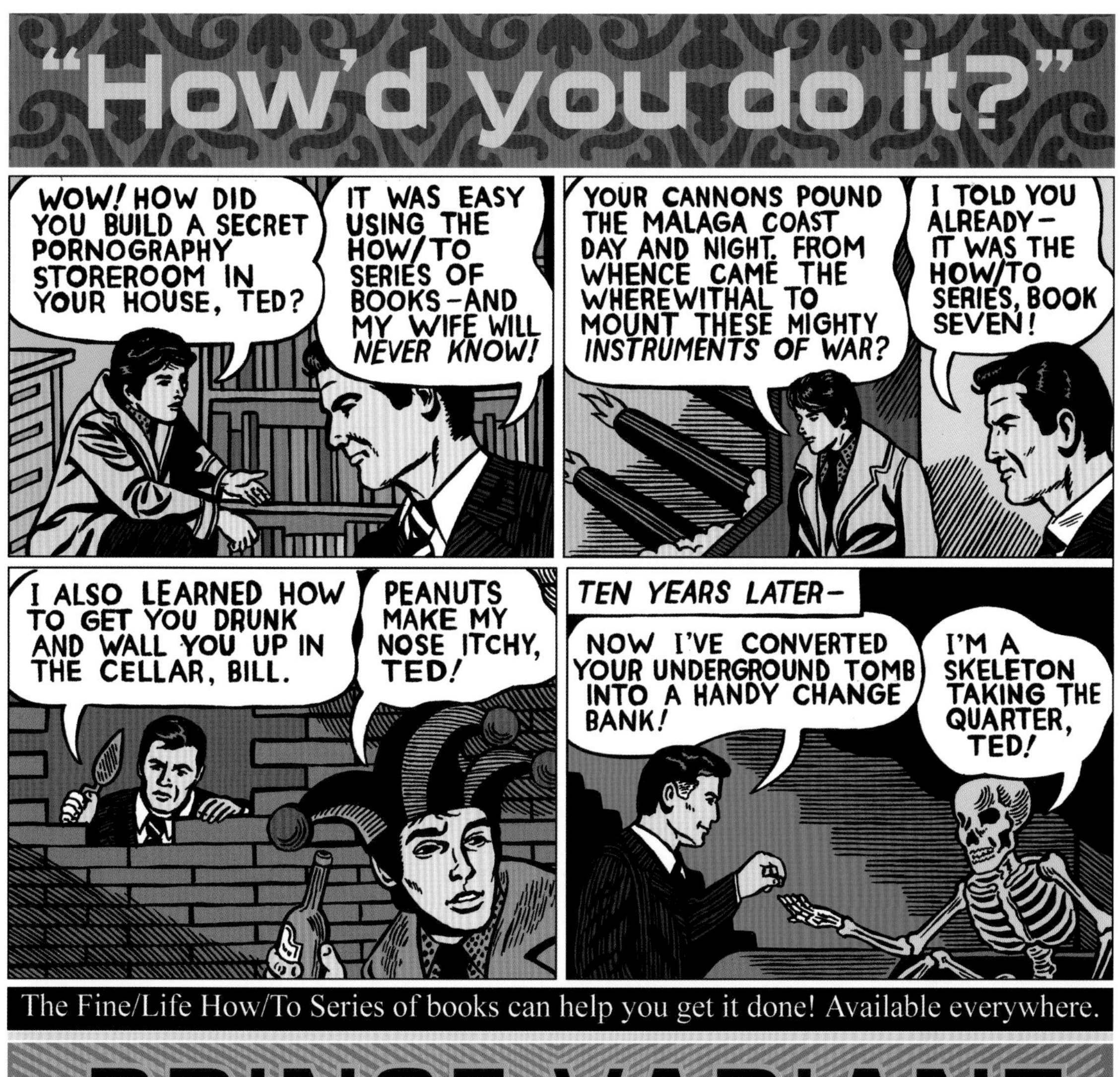

WOW! HOW DID YOU BUILD A SECRET PORNOGRAPHY STOREROOM IN YOUR HOUSE, TED?
IT WAS EASY USING THE HOW/TO SERIES OF BOOKS—AND MY WIFE WILL *NEVER KNOW!*
YOUR CANNONS POUND THE MALAGA COAST DAY AND NIGHT. FROM WHENCE CAME THE WHEREWITHAL TO MOUNT THESE MIGHTY *INSTRUMENTS OF WAR?*
I TOLD YOU ALREADY—IT WAS THE HOW/TO SERIES, BOOK SEVEN!
I ALSO LEARNED HOW TO GET YOU DRUNK AND WALL YOU UP IN THE CELLAR, BILL.
PEANUTS MAKE MY NOSE ITCHY, TED!
TEN YEARS LATER—
NOW I'VE CONVERTED YOUR UNDERGROUND TOMB INTO A HANDY CHANGE BANK!
I'M A SKELETON TAKING THE QUARTER, TED!

The Fine/Life How/To Series of books can help you get it done! Available everywhere.

PRINCE VARIANT

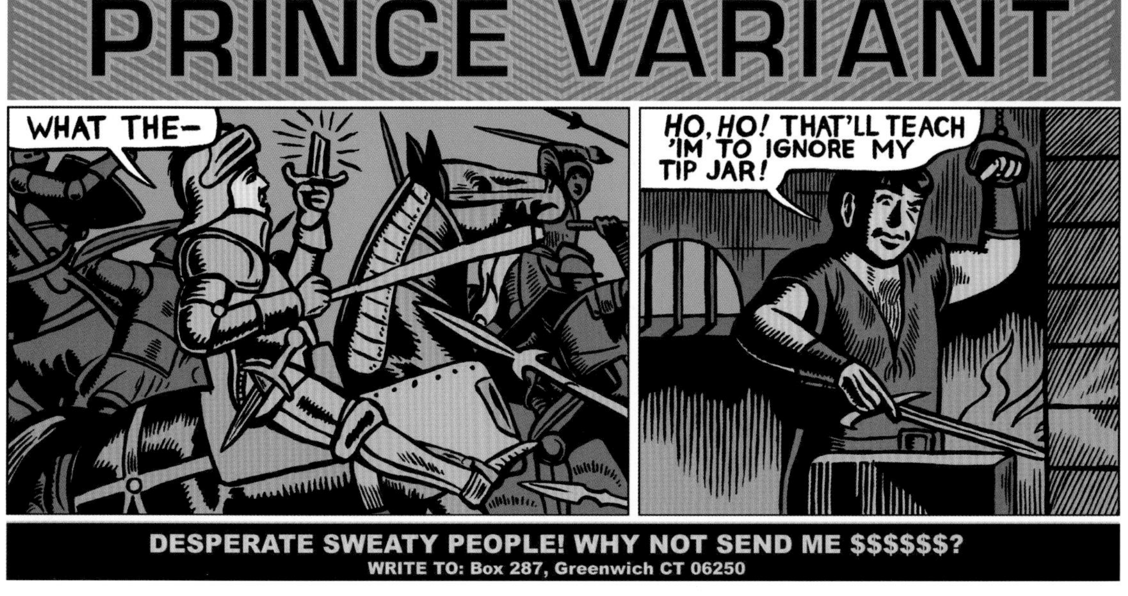

WHAT THE—
HO, HO! THAT'LL TEACH 'IM TO IGNORE MY TIP JAR!

DESPERATE SWEATY PEOPLE! WHY NOT SEND ME $$$$$$?

WRITE TO: Box 287, Greenwich CT 06250

THE HEISTY PEOPLE

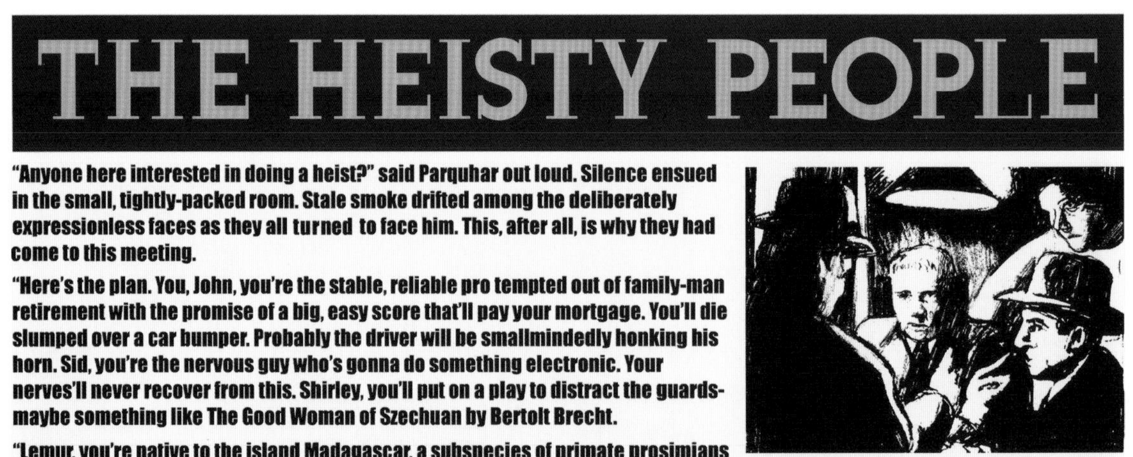

"Anyone here interested in doing a heist?" said Parquhar out loud. Silence ensued in the small, tightly-packed room. Stale smoke drifted among the deliberately expressionless faces as they all turned to face him. This, after all, is why they had come to this meeting.

"Here's the plan. You, John, you're the stable, reliable pro tempted out of family-man retirement with the promise of a big, easy score that'll pay your mortgage. You'll die slumped over a car bumper. Probably the driver will be smallmindedly honking his horn. Sid, you're the nervous guy who's gonna do something electronic. Your nerves'll never recover from this. Shirley, you'll put on a play to distract the guards- maybe something like The Good Woman of Szechuan by Bertolt Brecht.

"Lemur, you're native to the island Madagascar, a subspecies of primate prosimians constituting the order Lemuriformes. Squealy Ratzinger, you're being squeezed between the mob and the law. You'll betray us all, and die horribly as you whimper for mercy. And Rico, you're the loosely-wrapped psychotic with the itchy trigger finger who starts the carnage."

"Nobody disrespects me" mumbled Rico as he fingered his specially concealed holster within his chicken costume.

"So. Any questions?"

"Alright Joe, that's a splendid plan. Now let's enjoy some of that splendid Junior Senior's Canned Ribs'n'Rice," croaked Big Al. Shrimpy furrowed his brow. "Junior Senior's Canned Ribs'n'Rice? I heard about them" he commented gravely. "They're scientific, is what I heard."

Big Al beamed and nodded approvingly. "That's right, boys, it's scientific, see, so it's better'n'restaurant food. We gotta fortify our- selves for our big heist. Dig in, boys," he belched, producing a skillet full of steaming food. "And don't worry where it came from."

He chuckled. "I heisted it!"

Junior Senior's Canned Ribs'n'Rice..

So scientific you'll want to heist some for yourself.

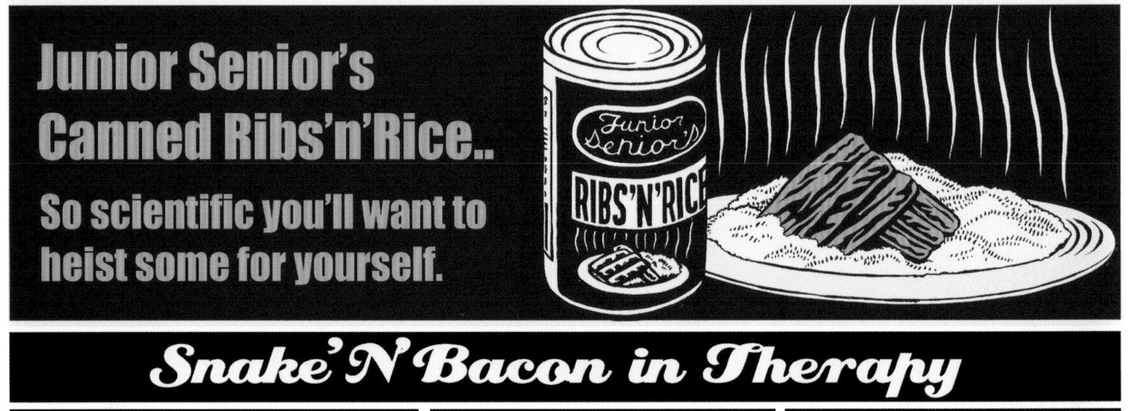
Junior Senior's
RIBS'N'RICE

Snake'N'Bacon in Therapy

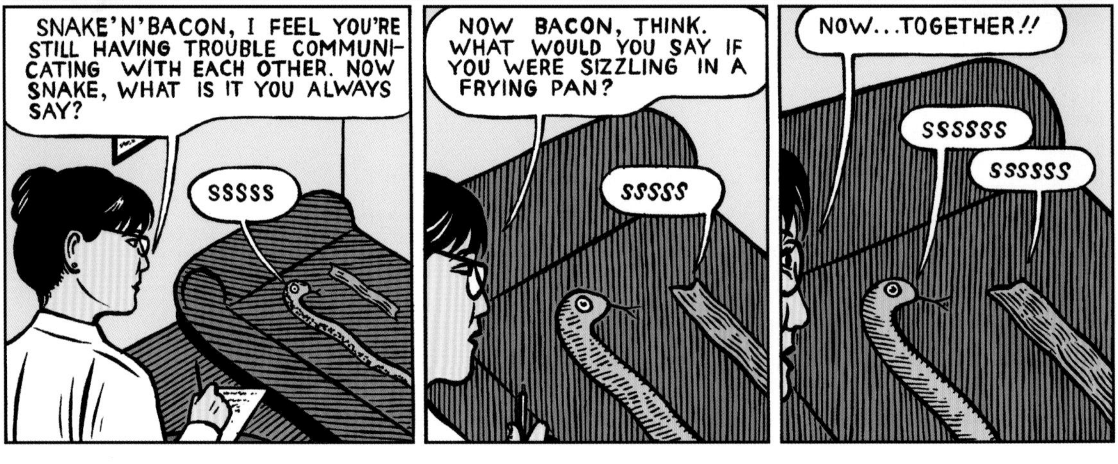
SNAKE'N'BACON, I FEEL YOU'RE STILL HAVING TROUBLE COMMUNICATING WITH EACH OTHER. NOW SNAKE, WHAT IS IT YOU ALWAYS SAY?
SSSSS
NOW BACON, THINK. WHAT WOULD YOU SAY IF YOU WERE SIZZLING IN A FRYING PAN?
SSSSS
NOW...TOGETHER!!
SSSSSS
SSSSSS

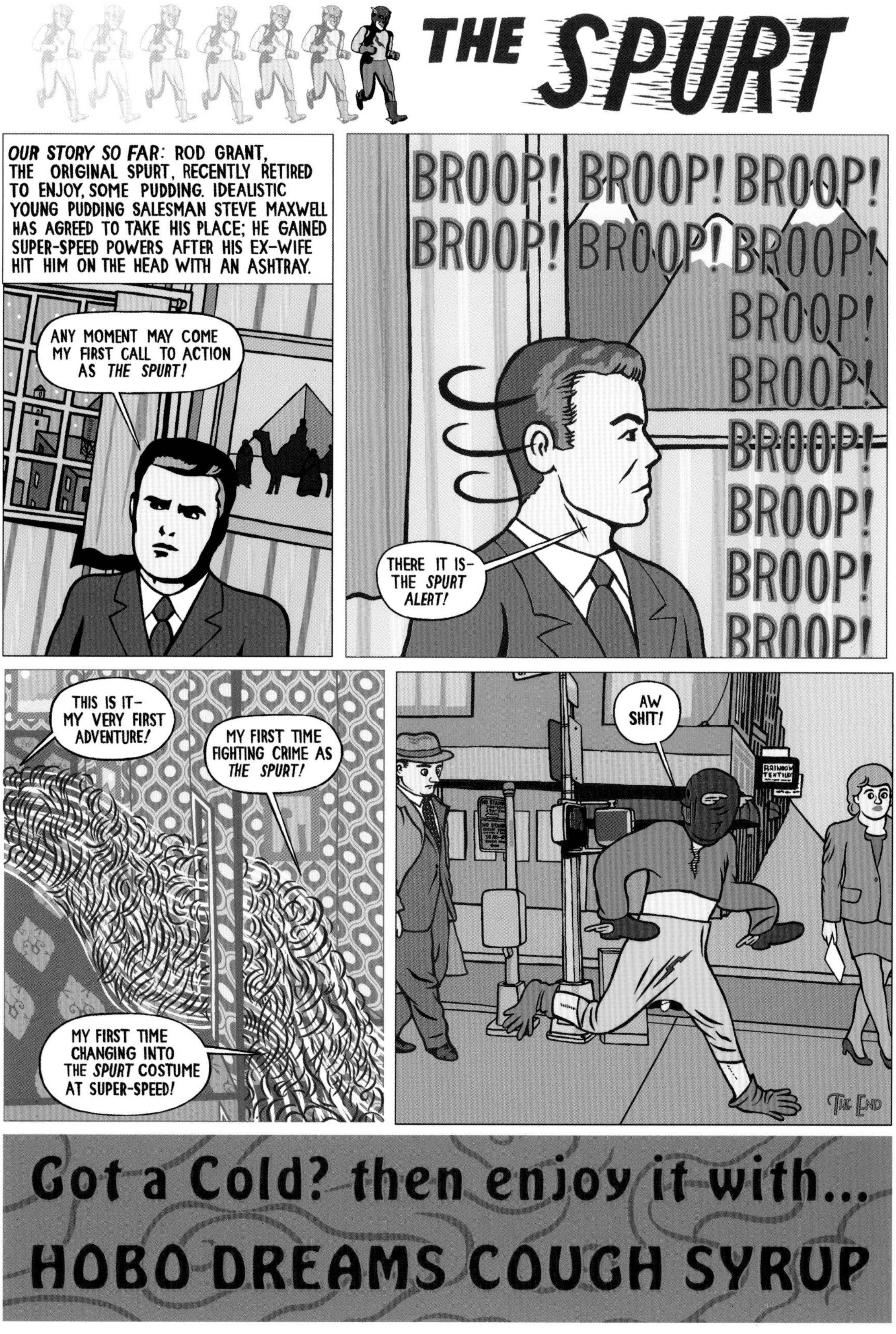
THE SPURT
OUR STORY SO FAR: ROD GRANT, THE ORIGINAL SPURT, RECENTLY RETIRED TO ENJOY SOME PUDDING. IDEALISTIC YOUNG PUDDING SALESMAN STEVE MAXWELL HAS AGREED TO TAKE HIS PLACE; HE GAINED SUPER-SPEED POWERS AFTER HIS EX-WIFE HIT HIM ON THE HEAD WITH AN ASHTRAY.
ANY MOMENT MAY COME MY FIRST CALL TO ACTION AS THE SPURT!
BROOP! BROOP! BROOP! BROOP! BROOP! BROOP! BROOP! BROOP! BROOP! BROOP! BROOP! BROOP!
THERE IT IS— THE SPURT ALERT!
THIS IS IT— MY VERY FIRST ADVENTURE!
MY FIRST TIME FIGHTING CRIME AS THE SPURT!
MY FIRST TIME CHANGING INTO THE SPURT COSTUME AT SUPER-SPEED!
AW SHIT!
THE END
Got a Cold? then enjoy it with...
HOBO DREAMS COUGH SYRUP

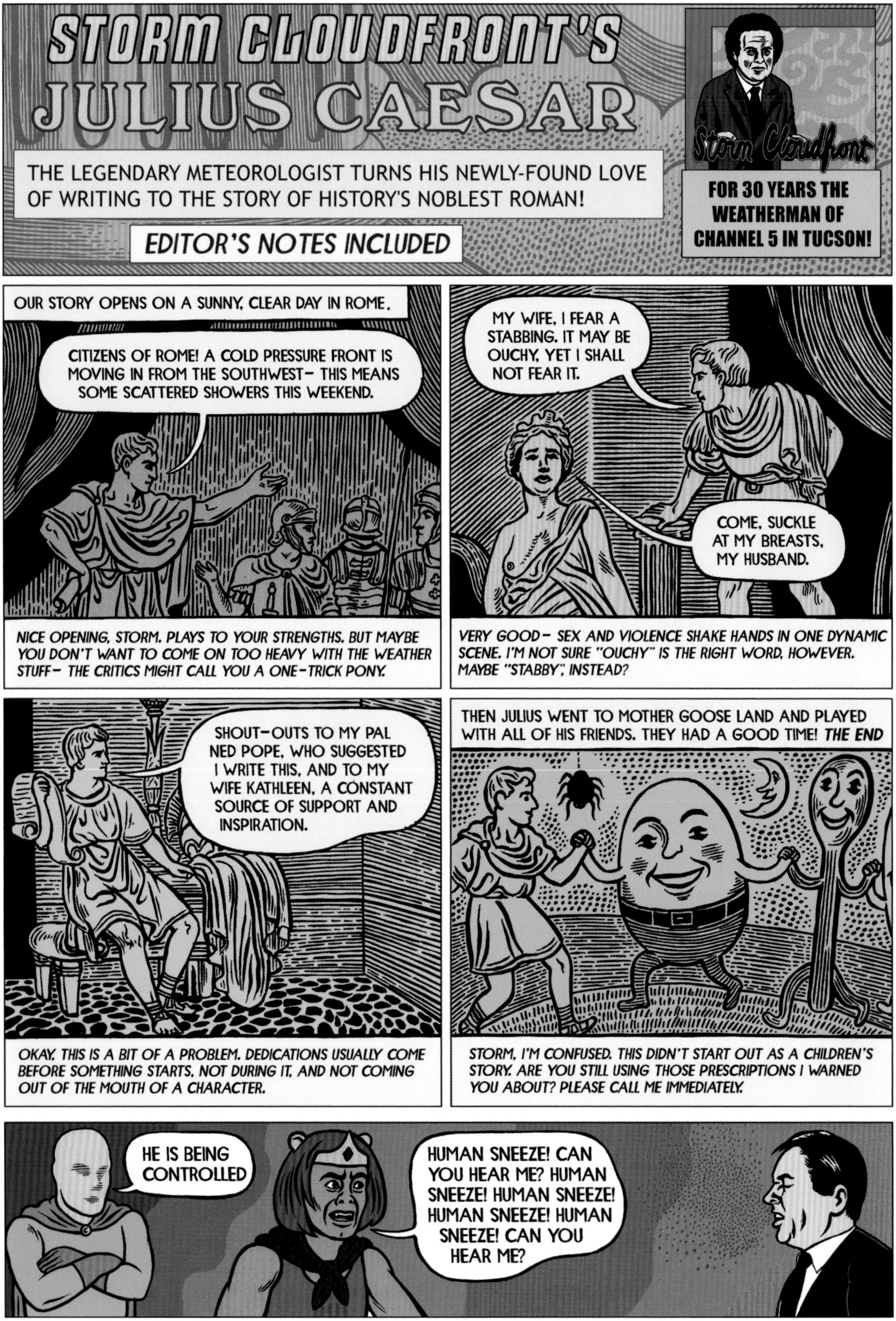
STORM CLOUDFRONT'S
JULIUS CAESAR
THE LEGENDARY METEOROLOGIST TURNS HIS NEWLY-FOUND LOVE OF WRITING TO THE STORY OF HISTORY'S NOBLEST ROMAN!
EDITOR'S NOTES INCLUDED
Storm Cloudfront
FOR 30 YEARS THE WEATHERMAN OF CHANNEL 5 IN TUCSON!
OUR STORY OPENS ON A SUNNY, CLEAR DAY IN ROME.
CITIZENS OF ROME! A COLD PRESSURE FRONT IS MOVING IN FROM THE SOUTHWEST– THIS MEANS SOME SCATTERED SHOWERS THIS WEEKEND.
NICE OPENING, STORM. PLAYS TO YOUR STRENGTHS. BUT MAYBE YOU DON'T WANT TO COME ON TOO HEAVY WITH THE WEATHER STUFF– THE CRITICS MIGHT CALL YOU A ONE-TRICK PONY.
MY WIFE, I FEAR A STABBING. IT MAY BE OUCHY, YET I SHALL NOT FEAR IT.
COME, SUCKLE AT MY BREASTS, MY HUSBAND.
VERY GOOD– SEX AND VIOLENCE SHAKE HANDS IN ONE DYNAMIC SCENE. I'M NOT SURE "OUCHY" IS THE RIGHT WORD, HOWEVER. MAYBE "STABBY", INSTEAD?
SHOUT-OUTS TO MY PAL NED POPE, WHO SUGGESTED I WRITE THIS, AND TO MY WIFE KATHLEEN, A CONSTANT SOURCE OF SUPPORT AND INSPIRATION.
OKAY, THIS IS A BIT OF A PROBLEM. DEDICATIONS USUALLY COME BEFORE SOMETHING STARTS, NOT DURING IT, AND NOT COMING OUT OF THE MOUTH OF A CHARACTER.
THEN JULIUS WENT TO MOTHER GOOSE LAND AND PLAYED WITH ALL OF HIS FRIENDS. THEY HAD A GOOD TIME! THE END
STORM, I'M CONFUSED. THIS DIDN'T START OUT AS A CHILDREN'S STORY. ARE YOU STILL USING THOSE PRESCRIPTIONS I WARNED YOU ABOUT? PLEASE CALL ME IMMEDIATELY.
HE IS BEING CONTROLLED
HUMAN SNEEZE! CAN YOU HEAR ME? HUMAN SNEEZE! HUMAN SNEEZE! HUMAN SNEEZE! HUMAN SNEEZE! CAN YOU HEAR ME?

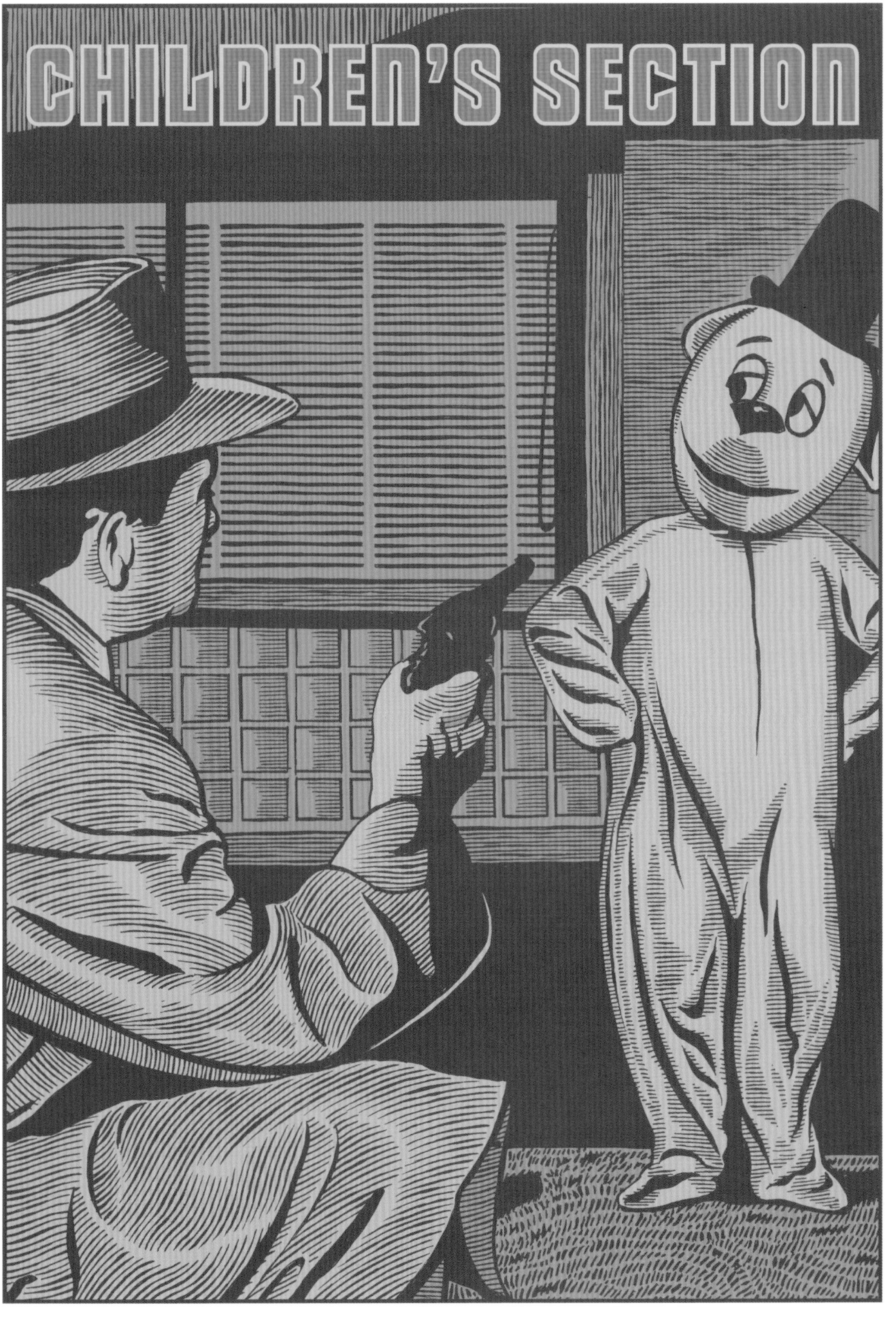
CHILDREN'S SECTION

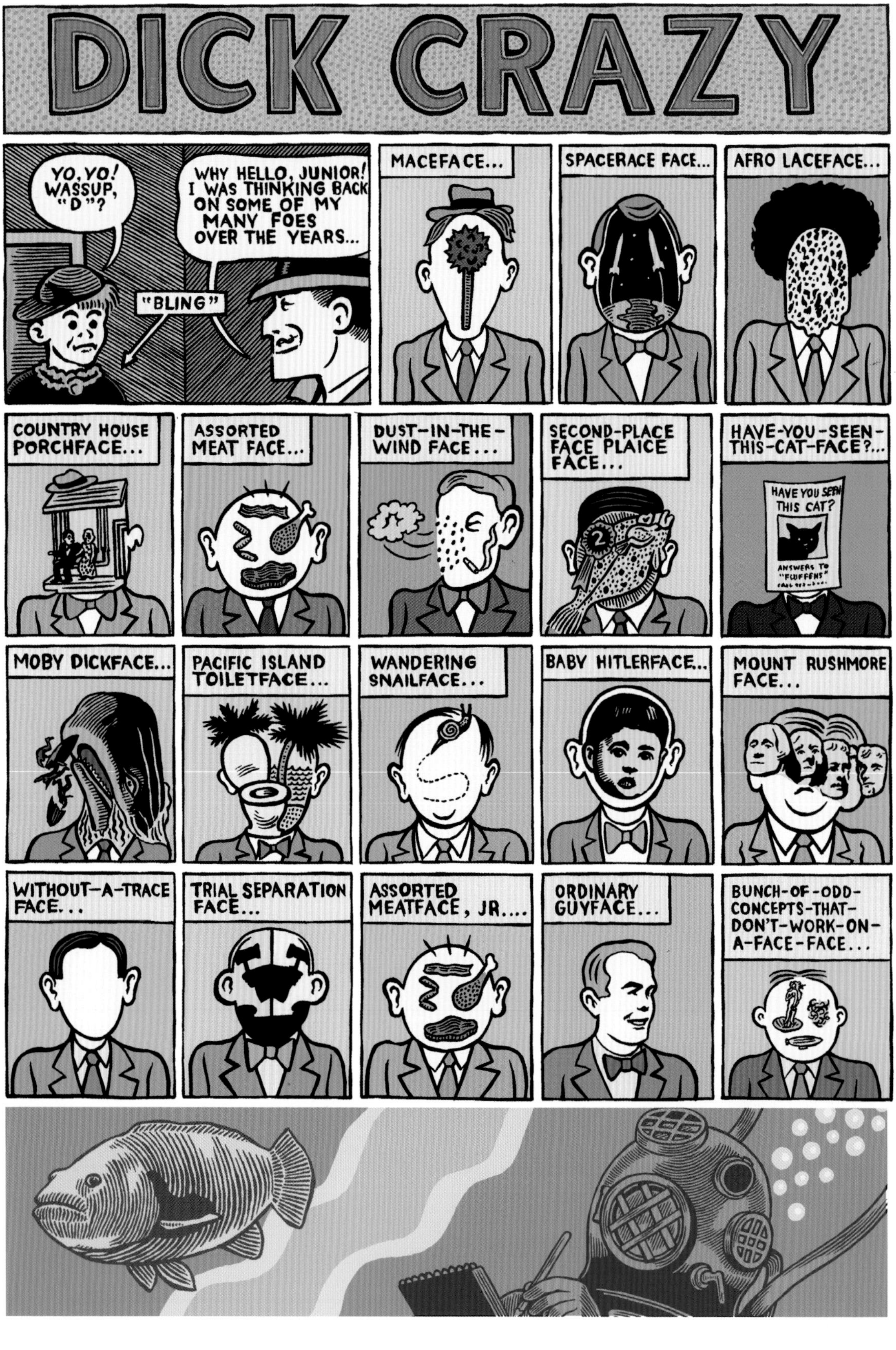
DICK CRAZY
YO, YO! WASSUP, "D"?
WHY HELLO, JUNIOR! I WAS THINKING BACK ON SOME OF MY MANY FOES OVER THE YEARS...
"BLING"
MACEFACE...
SPACERACE FACE...
AFRO LACEFACE...
COUNTRY HOUSE PORCHFACE...
ASSORTED MEAT FACE...
DUST-IN-THE-WIND FACE...
SECOND-PLACE FACE PLAICE FACE...
HAVE-YOU-SEEN-THIS-CAT-FACE?...
HAVE YOU SEEN THIS CAT?
ANSWERS TO "FLUFFENS"
MOBY DICKFACE...
PACIFIC ISLAND TOILETFACE...
WANDERING SNAILFACE...
BABY HITLERFACE...
MOUNT RUSHMORE FACE...
WITHOUT-A-TRACE FACE...
TRIAL SEPARATION FACE...
ASSORTED MEATFACE, JR....
ORDINARY GUYFACE...
BUNCH-OF-ODD-CONCEPTS-THAT-DON'T-WORK-ON-A-FACE-FACE...

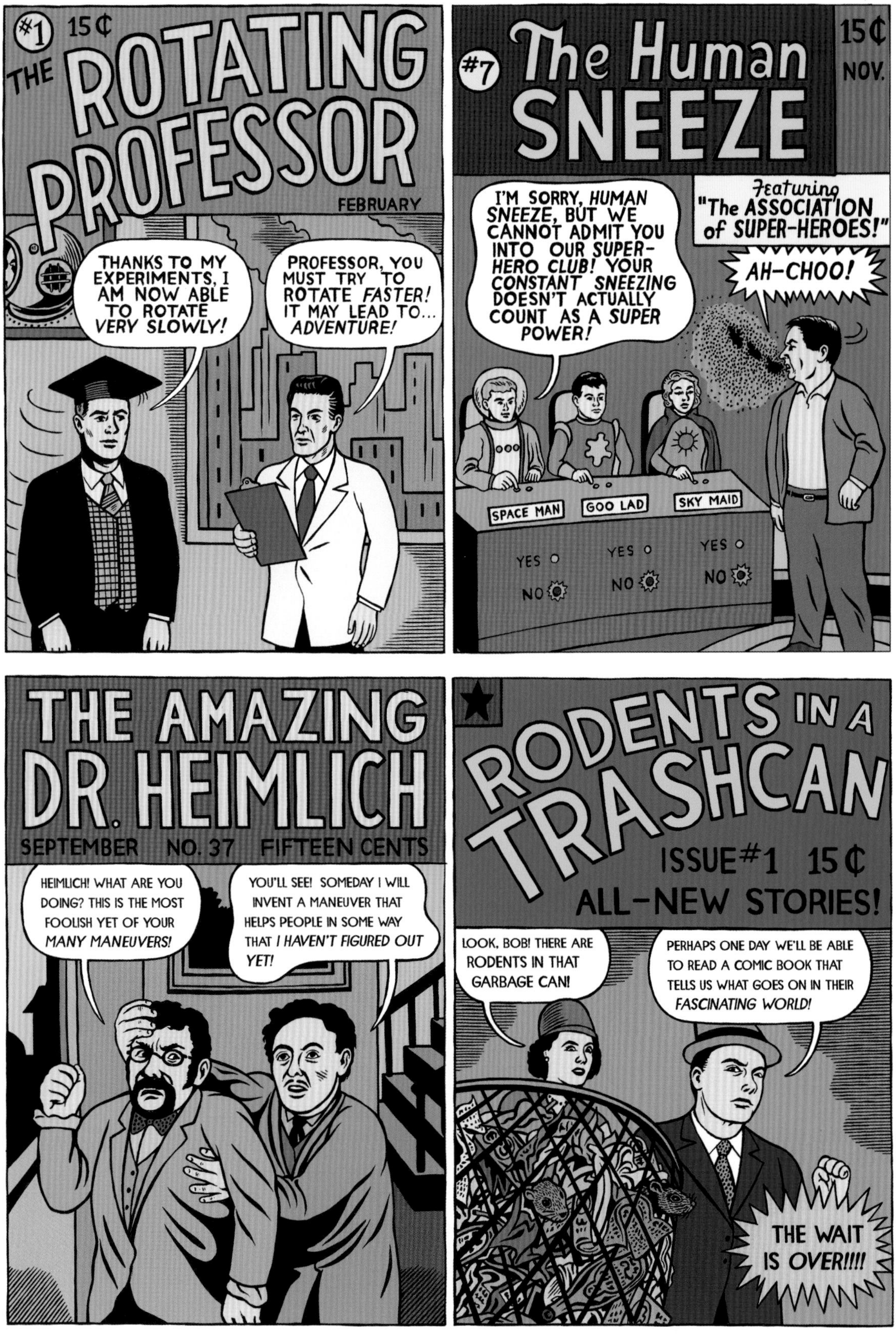
#1 15¢
THE ROTATING PROFESSOR
FEBRUARY
THANKS TO MY EXPERIMENTS, I AM NOW ABLE TO ROTATE VERY SLOWLY!
PROFESSOR, YOU MUST TRY TO ROTATE FASTER! IT MAY LEAD TO... ADVENTURE!
#7 The Human SNEEZE
15¢
NOV.
Featuring "The ASSOCIATION of SUPER-HEROES!"
I'M SORRY, HUMAN SNEEZE, BUT WE CANNOT ADMIT YOU INTO OUR SUPER-HERO CLUB! YOUR CONSTANT SNEEZING DOESN'T ACTUALLY COUNT AS A SUPER POWER!
AH-CHOO!
SPACE MAN
GOO LAD
SKY MAID
YES
NO
YES
NO
YES
NO
THE AMAZING DR. HEIMLICH
SEPTEMBER NO. 37 FIFTEEN CENTS
HEIMLICH! WHAT ARE YOU DOING? THIS IS THE MOST FOOLISH YET OF YOUR MANY MANEUVERS!
YOU'LL SEE! SOMEDAY I WILL INVENT A MANEUVER THAT HELPS PEOPLE IN SOME WAY THAT I HAVEN'T FIGURED OUT YET!
RODENTS IN A TRASHCAN
ISSUE #1 15¢
ALL-NEW STORIES!
LOOK, BOB! THERE ARE RODENTS IN THAT GARBAGE CAN!
PERHAPS ONE DAY WE'LL BE ABLE TO READ A COMIC BOOK THAT TELLS US WHAT GOES ON IN THEIR FASCINATING WORLD!
THE WAIT IS OVER!!!!

HOW TO RECOGNIZE CRIMINAL FINGERTALK

FINGERTALK IS ONE OF THE SECRET METHODS THAT CRIMINALS HAVE DEVELOPED SO THAT THEY CAN COMMUNICATE THEIR NEFARIOUS SCHEMES. BELOW ARE SOME EXAMPLES OF COMMONLY USED SIGNALS:

I'M PLANNING A NEW CRIMINAL CAPER.

IT'S A THREE-PERSON JOB.

I NEED A STRONG-ARM MAN...

...A DRIVER...

YOU CAN BE THE THIRD PERSON.

WE'LL SPLIT THE TAKE EVENLY.

I'VE GOT THE VAN CRESSWELL DIAMOND.

AND I'M KEEPING IT FOR MYSELF.

YOU'RE NEVER GOING TO SEE ME AGAIN.

YOU'VE DONE EXCELLENT WORK ON THIS CRIMINAL ENTERPRISE.

BUT WE'RE GOING TO HAVE TO GET RID OF YOU.

WE'RE GOING TO ROB A CHURCH.

IT'S GOT A STEEPLE.

WHEN WE OPEN THE DOOR...

WE MIGHT SEE SOME PEOPLE.

A LOOK INTO THE NEAR FUTURE

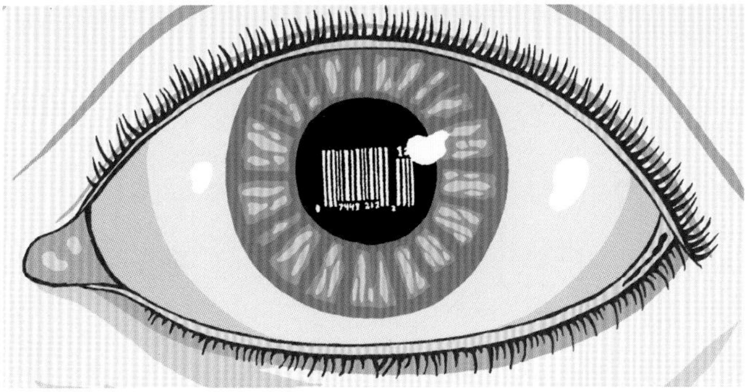
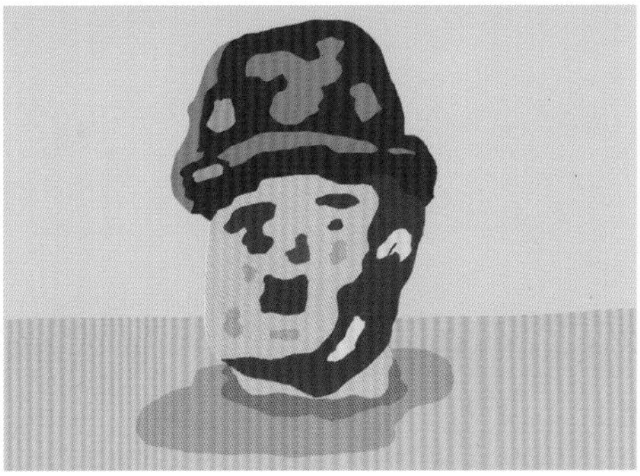

SCIENCE MARCHS ON. Left: New developments in retinal bar coding make it possible to use the supermarket price scanner to find out your current worth. Right: NASA unveils its most exciting discovery: "Charlie," a rock found in space that bears a remarkable resemblance to 20th-century performer Charles Chaplin. "Other than this, we've just found lots of dust and junk up there," complained a disgusted NASA official, explaining why they're giving up space exploration. "But this is kind of neat, huh? Look, he's got his little hat and everything."

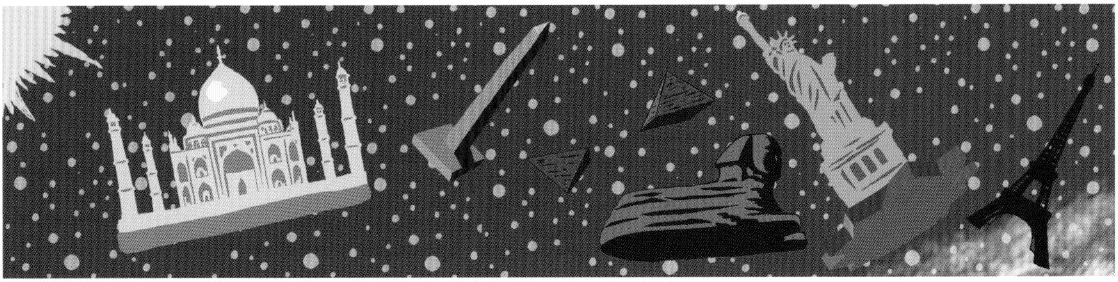

MONUMENTS IN SPACE. They've been placed there to free up valuable real estate, and can be viewed, free of charge, by anyone with a telescope.

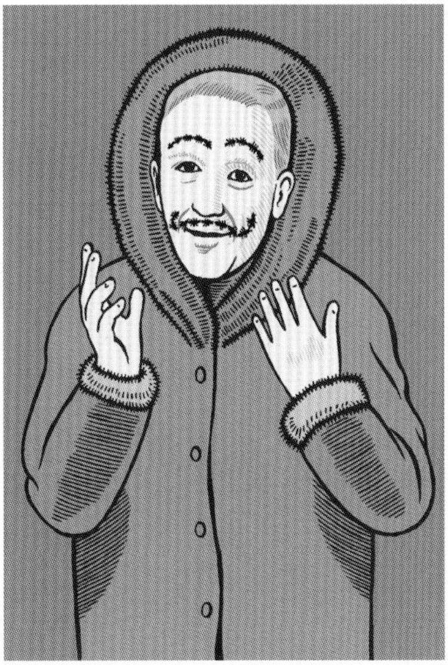
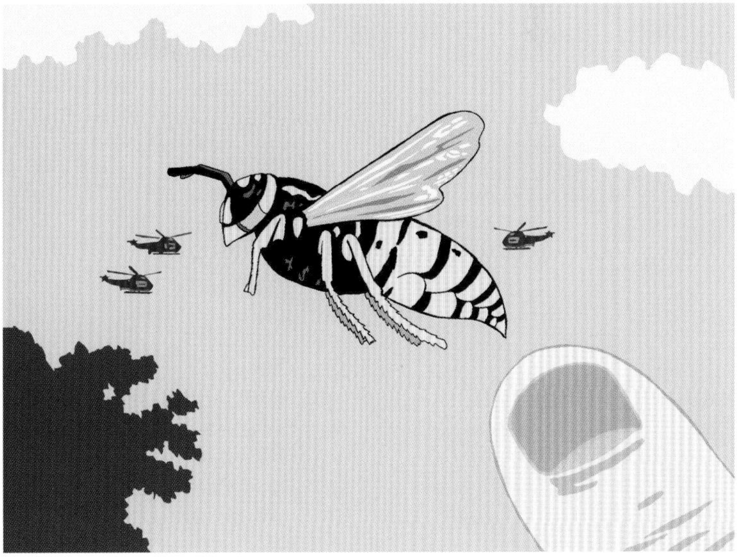

MAN GOES TO WAR WITH INSECTS. Left: This Eskimo Refrigerator salesman needs to look trustworthy, but ants have crawled onto his face and arranged themselves into eyebrows and a curly mustache. making him look ridiculous. Right: Helicopters battle a giant wasp outside Dayton (amateur photograph).

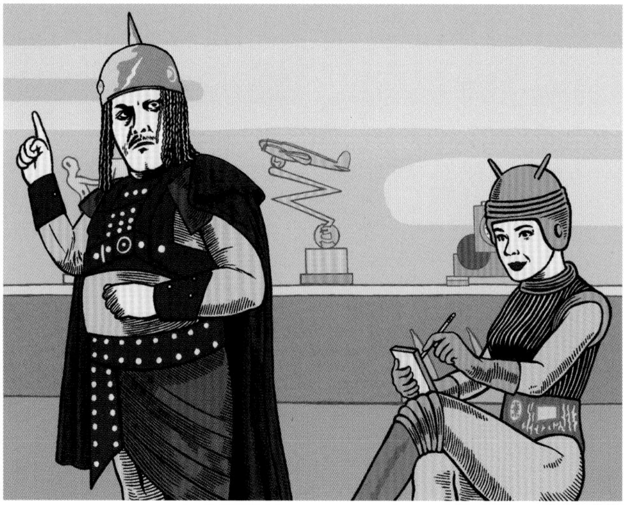

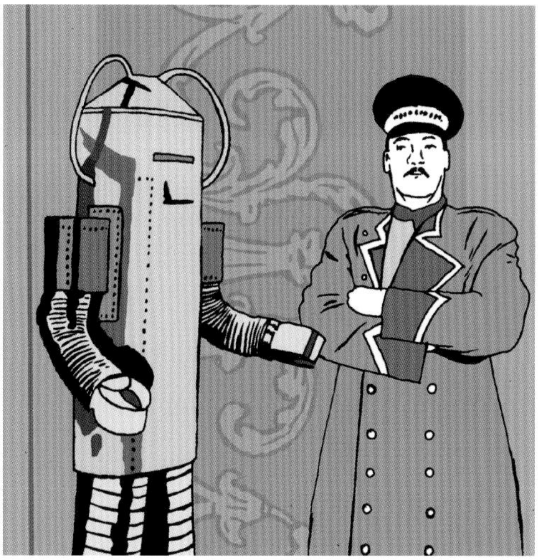

WHAT'S GOING ON HERE? Left: A businessman gives dictation to his secretary. Both are wearing the latest fashions. Right: A doorman refuses admission to a robot yesterday in the future.

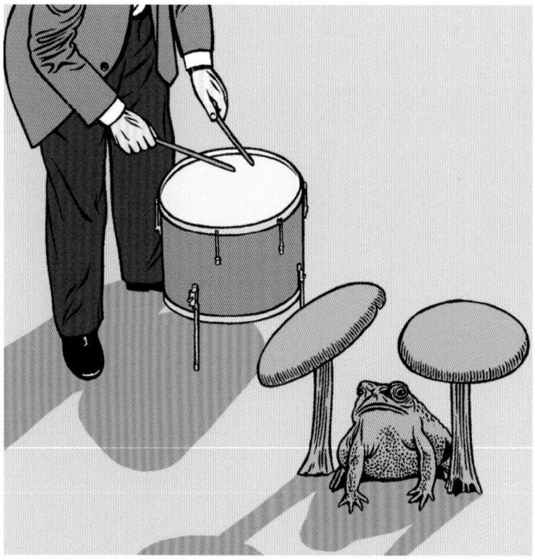

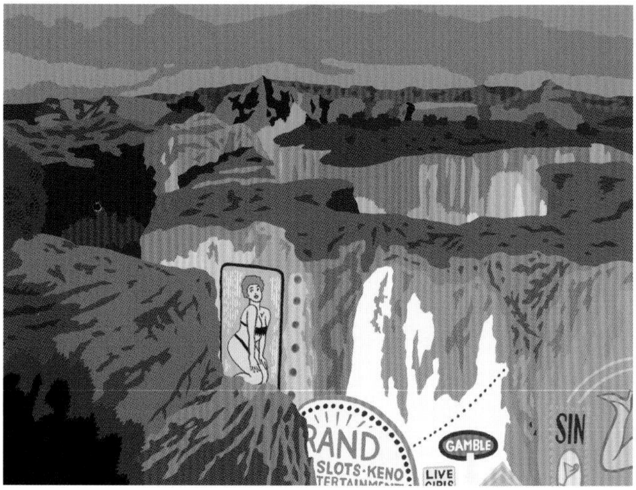
SLOTS·KENO
GAMBLE
LIVE
SIN

WE NEED FUN. Left: Annoying toads has become America's number-one pastime. Right: The Grand Canyon has changed greatly since prostitution and and gambling were legalized there.

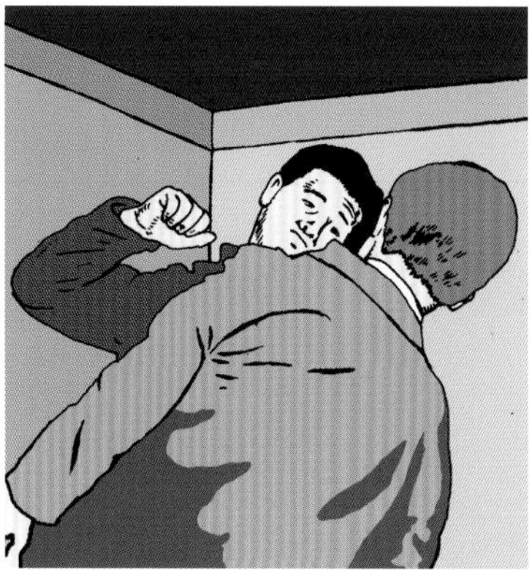

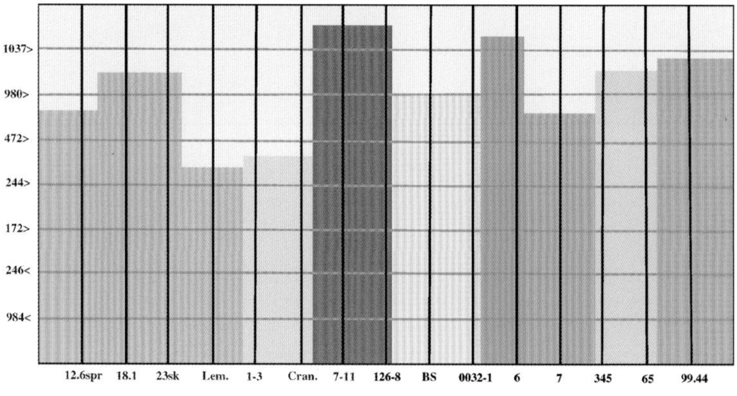
1037>
980>
472>
244>
172>
246<
984<
12.6spr
18.1
23sk
Lem.
1-3
Cran.
7-11
126-8
BS
0032-1
6
7
345
65
99.44

AND STLL THERE'S MORE. Left: Empathovision is sued out of existence after the special program "Beating of a Lifetime." Right: We have no idea what this graph means, because the person who made it was found this morning... murdered!

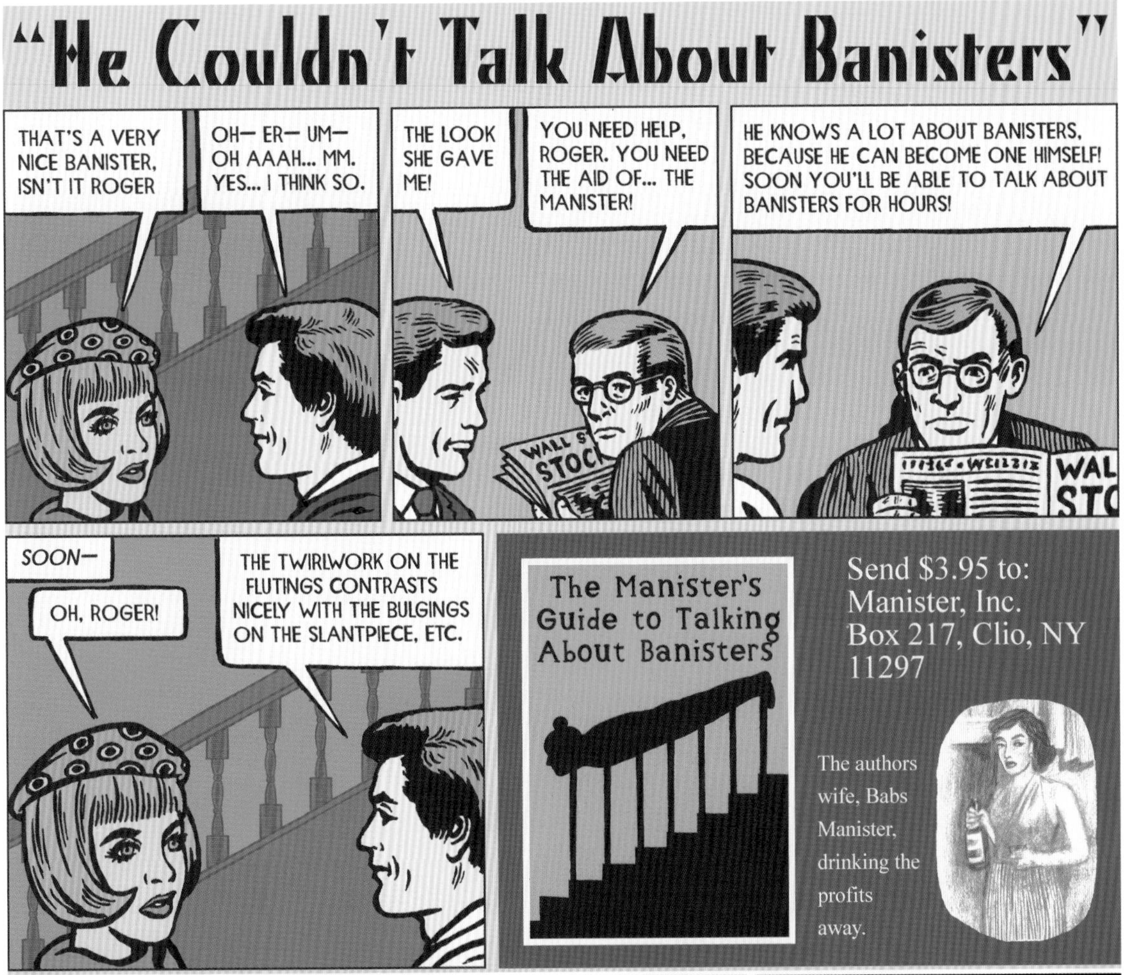
"He Couldn't Talk About Banisters"
THAT'S A VERY NICE BANISTER, ISN'T IT ROGER
OH— ER— UM— OH AAAH... MM. YES... I THINK SO.
THE LOOK SHE GAVE ME!
YOU NEED HELP, ROGER. YOU NEED THE AID OF... THE MANISTER!
HE KNOWS A LOT ABOUT BANISTERS, BECAUSE HE CAN BECOME ONE HIMSELF! SOON YOU'LL BE ABLE TO TALK ABOUT BANISTERS FOR HOURS!
SOON—
OH, ROGER!
THE TWIRLWORK ON THE FLUTINGS CONTRASTS NICELY WITH THE BULGINGS ON THE SLANTPIECE, ETC.
The Manister's Guide to Talking About Banisters
Send $3.95 to: Manister, Inc. Box 217, Clio, NY 11297
The authors wife, Babs Manister, drinking the profits away.

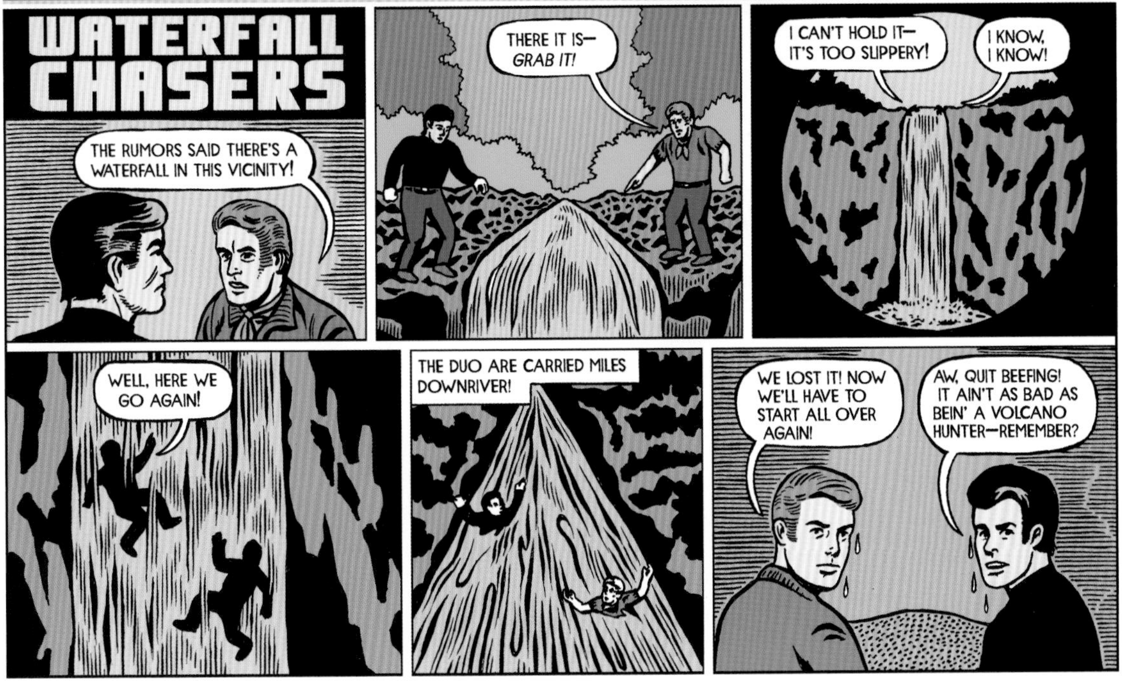
WATERFALL CHASERS
THE RUMORS SAID THERE'S A WATERFALL IN THIS VICINITY!
THERE IT IS— GRAB IT!
I CAN'T HOLD IT— IT'S TOO SLIPPERY!
I KNOW, I KNOW!
WELL, HERE WE GO AGAIN!
THE DUO ARE CARRIED MILES DOWNRIVER!
WE LOST IT! NOW WE'LL HAVE TO START ALL OVER AGAIN!
AW, QUIT BEEFING! IT AIN'T AS BAD AS BEIN' A VOLCANO HUNTER—REMEMBER?

The Story of Sammy the Crouton

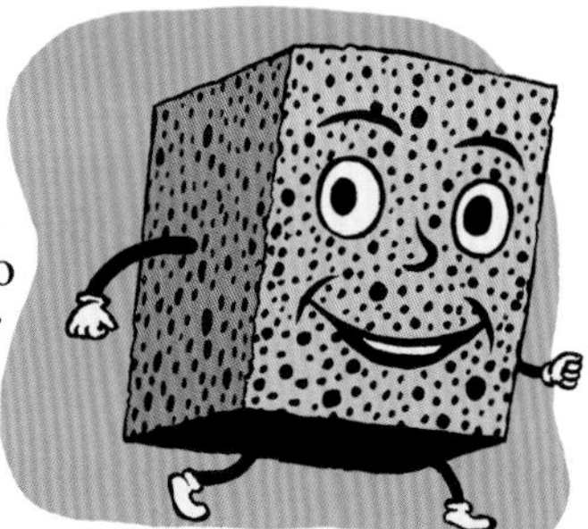

Sammy's life began as he was cut from a seasoned bread loaf on an automated assembly line. "My! What an interesting existence!" he thought as he was packed into a bag with several hundred other croutons. How they bickered and argued! Finally Sammy was placed in a salad with several of his fellows, a bunch of leaves, some tomato and mushroom slices, and some radish bits. Suddenly oil and vinegar was poured on them, and Sammy gasped.

As soon as the salad had been assembled, the maker left to the room to answer a phone call, and Sammy and the rest of the salad watched the TV, which was on. They saw almost all of "Ridin' Tall" (1958), a sudsy oater featuring two-star performances from Chester "Wombat" McLane and Giggly Jackson. Shortly before the end, the salad maker returned and began to masticate them mightily with her jaws. Sammy screamed as his small body was ground and smashed. "Why oh why isn't there an official society to prevent such cruelty?" he wondered as he lost consciousness for the final time.

This message is brought to you by the Official Society for the Prevention of Cruelty to Croutons.

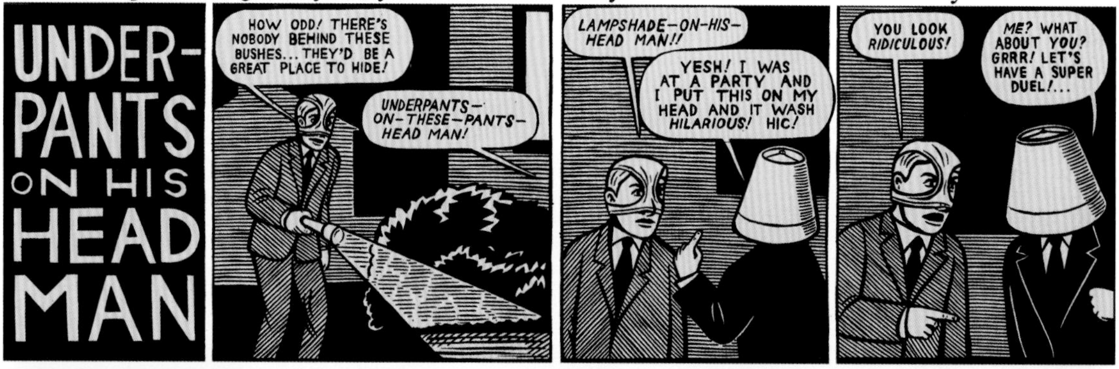
UNDER-PANTS ON HIS HEAD MAN
HOW ODD! THERE'S NOBODY BEHIND THESE BUSHES... THEY'D BE A GREAT PLACE TO HIDE!
UNDERPANTS—ON—THESE—PANTS—HEAD MAN!
LAMPSHADE—ON—HIS—HEAD MAN!!
YESH! I WAS AT A PARTY AND I PUT THIS ON MY HEAD AND IT WASH HILARIOUS! HIC!
YOU LOOK RIDICULOUS!
ME? WHAT ABOUT YOU? GRRR! LET'S HAVE A SUPER DUEL!...

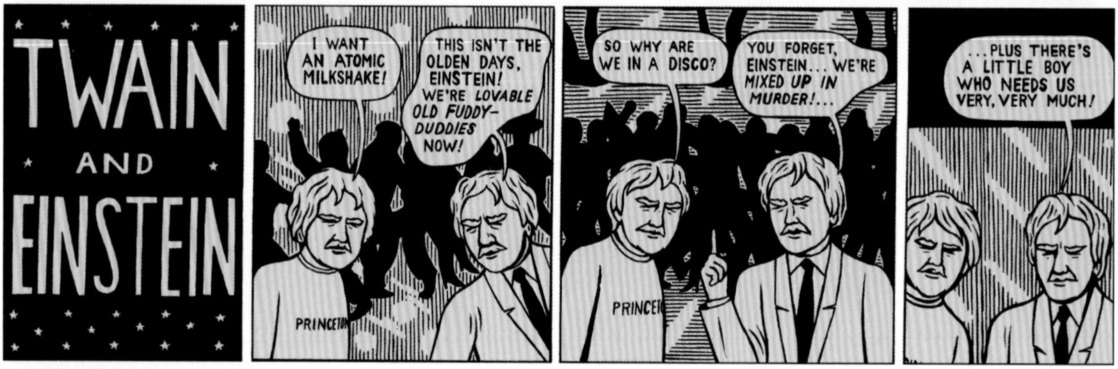
TWAIN AND EINSTEIN
I WANT AN ATOMIC MILKSHAKE!
THIS ISN'T THE OLDEN DAYS, EINSTEIN! WE'RE LOVABLE OLD FUDDY-DUDDIES NOW!
PRINCETON
SO WHY ARE WE IN A DISCO?
YOU FORGET, EINSTEIN... WE'RE MIXED UP IN MURDER!...
...PLUS THERE'S A LITTLE BOY WHO NEEDS US VERY, VERY MUCH!

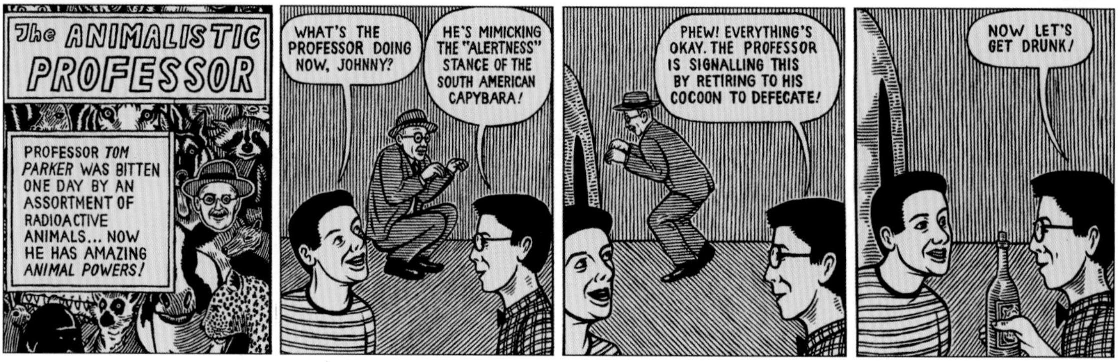
The ANIMALISTIC PROFESSOR
PROFESSOR TOM PARKER WAS BITTEN ONE DAY BY AN ASSORTMENT OF RADIOACTIVE ANIMALS... NOW HE HAS AMAZING ANIMAL POWERS!
WHAT'S THE PROFESSOR DOING NOW, JOHNNY?
HE'S MIMICKING THE "ALERTNESS" STANCE OF THE SOUTH AMERICAN CAPYBARA!
PHEW! EVERYTHING'S OKAY. THE PROFESSOR IS SIGNALLING THIS BY RETIRING TO HIS COCOON TO DEFECATE!
NOW LET'S GET DRUNK!

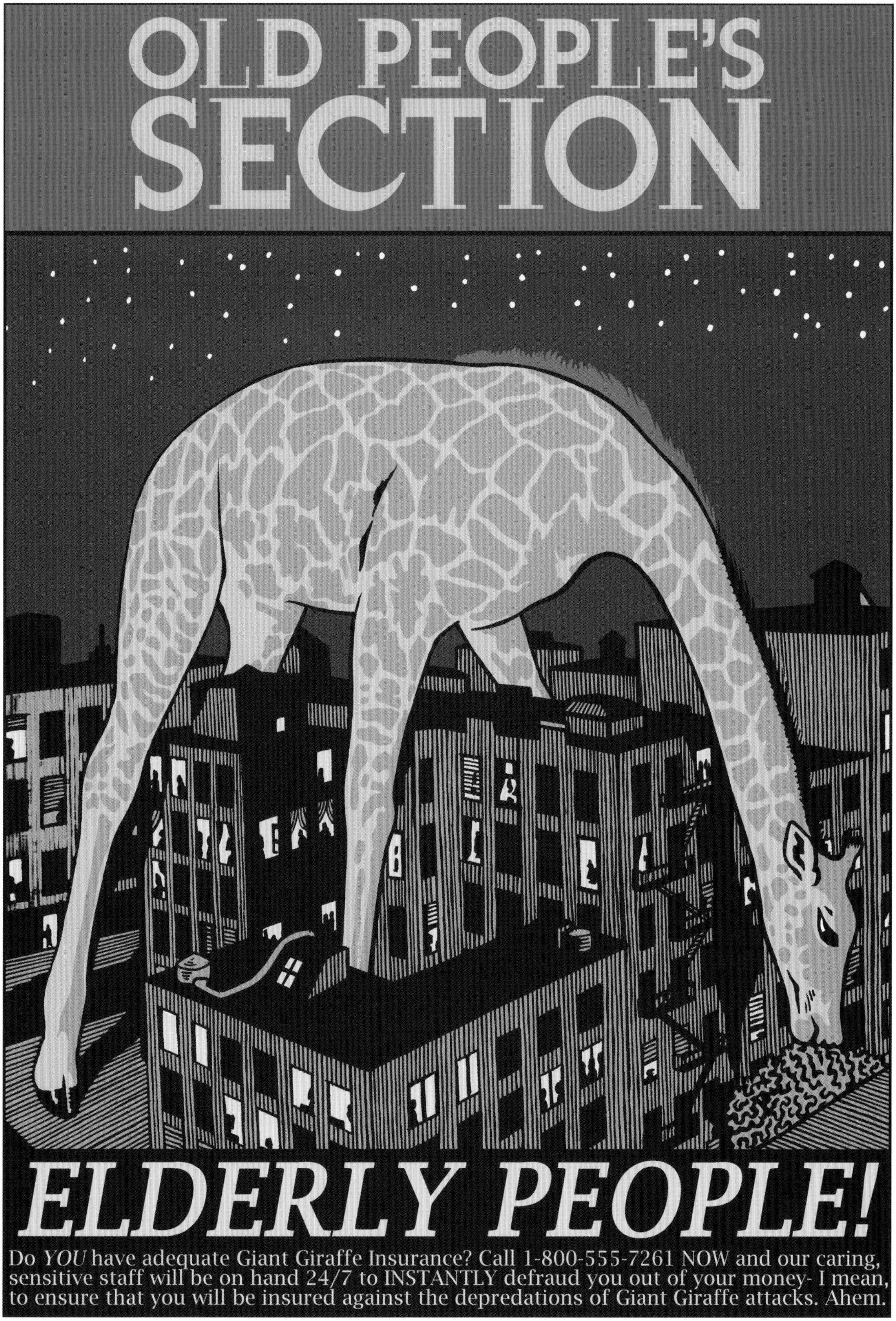
OLD PEOPLE'S SECTION
ELDERLY PEOPLE!
Do YOU have adequate Giant Giraffe Insurance? Call 1-800-555-7261 NOW and our caring, sensitive staff will be on hand 24/7 to INSTANTLY defraud you out of your money- I mean, to ensure that you will be insured against the depredations of Giant Giraffe attacks. Ahem.

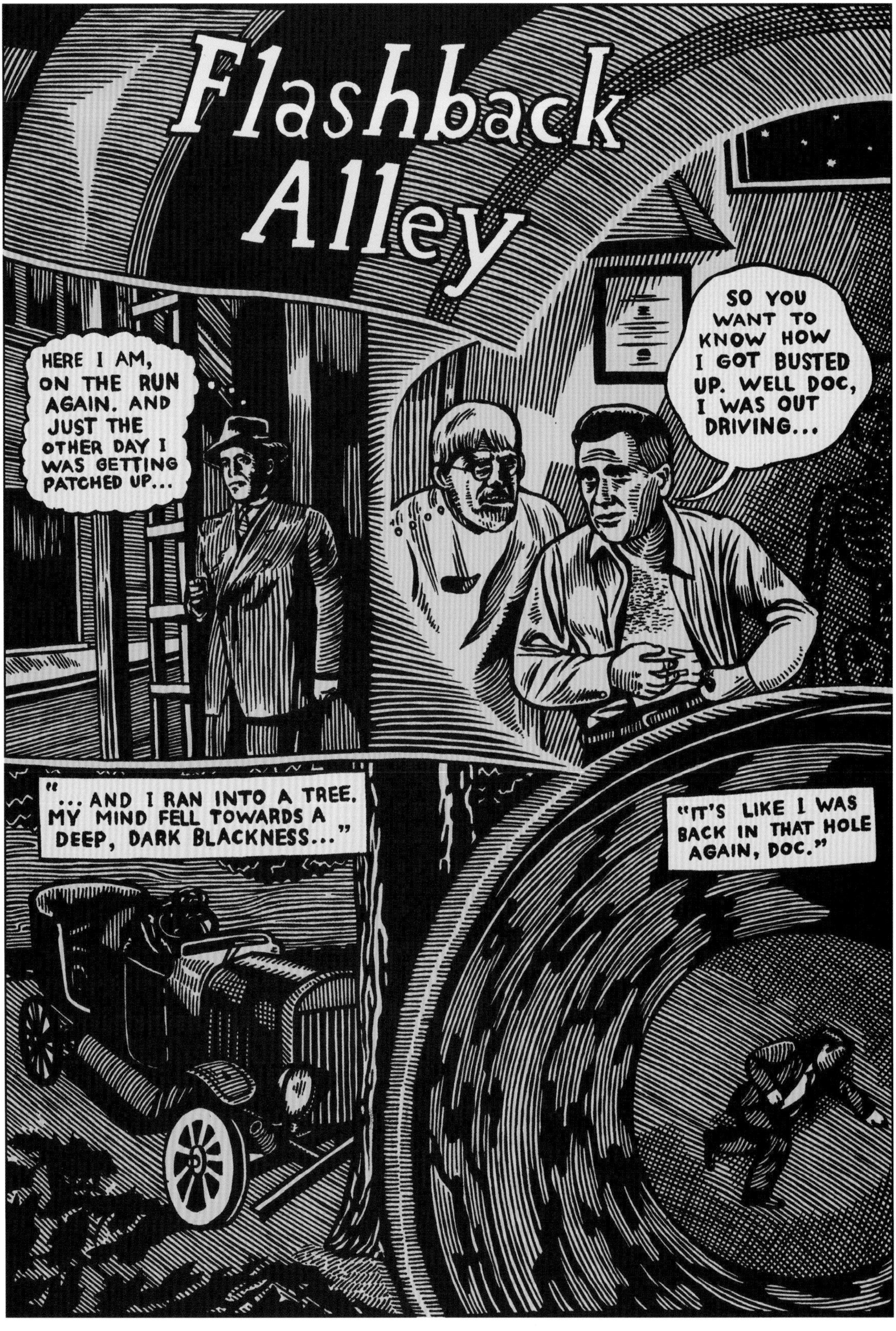

Flashback Alley
HERE I AM, ON THE RUN AGAIN. AND JUST THE OTHER DAY I WAS GETTING PATCHED UP...
SO YOU WANT TO KNOW HOW I GOT BUSTED UP. WELL DOC, I WAS OUT DRIVING...
"... AND I RAN INTO A TREE. MY MIND FELL TOWARDS A DEEP, DARK BLACKNESS..."
"IT'S LIKE I WAS BACK IN THAT HOLE AGAIN, DOC."

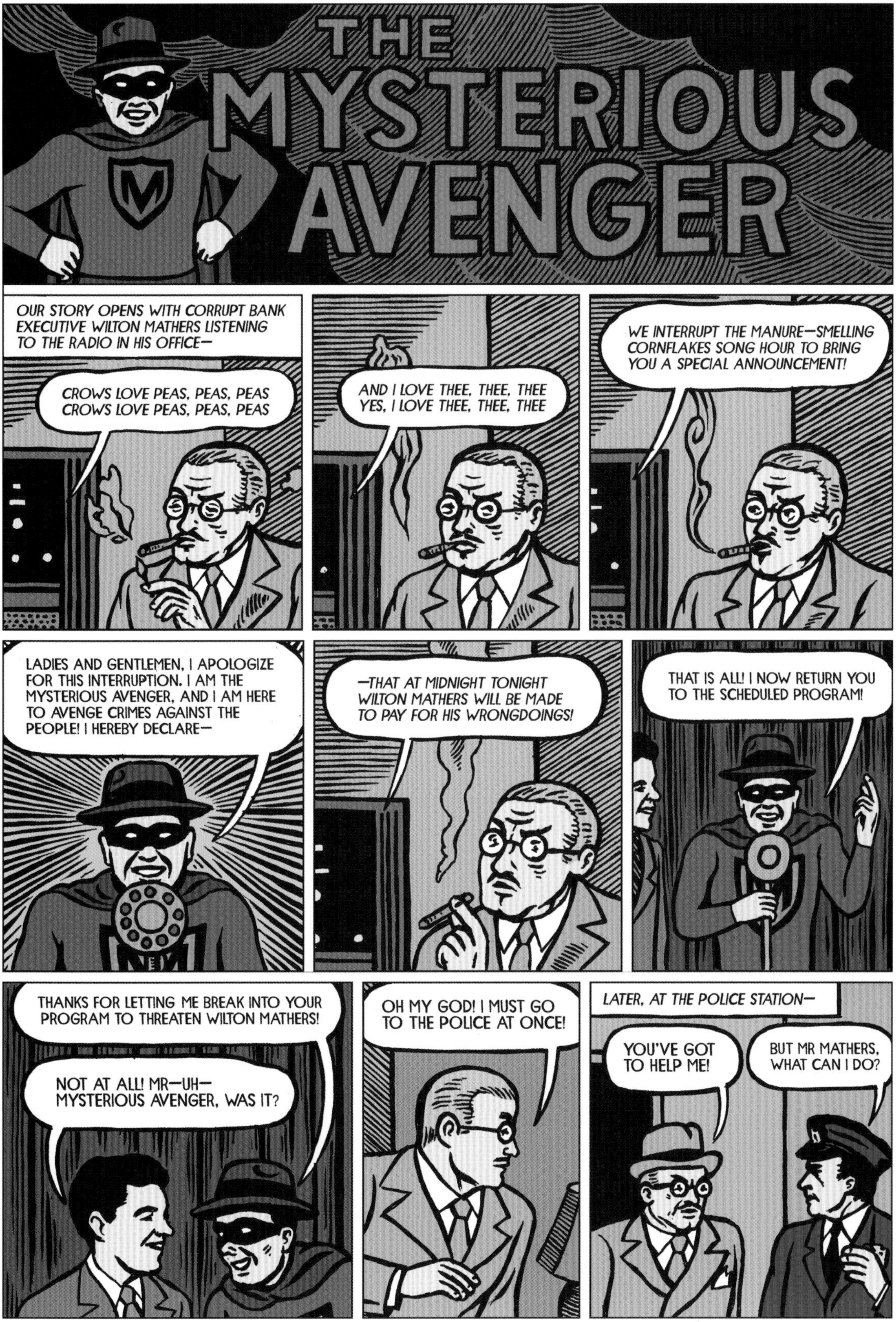
THE MYSTERIOUS AVENGER
OUR STORY OPENS WITH CORRUPT BANK EXECUTIVE WILTON MATHERS LISTENING TO THE RADIO IN HIS OFFICE—
CROWS LOVE PEAS, PEAS, PEAS CROWS LOVE PEAS, PEAS, PEAS
AND I LOVE THEE, THEE, THEE YES, I LOVE THEE, THEE, THEE
WE INTERRUPT THE MANURE—SMELLING CORNFLAKES SONG HOUR TO BRING YOU A SPECIAL ANNOUNCEMENT!
LADIES AND GENTLEMEN, I APOLOGIZE FOR THIS INTERRUPTION. I AM THE MYSTERIOUS AVENGER, AND I AM HERE TO AVENGE CRIMES AGAINST THE PEOPLE! I HEREBY DECLARE—
—THAT AT MIDNIGHT TONIGHT WILTON MATHERS WILL BE MADE TO PAY FOR HIS WRONGDOINGS!
THAT IS ALL! I NOW RETURN YOU TO THE SCHEDULED PROGRAM!
THANKS FOR LETTING ME BREAK INTO YOUR PROGRAM TO THREATEN WILTON MATHERS!
NOT AT ALL! MR—UH— MYSTERIOUS AVENGER, WAS IT?
OH MY GOD! I MUST GO TO THE POLICE AT ONCE!
LATER, AT THE POLICE STATION—
YOU'VE GOT TO HELP ME!
BUT MR MATHERS, WHAT CAN I DO?

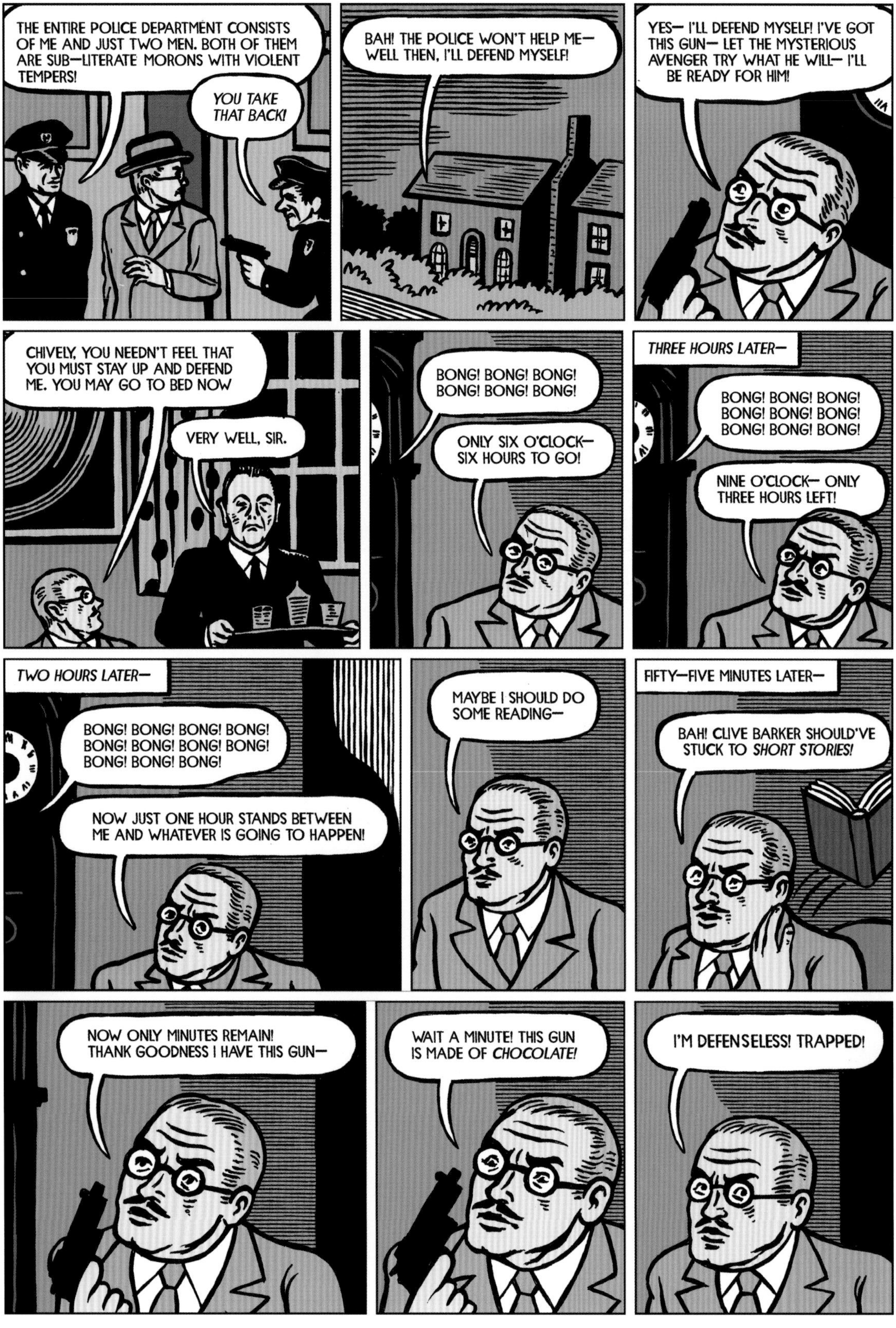
THE ENTIRE POLICE DEPARTMENT CONSISTS OF ME AND JUST TWO MEN. BOTH OF THEM ARE SUB—LITERATE MORONS WITH VIOLENT TEMPERS!
YOU TAKE THAT BACK!
BAH! THE POLICE WON'T HELP ME— WELL THEN, I'LL DEFEND MYSELF!
YES— I'LL DEFEND MYSELF! I'VE GOT THIS GUN— LET THE MYSTERIOUS AVENGER TRY WHAT HE WILL— I'LL BE READY FOR HIM!
CHIVELY, YOU NEEDN'T FEEL THAT YOU MUST STAY UP AND DEFEND ME. YOU MAY GO TO BED NOW
VERY WELL, SIR.
BONG! BONG! BONG! BONG! BONG! BONG!
ONLY SIX O'CLOCK— SIX HOURS TO GO!
THREE HOURS LATER—
BONG! BONG! BONG! BONG! BONG! BONG! BONG! BONG! BONG!
NINE O'CLOCK— ONLY THREE HOURS LEFT!
TWO HOURS LATER—
BONG! BONG! BONG! BONG! BONG! BONG! BONG! BONG! BONG! BONG! BONG!
NOW JUST ONE HOUR STANDS BETWEEN ME AND WHATEVER IS GOING TO HAPPEN!
MAYBE I SHOULD DO SOME READING—
FIFTY—FIVE MINUTES LATER—
BAH! CLIVE BARKER SHOULD'VE STUCK TO SHORT STORIES!
NOW ONLY MINUTES REMAIN! THANK GOODNESS I HAVE THIS GUN—
WAIT A MINUTE! THIS GUN IS MADE OF CHOCOLATE!
I'M DEFENSELESS! TRAPPED!

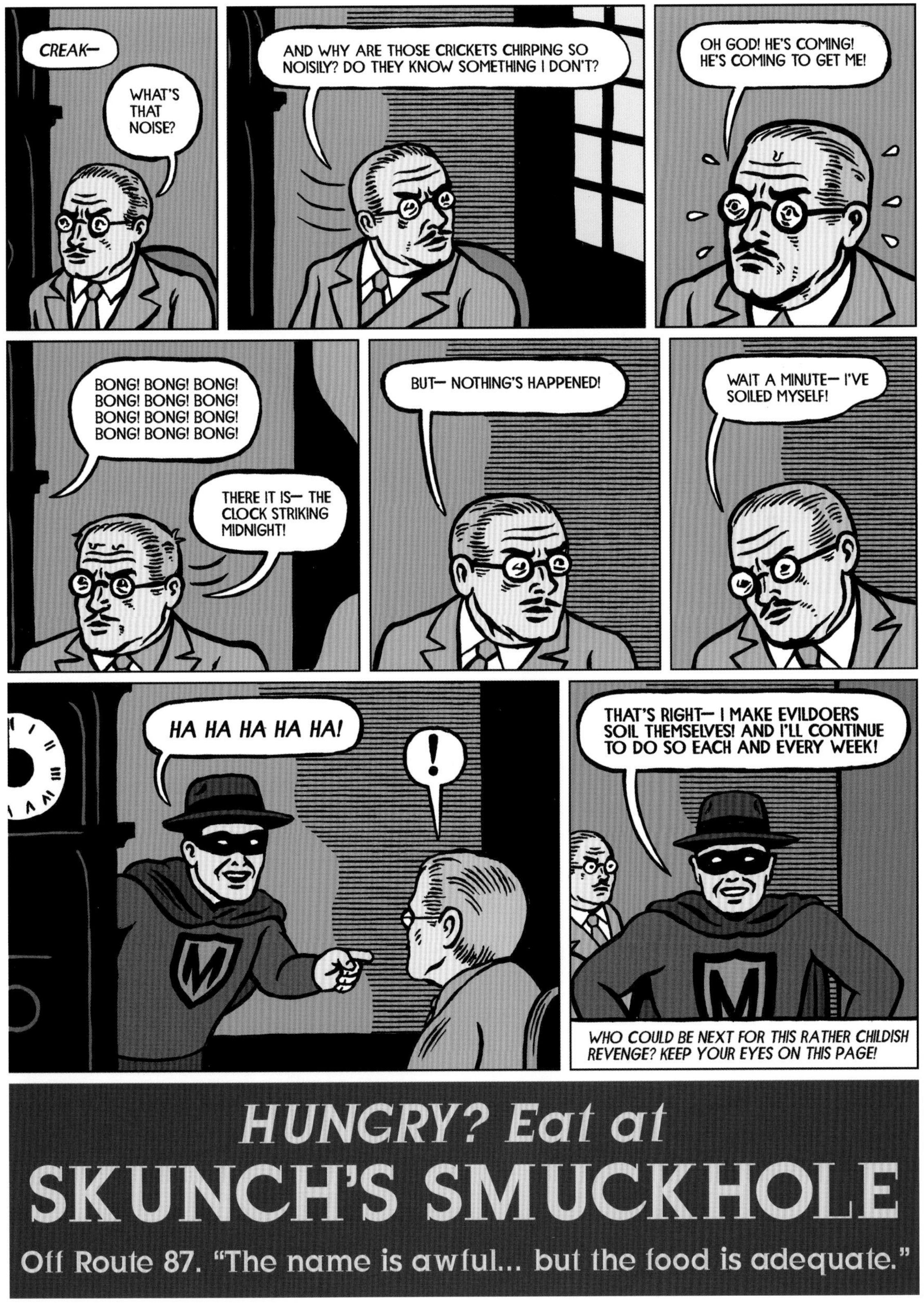
CREAK—
WHAT'S THAT NOISE?
AND WHY ARE THOSE CRICKETS CHIRPING SO NOISILY? DO THEY KNOW SOMETHING I DON'T?
OH GOD! HE'S COMING! HE'S COMING TO GET ME!
BONG! BONG! BONG! BONG! BONG! BONG! BONG! BONG! BONG! BONG! BONG! BONG!
THERE IT IS— THE CLOCK STRIKING MIDNIGHT!
BUT— NOTHING'S HAPPENED!
WAIT A MINUTE— I'VE SOILED MYSELF!
HA HA HA HA HA!
!
THAT'S RIGHT— I MAKE EVILDOERS SOIL THEMSELVES! AND I'LL CONTINUE TO DO SO EACH AND EVERY WEEK!
WHO COULD BE NEXT FOR THIS RATHER CHILDISH REVENGE? KEEP YOUR EYES ON THIS PAGE!

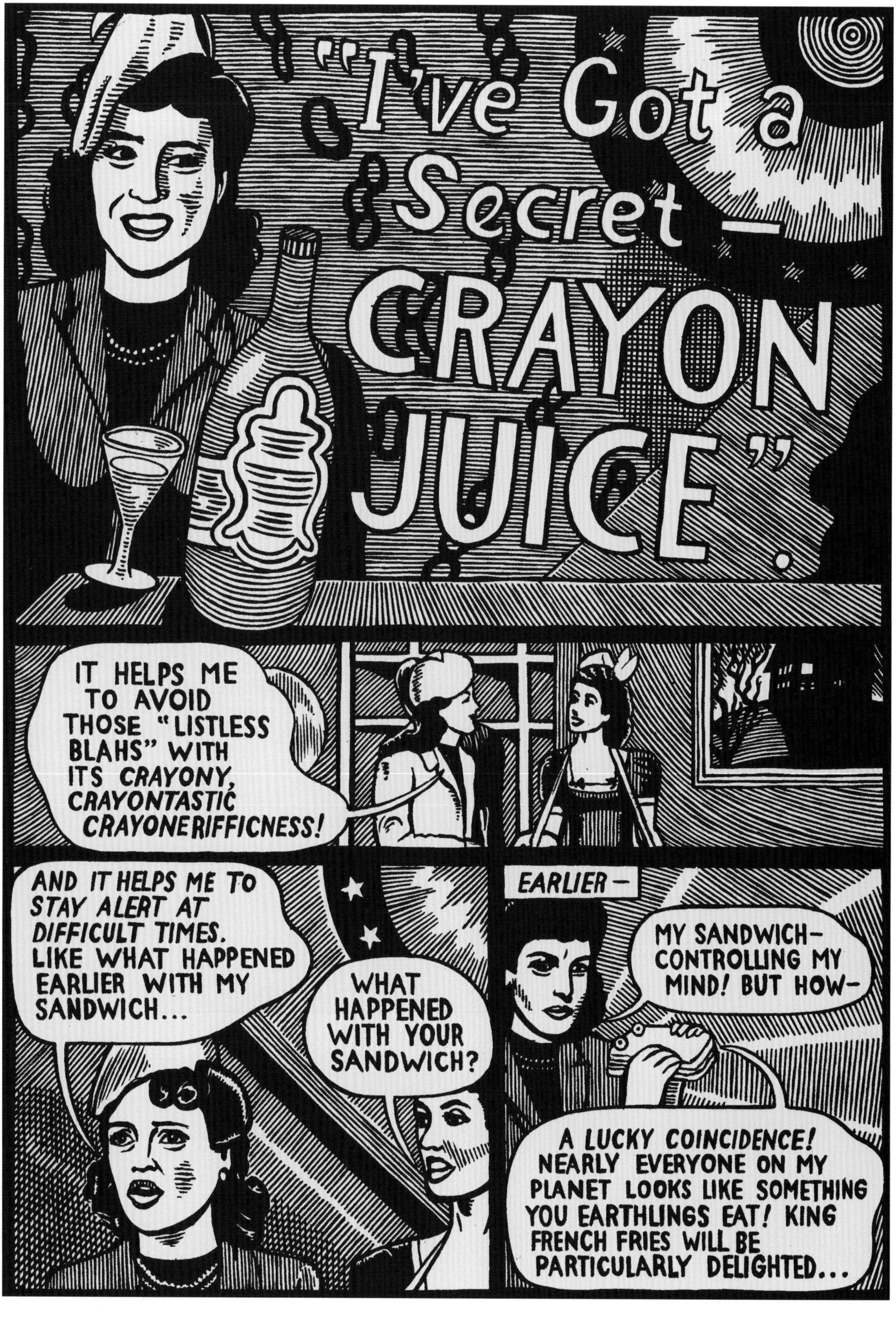
"I've Got a Secret — CRAYON JUICE".
IT HELPS ME TO AVOID THOSE "LISTLESS BLAHS" WITH ITS CRAYONY, CRAYONTASTIC CRAYONERIFFICNESS!
AND IT HELPS ME TO STAY ALERT AT DIFFICULT TIMES. LIKE WHAT HAPPENED EARLIER WITH MY SANDWICH...
WHAT HAPPENED WITH YOUR SANDWICH?
EARLIER —
MY SANDWICH— CONTROLLING MY MIND! BUT HOW—
A LUCKY COINCIDENCE! NEARLY EVERYONE ON MY PLANET LOOKS LIKE SOMETHING YOU EARTHLINGS EAT! KING FRENCH FRIES WILL BE PARTICULARLY DELIGHTED...

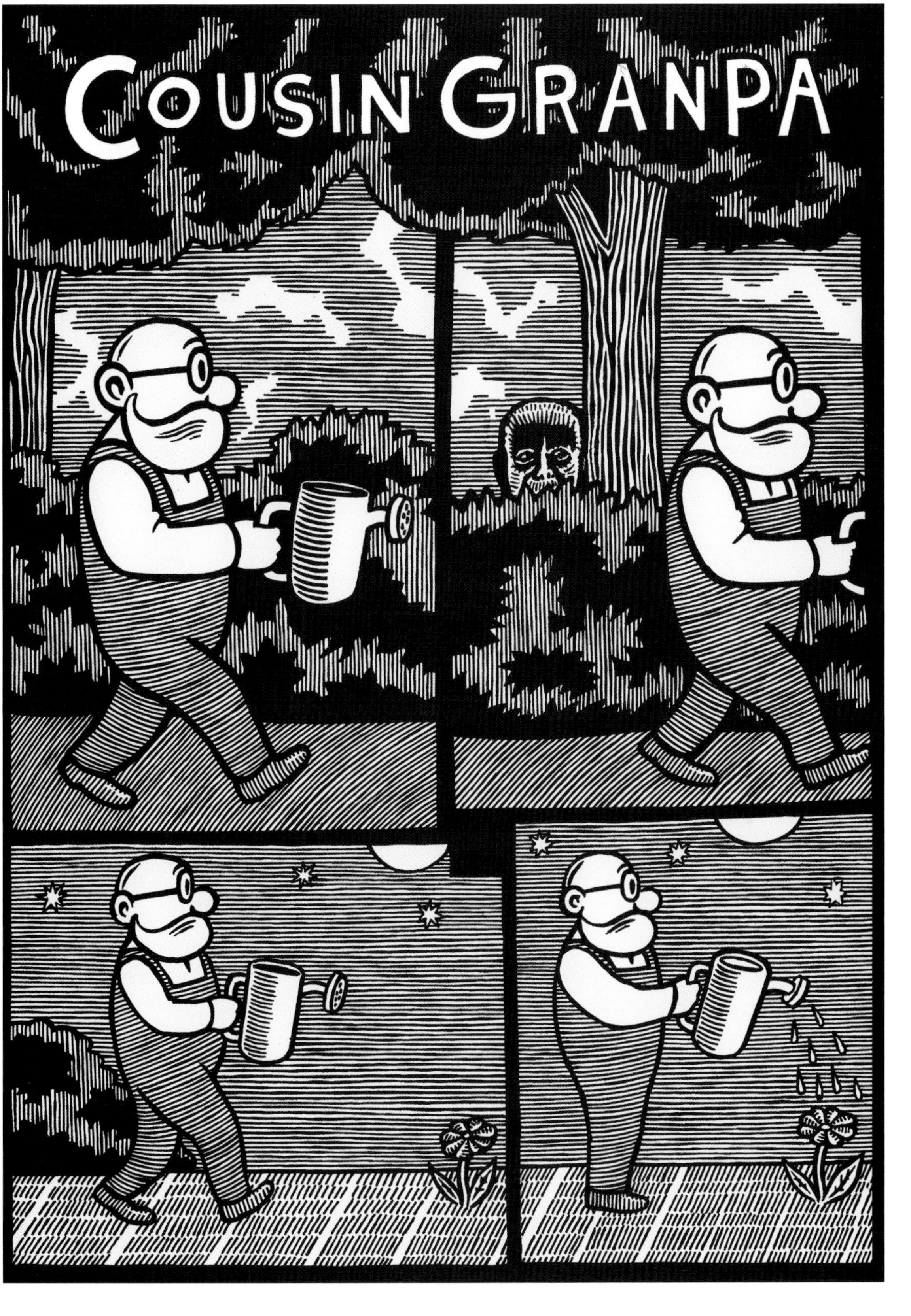
COUSIN GRANPA

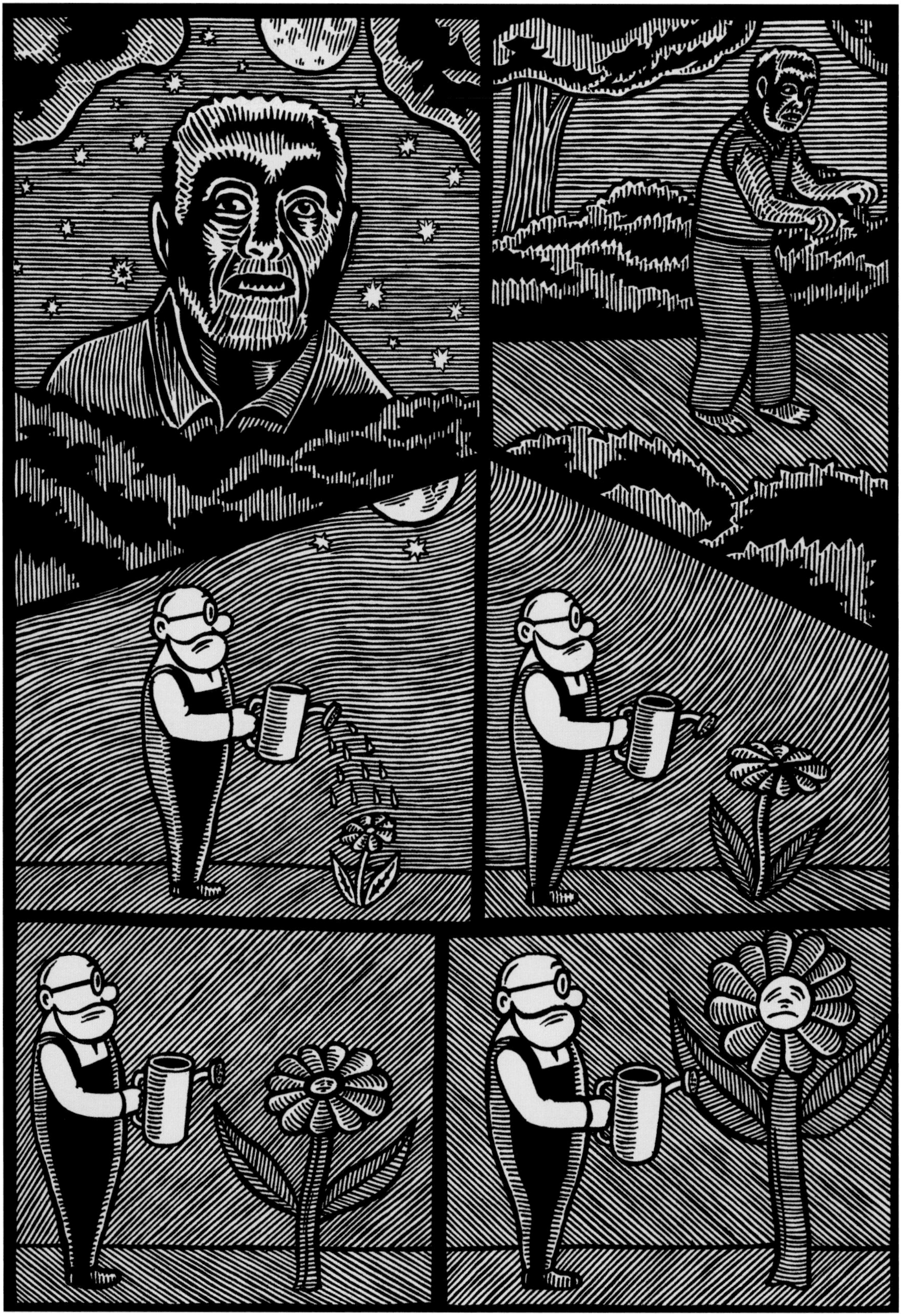

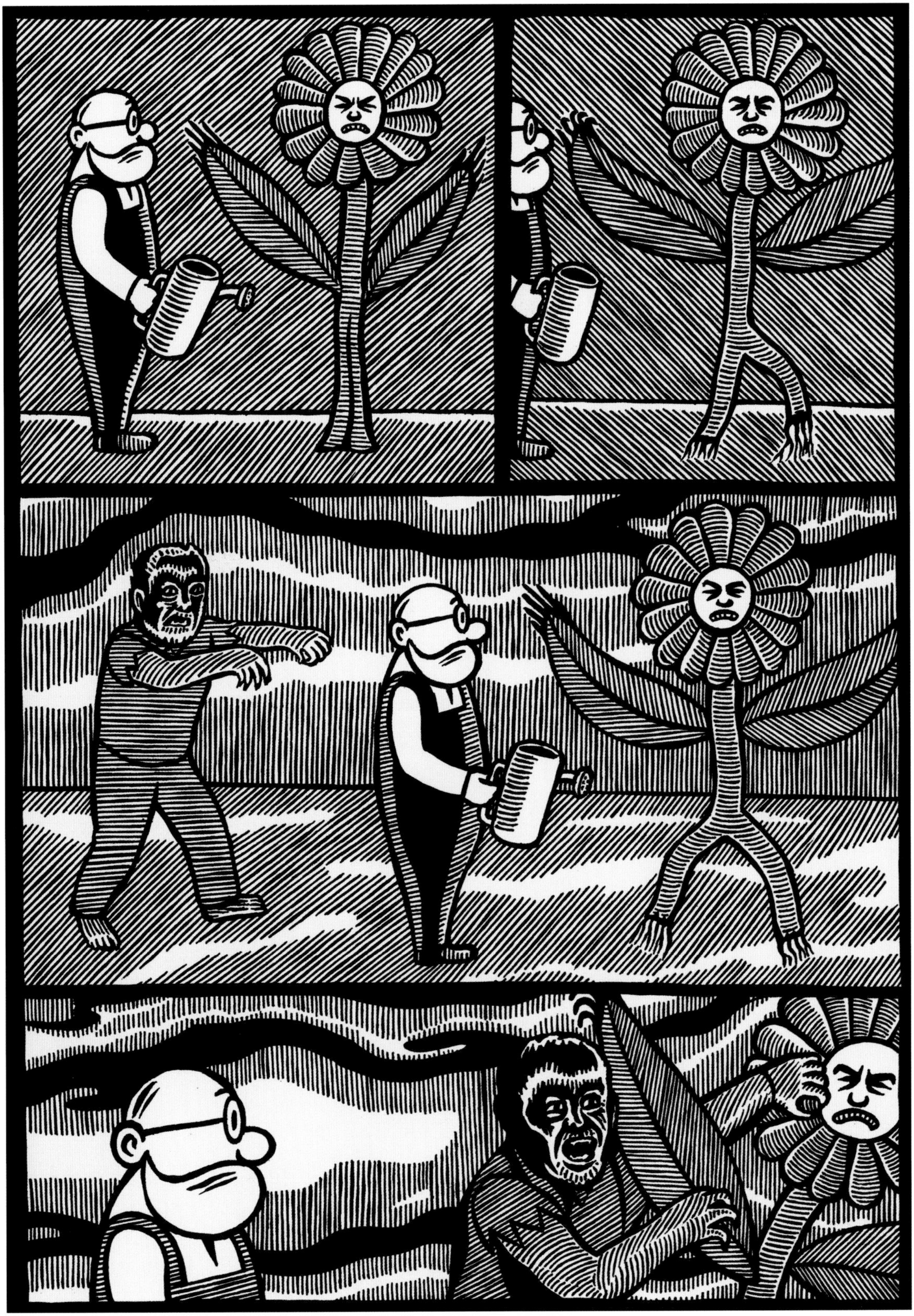

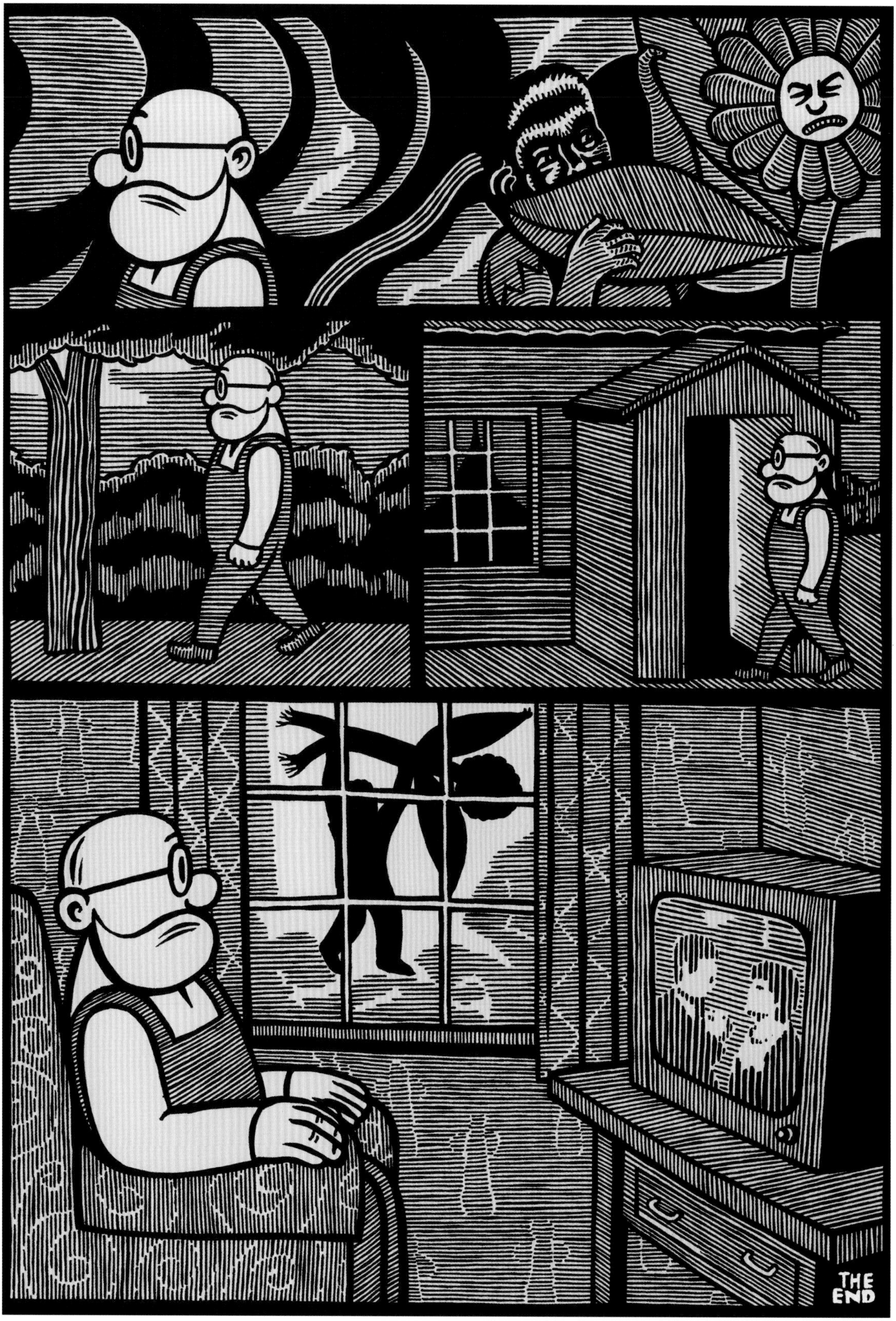
THE
END

BOOK REVIEW CORNER

THE HISTORY OF FOOD By Lazlo Haggard.
St. Dotard's Press, 29.95

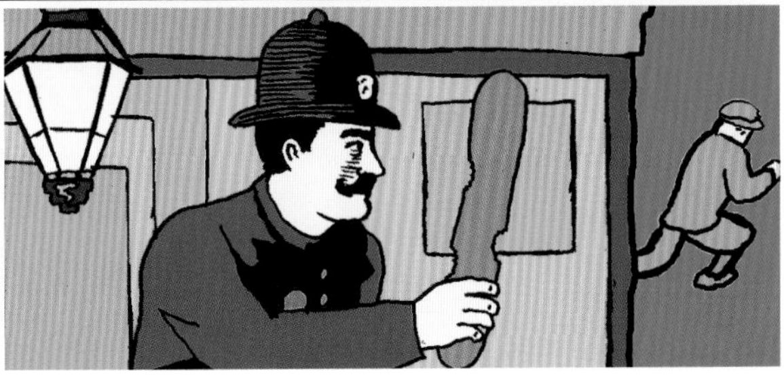
The policeman's nightstick was originally a large salami.

Lively and entertaining, Lazlo Haggard's latest book takes us right back to the days of caveman cuisine, and then moves forward again in a well-illustrated tour of the story of eating. When it all began, Haggard points out, many basic lessons we take for granted had yet to be learned, such as the size of an object determining a person's ability to put it in his or her mouth. As he puts it: "To discover the difference between something being edible or inedible, there was only one method: to eat it, or try to. Sometimes the combination of edible with inedible substances survived because the one made the other possible, a late example being the pebble and cheese omelettes still popular in France up to the late nineteenth century."

As food came to be better understood, it also became an avenue by which the ambitions of merchant adventurers could be realized. Following the invention of the sandwich by the Earl of Sandwich in 1652, ambitious men from all over Europe competed to present to the world the latest refinement on this startling invention. One man who underwent severe hardship as a result was the Count of Monte Cristos, who was jailed for attempting the merchandise of a sandwich containing ham, cheese and powered sugar; his story was later made into a famous novel, although they left out the sandwich parts. Haggard maintains that the imprisonment was probably the work of Monte Cristo's powerful rival, the ruthless Duke of Reubens, who was himself later killed during a scuffle with members of the sinister Garnish faction.

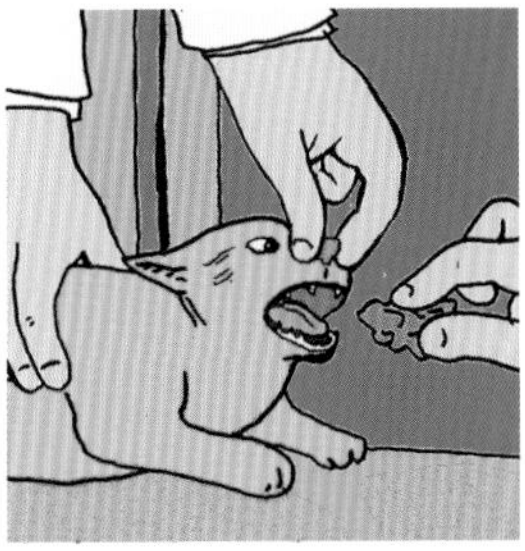
Cats are force-fed arugula.

Another theme of the book is the idea of food as tool. Even now, Haggard points out, we will still occasionally use a chicken leg as a baton, or map out an elaborate armored truck robbery scheme for our confederates using a plate of meatloaf, mashed potatoes, peas, and gravy; the peas represent the guards. But did you know the New York policeman's nightstick was originally a sausage? In 1837 police commissioner Thomas Haybright ordered that "each man on the force be given a large salami every week, of a size and hardship suitable for their personal defense; and let them eat what is left and thereby feed themselves". Criminals responded by carrying hunks of paté in their fists, which they would mush into the copper's faces if provoked. Another surprise is the early use of soup as currency.

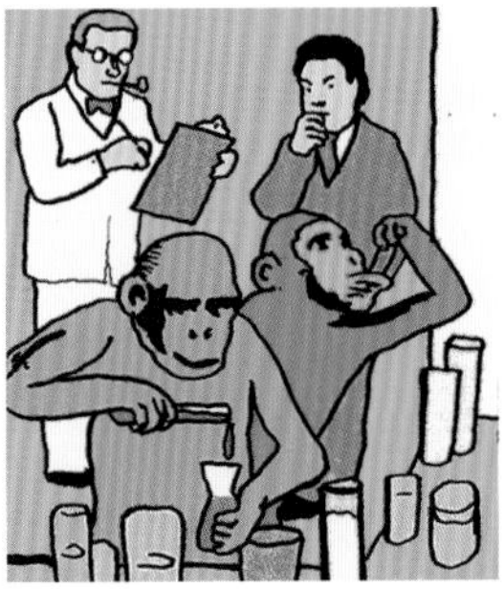
Chimpanzees: good at it?

Our current age Haggard defines as the Synthetic Age. He takes us through the new foods introduced by NASA as a side benefit of the space program, while explaining the reasons why such progress was initially flawed: "Artificial proteins were being produced at the outset which had been calculated to appeal to the astronauts, who were mostly hillbillies. This explains why Powdered Possum Vittles was the first space food to be introduced to the public.

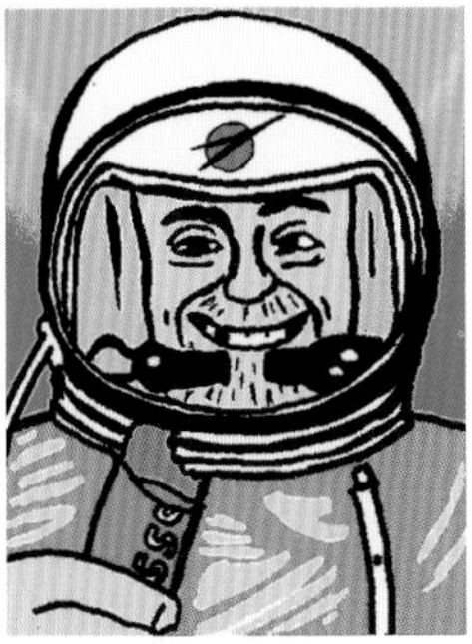
Hillbilly astronauts.

Experimental chimpanzees were also put to work in the lab, to test the theory that they would be good at it, and succeeded only in creating the astoundingly unpopular "ChocoSturgeon."TM Haggard then provides a surprising list of popular food substances of today which are synthetic, such as licorice, which is actually a mixture of mint and grape; and ones which involve animal-related procedures, such as capers, which are created by force-feeding arugula to cats and then waiting three hours.

But what does the future hold? Haggard scoffs at the popular image of people in silver jumpsuits swallowing pills; to him the coming years see an increase of radical new "super-diets." This chapter is the strangest of the book, filled with bizarre blueprints of theoretical soufflés and terrines, and an extended diatribe on the possible use of 'Star Trek' style matter transporters as a method of food delivery. It's an odd ending note to an otherwise solid and well-researched work.

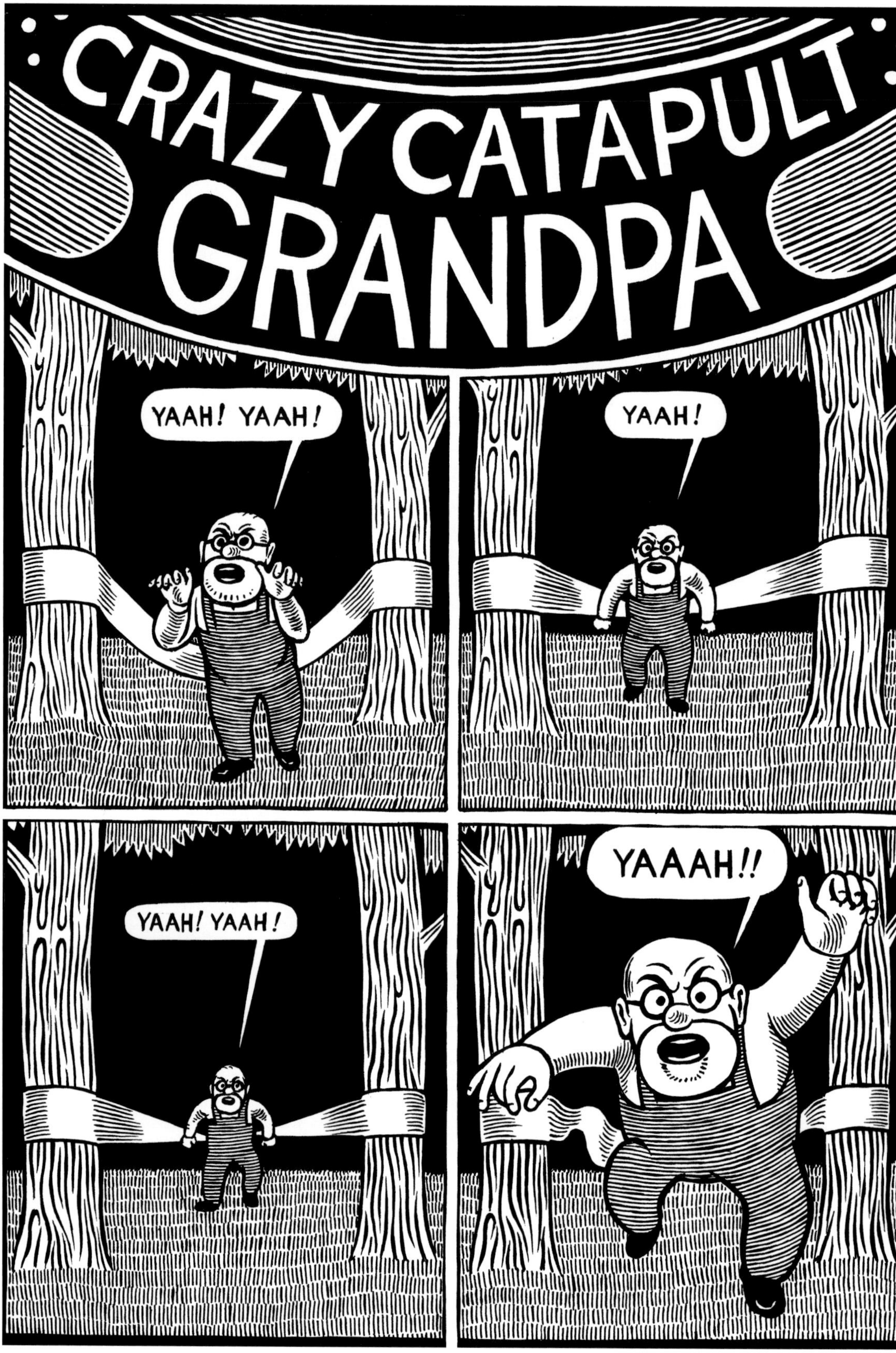
CRAZY CATAPULT GRANDPA
YAAH! YAAH!
YAAH!
YAAH! YAAH!
YAAAH!!

OSCAR MADNESS!!!

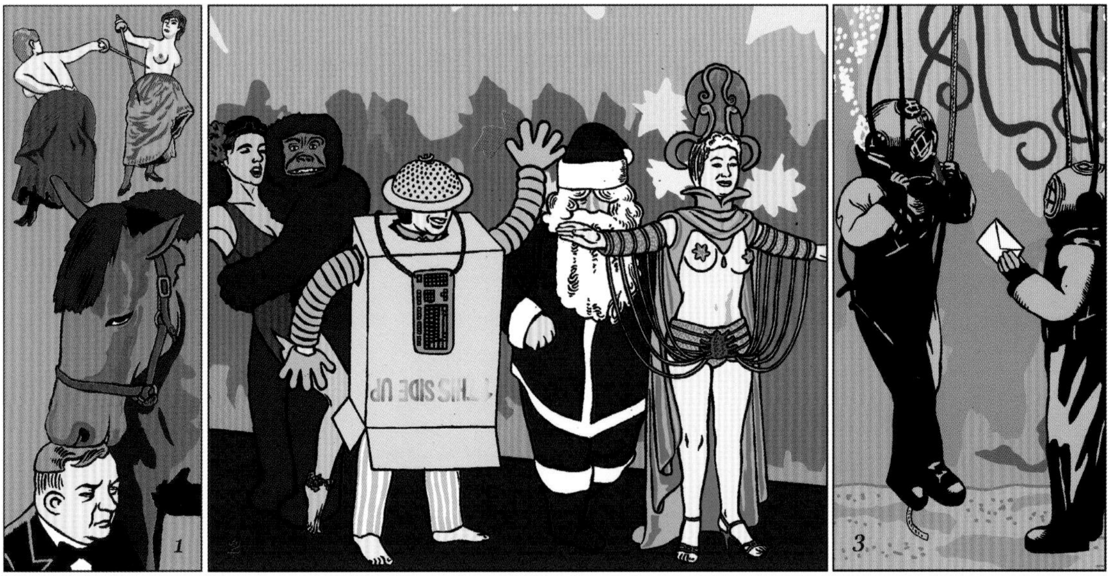
1
3

The Oscars are coming, and everyone is full of anticipation! (1) Will there be topless swordfighting? Will a horse eat a toupee? (2) What will the stars be wearing? We certainly saw some interesting outfits last year. (3) Everyone was wearing the same outfit at the 1947 Oscars - a diving suit! That's because the Oscars happened at the bottom of the ocean that year, for security reasons.

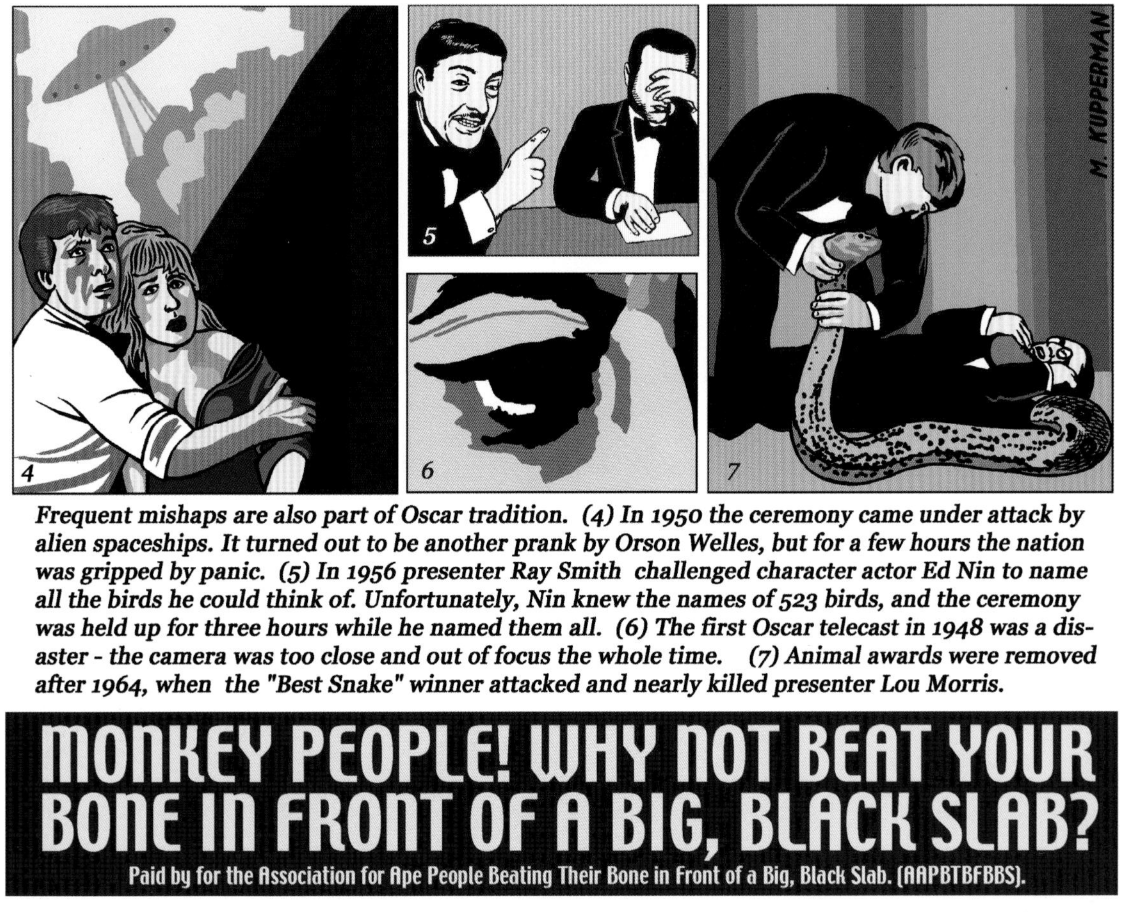
M. KUPPERMAN
4
5
6
7

Frequent mishaps are also part of Oscar tradition. (4) In 1950 the ceremony came under attack by alien spaceships. It turned out to be another prank by Orson Welles, but for a few hours the nation was gripped by panic. (5) In 1956 presenter Ray Smith challenged character actor Ed Nin to name all the birds he could think of. Unfortunately, Nin knew the names of 523 birds, and the ceremony was held up for three hours while he named them all. (6) The first Oscar telecast in 1948 was a disaster - the camera was too close and out of focus the whole time. (7) Animal awards were removed after 1964, when the "Best Snake" winner attacked and nearly killed presenter Lou Morris.

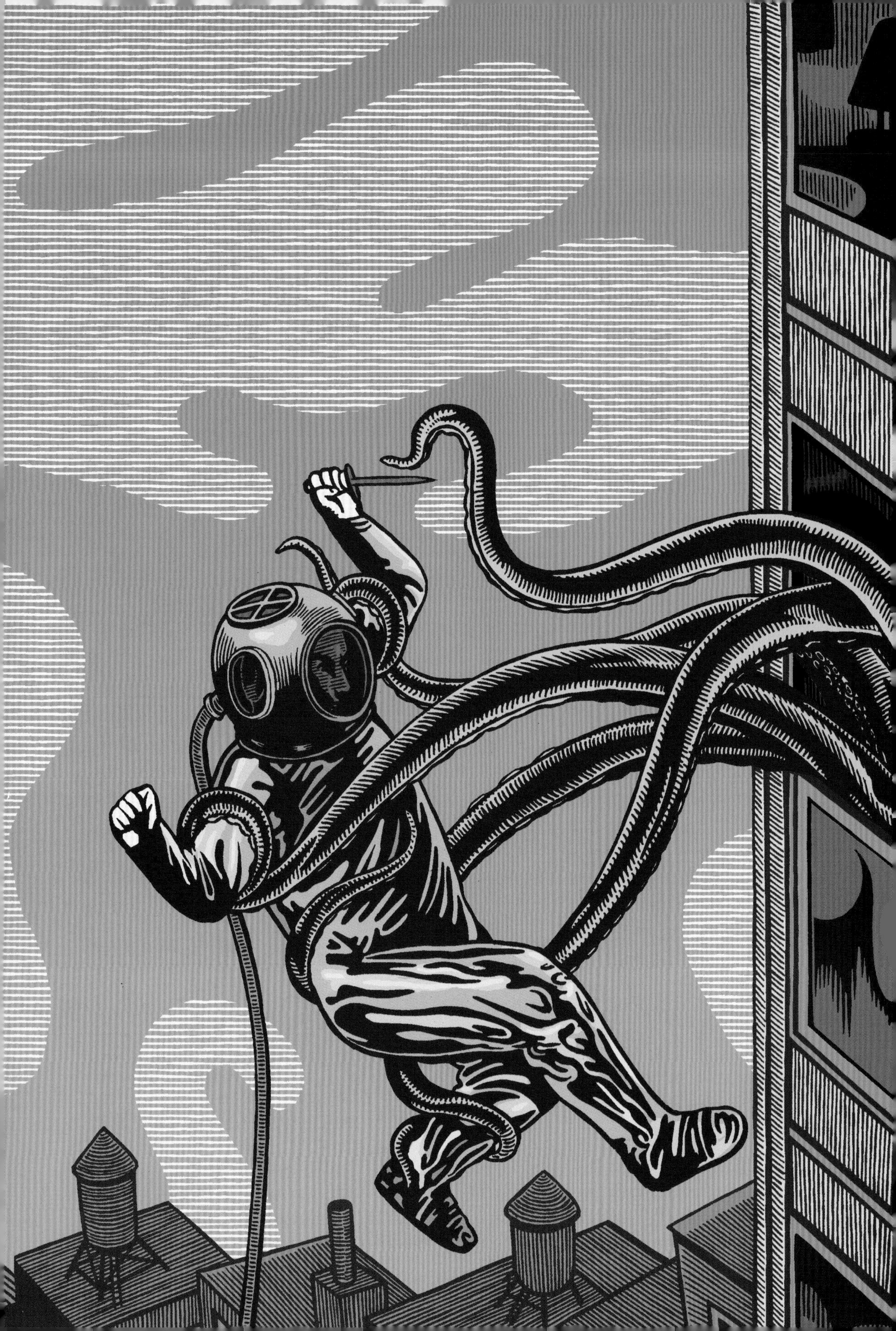

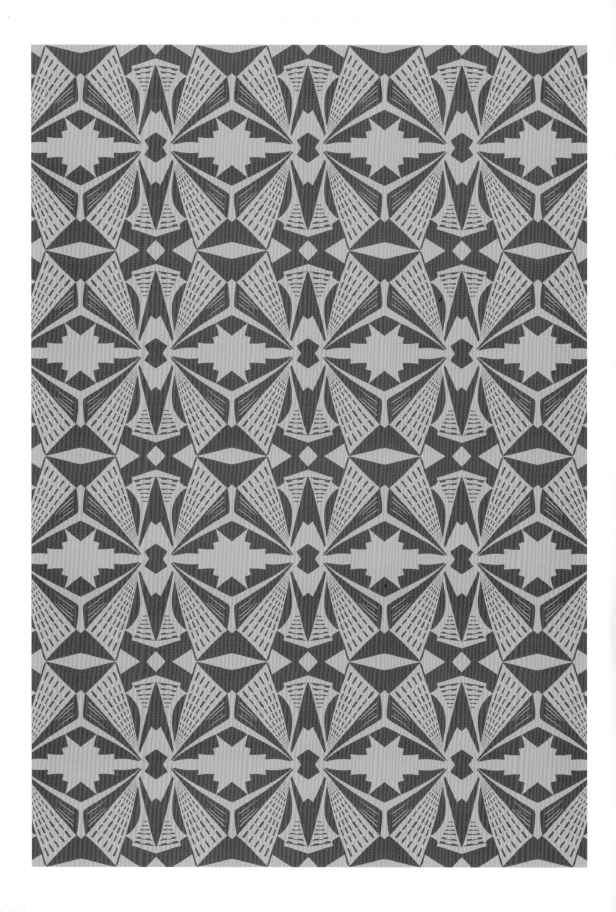

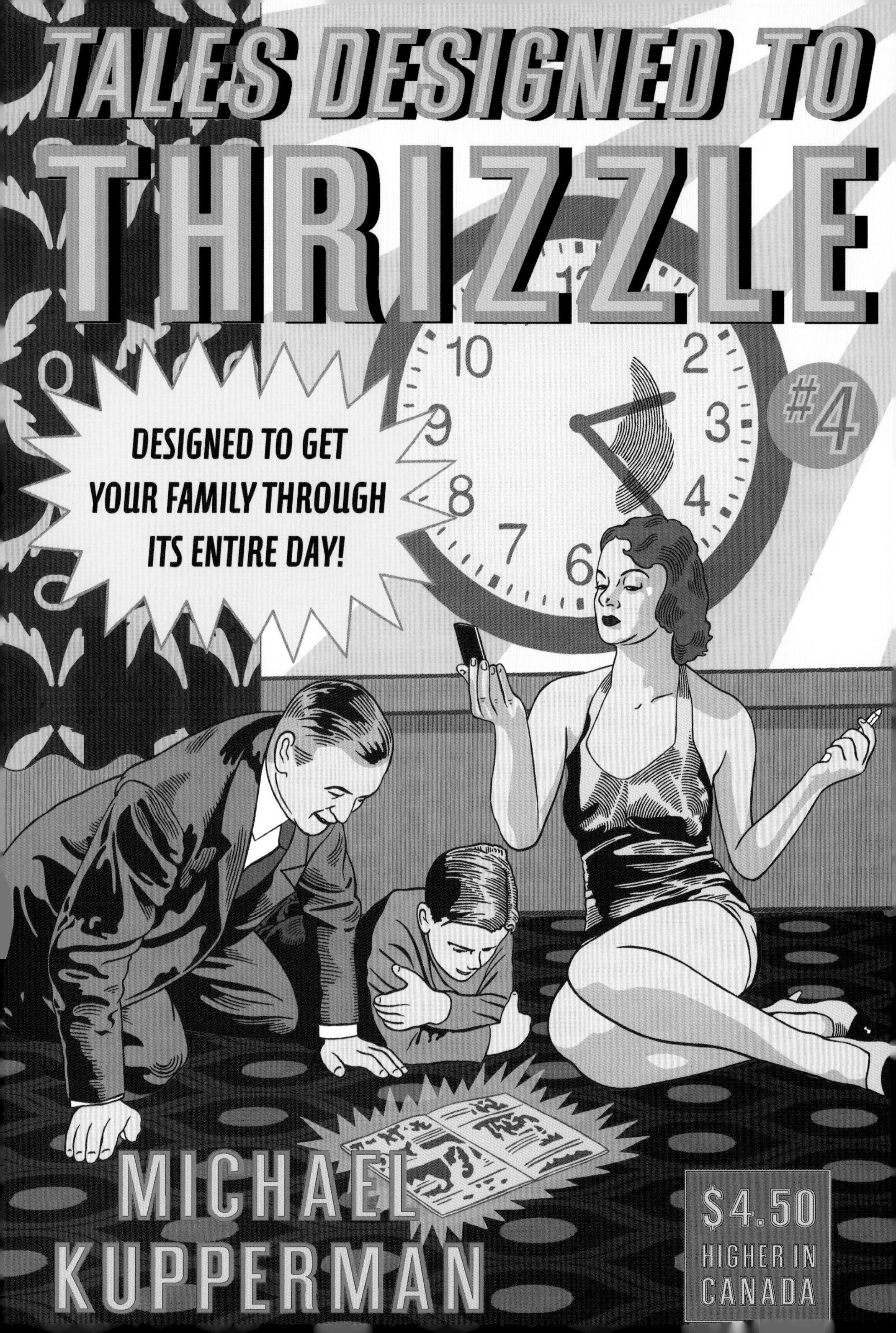

TALES DESIGNED TO
THRIZZLE
DESIGNED TO GET YOUR FAMILY THROUGH ITS ENTIRE DAY!
#4
MICHAEL KUPPERMAN
$4.50
HIGHER IN CANADA

A NEW FORMAT FOR THRIZZLE!

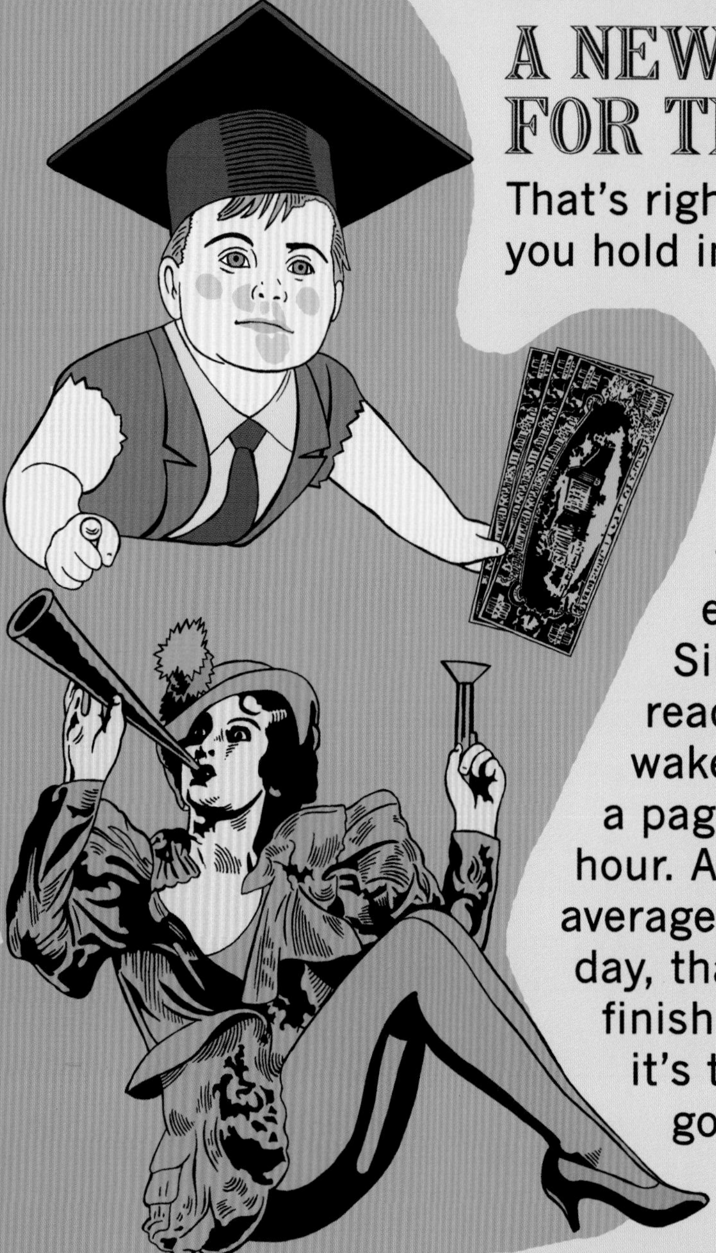

That's right! The Thrizzle you hold in your hands right now has been specially designed to help you through your entire day! Simply start reading when you wake up, and read a page every half hour. Assuming an average sixteen-hour day, that means you'll finish reading just as it's time for you to go to bed. It's just that simple.

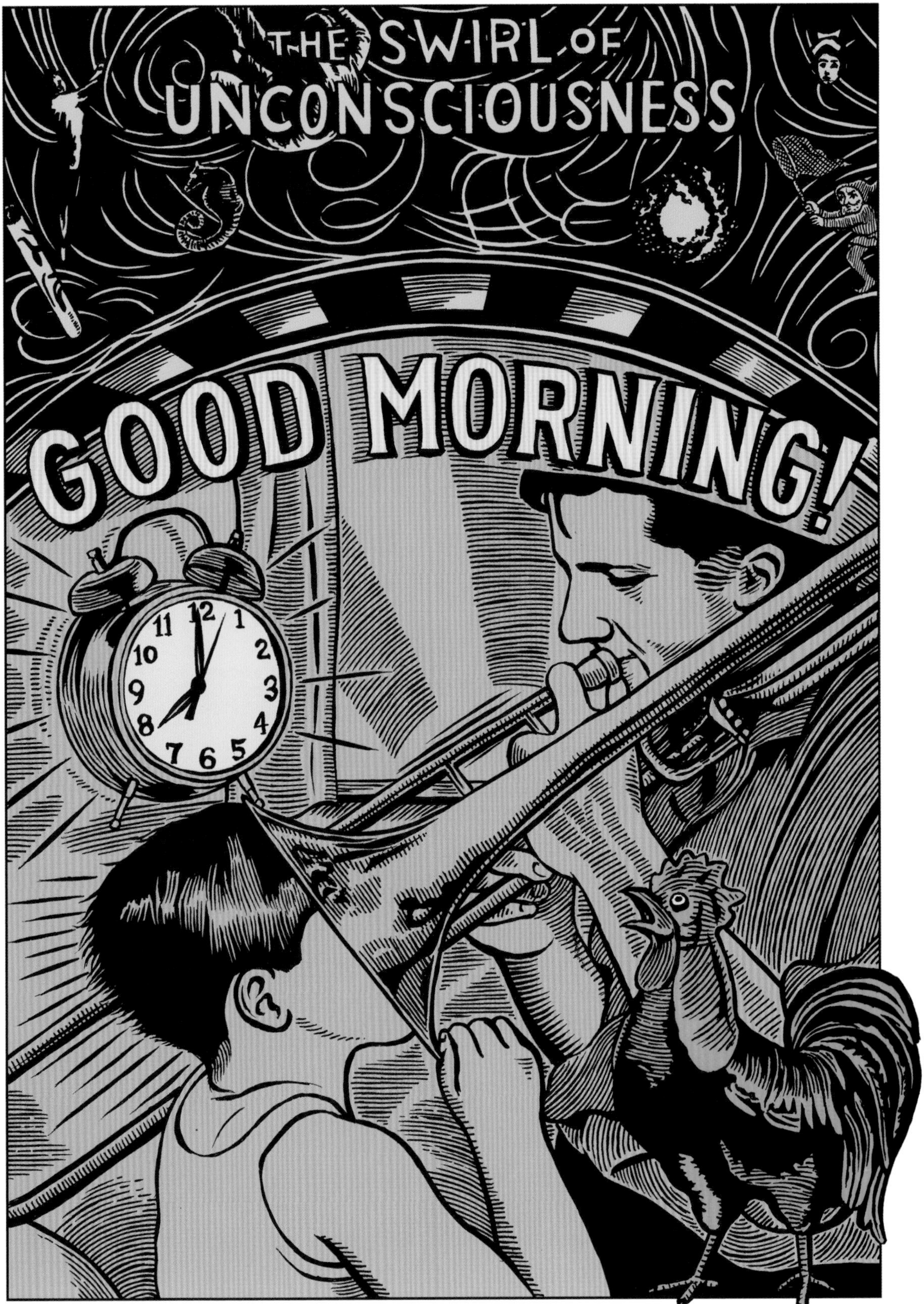
THE SWIRL OF
UNCONSCIOUSNESS
GOOD MORNING!
12 1 2 3 4 5 6 7 8 9 10 11

A.M. KIPPLE

A machine which scientists invented yesterday.

Morning Poem

Hey, Rosy-Fingered Dawn-
Knock it off, already.

AWAKE?

QUOTE FOR THE DAY
"Let each and every day mimic the full evolution of human history. I am a baboon in the morning and a caveman at breakfast. By the afternoon, I am enjoying the splendors of the Renaissance, and at night I fully enter the present age."
-Sir Alfred Chutney-Waistcoat

ASK PROFESSOR SEXY
Dear Professor Sexy: My brother-in-law hurt his leg over two months ago, and he still won't leave our basement. What should I do?
P.B., Duluth, WI.
Professor Sexy says: Why not have sex?

Isn't it time you went to the BATHROOM?
Paid for by the bathroom council.

EDITORIAL. Well, the bathroom council has been at it again. From what they tell us, you might be excused for thinking that "going to the bathroom" is a pure, natural thing, like drinking some water or abusing a prostitute. But "going to the bathroom" doesn't always mean going to the bathroom any more. Now many people go the bathroom where they shouldn't, which is to say they don't go to the bathroom at all. They go to the bathroom without going to the bathroom, if you catch my drift. Don't get me wrong, it's just that- (continued on page 138)

MY TWO CENTS *by an Average Joe*
No, it's not going to be like that this time. I'll tell you when we get there. Alright then goddamnit, forget it!

TRACK PREDICTIONS Chocolate Buttered Biscuit, Queen Nabob, 8 ½, Dom Bedooby, Snout the Whistler.

TODAY'S WEATHER

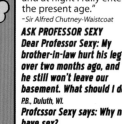

MORNING CHUCKLE

"Carrion, my wayward son!"

HUNGRY?
Why not eat some
BREAK FAST?

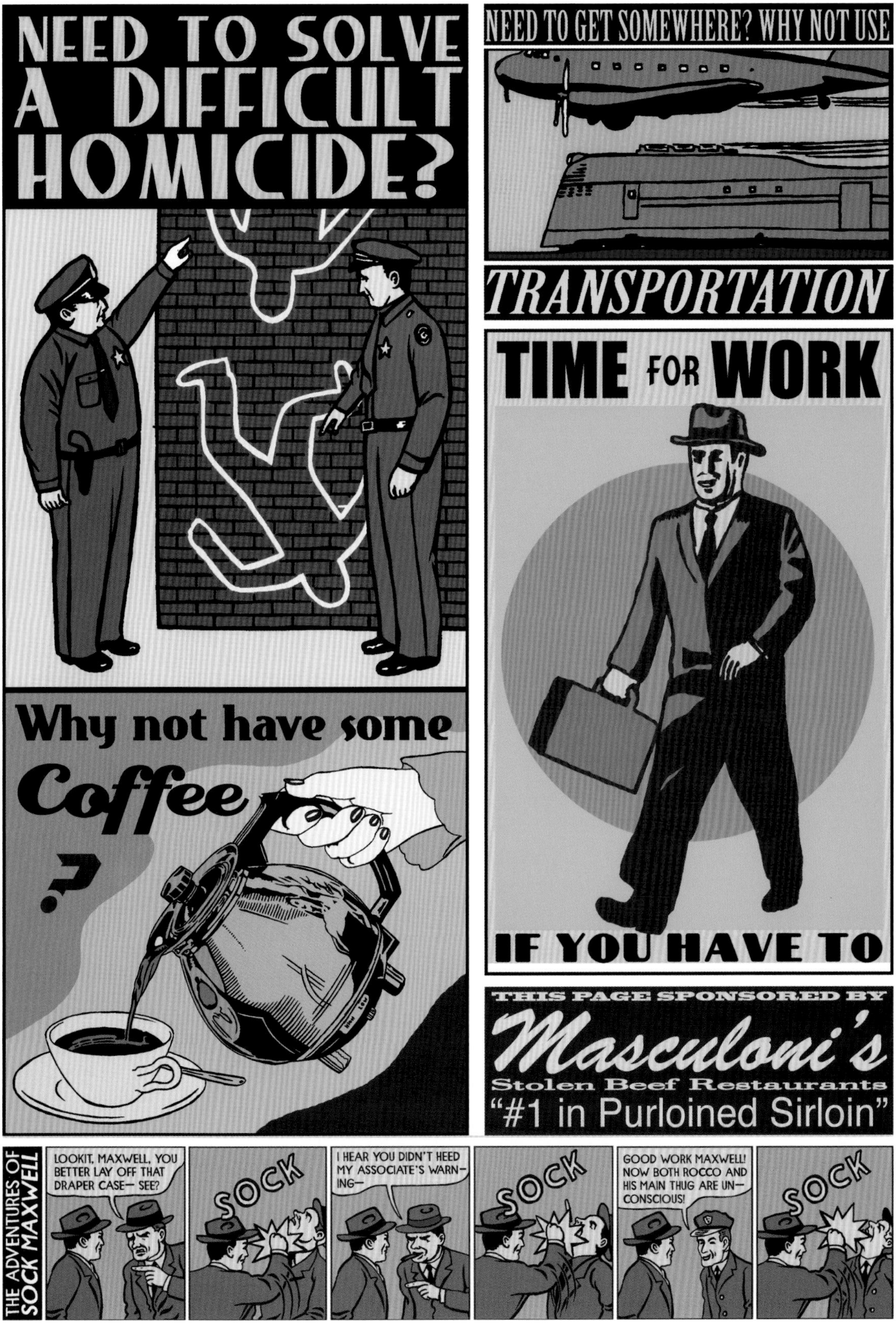

NEED TO SOLVE A DIFFICULT HOMICIDE?
Why not have some
Coffee
?
NEED TO GET SOMEWHERE? WHY NOT USE
TRANSPORTATION
TIME FOR WORK
IF YOU HAVE TO
THIS PAGE SPONSORED BY
Masculoni's
Stolen Beef Restaurants
"#1 in Purloined Sirloin"
THE ADVENTURES OF SOCK MAXWELL
LOOKIT, MAXWELL, YOU BETTER LAY OFF THAT DRAPER CASE— SEE?
SOCK
I HEAR YOU DIDN'T HEED MY ASSOCIATE'S WARN-ING—
SOCK
GOOD WORK MAXWELL! NOW BOTH ROCCO AND HIS MAIN THUG ARE UN-CONSCIOUS!
SOCK

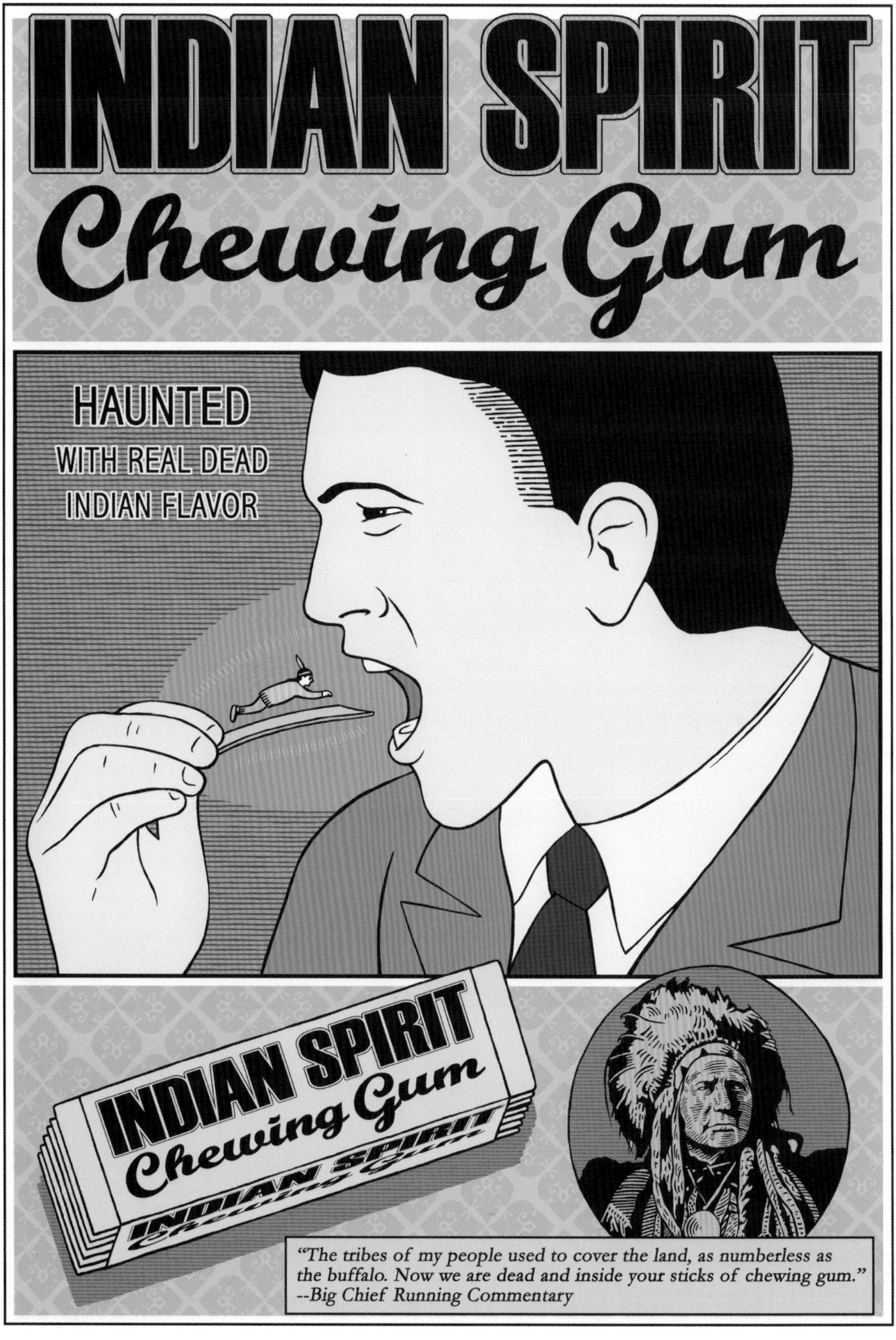
INDIAN SPIRIT
Chewing Gum
HAUNTED
WITH REAL DEAD
INDIAN FLAVOR
INDIAN SPIRIT
Chewing Gum
"The tribes of my people used to cover the land, as numberless as the buffalo. Now we are dead and inside your sticks of chewing gum."
--Big Chief Running Commentary

OFFICE LAFFS

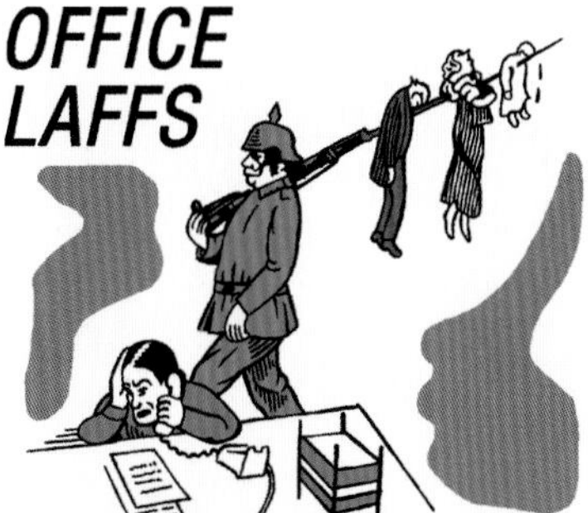

"I can't talk to you right now, Barry- my new boss is a murdering Hun!"

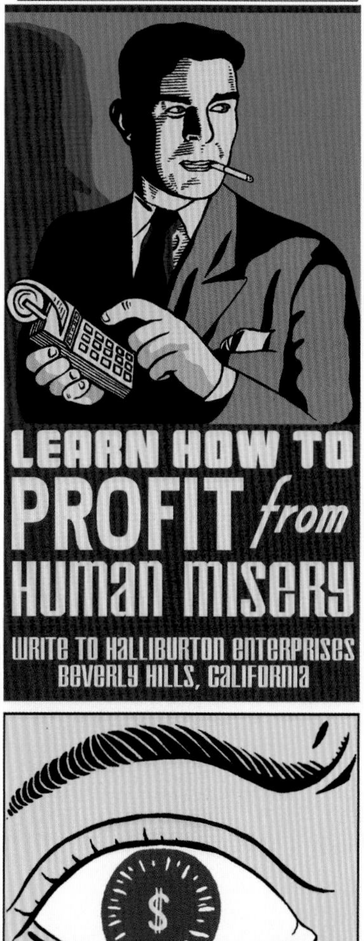

LEARN HOW TO
PROFIT from
HUMAN MISERY
WRITE TO HALLIBURTON ENTERPRISES
BEVERLY HILLS, CALIFORNIA

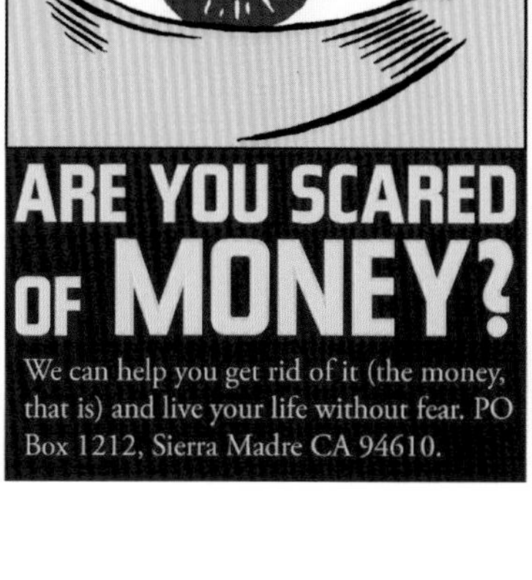

$
ARE YOU SCARED
OF MONEY?
We can help you get rid of it (the money, that is) and live your life without fear. PO Box 1212, Sierra Madre CA 94610.

Hey! Remember the 70s? Tuna Mac'n'Cheese, Flashing Mags, and those TV cops Twain & Einstein! Join us now for some selections from their comic book adventures.

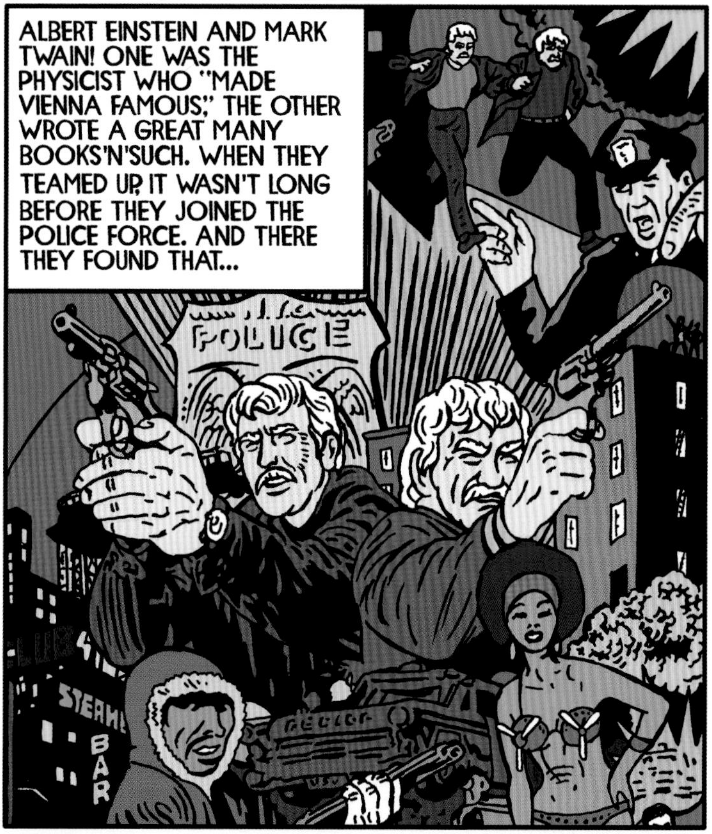

ALBERT EINSTEIN AND MARK TWAIN! ONE WAS THE PHYSICIST WHO "MADE VIENNA FAMOUS," THE OTHER WROTE A GREAT MANY BOOKS'N'SUCH. WHEN THEY TEAMED UP, IT WASN'T LONG BEFORE THEY JOINED THE POLICE FORCE. AND THERE THEY FOUND THAT...
POLICE
BAR

CRIME IS PUSHING THE LIMITS!

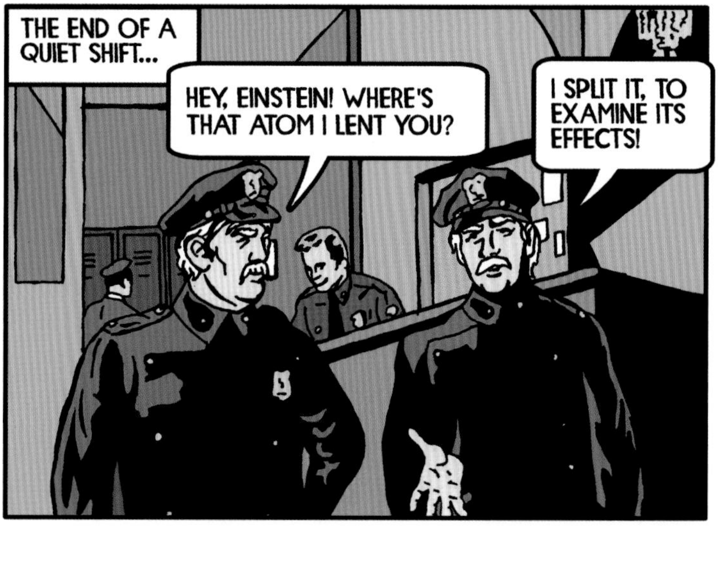

THE END OF A QUIET SHIFT...
HEY, EINSTEIN! WHERE'S THAT ATOM I LENT YOU?
I SPLIT IT, TO EXAMINE ITS EFFECTS!

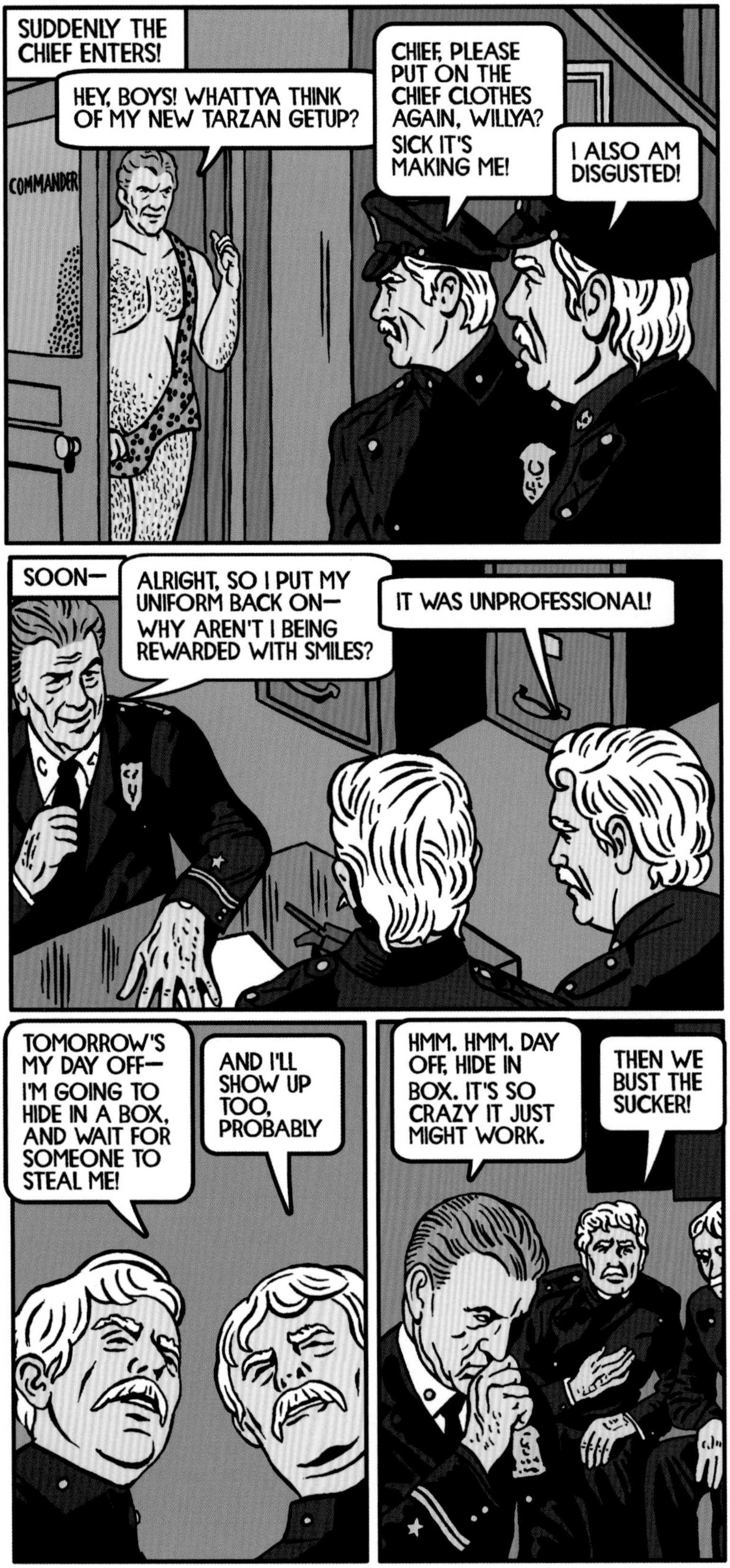
SUDDENLY THE CHIEF ENTERS!
HEY, BOYS! WHATTYA THINK OF MY NEW TARZAN GETUP?
COMMANDER
CHIEF, PLEASE PUT ON THE CHIEF CLOTHES AGAIN, WILLYA? SICK IT'S MAKING ME!
I ALSO AM DISGUSTED!
SOON—
ALRIGHT, SO I PUT MY UNIFORM BACK ON— WHY AREN'T I BEING REWARDED WITH SMILES?
IT WAS UNPROFESSIONAL!
TOMORROW'S MY DAY OFF— I'M GOING TO HIDE IN A BOX, AND WAIT FOR SOMEONE TO STEAL ME!
AND I'LL SHOW UP TOO, PROBABLY
HMM. HMM. DAY OFF, HIDE IN BOX. IT'S SO CRAZY IT JUST MIGHT WORK.
THEN WE BUST THE SUCKER!

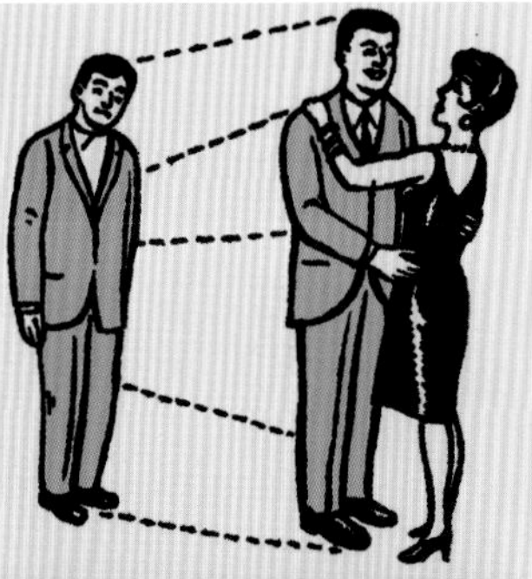

HOW TO AVOID BEING DOMINATED BY OTHERS

"Shut up, you worm! Listen to me!" How often have you heard those words? Prepare to hear them again! Shut up, you worm! Listen to me!

What's that, worm? You do not wish to be addressed as such? Such pain those words cause! You are constantly being crushed beneath the heel of life's boot., and therefore are a worm and hate to be addressed as such. It burns!

Pardon me, worm. You wish not to be dominated by others? Ah... ha ha ha ha ha ha ha ha ha! Very well, worm! Send $3.95 to: The Master, Suite 351, Royal Carp Hotel, NYC, and I shall tell you how. Ah ha ha ha ha ha ha ha ha ha!

Worm!

Learn to PICK POCKETS for FUN and PROFIT

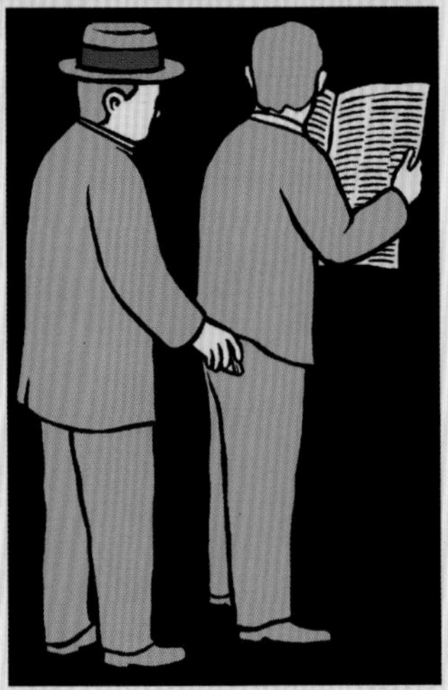

Write to Lefty, 10 Hangover Rd, New York

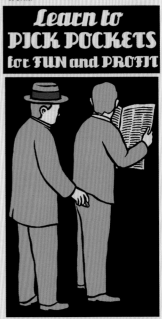

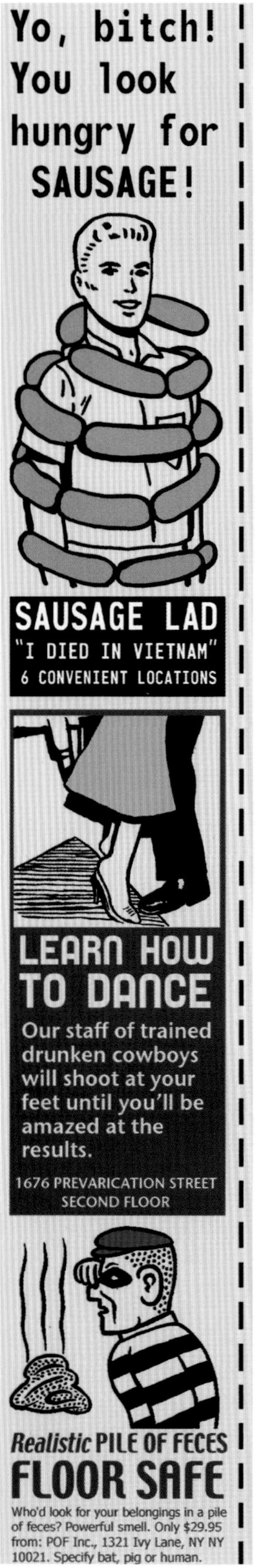
Yo, bitch! You look hungry for SAUSAGE!
SAUSAGE LAD
"I DIED IN VIETNAM"
6 CONVENIENT LOCATIONS
LEARN HOW TO DANCE
Our staff of trained drunken cowboys will shoot at your feet until you'll be amazed at the results.
1676 PREVARICATION STREET
SECOND FLOOR
Realistic PILE OF FECES
FLOOR SAFE
Who'd look for your belongings in a pile of feces? Powerful smell. Only $29.95 from: POF Inc., 1321 Ivy Lane, NY NY 10021. Specify bat, pig or human.

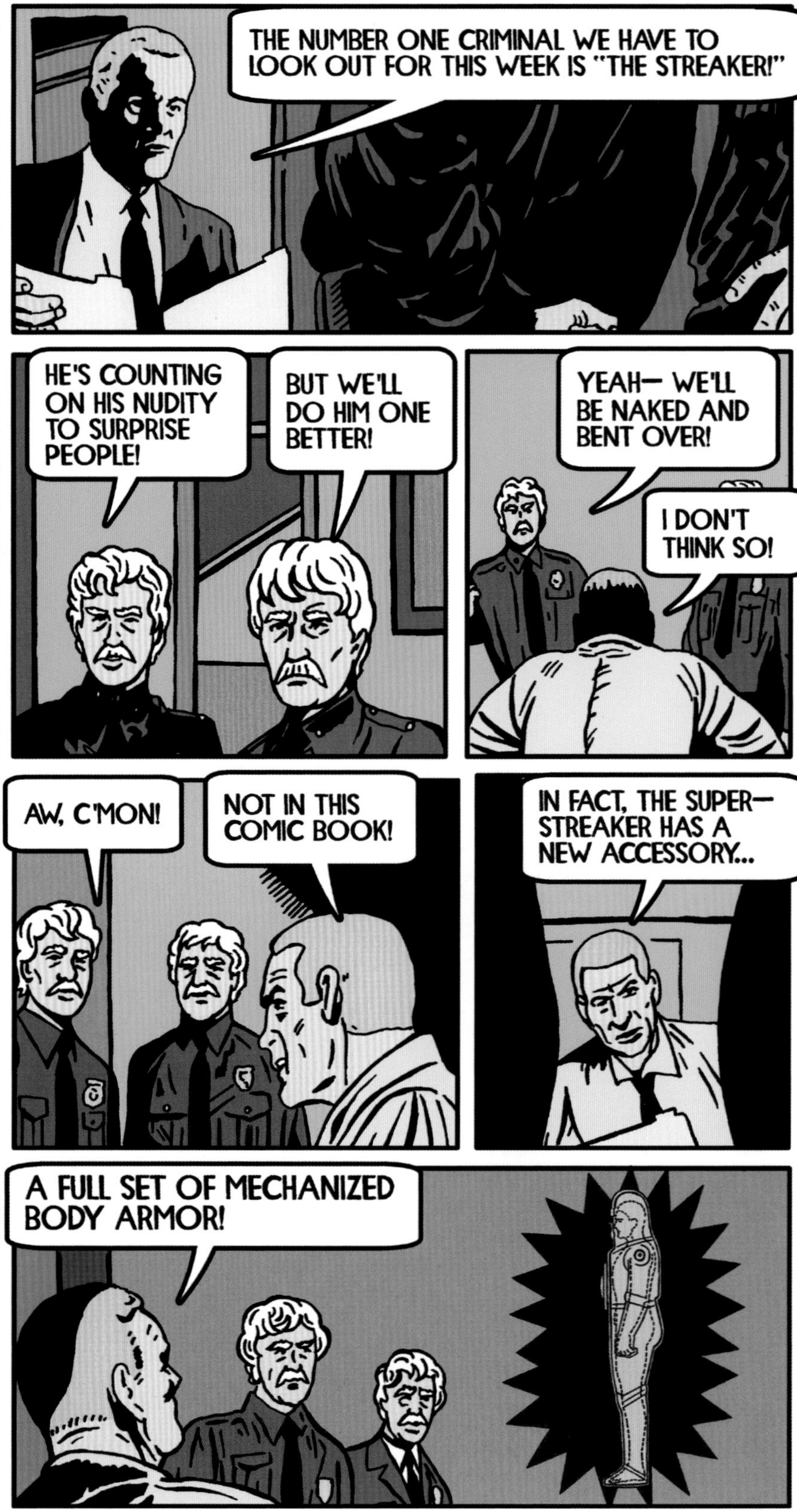
THE NUMBER ONE CRIMINAL WE HAVE TO LOOK OUT FOR THIS WEEK IS "THE STREAKER!"
HE'S COUNTING ON HIS NUDITY TO SURPRISE PEOPLE!
BUT WE'LL DO HIM ONE BETTER!
YEAH— WE'LL BE NAKED AND BENT OVER!
I DON'T THINK SO!
AW, C'MON!
NOT IN THIS COMIC BOOK!
IN FACT, THE SUPER— STREAKER HAS A NEW ACCESSORY...
A FULL SET OF MECHANIZED BODY ARMOR!

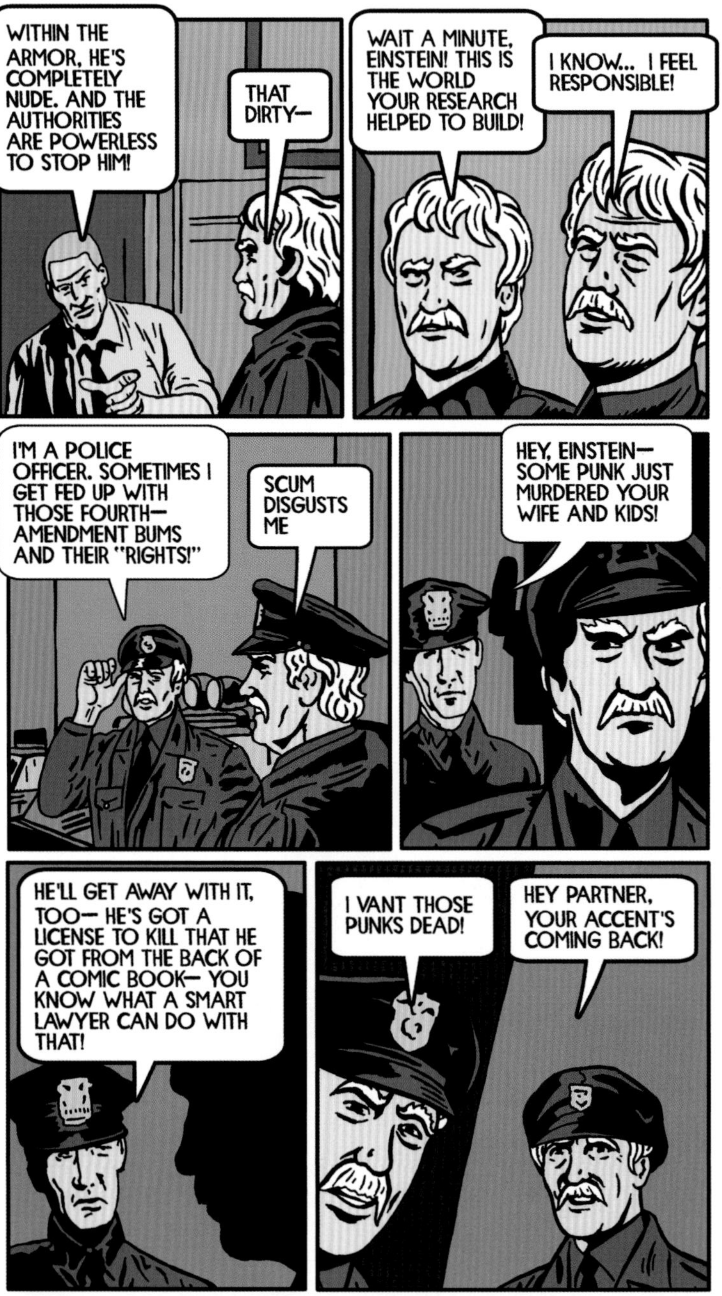
WITHIN THE ARMOR, HE'S COMPLETELY NUDE. AND THE AUTHORITIES ARE POWERLESS TO STOP HIM!
THAT DIRTY—
WAIT A MINUTE, EINSTEIN! THIS IS THE WORLD YOUR RESEARCH HELPED TO BUILD!
I KNOW... I FEEL RESPONSIBLE!
I'M A POLICE OFFICER. SOMETIMES I GET FED UP WITH THOSE FOURTH-AMENDMENT BUMS AND THEIR "RIGHTS!"
SCUM DISGUSTS ME
HEY, EINSTEIN— SOME PUNK JUST MURDERED YOUR WIFE AND KIDS!
HE'LL GET AWAY WITH IT, TOO— HE'S GOT A LICENSE TO KILL THAT HE GOT FROM THE BACK OF A COMIC BOOK— YOU KNOW WHAT A SMART LAWYER CAN DO WITH THAT!
I VANT THOSE PUNKS DEAD!
HEY PARTNER, YOUR ACCENT'S COMING BACK!

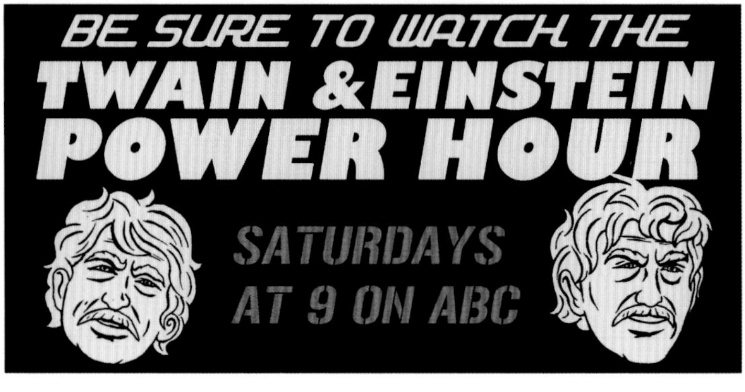
BE SURE TO WATCH THE
TWAIN &EINSTEIN POWER HOUR
SATURDAYS AT 9 ON ABC

ASK SWELLY

Dear Swelly,
The other day I mistakenly drank while standing in a freshly varnished storeroom. When I came to, my roommate Clive, who looks like a dressed-up fish, was standing in the doorway.

"Wuh... I had such an awful bump on my head." I said. "So... what's happening?"
"Was I in your dream?" he asked.
"Yeah, you were... you were delivering weird, non-sensical gossip in a shrill, unpleasant voice."
"Was I? Then hold on to your bits, love." he smirked.

"Shirley Pablum *has been loining it up with* Jason Rotunda, *despite his being fictional and a rotunda.*
Who was out the other night at super-hot club Dunghole until 9:30 the following evening? Not super-hot Paul Giamatti, *who got very angry when he found us lurking in his bushes... Spotted at Replica:* Lindsay Lohan *partying with* The Human Sneeze...*Hot new sensation* Celery Tomato *has been spotted incorporating himself, in contravention of several local regulations.*

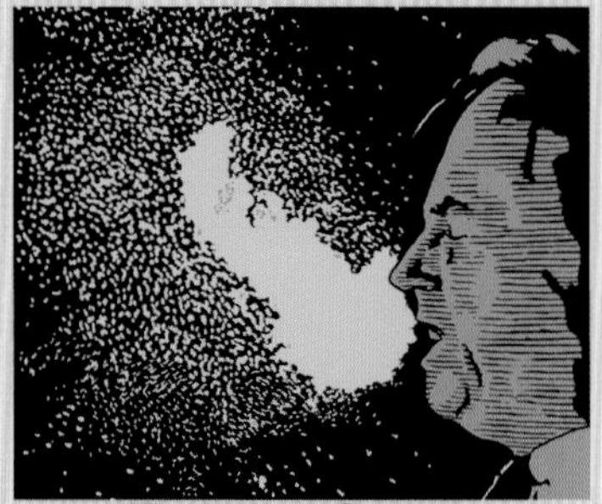
The Human Sneeze

"The other day I opened up a banana and there were raisins in it. Only in this town, kids, only in this town...
This is Oscar Wilde IV, saying don't be tiresome! I hate it when people are tiresome."

MICROSCOPIC GOINGS—ON ABOUT TOWN

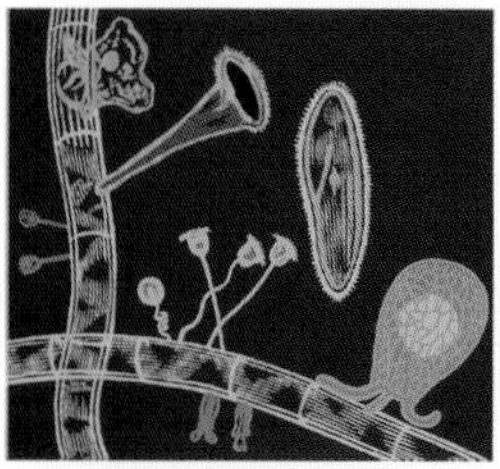

DOWNTOWN

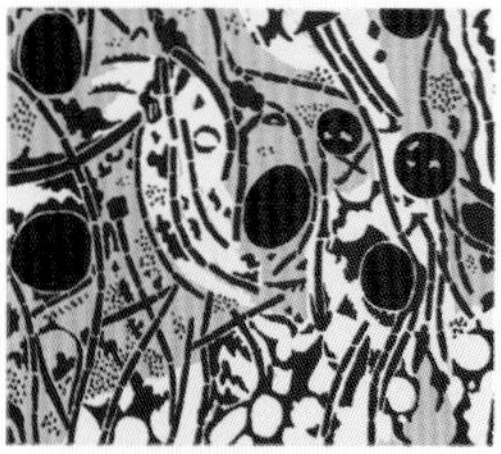

UPTOWN

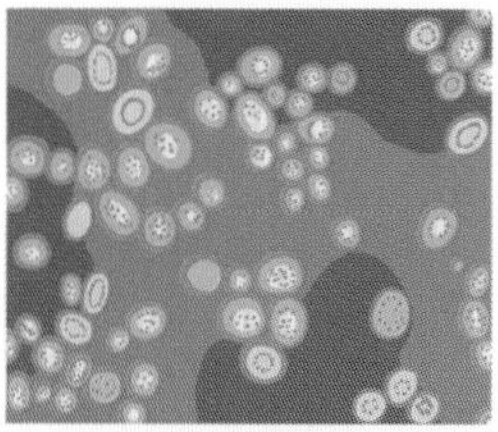

BROOKLYN

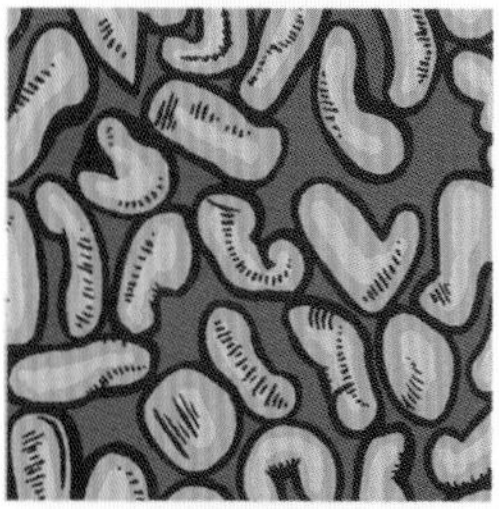

QUEENS

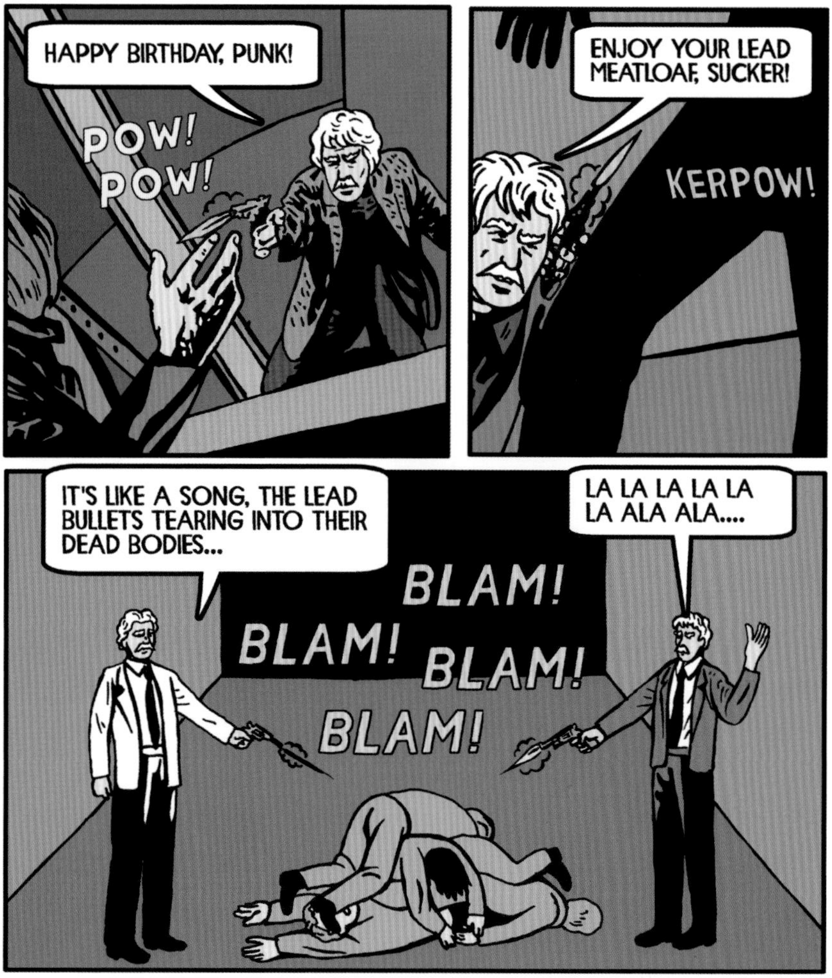
HAPPY BIRTHDAY, PUNK!
POW! POW!
ENJOY YOUR LEAD MEATLOAF, SUCKER!
KERPOW!
IT'S LIKE A SONG, THE LEAD BULLETS TEARING INTO THEIR DEAD BODIES...
LA LA LA LA LA LA ALA ALA....
BLAM! BLAM! BLAM! BLAM!

WE APOLOGIZE FOR THE UNUSUALLY HIGH LEVEL OF VIOLENCE IN THIS EPISODE OF **TWAIN AND EINSTEIN!** WE HAVE FIRED THE WRITER, AND RE—PLACED HIM WITH A NEW WRITER, WHO SEEMS FINE, EXCEPT THAT HE HAS AN OBSESSION WITH HIS NEIGHBOR, ONE NED R. FEINBERG. WE HOPE THIS WILL NOT HAVE AN ADVERSE EFFECT UPON HIS WRITING AS WE RETURN TO THE EXCITING ADVENTURES OF **TWAIN AND EINSTEIN!**

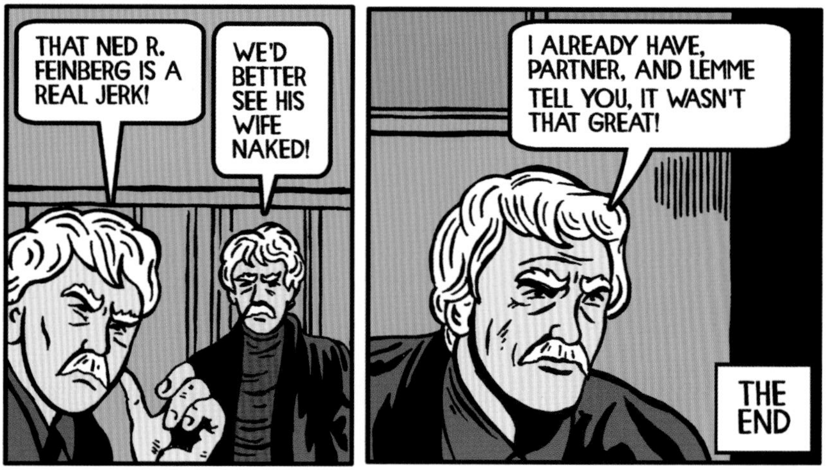
THAT NED R. FEINBERG IS A REAL JERK!
WE'D BETTER SEE HIS WIFE NAKED!
I ALREADY HAVE, PARTNER, AND LEMME TELL YOU, IT WASN'T THAT GREAT!
THE END

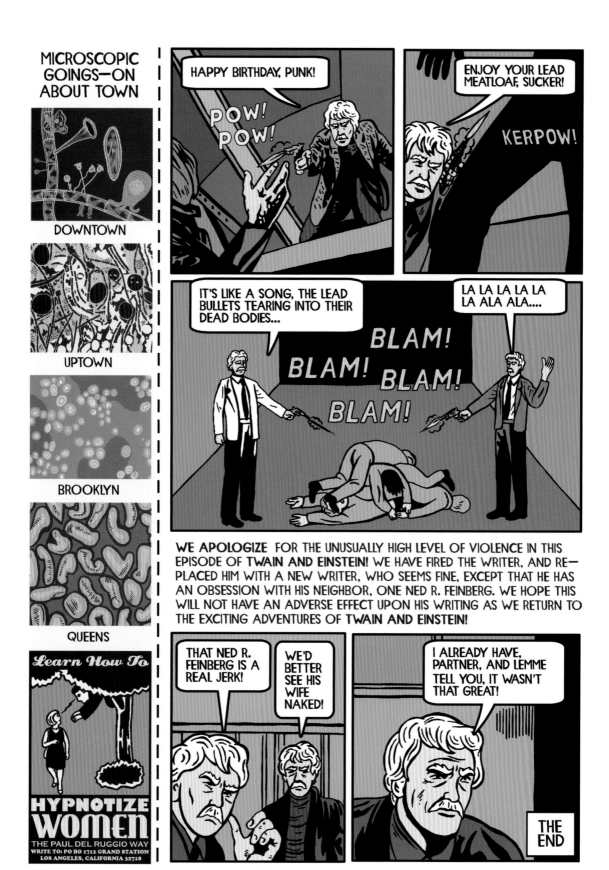

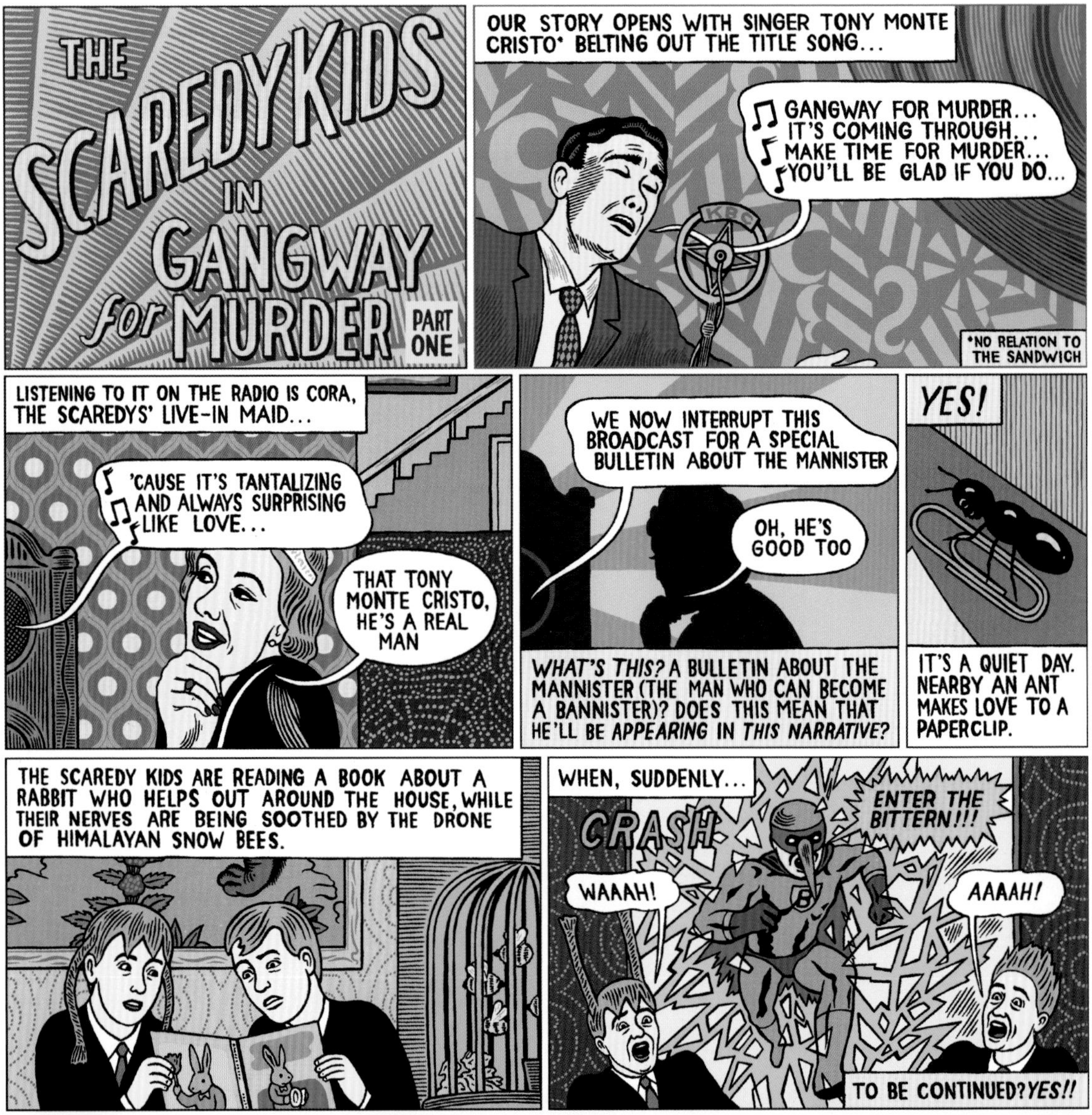
THE SCAREDY KIDS IN GANGWAY for MURDER PART ONE
OUR STORY OPENS WITH SINGER TONY MONTE CRISTO* BELTING OUT THE TITLE SONG...
♫ GANGWAY FOR MURDER... IT'S COMING THROUGH... MAKE TIME FOR MURDER... YOU'LL BE GLAD IF YOU DO...
*NO RELATION TO THE SANDWICH
LISTENING TO IT ON THE RADIO IS CORA, THE SCAREDYS' LIVE-IN MAID...
♫ 'CAUSE IT'S TANTALIZING AND ALWAYS SURPRISING LIKE LOVE...
THAT TONY MONTE CRISTO, HE'S A REAL MAN
WE NOW INTERRUPT THIS BROADCAST FOR A SPECIAL BULLETIN ABOUT THE MANNISTER
OH, HE'S GOOD TOO
WHAT'S THIS? A BULLETIN ABOUT THE MANNISTER (THE MAN WHO CAN BECOME A BANNISTER)? DOES THIS MEAN THAT HE'LL BE APPEARING IN THIS NARRATIVE?
YES!
IT'S A QUIET DAY. NEARBY AN ANT MAKES LOVE TO A PAPERCLIP.
THE SCAREDY KIDS ARE READING A BOOK ABOUT A RABBIT WHO HELPS OUT AROUND THE HOUSE, WHILE THEIR NERVES ARE BEING SOOTHED BY THE DRONE OF HIMALAYAN SNOW BEES.
WHEN, SUDDENLY...
CRASH
ENTER THE BITTERN!!!
WAAAH!
AAAAH!
TO BE CONTINUED? YES!!

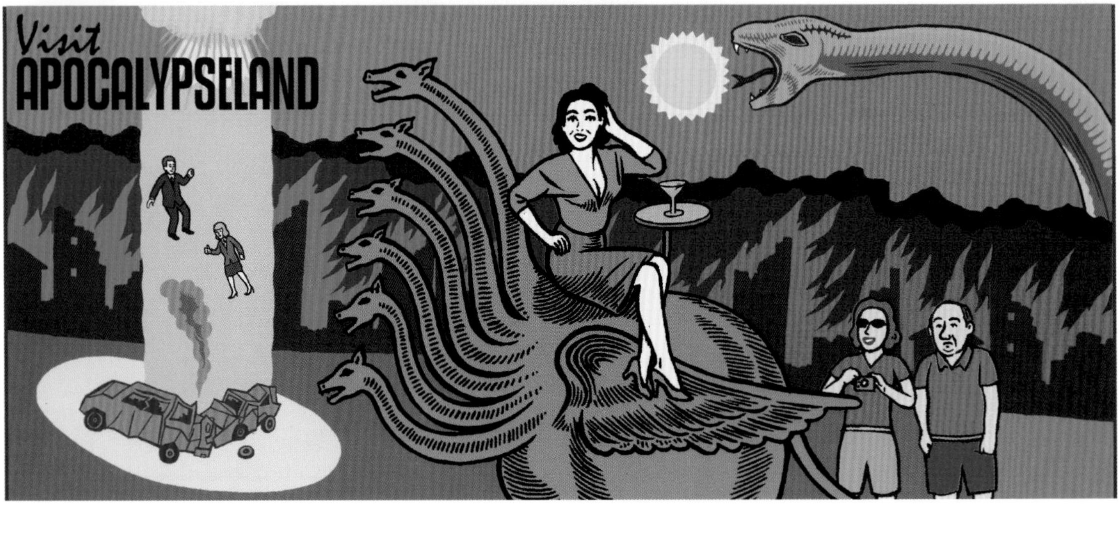
Visit
APOCALYPSELAND

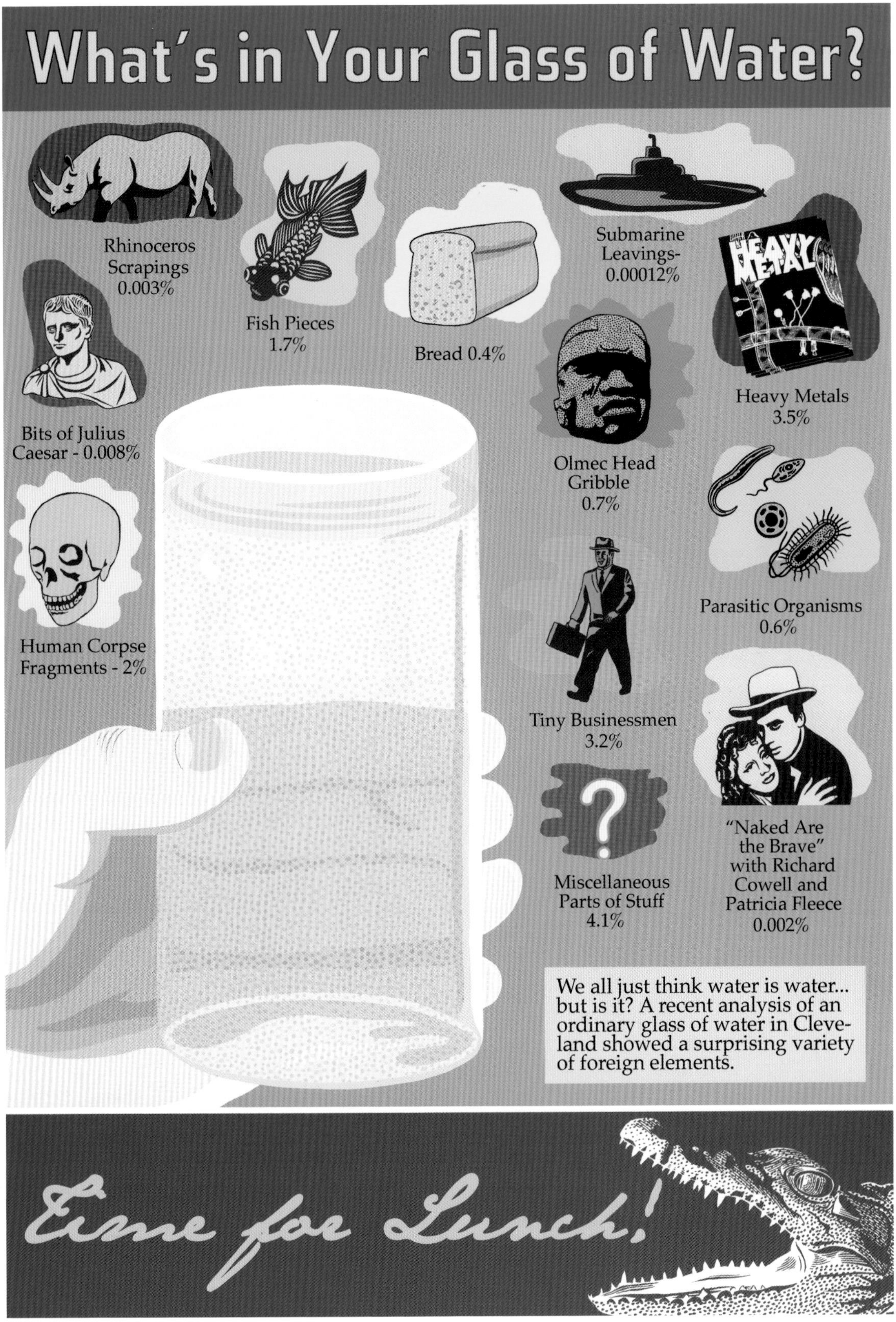
What's in Your Glass of Water?
Rhinoceros Scrapings 0.003%
Fish Pieces 1.7%
Bread 0.4%
Submarine Leavings- 0.00012%
HEAVY METAL
Bits of Julius Caesar - 0.008%
Heavy Metals 3.5%
Olmec Head Gribble 0.7%
Human Corpse Fragments - 2%
Parasitic Organisms 0.6%
Tiny Businessmen 3.2%
?
"Naked Are the Brave" with Richard Cowell and Patricia Fleece 0.002%
Miscellaneous Parts of Stuff 4.1%
We all just think water is water... but is it? A recent analysis of an ordinary glass of water in Cleveland showed a surprising variety of foreign elements.
Time for Lunch!

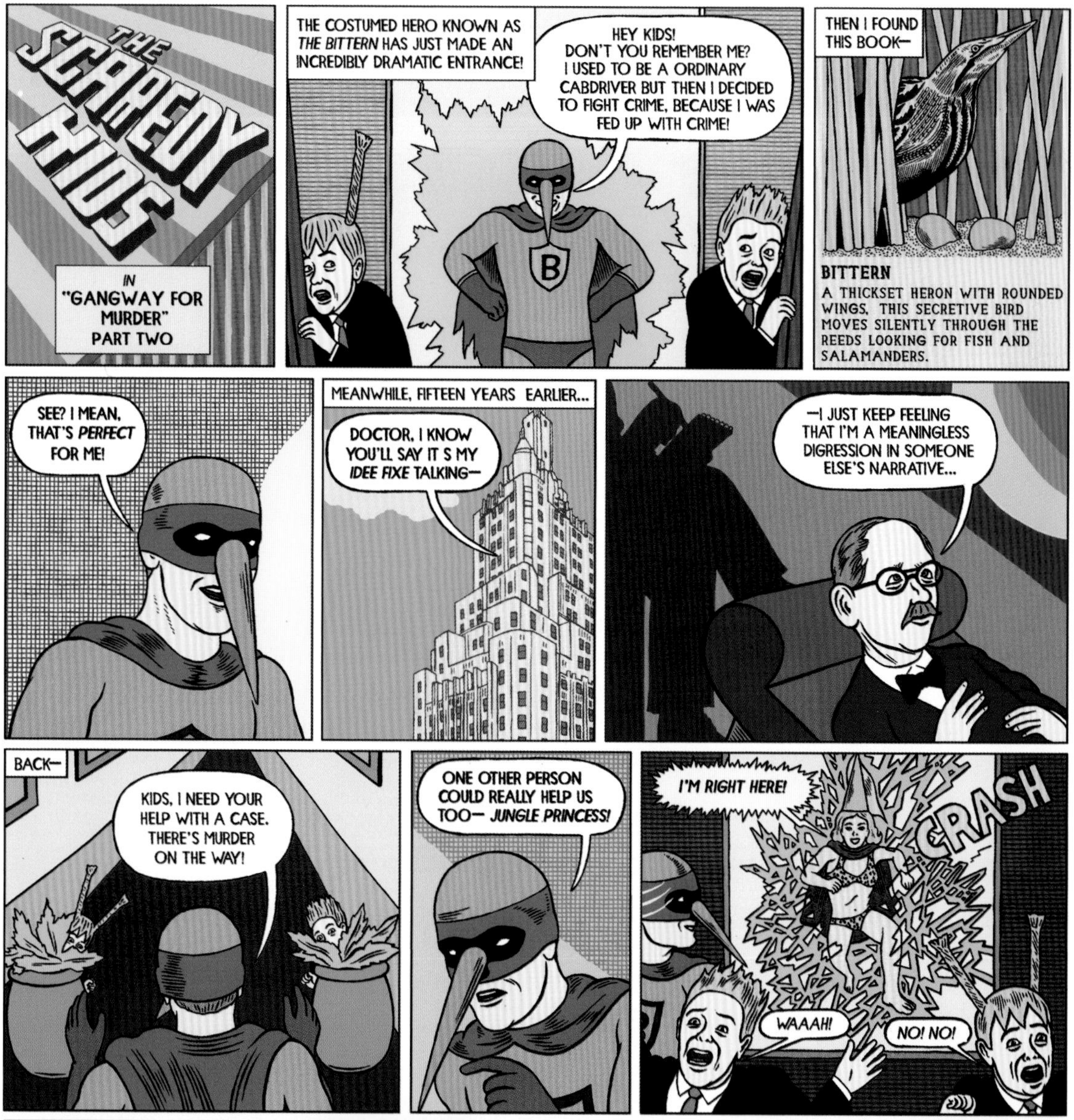
THE SCAREDY KIDS
IN "GANGWAY FOR MURDER" PART TWO
THE COSTUMED HERO KNOWN AS *THE BITTERN* HAS JUST MADE AN INCREDIBLY DRAMATIC ENTRANCE!
HEY KIDS! DON'T YOU REMEMBER ME? I USED TO BE A ORDINARY CABDRIVER BUT THEN I DECIDED TO FIGHT CRIME, BECAUSE I WAS FED UP WITH CRIME!
B
THEN I FOUND THIS BOOK—
BITTERN
A THICKSET HERON WITH ROUNDED WINGS, THIS SECRETIVE BIRD MOVES SILENTLY THROUGH THE REEDS LOOKING FOR FISH AND SALAMANDERS.
SEE? I MEAN, THAT'S *PERFECT* FOR ME!
MEANWHILE, FIFTEEN YEARS EARLIER...
DOCTOR, I KNOW YOU'LL SAY IT S MY *IDEE FIXE* TALKING—
—I JUST KEEP FEELING THAT I'M A MEANINGLESS DIGRESSION IN SOMEONE ELSE'S NARRATIVE...
BACK—
KIDS, I NEED YOUR HELP WITH A CASE. THERE'S MURDER ON THE WAY!
ONE OTHER PERSON COULD REALLY HELP US TOO— *JUNGLE PRINCESS!*
I'M RIGHT HERE!
CRASH
WAAAH!
NO! NO!

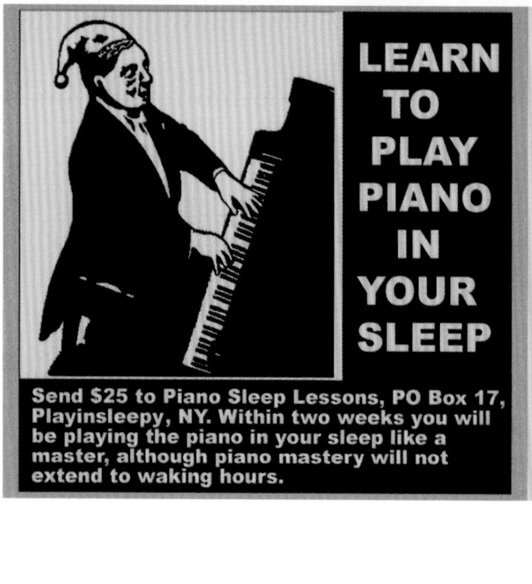
LEARN TO PLAY PIANO IN YOUR SLEEP
Send $25 to Piano Sleep Lessons, PO Box 17, Playinsleepy, NY. Within two weeks you will be playing the piano in your sleep like a master, although piano mastery will not extend to waking hours.

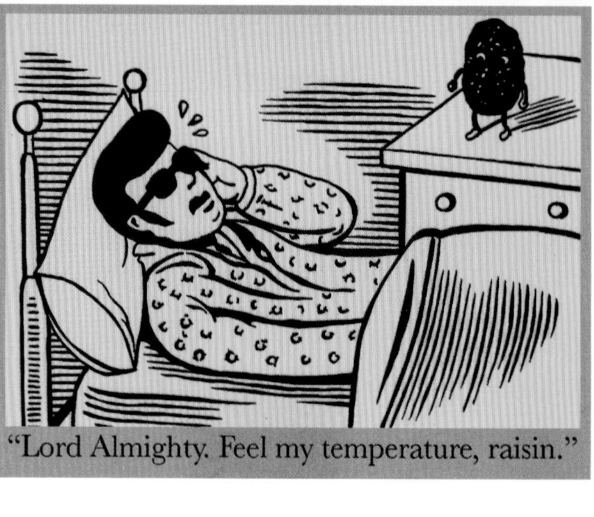
"Lord Almighty. Feel my temperature, raisin."

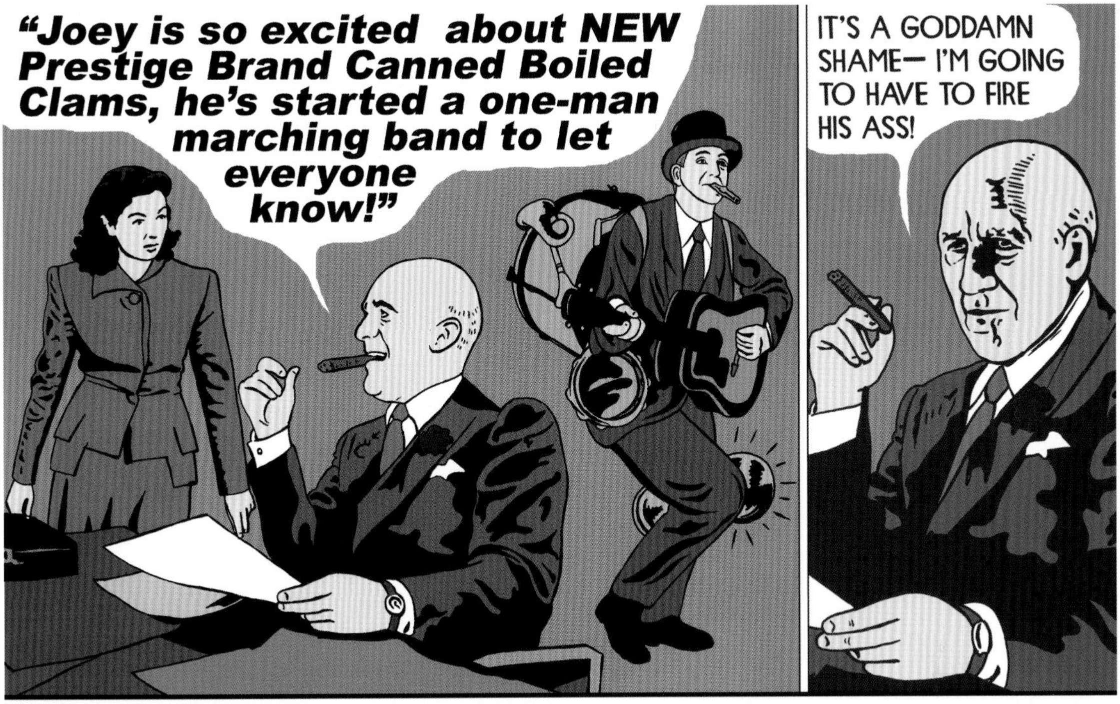
"Joey is so excited about NEW Prestige Brand Canned Boiled Clams, he's started a one-man marching band to let everyone know!"
IT'S A GODDAMN SHAME— I'M GOING TO HAVE TO FIRE HIS ASS!

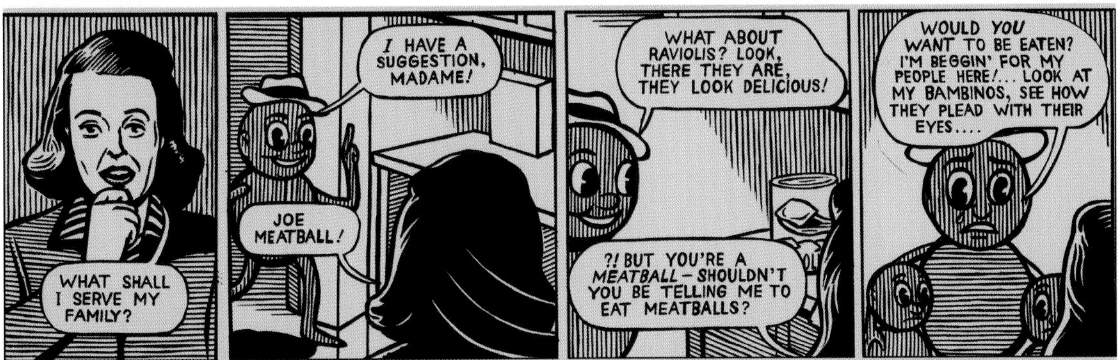
WHAT SHALL I SERVE MY FAMILY?
I HAVE A SUGGESTION, MADAME!
JOE MEATBALL!
WHAT ABOUT RAVIOLIS? LOOK, THERE THEY ARE, THEY LOOK DELICIOUS!
?! BUT YOU'RE A MEATBALL – SHOULDN'T YOU BE TELLING ME TO EAT MEATBALLS?
WOULD YOU WANT TO BE EATEN? I'M BEGGIN' FOR MY PEOPLE HERE!... LOOK AT MY BAMBINOS, SEE HOW THEY PLEAD WITH THEIR EYES....

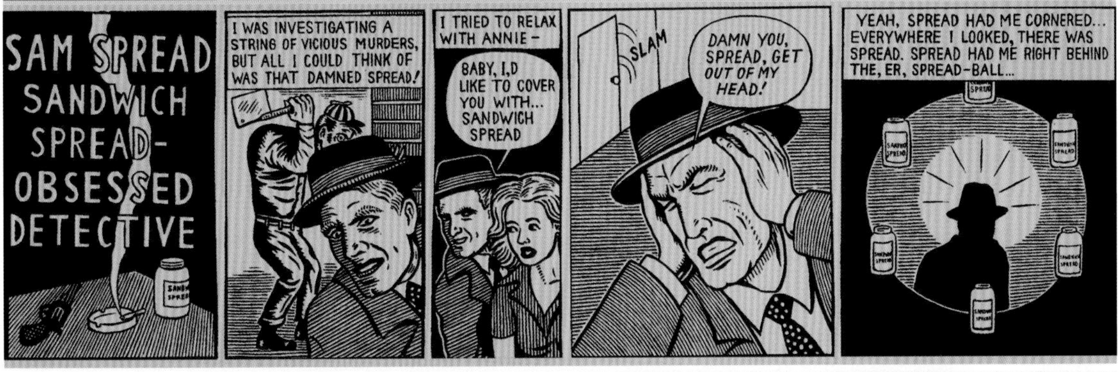
SAM SPREAD
SANDWICH SPREAD-OBSESSED DETECTIVE
I WAS INVESTIGATING A STRING OF VICIOUS MURDERS, BUT ALL I COULD THINK OF WAS THAT DAMNED SPREAD!
I TRIED TO RELAX WITH ANNIE –
BABY, I,D LIKE TO COVER YOU WITH... SANDWICH SPREAD
SLAM
DAMN YOU, SPREAD, GET OUT OF MY HEAD!
YEAH, SPREAD HAD ME CORNERED... EVERYWHERE I LOOKED, THERE WAS SPREAD. SPREAD HAD ME RIGHT BEHIND THE, ER, SPREAD-BALL...

Toilet Whore. More than the name implies.

When we first started Toilet Whore, we only dealt with two things: toilets and whores. Then we moved into toilet whores.

Now we're involved in many industries: Housing, Medicine, Media, Banking, Munitions, Aerospace, and much, much more.

And yes, we're still involved with toilets and whores. It's in our name.

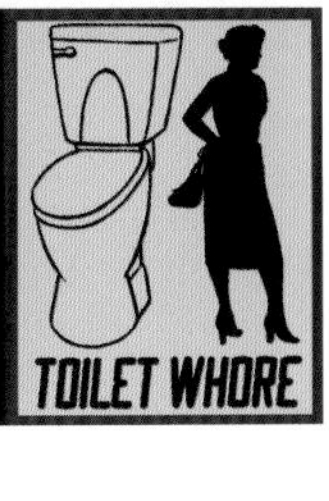
TOILET WHORE

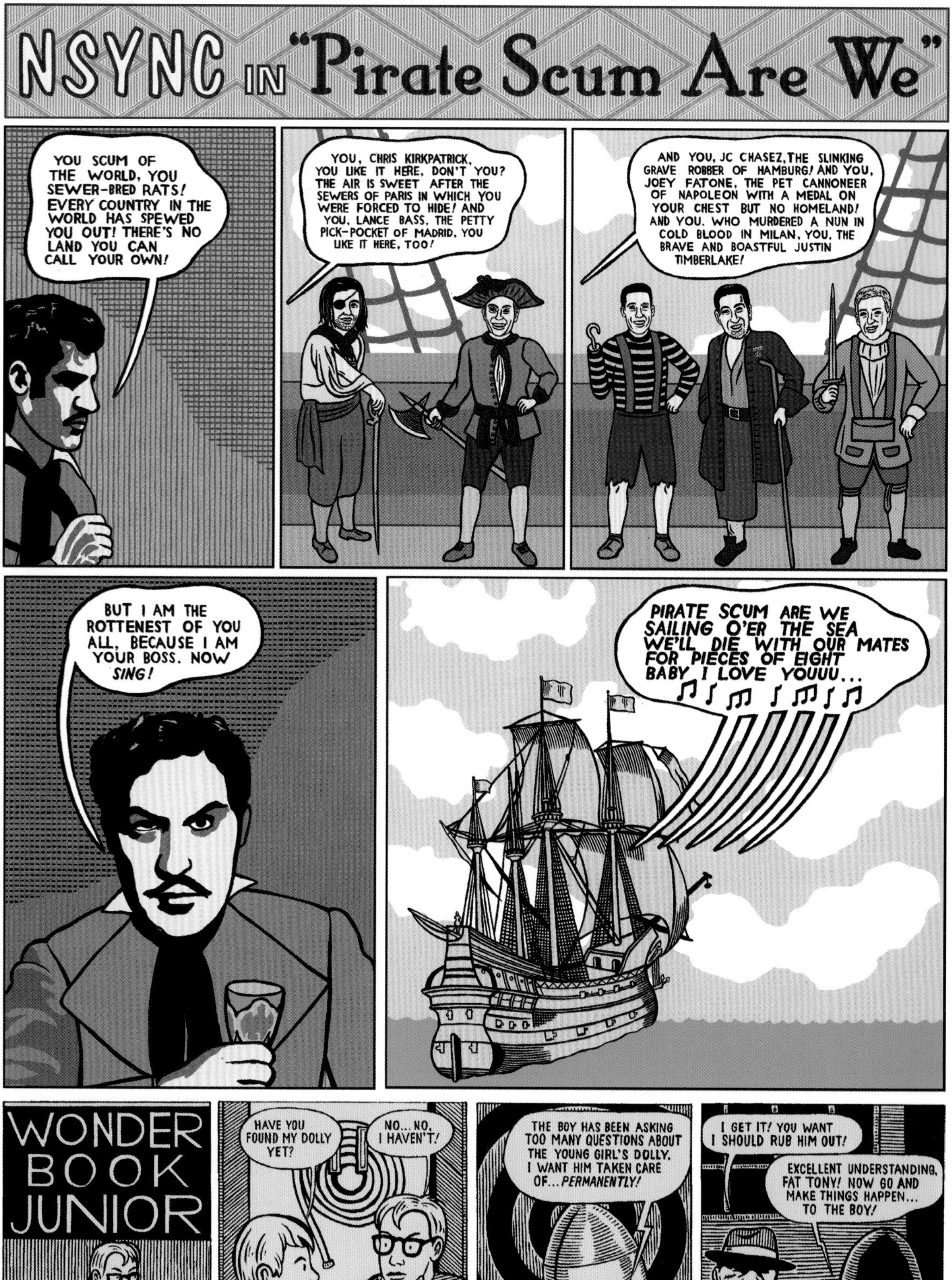
NSYNC IN "Pirate Scum Are We"
YOU SCUM OF THE WORLD, YOU SEWER-BRED RATS! EVERY COUNTRY IN THE WORLD HAS SPEWED YOU OUT! THERE'S NO LAND YOU CAN CALL YOUR OWN!
YOU, CHRIS KIRKPATRICK, YOU LIKE IT HERE, DON'T YOU? THE AIR IS SWEET AFTER THE SEWERS OF PARIS IN WHICH YOU WERE FORCED TO HIDE! AND YOU, LANCE BASS, THE PETTY PICK-POCKET OF MADRID, YOU LIKE IT HERE, TOO!
AND YOU, JC CHASEZ, THE SLINKING GRAVE ROBBER OF HAMBURG! AND YOU, JOEY FATONE, THE PET CANNONEER OF NAPOLEON WITH A MEDAL ON YOUR CHEST BUT NO HOMELAND! AND YOU, WHO MURDERED A NUN IN COLD BLOOD IN MILAN, YOU, THE BRAVE AND BOASTFUL JUSTIN TIMBERLAKE!
BUT I AM THE ROTTENEST OF YOU ALL, BECAUSE I AM YOUR BOSS. NOW SING!
PIRATE SCUM ARE WE SAILING O'ER THE SEA WE'LL DIE WITH OUR MATES FOR PIECES OF EIGHT BABY I LOVE YOUUU...

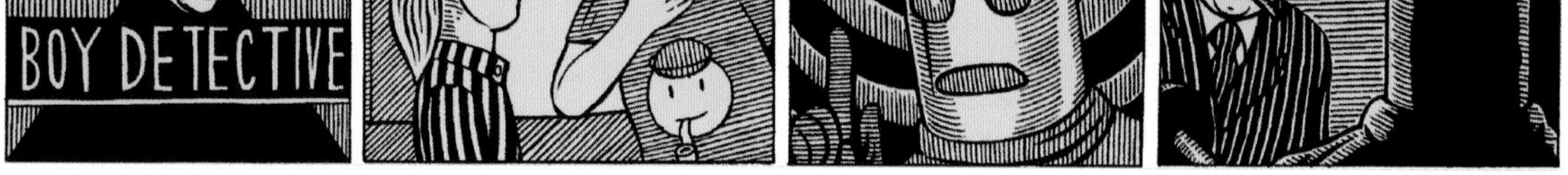
WONDER BOOK JUNIOR
BOY DETECTIVE
HAVE YOU FOUND MY DOLLY YET?
NO... NO, I HAVEN'T!
THE BOY HAS BEEN ASKING TOO MANY QUESTIONS ABOUT THE YOUNG GIRL'S DOLLY. I WANT HIM TAKEN CARE OF... PERMANENTLY!
I GET IT! YOU WANT I SHOULD RUB HIM OUT!
EXCELLENT UNDERSTANDING, FAT TONY! NOW GO AND MAKE THINGS HAPPEN... TO THE BOY!

Afternoon Childrens Corner

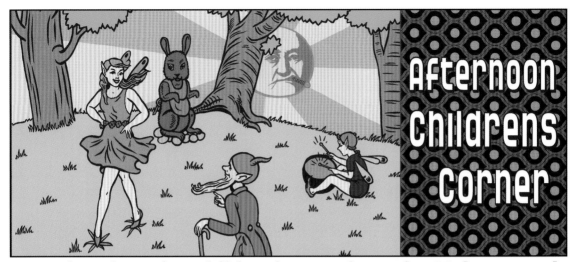

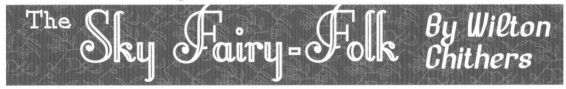

Here's a charming children's story from the 19th century!

The Sky Fairy-Folk

By Wilton Chithers

Little Joseph lay trembling on the hard wooden floor. Although it was very cold, he was shivering from the fever that hunger brings, for he had eaten nothing but a little turnip paste a few days earlier. He lived on the floor of a man named Grimwich, who had added him to his collection of boys after his Mother had been bitten by an Irishman and died in terrible pain, first losing her wits and foaming at the mouth. Grimwich trained the boys to do crimes, and beat them regularly; it was a hard life for a little lad like Joseph, who was six years old and slightly built.

Grimwich entered the room and grabbed the boy by the scraps of his collar. "Get up!" he snarled, "I'm selling you to the Jew." The Jew was actually a Chinaman, noted for his meanness, who ran a number of carts in the wharf district. Joseph tightened with misery as he was dragged out the door. He stepped on a rat, who bit him in frustration, and the mud outside the door sucked at the scabs on his ankles.

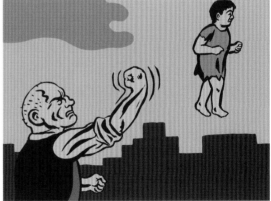

Suddenly an amazing thing happened- Joseph began to float into the sky! Grimwich made an attempt to capture him, but he was too slow, and Joseph rose steadily upwards. Soon he was among the clouds, and the fluffy, pristine whiteness was a stark contrast to the filthy, grimy world he had left behind, with its constant excrement and brutal vomit. His progress slowed, and he found himself gently placed on one of the clouds.

Then the sky fairy-folk came out to greet him, and oh! how magnificent their clothing was, all made out of rainbows and cloud pieces and loose scraps of weather. They were smiling at Joseph, and making gestures of friendship, and no-one was kicking or beating him. Joseph cleared his throat nervously. "Am I to live here now?"

"No," came the reply. "You are dead now, and although you may stay here for a short while, you must soon return to the ground to be eaten by worms."

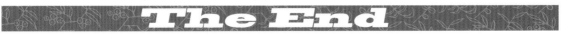

The End

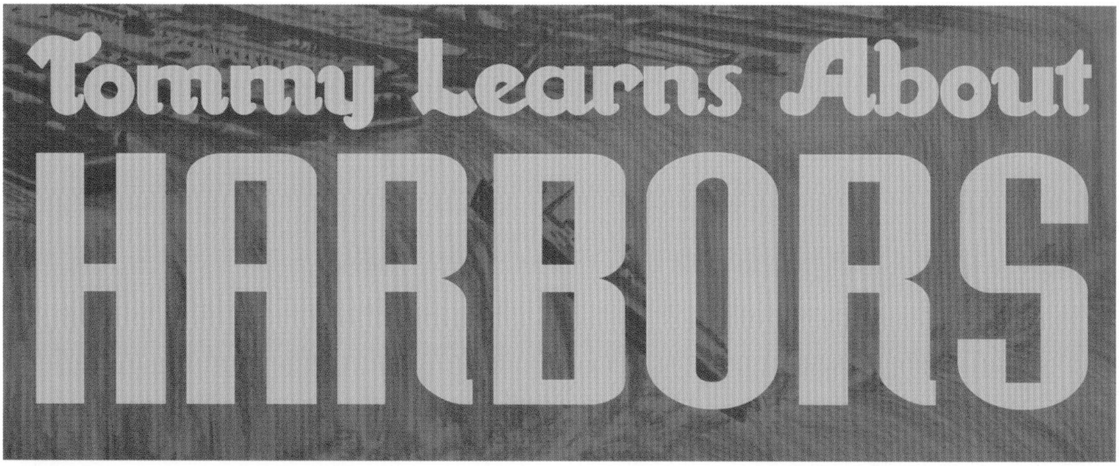
Tommy Learns About
HARBORS

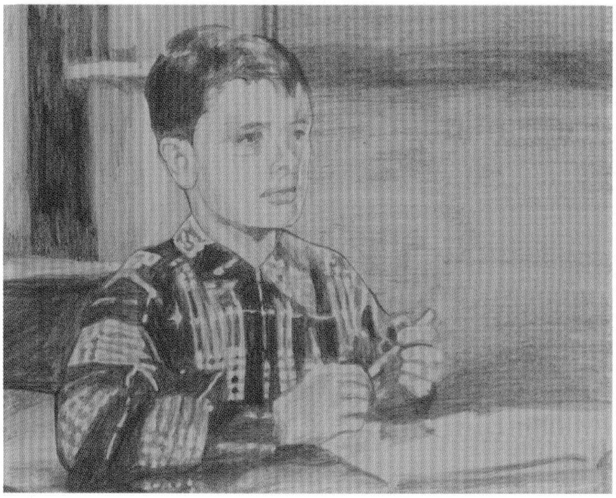

Tommy is bored. "Why can't school be over?" he sits and wonders.

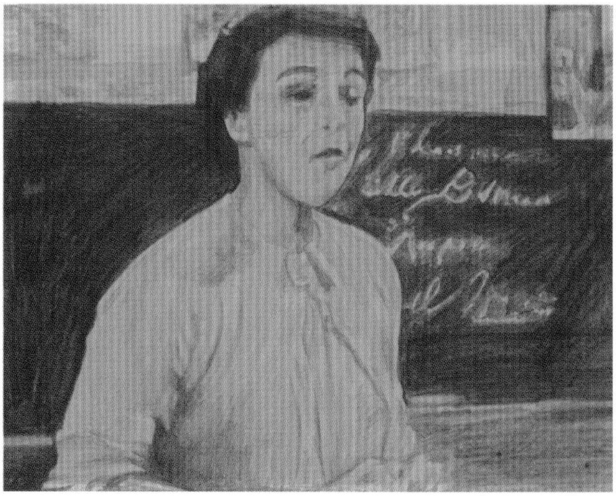

But Mrs. Monroe just keeps talking! Her voice drones on and on, and soon Tommy is dragged into the fascinating world of harbors.

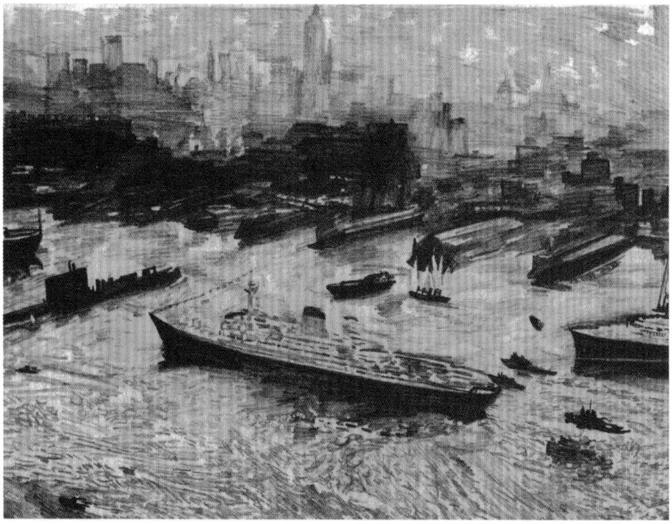

You might already know that a harbor is a place where a ship can get into a city. But did you know that the man who invented harbors got the idea from an animal?

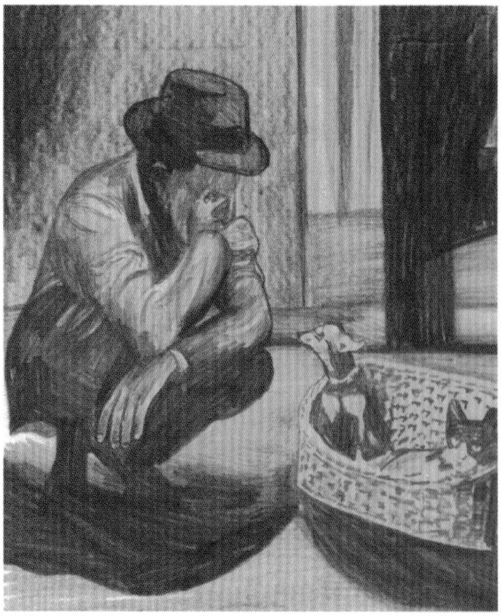

That's right– the man who invented harbors said he got the idea from an animal!

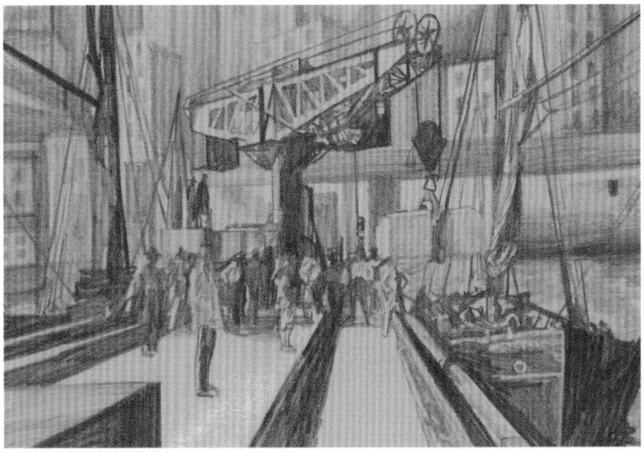

Ships and boats come into harbors and deposit all kinds of things: Keys, spices, grapefruit, hats, raccoons, balls.

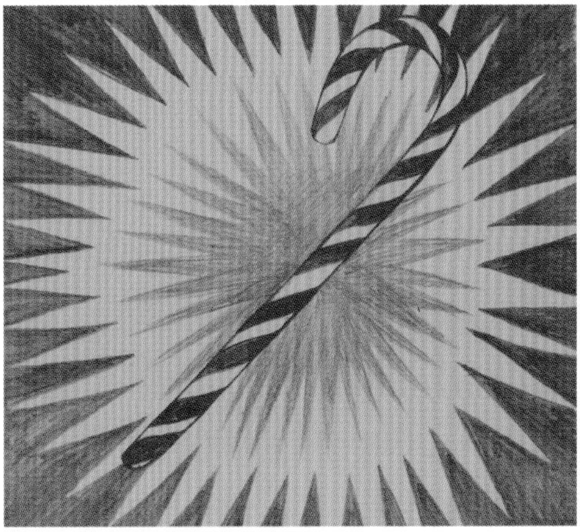

"And Candy?" asks Tommy, eagerly. "Yes, Tommy, even candy," answers Mrs. Monroe.

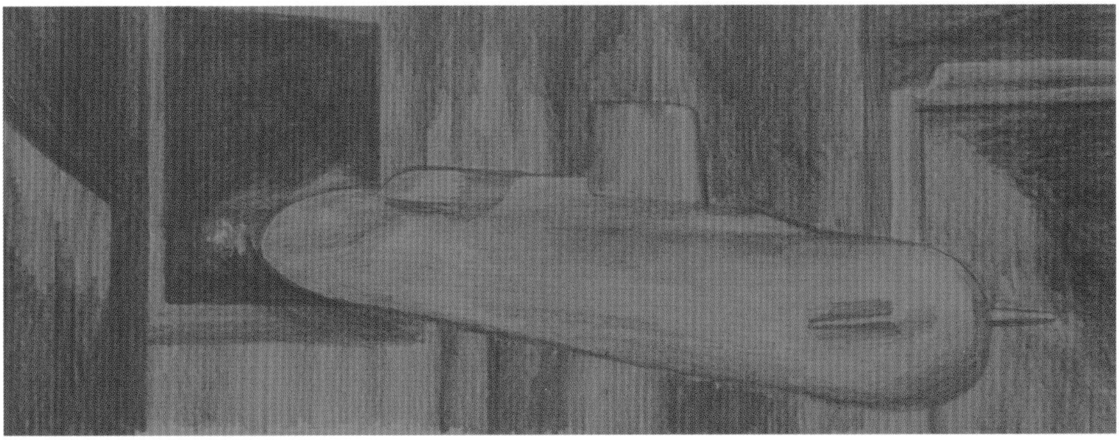

Submarines, which are used to transport cheese because of their pressurization, enter the harbor through a special underwater entrance.

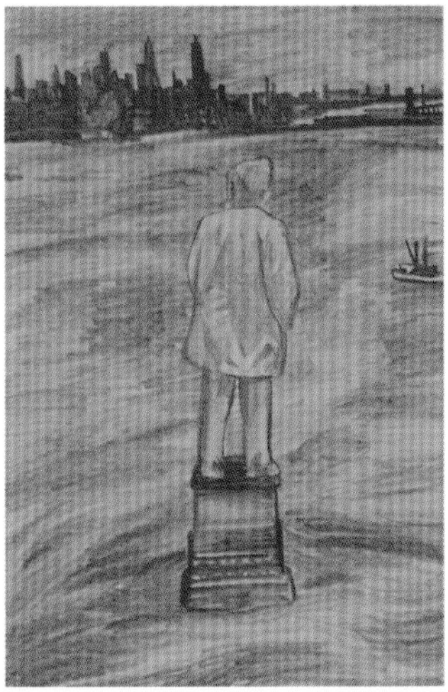

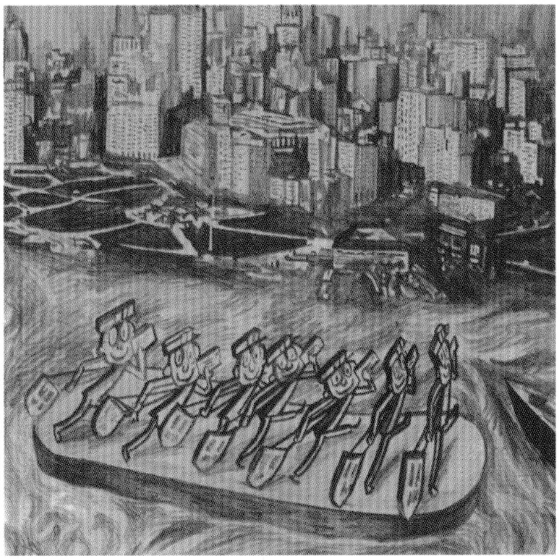

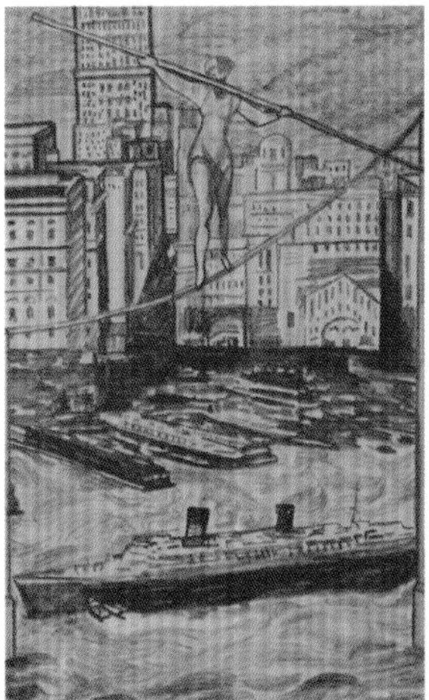

Harbors are also places where huge statues can be placed. The US has the Statue of Liberty, of course, but many other harbors have their own statues. Paraguay City has the eighty-seven foot statue of Columbo; New Madrid has the Seven Postal Regulations; and Lower Australia City has that structural marvel, The Tightrope Walker.

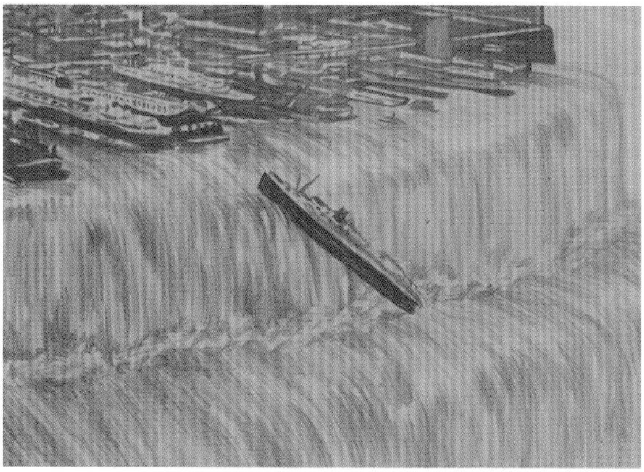

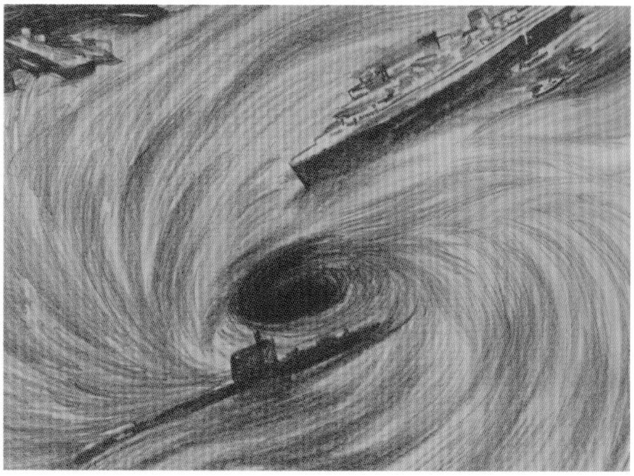

Flat harbors have been the most successful. Failed experimental harbors include the terraced harbor of Tierra del Fuego and the badly-planned Whirlpool City Harbor.

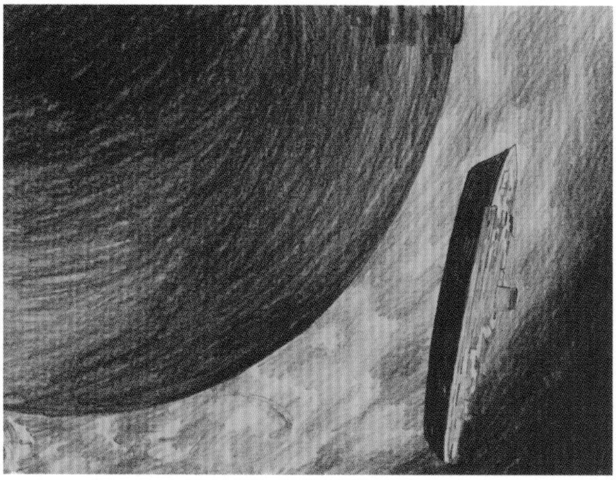

And harbors placed at the wrong angle on the globe can result in the ships falling off.

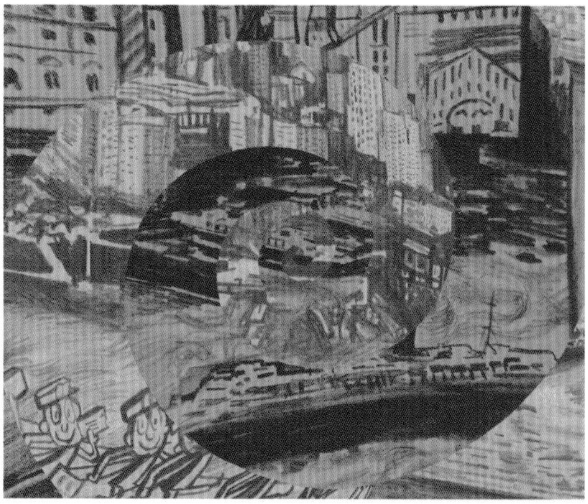

Harbors! Harbors! Harbors! Harbors! Harbors! Harbors! Harbors! Harbors...

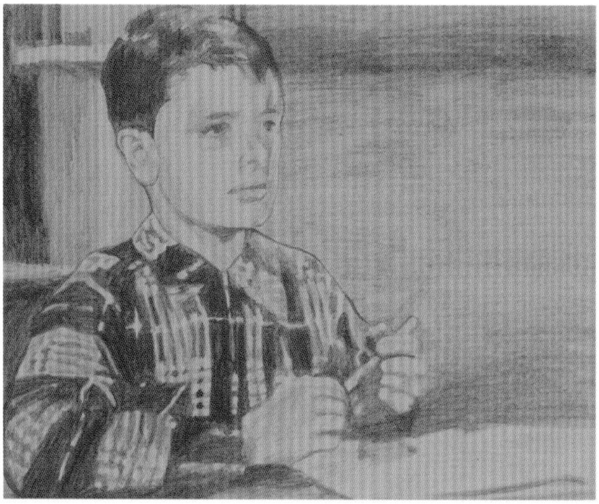

Suddenly Tommy wakes up. It was all a dream! Mrs. Monroe hadn't even started talking yet.

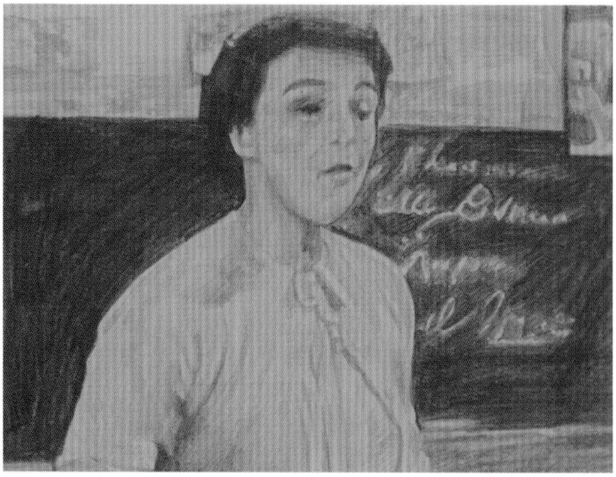

But then Mrs. Monroe starts talking, and drones on and on, and soon Tommy is dragged into the fascinating world of harbors.

THE END?

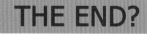

AROUND OUR COUNTRY

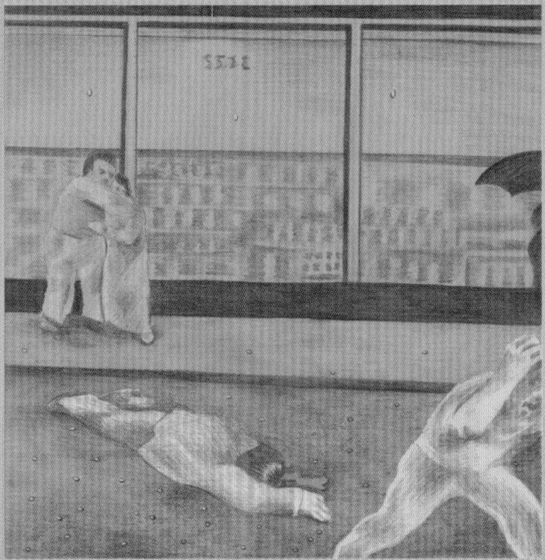

NEW YORK, NY. Another pedestrian lies dead, the victim of deadly "pennystorms" on the streets surrounding the Empire State building. Teenagers on the roof throw hundreds of pennies every hour; police seem helpless to stop them. "They run so fast" says a police spokesman.

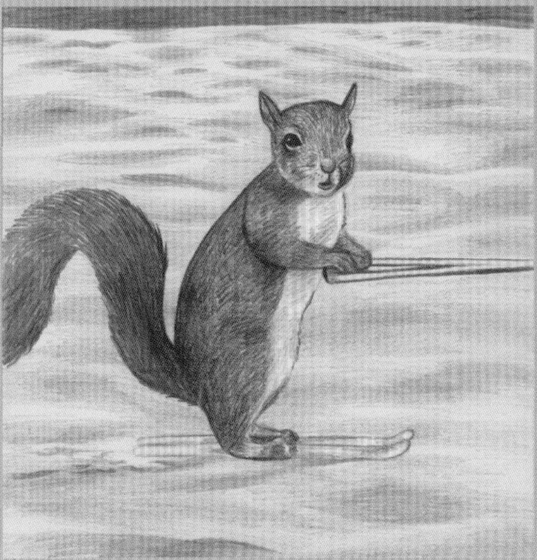

DULUTH, MN. The big news again this year: 'Sparkles', the water-skiing squirrel. Said mayor Paxton Bluthwell, "That squirrel's smarter than me! I can't waterski." Upon hearing this remark, the citizens voted Bluthwell out of office and the squirrel in. Unfortunately, the squirrel had just been killed by a speedboat driven by a chinchilla.

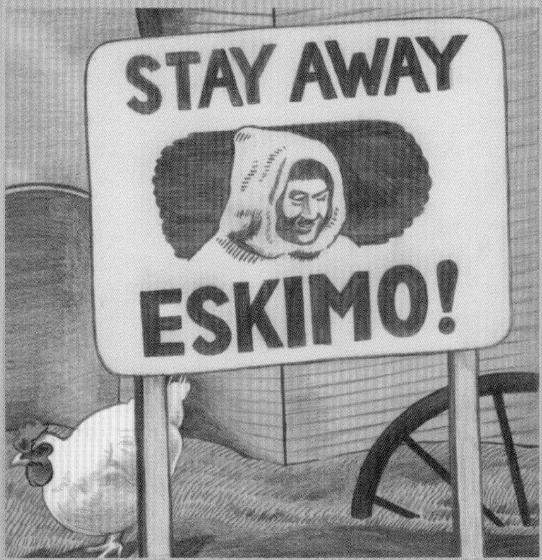
STAY AWAY
ESKIMO!

DIRTWELL, GA. The town council here has voted to adopt an official "Keep Eskimos Out of Dirtwell" campaign. Explained town councillor Referum Matthews, "I read about them one time in National Geographic. See, if they was to come here, they's raw fish'd be stinkin', and they'd be disorientated in the hot sun with them furs they got on."

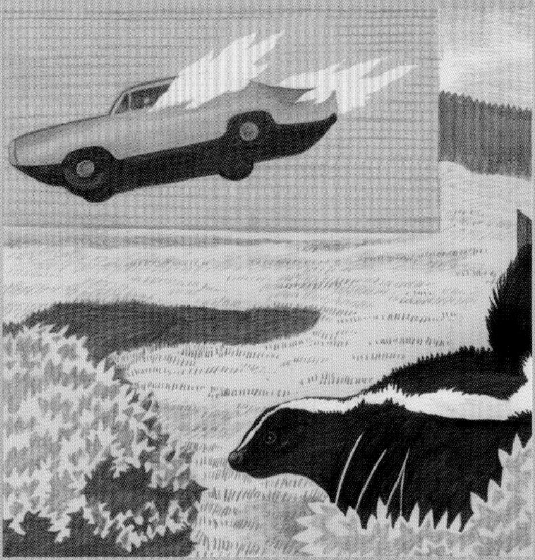

LOS ANGELES, CA. Skunks wandering onto people's lawns has for a long time been a problem and nuisance for the people in Tinseltown. Now they've found a new solution: stunts. "Skunks stay away from stunts," explained resident Abe Lim. "A skunk won't come onto a lawn where there's a Dodge Charger doing a flaming 360 jump."

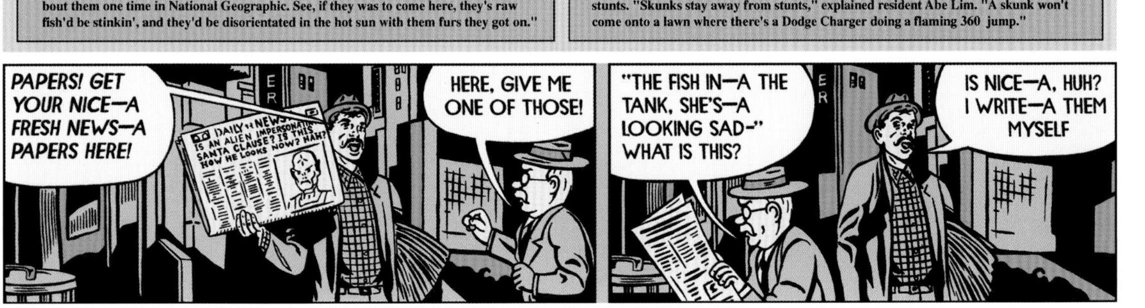
PAPERS! GET YOUR NICE—A FRESH NEWS—A PAPERS HERE!
HERE, GIVE ME ONE OF THOSE!
"THE FISH IN—A THE TANK, SHE'S—A LOOKING SAD-" WHAT IS THIS?
IS NICE—A, HUH? I WRITE—A THEM MYSELF

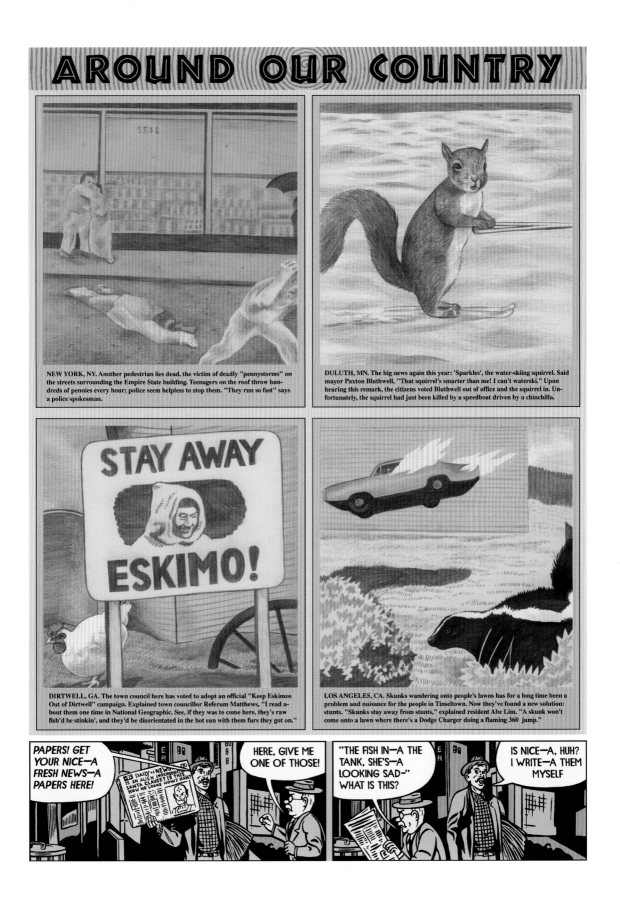

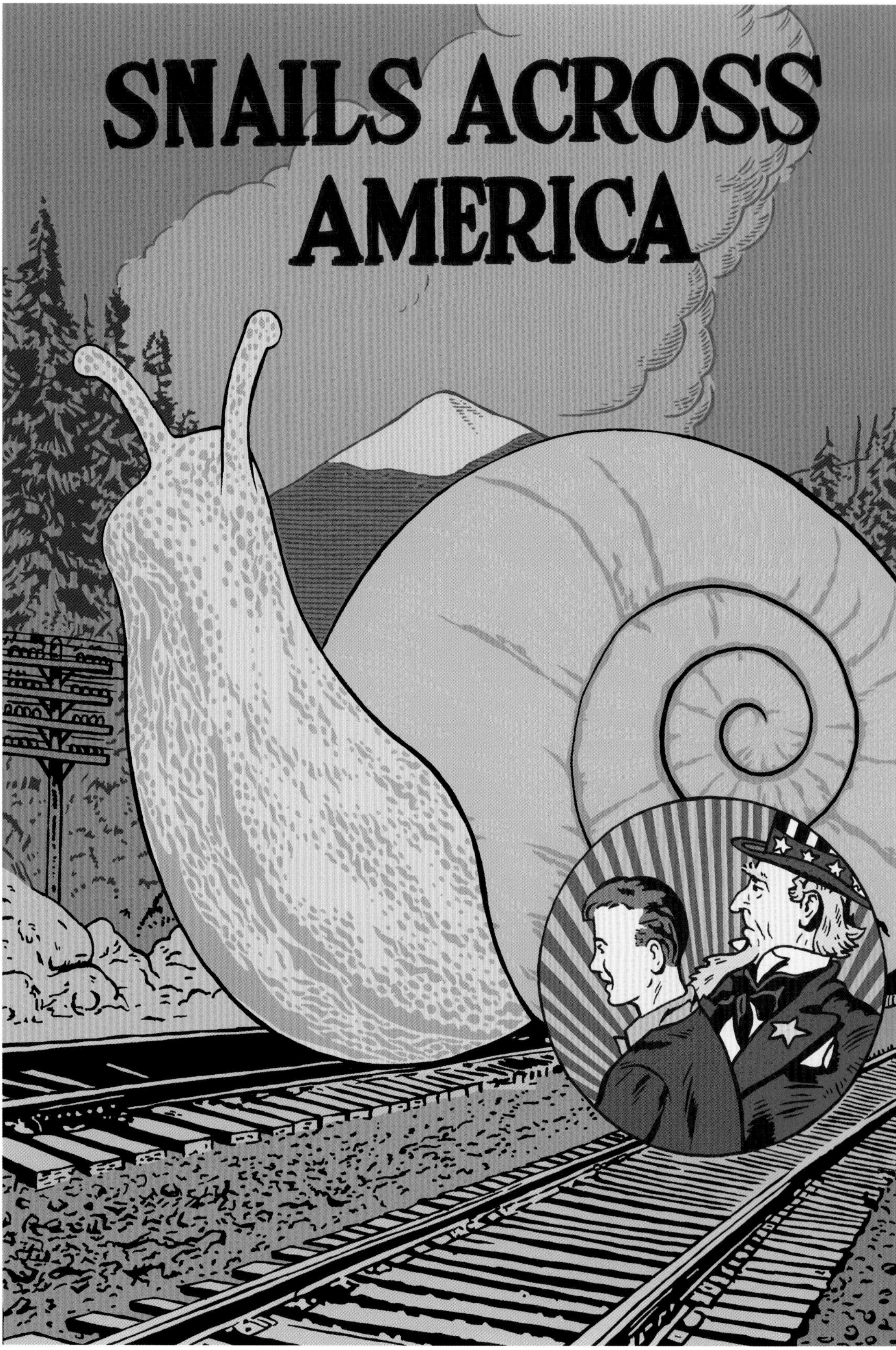
SNAILS ACROSS AMERICA

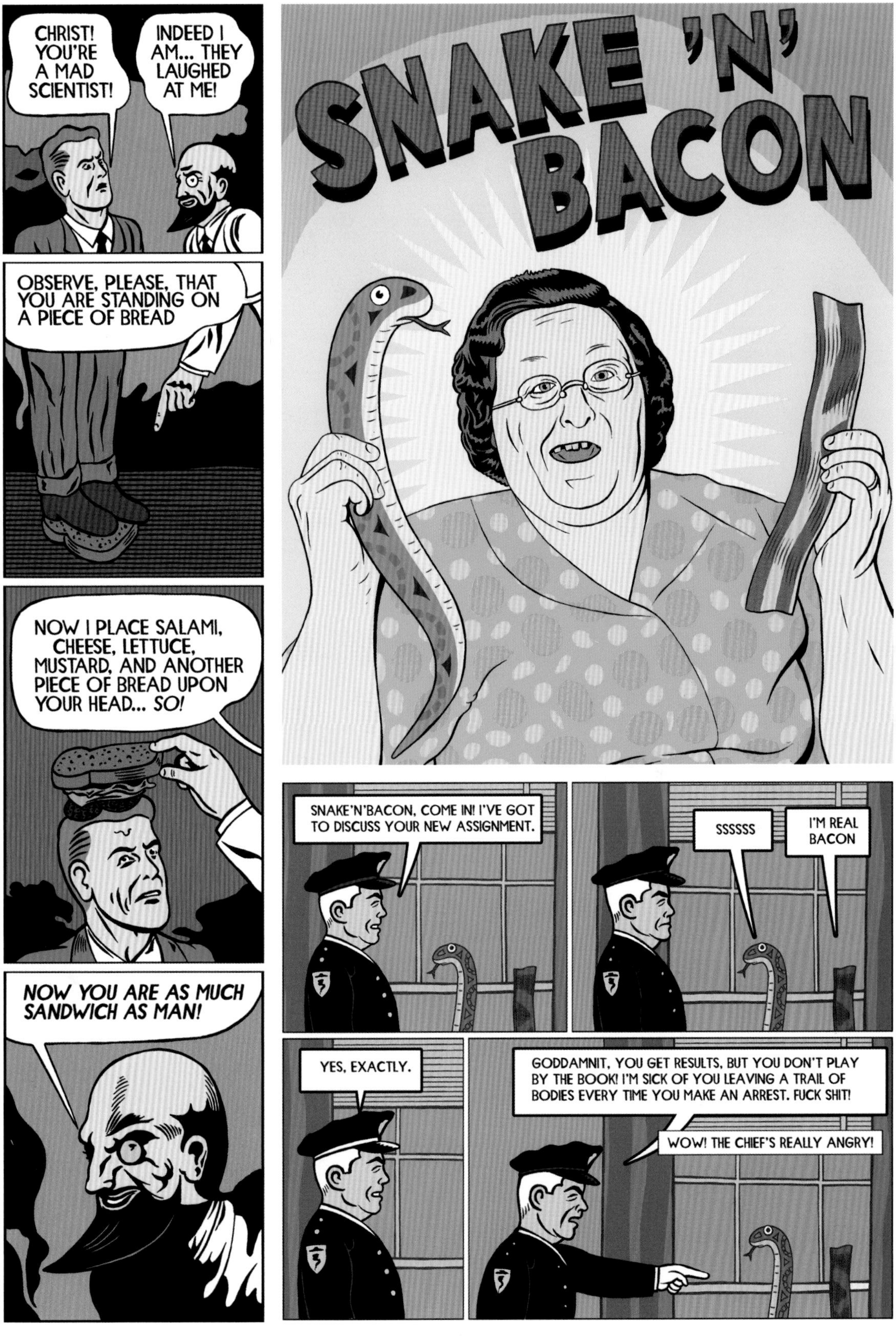
CHRIST! YOU'RE A MAD SCIENTIST!
INDEED I AM... THEY LAUGHED AT ME!
OBSERVE, PLEASE, THAT YOU ARE STANDING ON A PIECE OF BREAD
NOW I PLACE SALAMI, CHEESE, LETTUCE, MUSTARD, AND ANOTHER PIECE OF BREAD UPON YOUR HEAD... SO!
NOW YOU ARE AS MUCH SANDWICH AS MAN!
SNAKE 'N' BACON
SNAKE'N'BACON, COME IN! I'VE GOT TO DISCUSS YOUR NEW ASSIGNMENT.
SSSSSS
I'M REAL BACON
YES, EXACTLY.
GODDAMNIT, YOU GET RESULTS, BUT YOU DON'T PLAY BY THE BOOK! I'M SICK OF YOU LEAVING A TRAIL OF BODIES EVERY TIME YOU MAKE AN ARREST. FUCK SHIT!
WOW! THE CHIEF'S REALLY ANGRY!

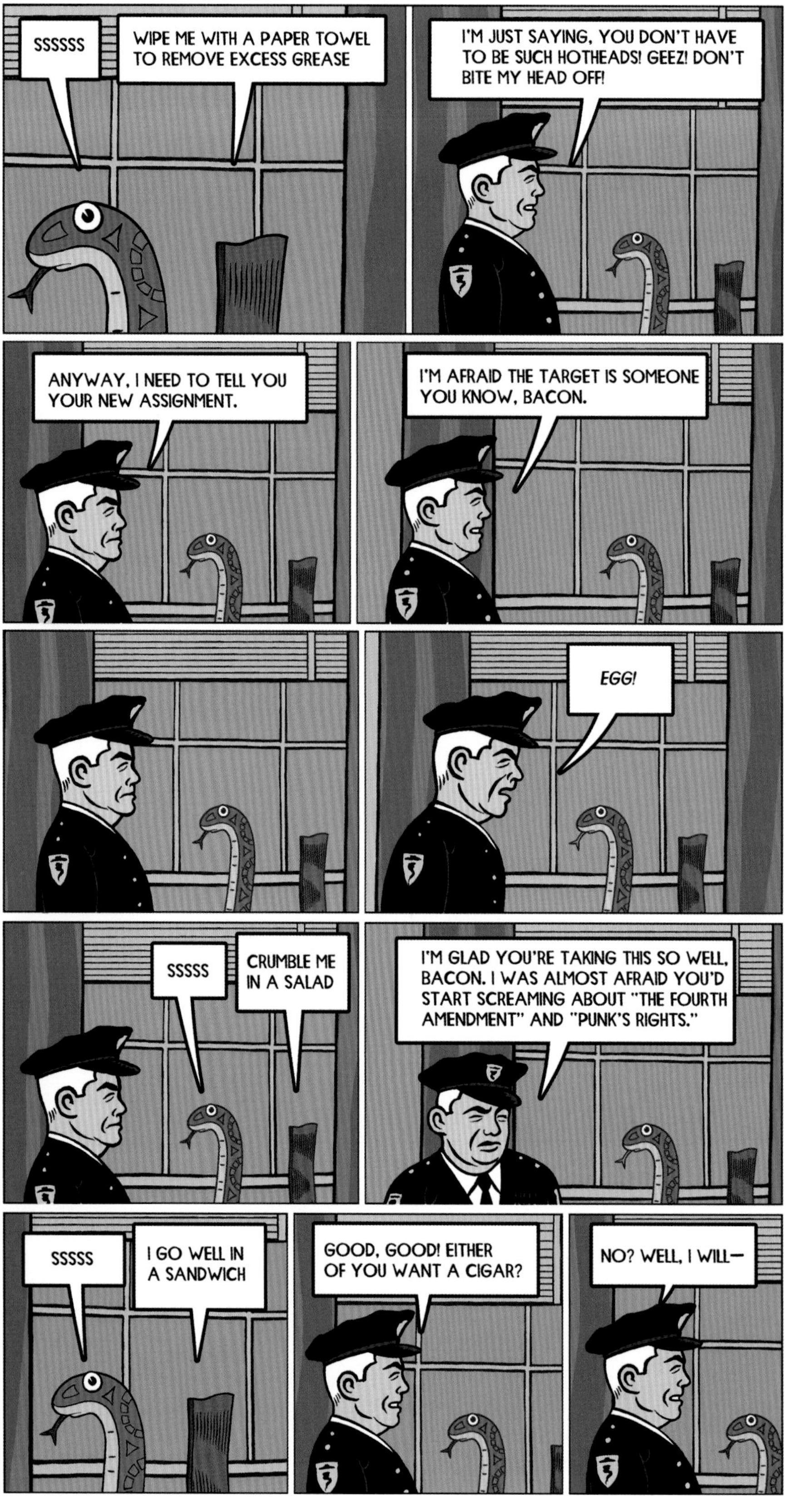
SSSSSS
WIPE ME WITH A PAPER TOWEL TO REMOVE EXCESS GREASE
I'M JUST SAYING, YOU DON'T HAVE TO BE SUCH HOTHEADS! GEEZ! DON'T BITE MY HEAD OFF!
ANYWAY, I NEED TO TELL YOU YOUR NEW ASSIGNMENT.
I'M AFRAID THE TARGET IS SOMEONE YOU KNOW, BACON.
EGG!
SSSSS
CRUMBLE ME IN A SALAD
I'M GLAD YOU'RE TAKING THIS SO WELL, BACON. I WAS ALMOST AFRAID YOU'D START SCREAMING ABOUT "THE FOURTH AMENDMENT" AND "PUNK'S RIGHTS."
SSSSS
I GO WELL IN A SANDWICH
GOOD, GOOD! EITHER OF YOU WANT A CIGAR?
NO? WELL, I WILL—

NEW GAMES FOR YOUR COMPUTER FROM QUALCO

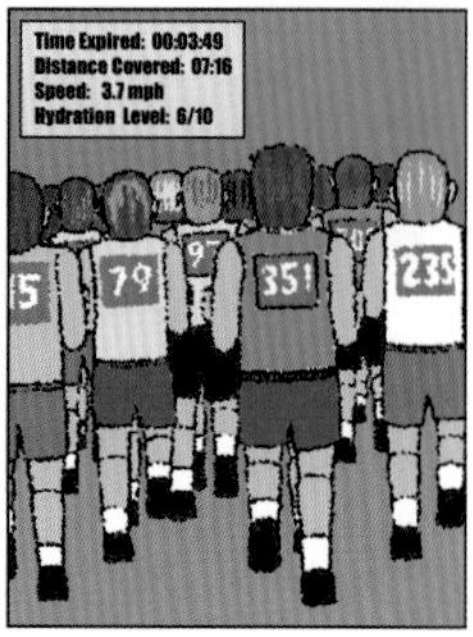
Time Expired: 00:03:49
Distance Covered: 07:16
Speed: 3.7 mph
Hydration Level: 6/10

Big City Marathon. Keep your finger on the forward arrow key for 26 hours to win this exciting game.

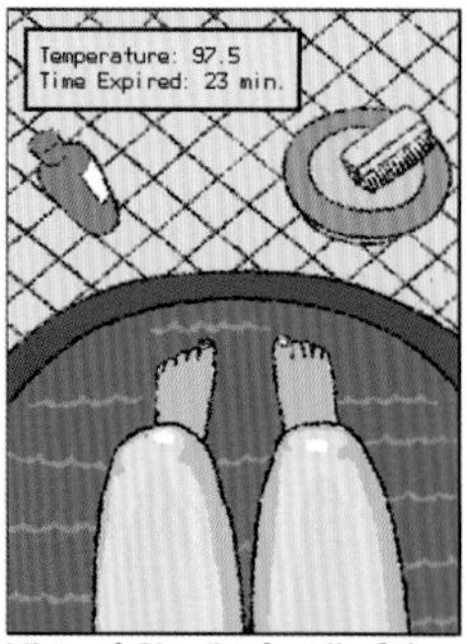
Temperature: 97.5
Time Expired: 23 min.

Virtual Sitz Bath. All of the excitement of an actual sitz bath, brought to a computer game.

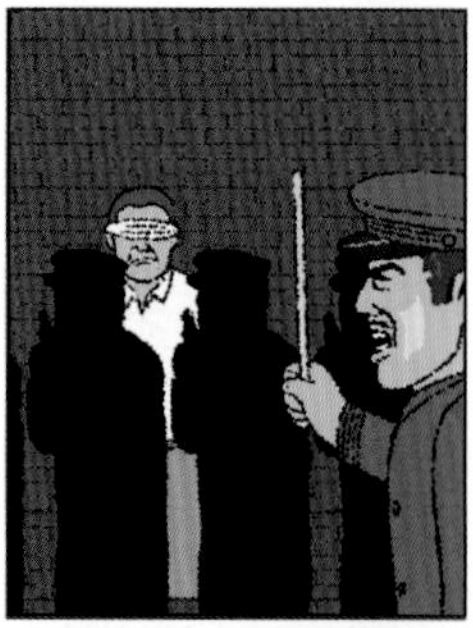

Firing Squad. *You* control the junta's death machinery.

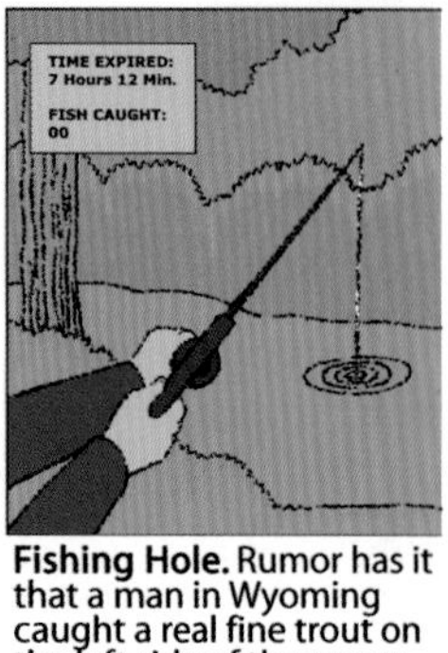
TIME EXPIRED:
7 Hours 12 Min.
FISH CAUGHT:
00

Fishing Hole. Rumor has it that a man in Wyoming caught a real fine trout on the left side of the screen, just last year.

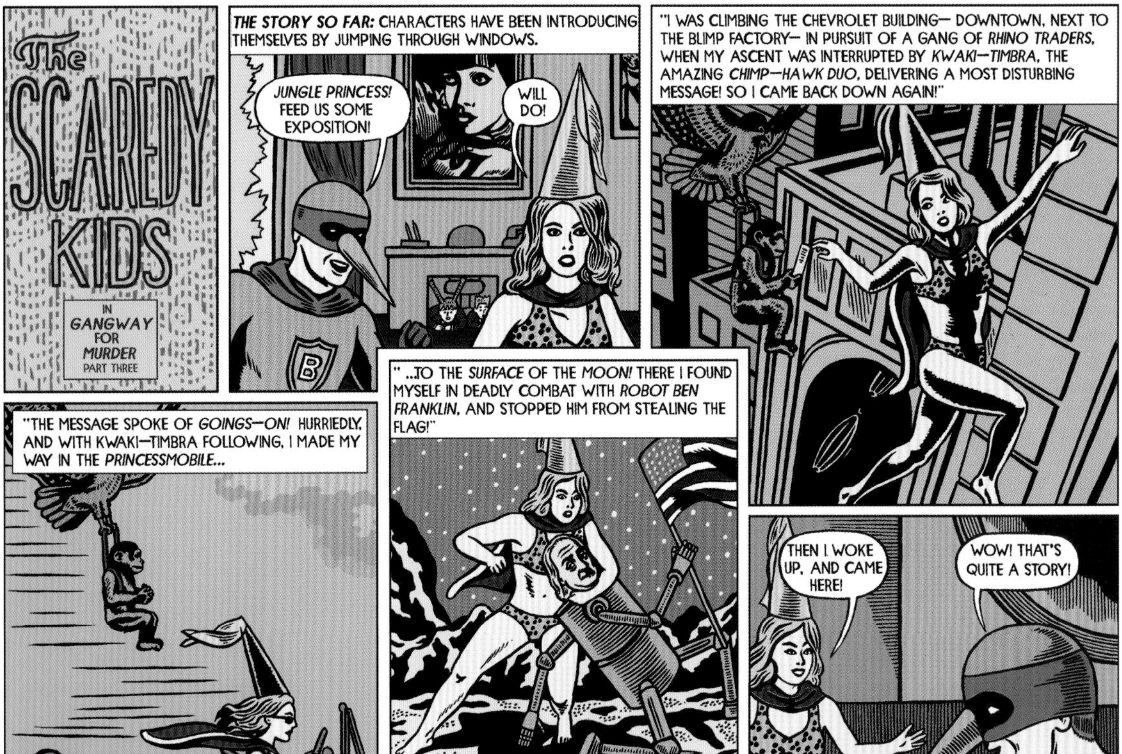
The
SCAREDY
KIDS
IN
GANGWAY
FOR
MURDER
PART THREE
THE STORY SO FAR: CHARACTERS HAVE BEEN INTRODUCING THEMSELVES BY JUMPING THROUGH WINDOWS.
JUNGLE PRINCESS! FEED US SOME EXPOSITION!
WILL DO!
"I WAS CLIMBING THE CHEVROLET BUILDING— DOWNTOWN, NEXT TO THE BLIMP FACTORY— IN PURSUIT OF A GANG OF RHINO TRADERS, WHEN MY ASCENT WAS INTERRUPTED BY KWAKI—TIMBRA, THE AMAZING CHIMP—HAWK DUO, DELIVERING A MOST DISTURBING MESSAGE! SO I CAME BACK DOWN AGAIN!"
"THE MESSAGE SPOKE OF GOINGS—ON! HURRIEDLY, AND WITH KWAKI—TIMBRA FOLLOWING, I MADE MY WAY IN THE PRINCESSMOBILE...
" ...TO THE SURFACE OF THE MOON! THERE I FOUND MYSELF IN DEADLY COMBAT WITH ROBOT BEN FRANKLIN, AND STOPPED HIM FROM STEALING THE FLAG!"
THEN I WOKE UP, AND CAME HERE!
WOW! THAT'S QUITE A STORY!
WELL, WE SHOULD GET GOING. BUT IF WE'RE GOING TO TAKE THE KIDS WITH US, WE SHOULD TELL THE MAID. WHERE IS SHE?
WHO'S BEEN JUMPING THROUGH THE WINDOWS?
CRASH
UH— THAT IS TO SAY, WE—
AW, FORGET IT! GAVE ME A CHANCE TO LIVE MY LIFE—LONG DREAM OF JUMPING THROUGH A WINDOW IN A REAL DRAMATIC WAY! EVER SINCE I WAS A KID, WATCHING MOVIES WHERE GINGER ROGERS AND FRED ASTAIRE JUMP THROUGH A WINDOW! AND WHEN I SAW THAT TWO WINDOWS HAD ALREADY BEEN JUMPED THROUGH, AND I REMEMBERED THAT THREE FOR TWO WINDOW SALE AT LOHMANS, WELL I JUST HAD TO DO IT AND GLAD I DID. SAY, THIS TEXT BALLOON GOT AWFULLY LARGE.

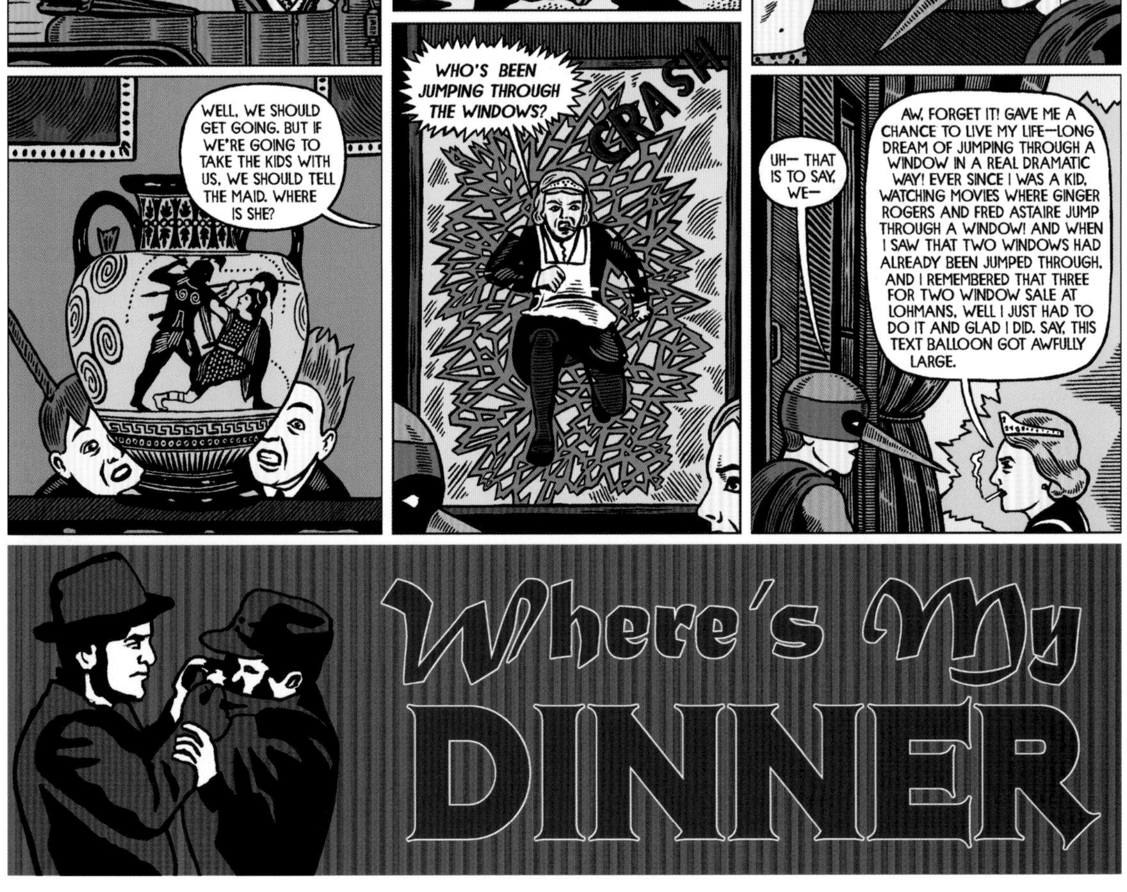
Where's My
DINNER

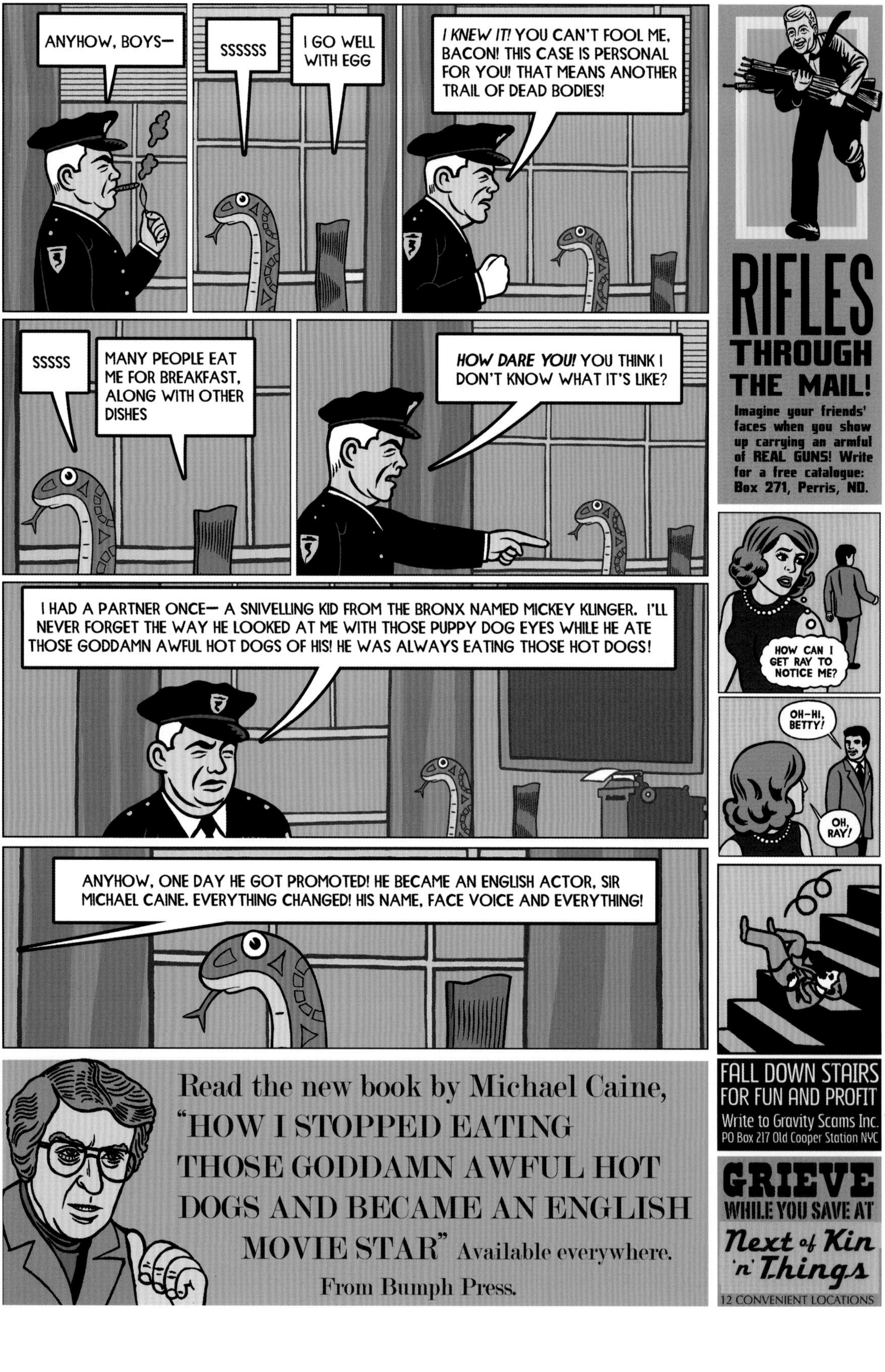
ANYHOW, BOYS—
SSSSSS
I GO WELL WITH EGG
I KNEW IT! YOU CAN'T FOOL ME, BACON! THIS CASE IS PERSONAL FOR YOU! THAT MEANS ANOTHER TRAIL OF DEAD BODIES!
SSSSS
MANY PEOPLE EAT ME FOR BREAKFAST, ALONG WITH OTHER DISHES
HOW DARE YOU! YOU THINK I DON'T KNOW WHAT IT'S LIKE?
I HAD A PARTNER ONCE— A SNIVELLING KID FROM THE BRONX NAMED MICKEY KLINGER. I'LL NEVER FORGET THE WAY HE LOOKED AT ME WITH THOSE PUPPY DOG EYES WHILE HE ATE THOSE GODDAMN AWFUL HOT DOGS OF HIS! HE WAS ALWAYS EATING THOSE HOT DOGS!
ANYHOW, ONE DAY HE GOT PROMOTED! HE BECAME AN ENGLISH ACTOR, SIR MICHAEL CAINE. EVERYTHING CHANGED! HIS NAME, FACE VOICE AND EVERYTHING!
Read the new book by Michael Caine, "HOW I STOPPED EATING THOSE GODDAMN AWFUL HOT DOGS AND BECAME AN ENGLISH MOVIE STAR" Available everywhere.
From Bumph Press.
RIFLES THROUGH THE MAIL!
Imagine your friends' faces when you show up carrying an armful of REAL GUNS! Write for a free catalogue: Box 271, Perris, ND.
HOW CAN I GET RAY TO NOTICE ME?
OH—HI, BETTY!
OH, RAY!
FALL DOWN STAIRS FOR FUN AND PROFIT
Write to Gravity Scams Inc.
PO Box 217 Old Cooper Station NYC
GRIEVE WHILE YOU SAVE AT
Next of Kin 'n' Things
12 CONVENIENT LOCATIONS

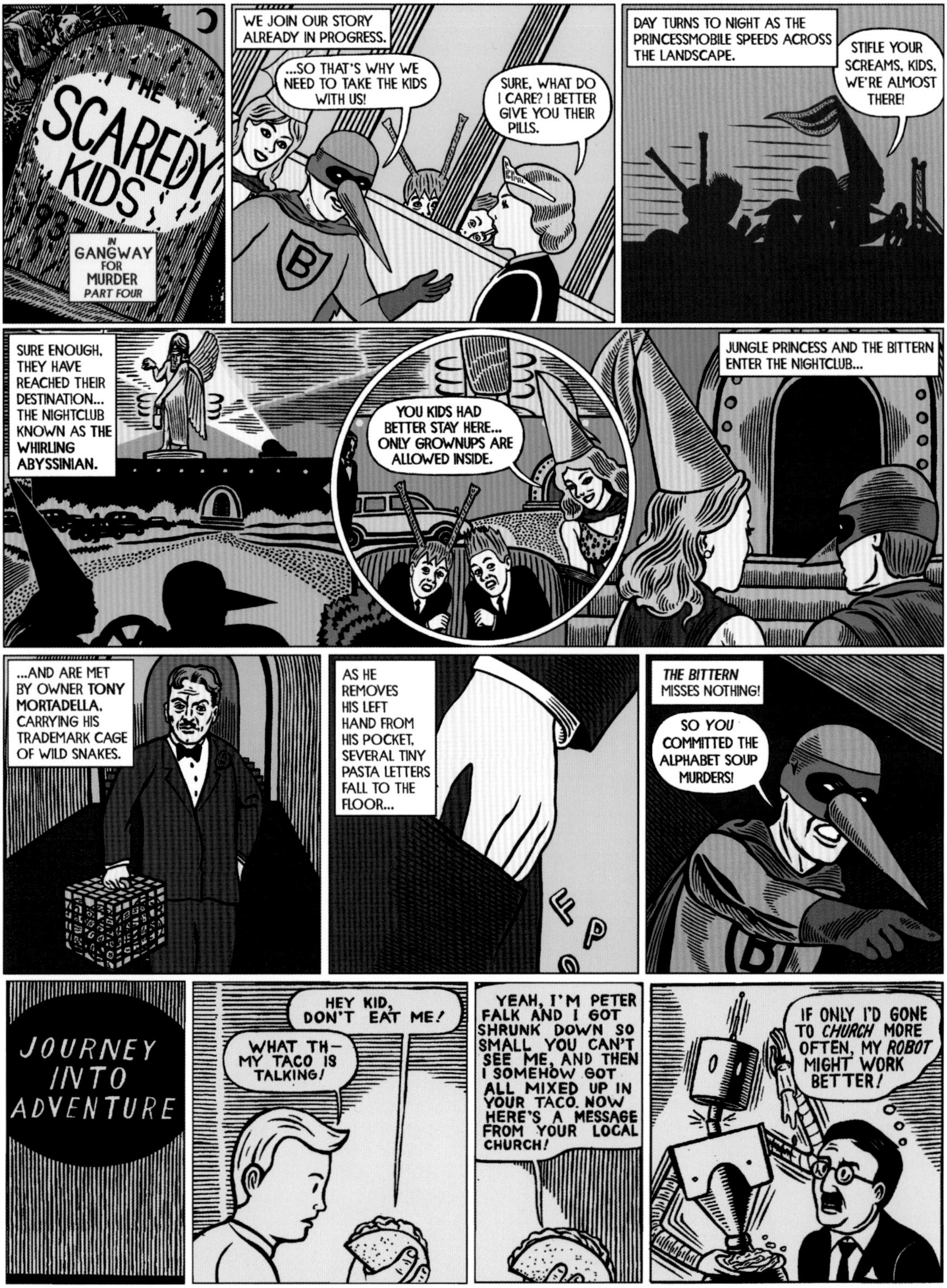
THE SCAREDY KIDS
1937
IN GANGWAY FOR MURDER PART FOUR
WE JOIN OUR STORY ALREADY IN PROGRESS.
...SO THAT'S WHY WE NEED TO TAKE THE KIDS WITH US!
SURE, WHAT DO I CARE? I BETTER GIVE YOU THEIR PILLS.
DAY TURNS TO NIGHT AS THE PRINCESSMOBILE SPEEDS ACROSS THE LANDSCAPE.
STIFLE YOUR SCREAMS, KIDS, WE'RE ALMOST THERE!
SURE ENOUGH, THEY HAVE REACHED THEIR DESTINATION... THE NIGHTCLUB KNOWN AS THE WHIRLING ABYSSINIAN.
YOU KIDS HAD BETTER STAY HERE... ONLY GROWNUPS ARE ALLOWED INSIDE.
JUNGLE PRINCESS AND THE BITTERN ENTER THE NIGHTCLUB...
...AND ARE MET BY OWNER TONY MORTADELLA, CARRYING HIS TRADEMARK CAGE OF WILD SNAKES.
AS HE REMOVES HIS LEFT HAND FROM HIS POCKET, SEVERAL TINY PASTA LETTERS FALL TO THE FLOOR...
THE BITTERN MISSES NOTHING!
SO YOU COMMITTED THE ALPHABET SOUP MURDERS!
JOURNEY INTO ADVENTURE
HEY KID, DON'T EAT ME!
WHAT TH— MY TACO IS TALKING!
YEAH, I'M PETER FALK AND I GOT SHRUNK DOWN SO SMALL YOU CAN'T SEE ME, AND THEN I SOMEHOW GOT ALL MIXED UP IN YOUR TACO. NOW HERE'S A MESSAGE FROM YOUR LOCAL CHURCH!
IF ONLY I'D GONE TO CHURCH MORE OFTEN, MY ROBOT MIGHT WORK BETTER!

HELPFUL HINT If you're going to call someone a walrus, but halfway through you realize that might upset them, you can always call them a walnut instead. That probably won't upset them so much.

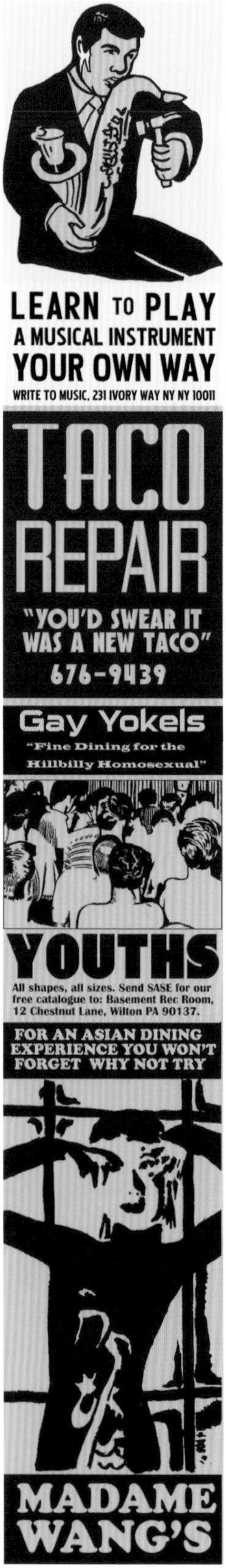
LEARN TO PLAY
A MUSICAL INSTRUMENT
YOUR OWN WAY
WRITE TO MUSIC, 231 IVORY WAY NY NY 10011
TACO
REPAIR
"YOU'D SWEAR IT WAS A NEW TACO"
676-9439
Gay Yokels
"Fine Dining for the Hillbilly Homosexual"
YOUTHS
All shapes, all sizes. Send SASE for our free catalogue to: Basement Rec Room, 12 Chestnut Lane, Wilton PA 90137.
FOR AN ASIAN DINING EXPERIENCE YOU WON'T FORGET WHY NOT TRY
MADAME WANG'S

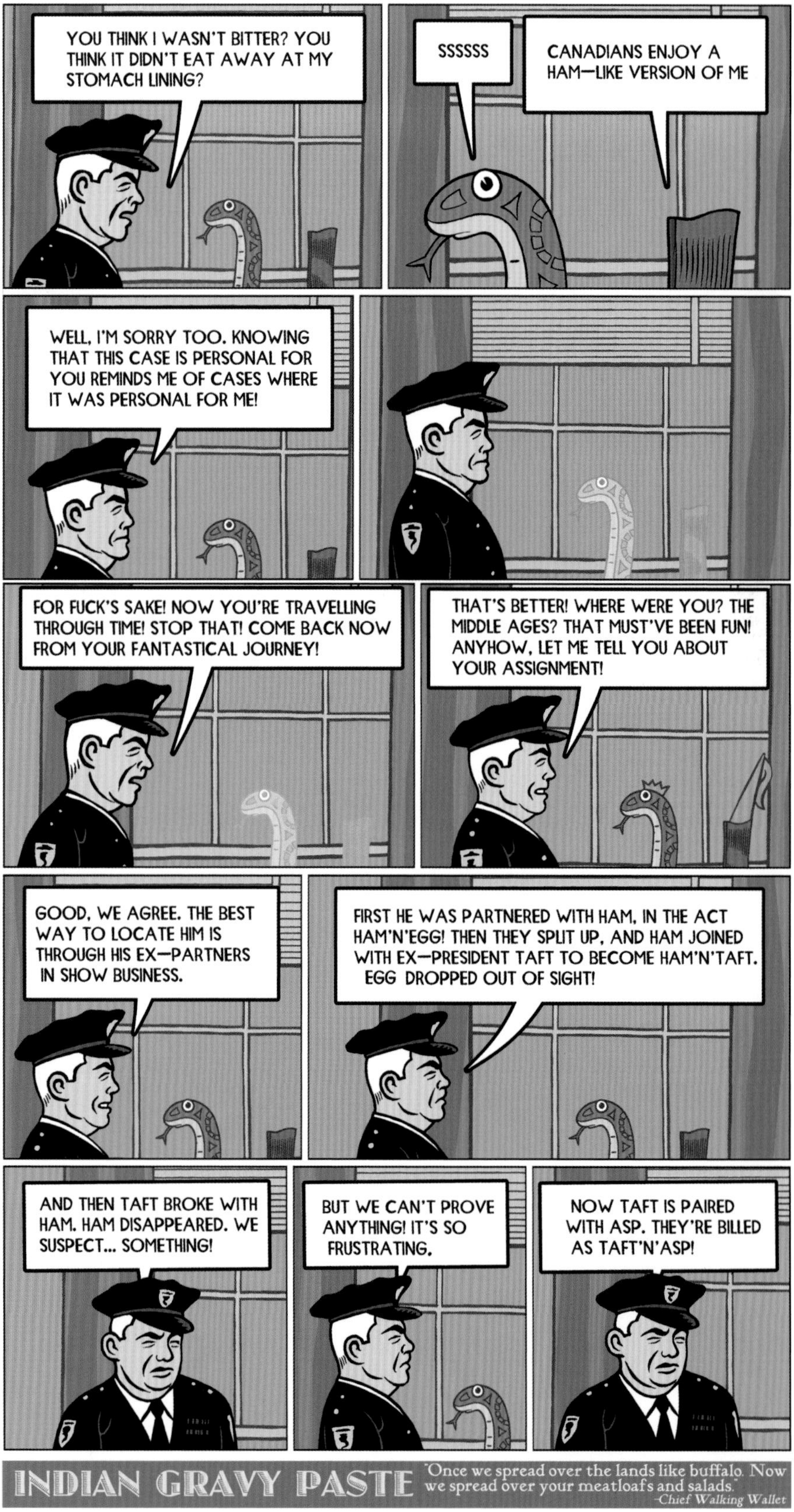
YOU THINK I WASN'T BITTER? YOU THINK IT DIDN'T EAT AWAY AT MY STOMACH LINING?
SSSSSS
CANADIANS ENJOY A HAM—LIKE VERSION OF ME
WELL, I'M SORRY TOO. KNOWING THAT THIS CASE IS PERSONAL FOR YOU REMINDS ME OF CASES WHERE IT WAS PERSONAL FOR ME!
FOR FUCK'S SAKE! NOW YOU'RE TRAVELLING THROUGH TIME! STOP THAT! COME BACK NOW FROM YOUR FANTASTICAL JOURNEY!
THAT'S BETTER! WHERE WERE YOU? THE MIDDLE AGES? THAT MUST'VE BEEN FUN! ANYHOW, LET ME TELL YOU ABOUT YOUR ASSIGNMENT!
GOOD, WE AGREE. THE BEST WAY TO LOCATE HIM IS THROUGH HIS EX—PARTNERS IN SHOW BUSINESS.
FIRST HE WAS PARTNERED WITH HAM, IN THE ACT HAM'N'EGG! THEN THEY SPLIT UP, AND HAM JOINED WITH EX—PRESIDENT TAFT TO BECOME HAM'N'TAFT. EGG DROPPED OUT OF SIGHT!
AND THEN TAFT BROKE WITH HAM. HAM DISAPPEARED. WE SUSPECT... SOMETHING!
BUT WE CAN'T PROVE ANYTHING! IT'S SO FRUSTRATING.
NOW TAFT IS PAIRED WITH ASP. THEY'RE BILLED AS TAFT'N'ASP!
INDIAN GRAVY PASTE
"Once we spread over the lands like buffalo. Now we spread over your meatloafs and salads."
-Chief Walking Wallet

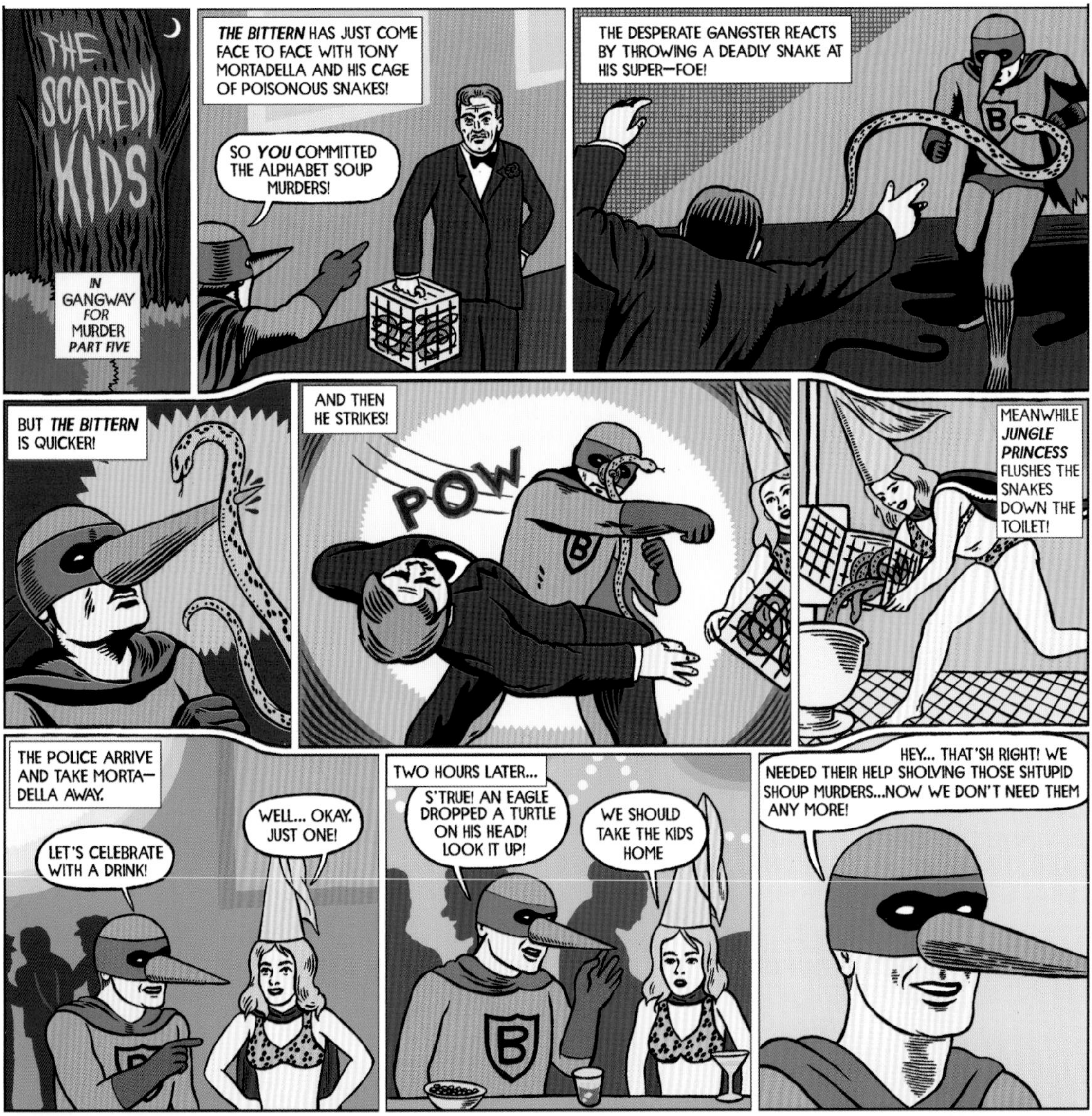
THE SCAREDY KIDS
IN GANGWAY FOR MURDER PART FIVE
THE BITTERN HAS JUST COME FACE TO FACE WITH TONY MORTADELLA AND HIS CAGE OF POISONOUS SNAKES!
SO YOU COMMITTED THE ALPHABET SOUP MURDERS!
THE DESPERATE GANGSTER REACTS BY THROWING A DEADLY SNAKE AT HIS SUPER—FOE!
BUT THE BITTERN IS QUICKER!
AND THEN HE STRIKES!
POW
MEANWHILE JUNGLE PRINCESS FLUSHES THE SNAKES DOWN THE TOILET!
THE POLICE ARRIVE AND TAKE MORTA—DELLA AWAY.
LET'S CELEBRATE WITH A DRINK!
WELL... OKAY. JUST ONE!
TWO HOURS LATER...
S'TRUE! AN EAGLE DROPPED A TURTLE ON HIS HEAD! LOOK IT UP!
WE SHOULD TAKE THE KIDS HOME
HEY... THAT'SH RIGHT! WE NEEDED THEIR HELP SHOLVING THOSE SHTUPID SHOUP MURDERS...NOW WE DON'T NEED THEM ANY MORE!

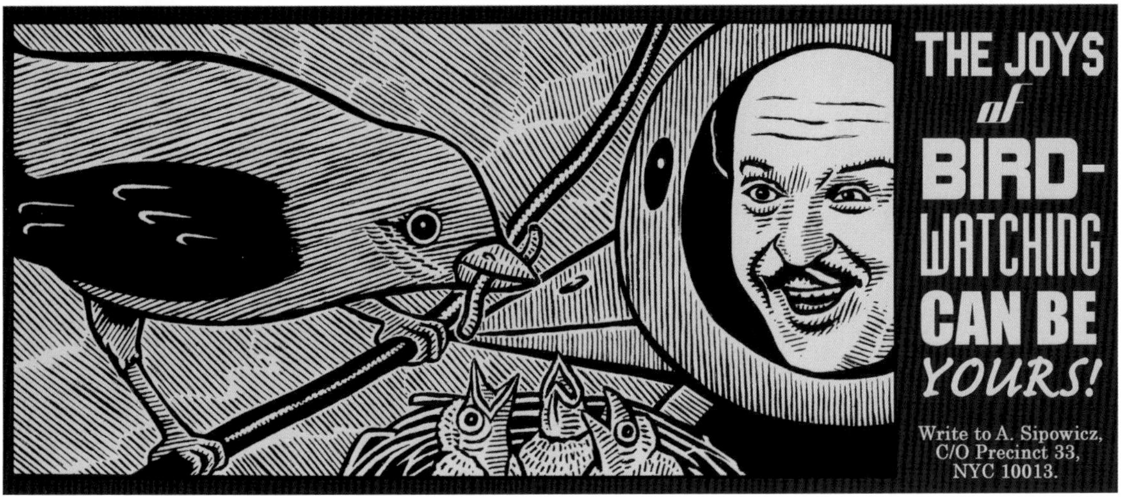
THE JOYS of BIRD-WATCHING CAN BE YOURS!
Write to A. Sipowicz, C/O Precinct 33, NYC 10013.

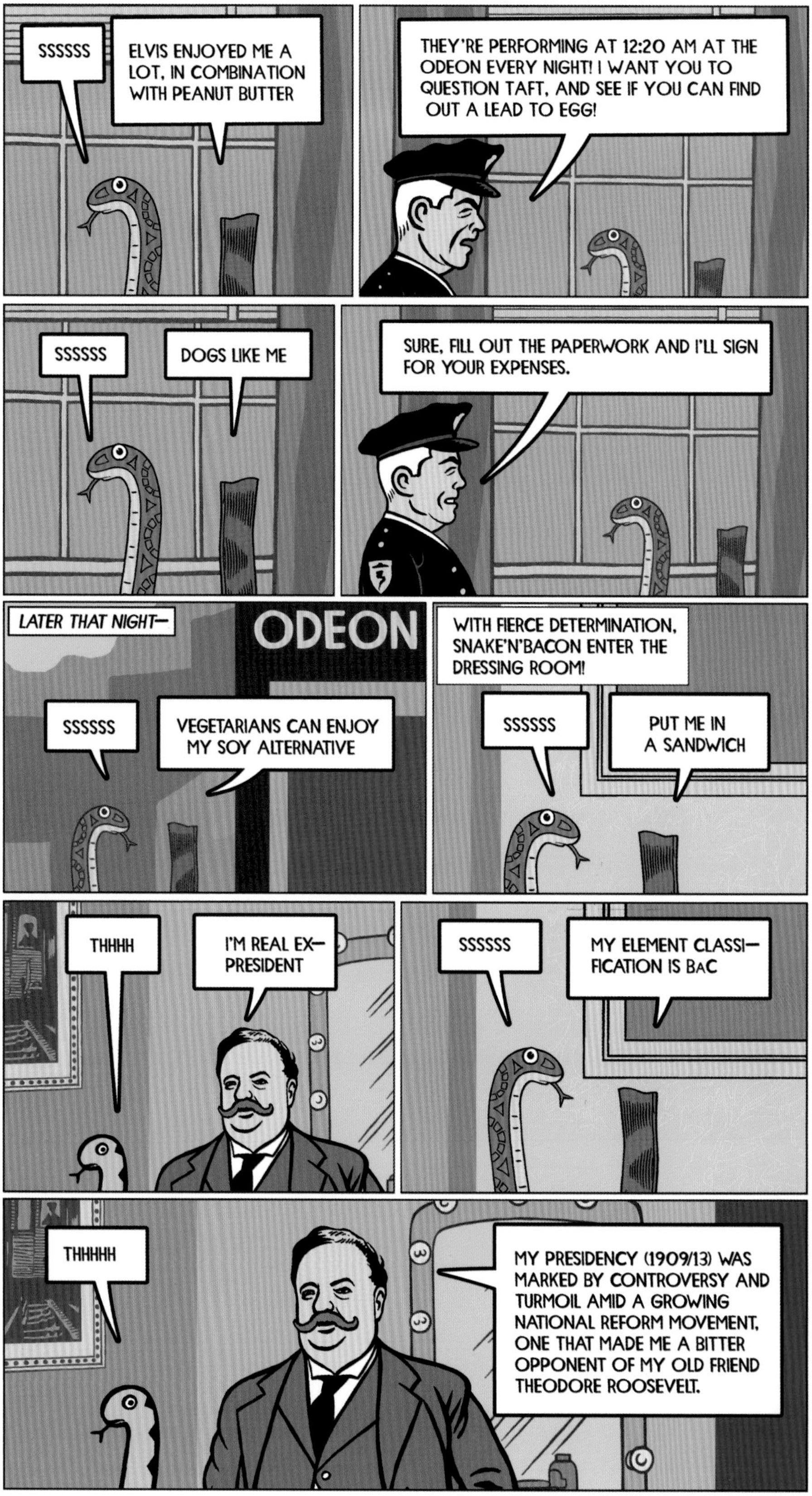
SSSSSS
ELVIS ENJOYED ME A LOT, IN COMBINATION WITH PEANUT BUTTER
THEY'RE PERFORMING AT 12:20 AM AT THE ODEON EVERY NIGHT! I WANT YOU TO QUESTION TAFT, AND SEE IF YOU CAN FIND OUT A LEAD TO EGG!
SSSSSS
DOGS LIKE ME
SURE, FILL OUT THE PAPERWORK AND I'LL SIGN FOR YOUR EXPENSES.
LATER THAT NIGHT—
ODEON
SSSSSS
VEGETARIANS CAN ENJOY MY SOY ALTERNATIVE
WITH FIERCE DETERMINATION, SNAKE'N'BACON ENTER THE DRESSING ROOM!
SSSSSS
PUT ME IN A SANDWICH
THHHH
I'M REAL EX-PRESIDENT
SSSSSS
MY ELEMENT CLASSI-FICATION IS BaC
THHHHH
MY PRESIDENCY (1909/13) WAS MARKED BY CONTROVERSY AND TURMOIL AMID A GROWING NATIONAL REFORM MOVEMENT, ONE THAT MADE ME A BITTER OPPONENT OF MY OLD FRIEND THEODORE ROOSEVELT.

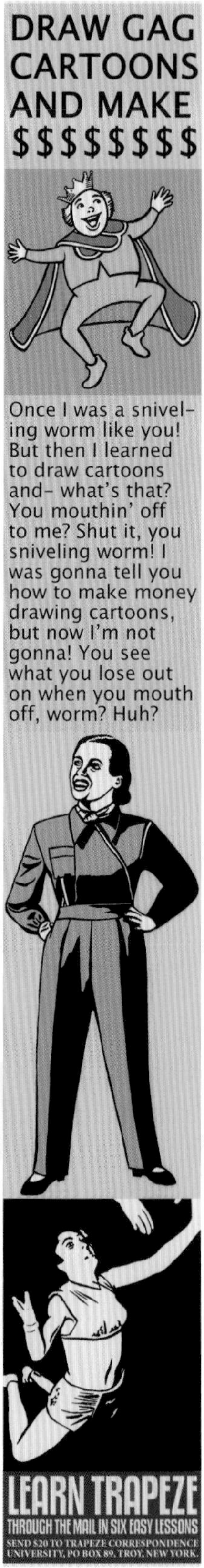
DRAW GAG CARTOONS AND MAKE $$$$$$$$
Once I was a sniveling worm like you! But then I learned to draw cartoons and– what's that? You mouthin' off to me? Shut it, you sniveling worm! I was gonna tell you how to make money drawing cartoons, but now I'm not gonna! You see what you lose out on when you mouth off, worm? Huh?
LEARN TRAPEZE
THROUGH THE MAIL IN SIX EASY LESSONS
SEND $20 TO TRAPEZE CORRESPONDENCE UNIVERSITY, PO BOX 89, TROY, NEW YORK.

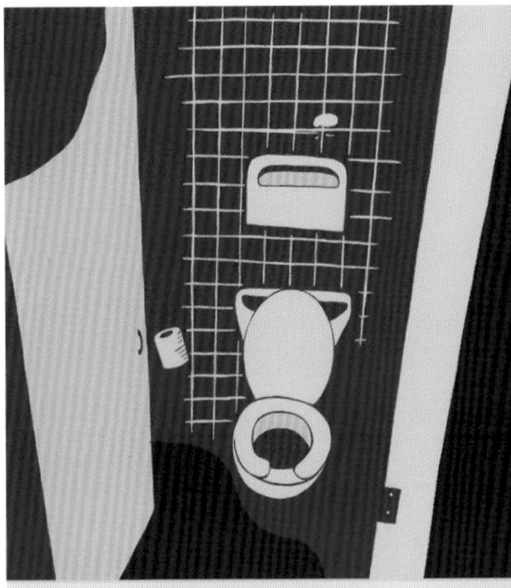

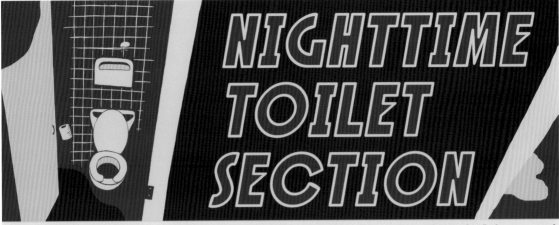

NIGHTTIME TOILET SECTION

"Going to the bathroom at night is a whole different game. It's got an element of danger and risk, yet it's sexier. It's got more attitude, it's in-your-face." – *Chazz Palamino*

IDEAL READING FOR THE GOING TO THE BATHROOM EXPERIENCE

The ALL-NEW *Sherlock Holmes* TOILET METAPHOR MYSTERIES

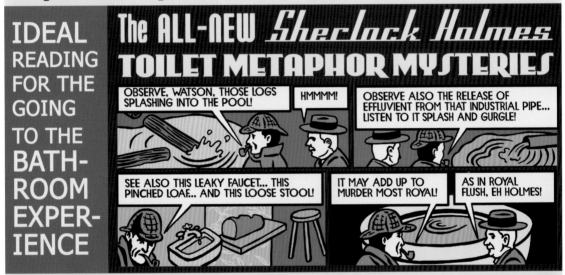

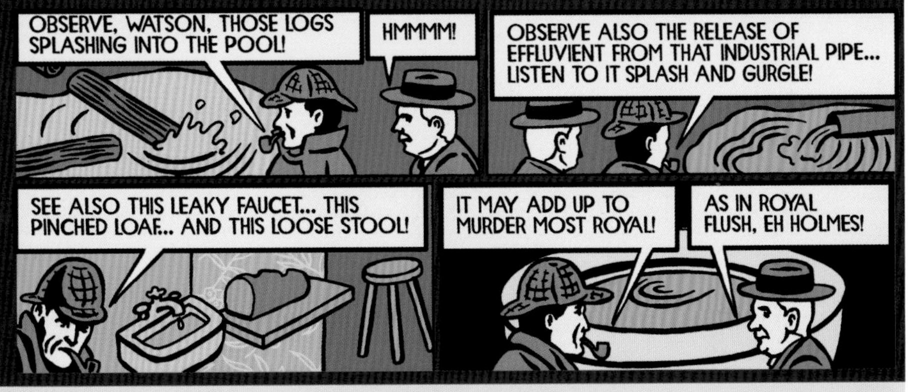
OBSERVE, WATSON, THOSE LOGS SPLASHING INTO THE POOL!
HMMMM!
OBSERVE ALSO THE RELEASE OF EFFLUVIENT FROM THAT INDUSTRIAL PIPE... LISTEN TO IT SPLASH AND GURGLE!
SEE ALSO THIS LEAKY FAUCET... THIS PINCHED LOAF... AND THIS LOOSE STOOL!
IT MAY ADD UP TO MURDER MOST ROYAL!
AS IN ROYAL FLUSH, EH HOLMES!

Pottie's

For the best of today's toilet comedians.

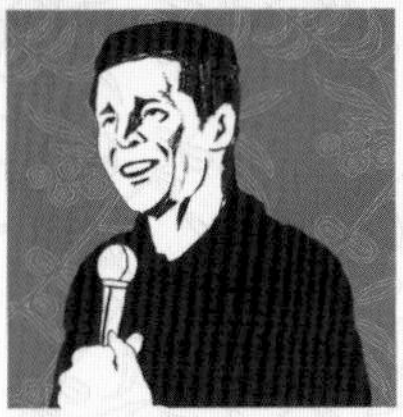

FEBRUARY 11TH

LARRY RONCO

"Don't you hate it when it won't go down?"

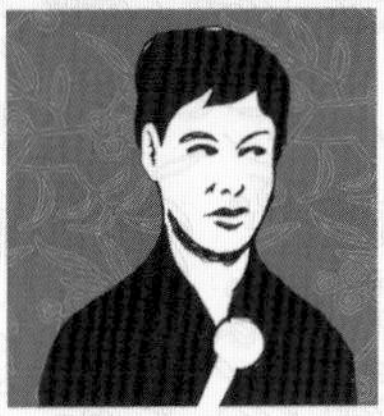

FEBRUARY 17TH

DAWN FUNKNALL

"I've dropped a deuce in some highly unusual places."

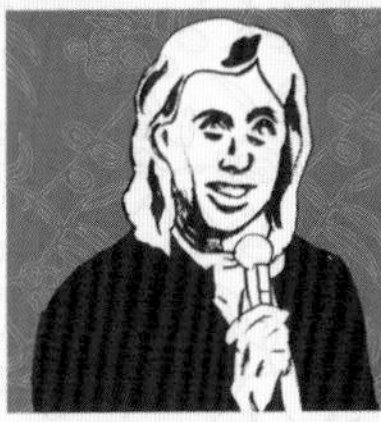

FEBRUARY 23RD

DON FUNKBUCK

"Poo-poo, ca-ca, doody... those are the tools of my trade."

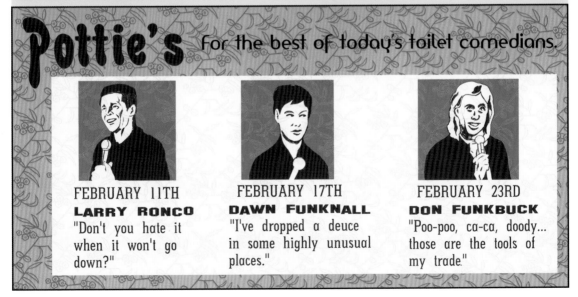

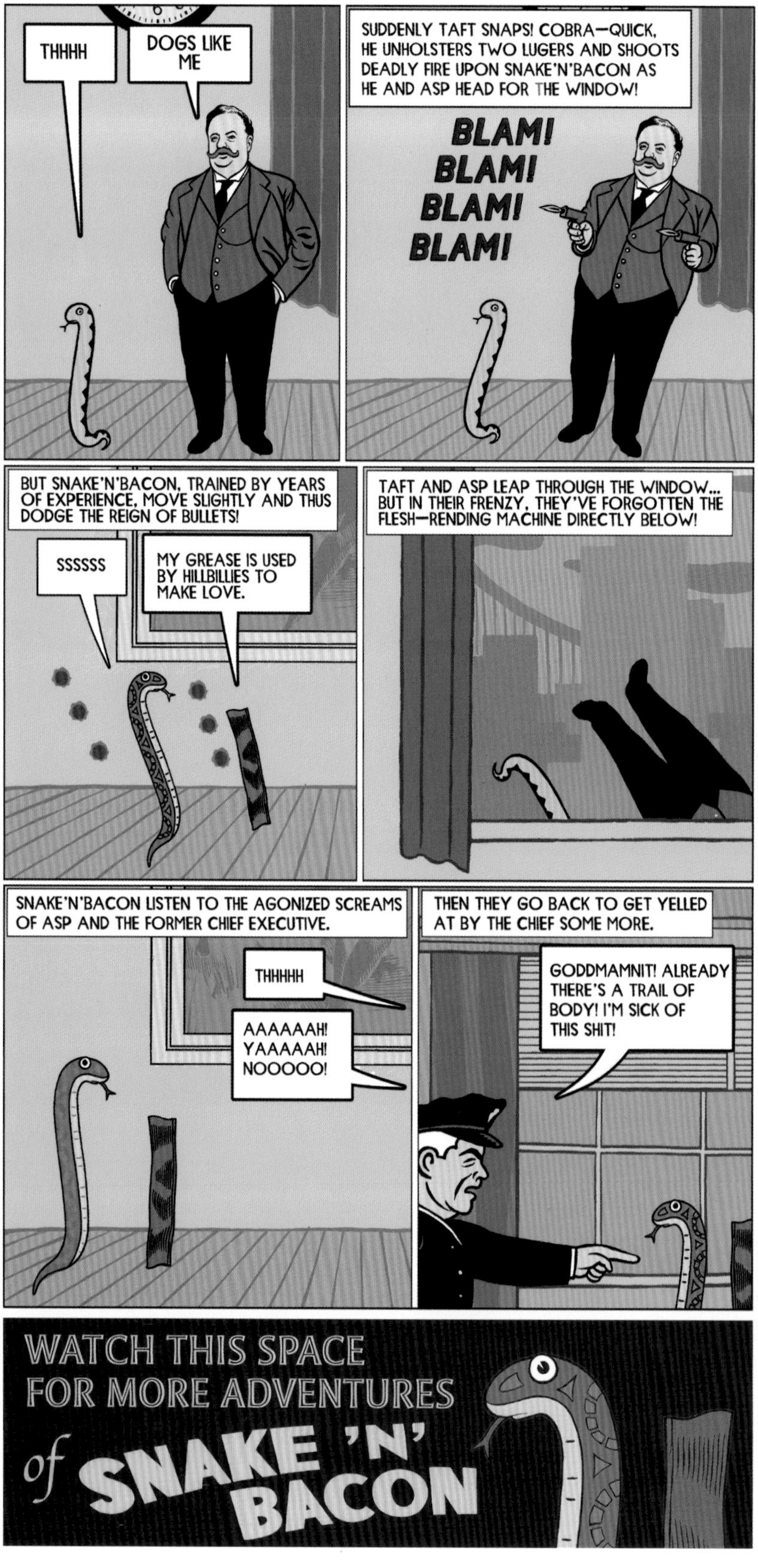
THHHH
DOGS LIKE ME
SUDDENLY TAFT SNAPS! COBRA—QUICK, HE UNHOLSTERS TWO LUGERS AND SHOOTS DEADLY FIRE UPON SNAKE'N'BACON AS HE AND ASP HEAD FOR THE WINDOW!
BLAM! BLAM! BLAM! BLAM!
BUT SNAKE'N'BACON, TRAINED BY YEARS OF EXPERIENCE, MOVE SLIGHTLY AND THUS DODGE THE REIGN OF BULLETS!
SSSSSS
MY GREASE IS USED BY HILLBILLIES TO MAKE LOVE.
TAFT AND ASP LEAP THROUGH THE WINDOW... BUT IN THEIR FRENZY, THEY'VE FORGOTTEN THE FLESH—RENDING MACHINE DIRECTLY BELOW!
SNAKE'N'BACON LISTEN TO THE AGONIZED SCREAMS OF ASP AND THE FORMER CHIEF EXECUTIVE.
THHHHH
AAAAAAH! YAAAAAH! NOOOOO!
THEN THEY GO BACK TO GET YELLED AT BY THE CHIEF SOME MORE.
GODDMAMNIT! ALREADY THERE'S A TRAIL OF BODY! I'M SICK OF THIS SHIT!
WATCH THIS SPACE FOR MORE ADVENTURES of SNAKE 'N' BACON

MOVIE REVIEW CORNER

With Feisty Grandpa.

Heck and tarnation! That boy wonder of an editor has been on my back again. "Why don't you review some new films?" he scowled. "The readers aren't interested in your descriptions of Hoot Gibson westerns you half-remember from sixty years ago," he saucily implied. Well, I can take a hint. So what've I done? Only gone and seen some of the most recent hottest releases, that's what.

CEREMONIOUS INTENTIONS (R)
Am I missing something or what? This was showing on that new-fangled pay-per-view. So I set that crazy VCR to catch it and I got to bed. When I wake up, what I got is about half-an-hour of static, and then a Matlock episode that looked mighty familiar to me. In fact, I could swear I watched it just last week! How does Hollywood expect to get away with this? My niece told me I "set the VCR wrong." I told her to stop doing so many drugs!

21ST CENTURY CARWASH (PG-13)
I noticed this playing in a drive-in near where I get sandwiches, so I went there the other day. Boy oh boy, that whole experience has changed. I went into a tunnel where there was all kinds of soap and brushes kept splashing all over my car. It was realistic, I guess, but where was the great acting? Three thumbs down!
My niece told me I'd "gone to a real car wash by mistake." "I'm not the one doing all the drugs!" I told her feistily.

RAPTORS IN THE RAFTERS (R)
Well, I wanted to show King Fancy-Pants I'm not scared of your new super-thrillers–and my heart ain't neither! So I actually went to see this in the brand new super-megaplex! That's right! But it was just another stinker. The noisetrack features a lotta screechings and screamings and hissings, and yellings and shoutings, with plenty of blowings-up. But the picture part weren't like that at all! It was just a bunch of greasy, slack-jawed moron people, staring into space while most of them ate in a disgusting, noisy fashion. Ten thumbs down!

My niece told me I'd been "facing in the wrong direction." I decided to show her–I called the police, and reported her for using drugs!

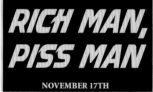

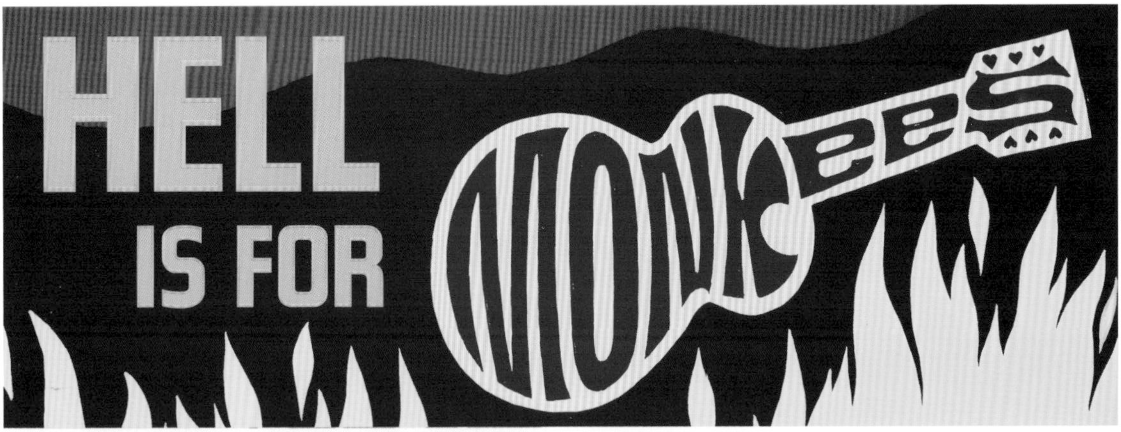
HELL
IS FOR
MONKEES

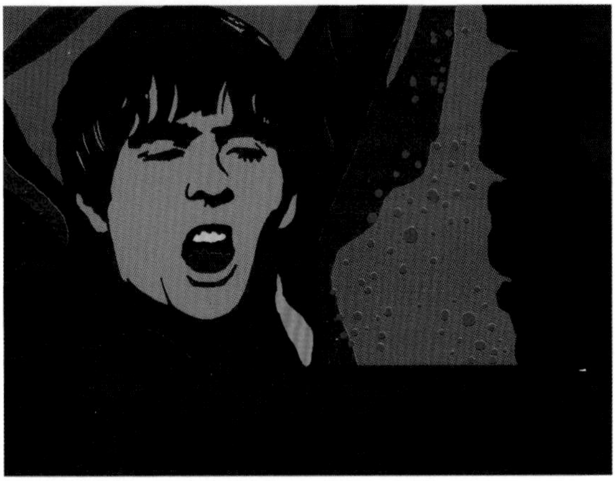

"Scream, Monkee, scream!" ordered Captain Hernandez as the lash bit again into Davy Jones' tender flesh. "Ugo wants to hear the Monkee scream, doesn't he, Ugo?" Ugo, the horribly bald, mute torturer, giggled obscenely and shook his whip. Davy knew that his pain was only beginning. Ugo was very, very bald.

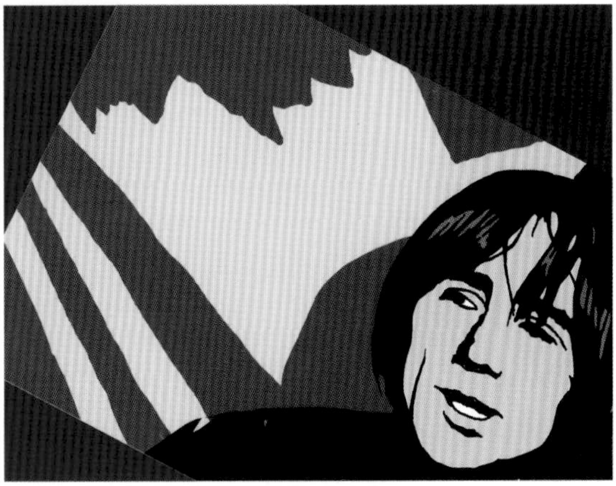

Meanwhile Peter Tork was cowering in his house. "Leave me alone!" he whimpered as bananas thudded against the windows, one of them breaking a pane and landing on the shabby carpet with a smelly thud. "Here's a banana for you, Monkee!" a male voice screamed. "Gonna crap in your hand and throw it at us, Monkee?" yelled another. The abuse was unending. He was sick to his stomach.

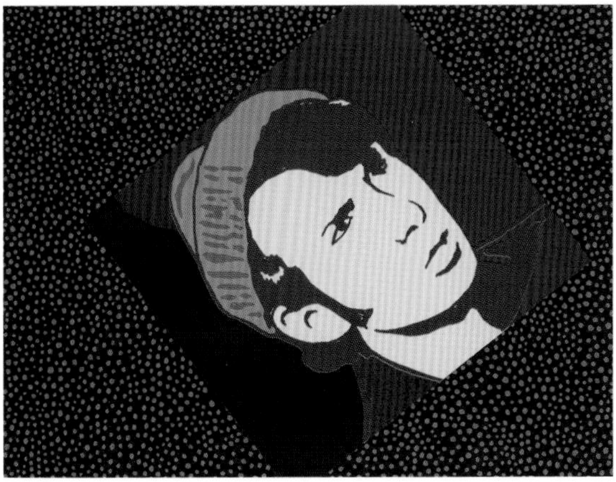

"Buried alive!" Mike Nesmith whispered softly. The words had a terrible finality. He had given up scrabbling at the rotten, collapsed earth and wood several minutes before, and now lay still, waiting to suffocate. "It won't be so bad, probably," he mused out loud. Then he heard the rats. They sounded quite excited, and in their weird, chattering voices he could almost hear a word... "Monkee." They were going to eat Monkee flesh!

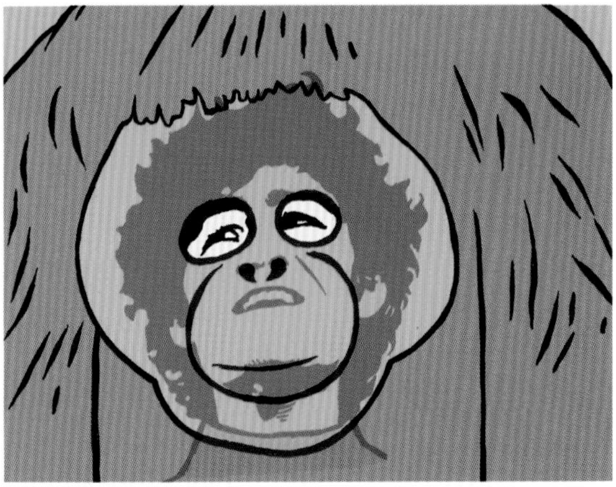

Mickey Dolenz felt nothing. Sealed inside the orangutang skin, he swung listlessly within the zoo cage, his senses dulled by the fortified wine the zoo keepers gave him. "Now you are a Monkee in fact as well as nomenclature" they had taunted him when they had covered him with the hot glue. He felt oddly at peace. Now he could take the last "e" of his name and replace it with a "y." And stop capitalizing the "m." Yes, finally.

Bedtime Thrills EXCLAMATION POINT SUSPENSE! "BLOODY CURSE OF THE SCREAM PEOPLE"

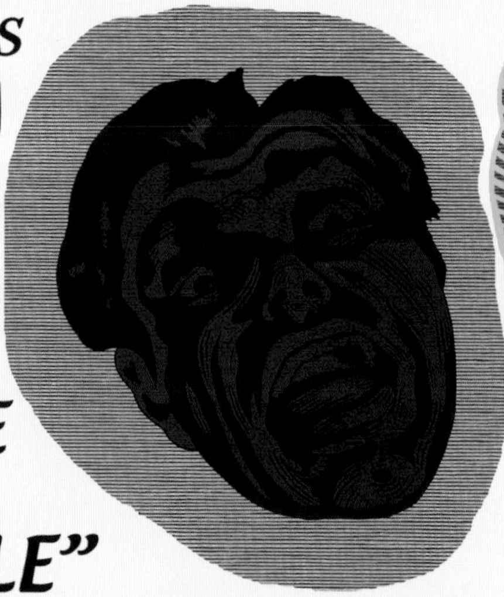

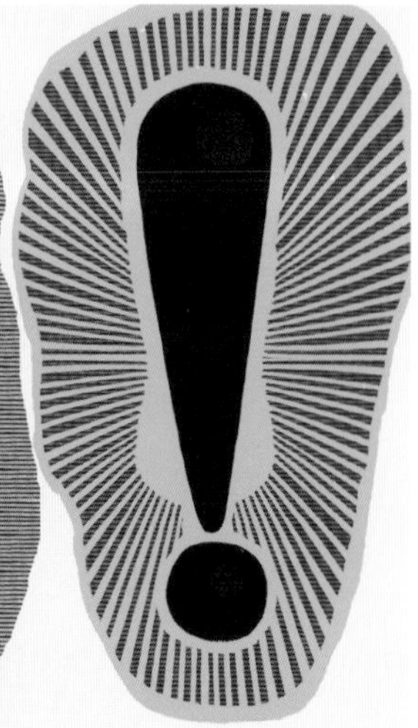

DOCTOR'S WARNING! Do not read this story shortly before you go to bed. Its excessive use of exclamation points and capital letters increases as the story goes on, and may cause excitement leading to sleeplessness.

Doctor Kalman put down his pen and looked at what he had written. It was a good warning! Let any who ignored it do so at their peril! For the story it was a warning to was a disturbing one, in which a man wrote a warning to a story and then found out that he was in the story. Doctor Kalman had thought briefly how much he would hate that happening to him!

Normally after writing a warning the Doctor would have relaxed with his wife–perhaps drinking a bottle of Riesling in front of the fireplace– but she had died two weeks ago! He missed her so much! He decided instead to listen to the radio!

Meanwhile, the asteroid the Doctor had found out in the field was in the basement pulsing with an eery, greenish light. Almost as if it was a SPACE EGG!!! The thing inside chuckled as it started to hatch.

The Doctor went back to his desk, for he had other warnings to work on. BEWARE!!!! he wrote; it was for a candy bar wrapper. His pen scratched so loudly he missed hearing the maniacal footsteps in the room behind him!! He also didn't hear the tentacles of THE SLIMY MEAT FROM SPACE as it squelched disgustingly up the stairs!!! It was only when he heard the BLOOD DRIPPING FROM THE AXE that he turned... JUST AS THE SLIME MONSTER USED ACID TO OPEN THE BASEMENT DOOR!!! AND THE SINGLE EYE WITHIN HIS MOUTH LOOKED... HUNGRRYYY!!!! OH, DEAR GOD HE SCREAMED! HELP MEEE! BUT THERE WAS NO HELP!!!!!! THEN HE REALIZED THAT THIS HAD HAPPENED BEFORE...

IT HAPPENED EVERY DAY, BECAUSE HE WAS IN HELL!!!!!!

Doctor Kalman put down his pen and looked at what he had written. It was a good warning!

THE END???

GO TO SLEEP!

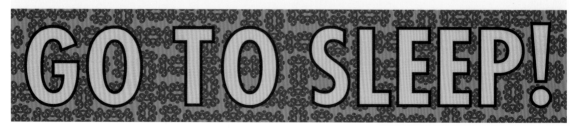

Read this if you have trouble falling asleep.

YOU ARE FALLING ASLEEP!

YOU are getting SLEEPY! YOU are TIRED and DROWSY!

YOU can hardly keep your EYES OPEN!

Your EYELIDS are getting VERY HEAVY! You're SLEEPY!

! I am going to COUNT BACKWARDS from 10 to 1.

10... 9...8...7...6...5...4...3...2...1. Go to sleep... NOW!

TIME TO DREAM

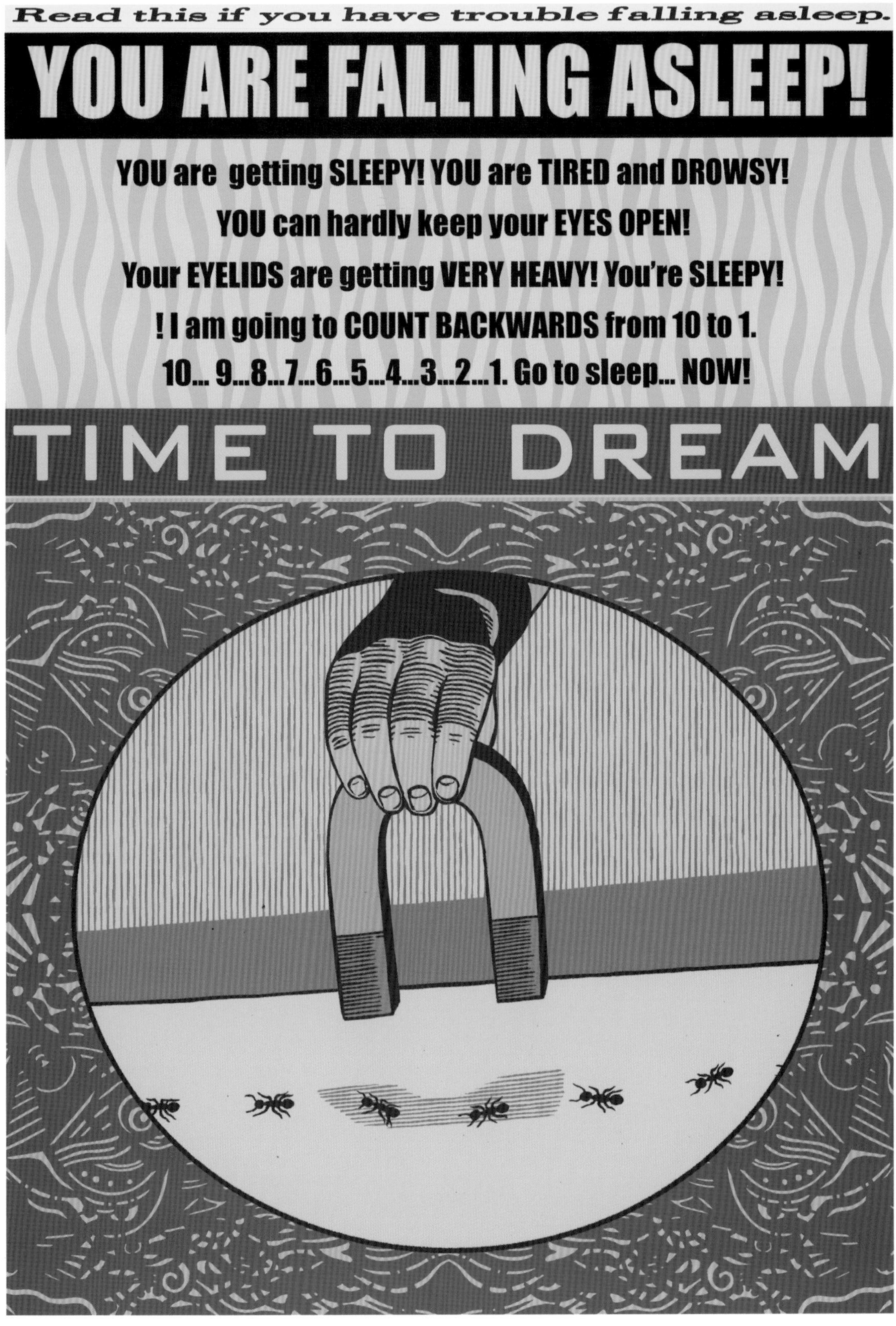

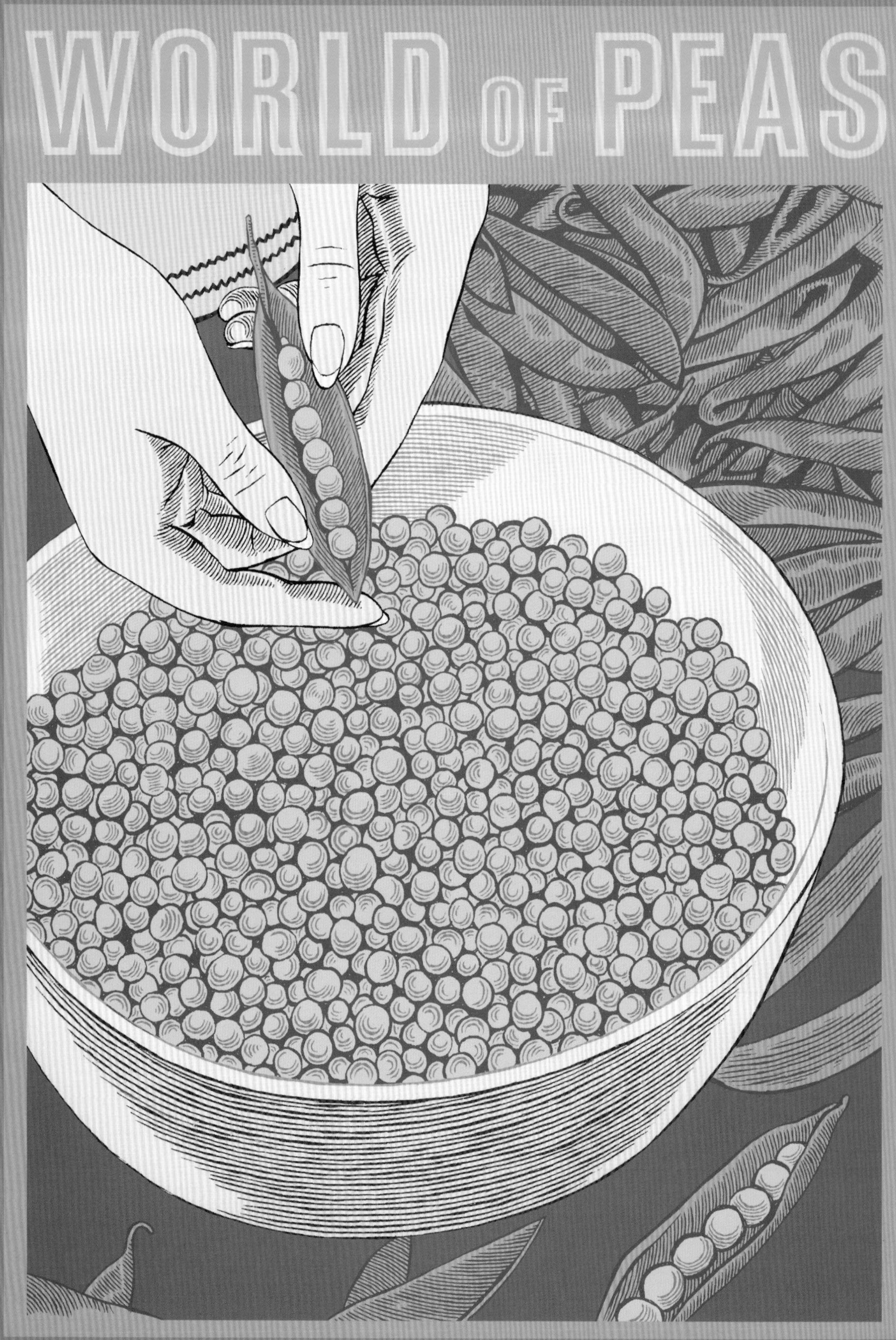
WORLD OF PEAS

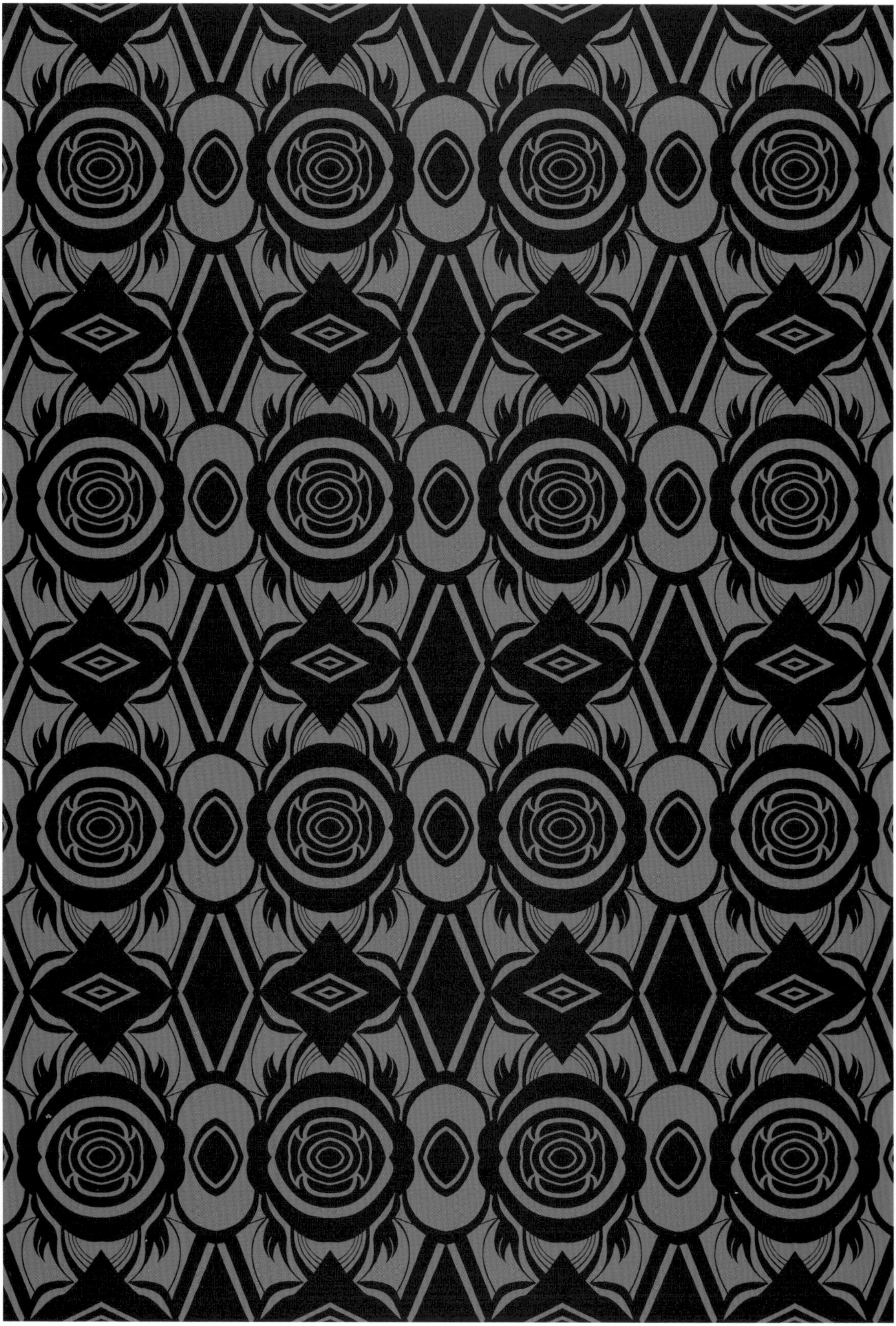

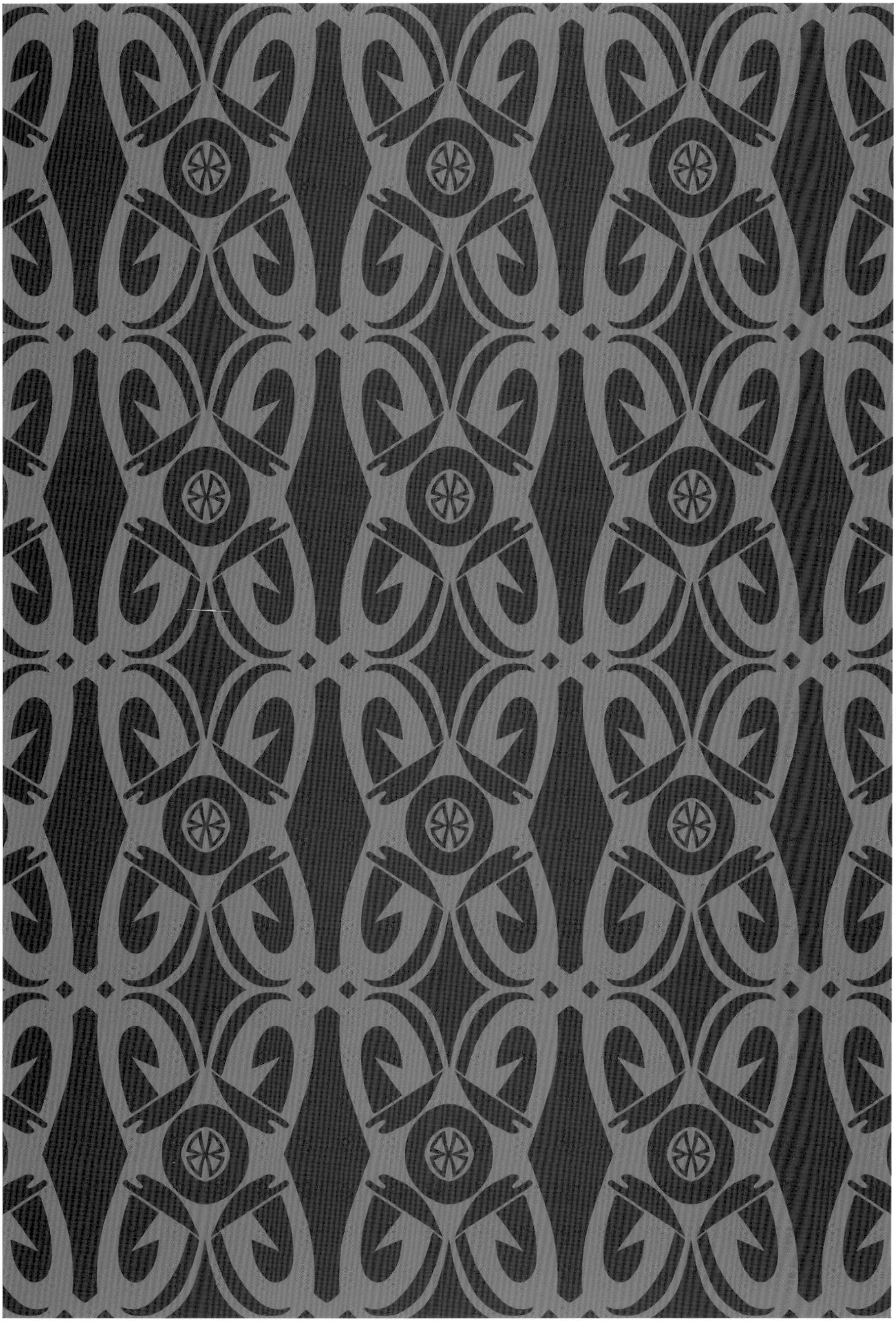

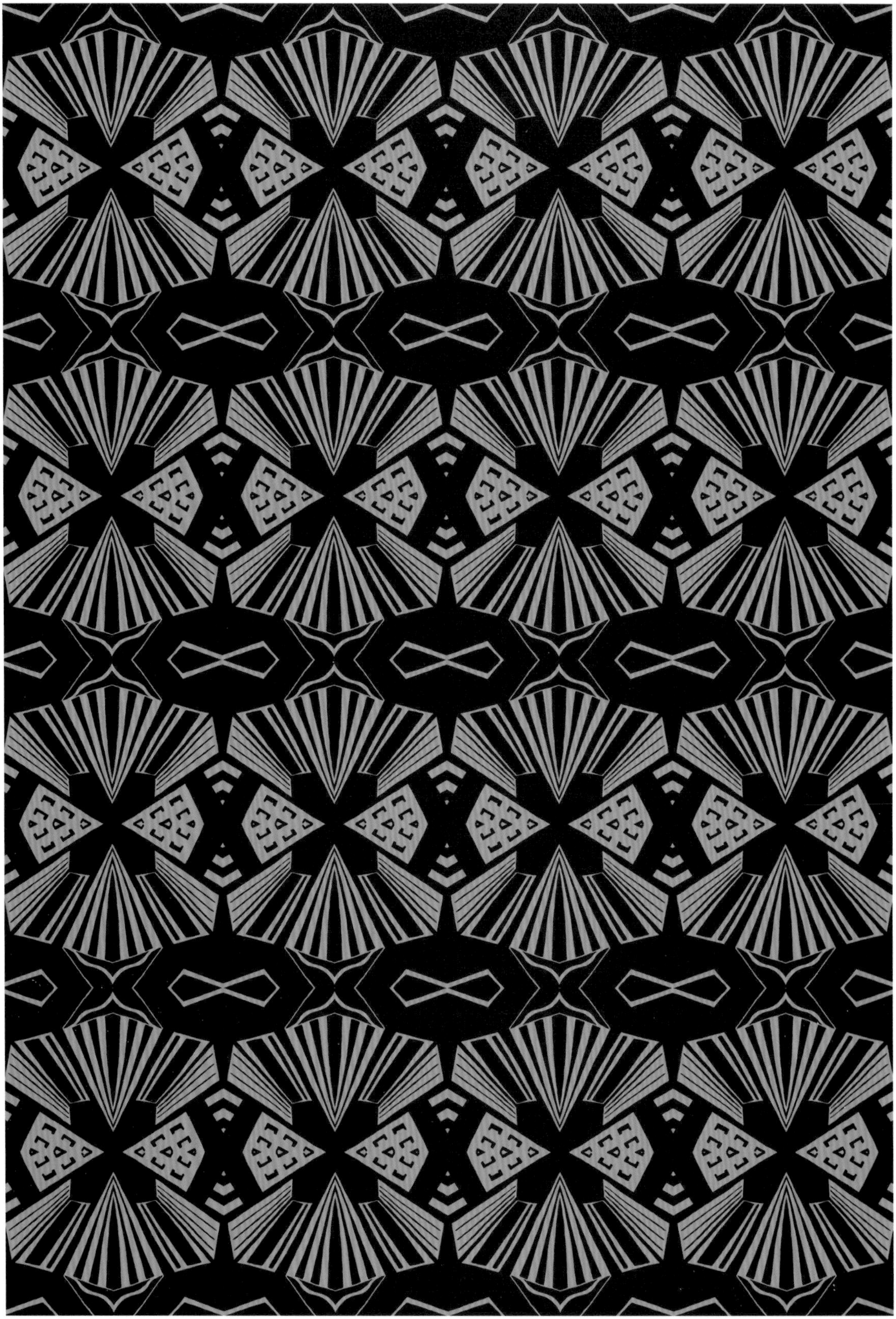